Introduction

Exploring the Taste of Scotland becomes a more fascinating and rewarding experience with each passing year. Against a backdrop of exciting cities, charming towns and villages, breathtaking landscapes and exhilarating seascapes you will find hotels, restaurants – and even the occasional seagoing vessel – which combine the very highest standards of cuisine with endless variations of presentation.

Only the best, those who have a true understanding of the essence of A Taste of Scotland, are accepted for membership. And we are delighted to welcome around sixty new members to the 1997 Guide.

All of the establishments listed between these covers have really had to earn the right to appear here – which is why you can be confident that each and every one of them will serve you with good quality, fresh Scottish produce. They have each been subjected to a stringent incognito assessment by one of our Inspectors, focusing mainly on the food but naturally looking at all other areas which play a part in the overall dining experience.

A word about our Inspectors – this dedicated team, all with professional qualifications in the culinary field, is recruited and reviewed annually. Their task is to put themselves in **your** place and ensure you're never disappointed when you visit a Taste of Scotland establishment. Once accepted, we require our members to maintain the levels of quality and service which allowed them entry to the Scheme in the first place.

Many apply but few are chosen, which is why our members are proud to display their current membership certificate. When you see that certificate you know that you have just arrived at an establishment which has met and exceeded our criteria.

As an independent, non-profit making organisation, Taste of Scotland is proud of what has been achieved to raise the standards and the profile of Scottish hospitality and cuisine. We are still working hard to foster a climate in which our members strive to be even better. You can help us gauge our success by returning the comment cards at the back of this guide – and, of course, by sampling a little more of the Taste of Scotland.

Amanda J Clark, Chief Executive, Taste of Scotland

HIGHLAND SPRING
NATURAL MINERAL WATER

❖

RESERVED FOR THE MOST EXCLUSIVE
TABLES IN THE WORLD

The finest food should be complemented with the finest water.
Which is why Highland Spring Natural Mineral Water is served at Scotland's prestigious
Gleneagles Hotel Resort, Paris's Restaurant Opéra and even on board Concorde.
Drawn from deep below the Ochil Hills in Scotland,
its crisp, clean taste is the natural choice for their tables. And we can recommend it
for the most exclusive table of them all, yours.

NATURAL MINERAL WATER

Contents

Taste of Scotland Scheme Ltd is grateful for the continued support of:

• S.T.B. • Scotch Quality Beef & Lamb Association • Scottish Salmon Board • Partners
• Trade Board Members:
Laurie Black (Chairman, Taste of Scotland Board), Fouters Bistro.
Annie Paul, Taychreggan Hotel. Eric Brown, Stakis Royal Deeside.
David Wilson, Peat Inn.

Taste of Scotland
current members are identified by
the 1997 Certificate of Membership
which should be on display

How to use this Guide

Entries

All members are listed in the Guide in alphabetical order under the nearest town or village. Island entries are shown alphabetically under Isle.

Dogs/Pets

Some establishments welcome guests with their pets – we advise that you check in advance to avoid any difficulties.

Meal Prices

We have this year introduced £ symbols which indicate the price category that the establishment has informed us they fall into. They are as follows:

£ =   up to £10 per person
££ =   £11 – £20 per person
£££ =   £21 – £30 per person
££££ = over £30 per person

Lunches

Lunchtime eating may be less formal in some establishments than others and thus the Taste of Scotland criteria extends to establishments who are open for a lighter lunch or bar snack. To avoid disappoint-ment please establish when booking whether lunchtime opening is for dining room lunch or bar meals.

Tips To Avoid Disappointment

Make an advance reservation whenever possible. Mention that you are using the Taste of Scotland Guide and check if price changes have taken place since publication. If you plan to pay by credit card – check that your card will be accepted.

Comments

Taste of Scotland welcomes comments – both good and bad – about your experiences using this Guide.

However, if you have an unsatisfactory meal we would always advise that you speak to the person in charge at the establishment concerned and let them know of your disappointment. It gives an immediate opportunity for the situation to be rectified or explained.

If this fails to resolve the problem, do write to Taste of Scotland. It is our policy to then pass a copy of your letter or comment form onto the establishment for investigation.

Please let us hear of your good experiences as we also pass these on to our members. There are comment forms at the rear of this Guide for your use.

Guide To Symbols

The symbols listed here indicate more information about the facilities available.

₳	Number of rooms	ⓤⓛ	Unlicensed	⬚	Packed meals provided
SP	Special rates available	⚲	Licensing status	₽	No parking
	(for accommodation	👑	Scottish Tourist Board	✸	Opening hours during
	rates, please enquire		Crown grading		local festival
	with establishment)	£	Credit Cards	🐕	Information on pets
✗	Information on meals	ℕ	Proprietor or manager	🐄	Member of the Scotch
Ⓥ	Vegetarians welcome	朩	Children		Beef Club
⚹	Smoking restrictions	♿	Facilities for disabled		
℞	Reservation required	⚓	Shipboard restaurant		

Map Reference	# Kinlochourn **124**

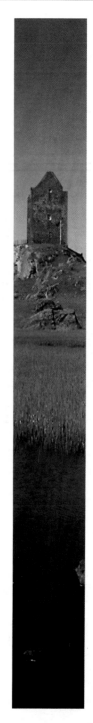

KINLOCHOURN
SKIARY

Address & Telephone Number, etc	Loch Hourn, Invergarry Inverness-shire PH35 4HD Tel: 01809 511214
How to get there	From Invergarry (on A82 Fort William–Inverness road) take A87 Invergarry–Kyle road. After 5 miles turn left to Kinlochourn. Proceed for 22 miles to end of single track road. You will then be met by boat by arrangement.
Brief description	**Remote, small guest house accessible only by boat or on foot.**
Type of building	• A unique guest house on the very shore of a dramatic West Highland sea-loch.
Style of cooking	• Home cooking.
Inspector's comment	• "The spectacular journey to this century old fisherman's cottage ends happily with a genuinely warm welcome to their home from John and Christina."
Description	This must be the most remote guest house in Scotland but the journey is worth it. Christina's cooking is miraculous, she uses excellent fresh local game, meat and fish. Vegetables, herbs and soft fruit come from the garden; and bread, scones and pastry are baked daily. The bedrooms are small but charming. Views from the house are truly spectacular with an abundance of wild life to be seen. A fantastic experience, not for the faint-hearted.
Seasonal limitations	Open 1 May to 30 Sep 🛏 Rooms: 3 SP Special rates available ✗ Residents only UL ♀ Unlicensed – guests welcome to take own wine ✗ Food served all day ✗ Lunch ✗ Dinner V Vegetarians welcome � Children welcome ♿ Downstairs bedroom suitable for mildly disabled visitors 🅿 No parking at establishment but parking at end of the road
Menu specialities	**Salmon and sour cream pie. Casserole of local venison with red wine and orange. Rhubarb and orange meringue pie.** 💳 No credit cards 👤 Owners: John & Christina Everett

Allt-Chaorain House

Crianlarich FK20 8RU
Telephone: 01838 300283
Fax: 01838 300238

"Welcome to my home"

Allt-Chaorain, is a compact and comfortable house noted for the warmth of its welcome and hospitality. Set high, it has level gardens and outstanding views of the surrounding mountains. Guests enjoy a "house party" atmosphere, helping themselves from the honesty bar and dining together in the evening.

The table d'hôte menu changes daily, usually offering a choice of dishes for the main course. The accent is on good home cooking with generous helpings and plenty of fresh vegetables. After enjoying dinner it is pleasant to sit in the sunroom and watch the evening light on the mountains, or, if the evening is chill, to enjoy the log fire burning in the lounge.

See entry Page 77

See entry Page 33

See entry Page 95

ARDOE HOUSE HOTEL

Ardoe House Hotel, a traditional Scottish Baronial Mansion stands enclosed by trees and leafy foliage amid seventeen acres of its own grounds. Situated on Royal Deeside yet only four miles from the centre of Aberdeen.

**South Deeside Road, Blairs, Aberdeen
Tel: (01224) 867355 Fax: (01224) 861283**

Edinburgh's Favourite Meeting Place

Princes Street, EH1 2AB
Tel: 0131 459 9988 Fax: 0131 225 6632

Historic Mansion, the home of Flora MacDonald preserver of Bonnie Prince Charlie.

Completely modernised, with electric light and heating.

Luxuriously furnished in up to date style.

FLODIGARRY HOTEL, ISLE OF SKYE 1928

CUISINE PERFECT

Unique and charming situation, with all the glamour of romance, near the famous Quiraing and Dunans.

TIMELESS

Wonderful views, unsurpassed in beauty, across the Little Minch to the islands of Rona and Raasay, with Gairloch and hills of Ross-shire in the distance.

No holiday home to equal Flodigarry in the British Isles

1928 TARIFF

Breakfast (early)	1/6
Breakfast Table d'hôte	3/-
Luncheon	3/6
Afternoon Tea	1/6
Dinner	5/-
*	
Bedroom, single	6/-
Bedroom, double	8/6 - 10/6
Fire in room	1/6
Servant's Board, per day	10/6
En Pension Terms, per week from	£5. 5/-

FLORA MACDONALDS COTTAGE 1928

'still a picture postcard'
'only the prices have changed'

FLODIGARRY COUNTRY HOUSE HOTEL
STAFFIN • ISLE OF SKYE • SCOTLAND • IV51 9HZ
TELEPHONE 01470 552 203 • FACSIMILE 01470 552 301

THE TASTE OF SCOTLAND

The Macallan Taste of Scotland Awards

The 1996 Winners Of The Macallan Taste of Scotland Awards are:

Hotel Of The Year	**Balbirnie House Hotel, Glenrothes**
Restaurant Of The Year	**The Symphony Room at the Beardmore Hotel, Clydebank (Glasgow outskirts)**
Country House Hotel Of The Year	**Ardsheal House, Kentallen**
Special Merit Award (Best Informal Lunch)	**East Haugh Country House Hotel & Restaurant, Pitlochry**
Special Merit Award for Hospitality	**Little Lodge, Gairloch**
The Macallan Personality of the Year	**Stewart Cameron, Turnberry Hotel**

Now in their tenth year the Awards were set up to encourage the pursuit of excellence and by so doing to encourage others to emulate the winners.

The Macallan Single Malt is known for its unique character and unrivalled quality and as such makes a perfect partner for these Awards. This partnership seems to capture the imagination of the public as every year a record number of nominations are received.

The Macallan Taste of Scotland Awards

Easter Elchies House, Home of The Macallan

The Awards are restricted to establishments which are listed in the Taste of Scotland Guide and thus are already highlighted as leaders in their specific category.

Once again this year we invite Taste of Scotland customers to nominate establishments in which you have received outstanding standards. In addition, Taste of Scotland Inspectors are asked to nominate their favourite places throughout the inspection season.

Please use the coupons at the rear of this Guide to nominate. Nominations cards may also be available at some Taste of Scotland establishments. Letters and postcards are also welcome and taken into consideration.

The categories for the 1997 Awards will remain the same. As in the past the Special Merit Awards will be decided based upon the recommendations received. Closing date for entries – 30 June 1997.

The 1996 Winners have been highlighted in the listings with this symbol:

Taste of Scotland
– in Partnership with only the best

As a reader of this latest Taste of Scotland publication you have already demonstrated your integrity as someone looking for quality. Taste of Scotland is committed to the quality of the establishments it represents but this commitment reaches wider still to the associations the organisation forms to help promote the name of quality in Scotland.

Some years ago now, Taste of Scotland made the decision to invite a selected number of prominent Scottish quality companies, majoring in the food and drink sector, as partners.

This association has now grown to a partnership in which representatives from each company come together to work with Taste of Scotland in the promotion of Scotland's quality food and drink and eating places.

The Macallan produces probably the finest malt whisky on Speyside and as partners and sponsors of the Taste of Scotland Awards they are generous in their support. It is a pleasure to be associated with such a fine product from

Scotland whose very name evokes the quality that Taste of Scotland is all about.

Walkers Shortbread, based in Speyside, is an extremely well known company both in Scotland and throughout the world.

It has the fine distinction of being run by the direct descendants of the founder and prides itself in the fact that, whilst being a world class name, it has not lost that family touch. Walkers produce a range of quality products from shortbread to traditional Scottish cakes.

Scotland is renowned worldwide for the quality of its farmed produce and eminently suitable landscape for producing fine Scotch beef, lamb, game not to mention the fabulous seafood to be sourced along the coastline.

Bain of Tarves is a long established, family business of catering butchers, game and venison suppliers. From its beginnings as a small butchers shop in the heart of Aberdeenshire, the company now delivers quality Scottish produce including Quality Assured and

Certified Aberdeen Angus Beef throughout Scotland from its base in Tarves and depot in Glasgow.

Deliveries are also made throughout the rest of the UK and wild Scottish game and venison is exported to over 20 major international markets.

Consumers also have the opportunity to sample some of these fine products direct from Bain of Tarves through their new mail order service. (For address and details see separate advertisement)

Matthew Algie have been perfecting the art of producing consistently excellent tea and coffee for over 130 years. Matthew Algie was born in Greenock in 1810 and in the 1850's he began importing tea directly to the Clyde for his grocery business and distributing it by the chest to other grocers in the area. Matthew Algie was founded in 1864 and remains to this day an independent, family-run business located in Glasgow, where the factory is still run by descendants of the founder.

Matthew Algie's guiding philosophy is to provide and influence all the elements that allow caterers to serve consistently excellent tea and coffee. As partners belonging to Taste of Scotland, the company is committed to raising the standards of tea and coffee service, to complement the already high food standards in Scotland.

Matthew Algie's Scottish Choice tea bags were awarded 'Drink Retail Product of 1996' in the recent Food from Scotland Excellence Awards and are available throughout Scotland.

Highland Spring is recognised as being one of the finest natural mineral waters as well as Britain's largest producer of mineral water. Established in 1979, today pure Highland Spring flows from its source deep below the Ochil Hills in Perthshire.

King James IV of Scotland ordered that celebration ale for his Coronation in 1488 should be made from 'Blackford water' and in 1503 King James issued a Royal Charter sanctioning the brewing of Blackford beer! Available in both still and sparkling, Highland Spring is the ideal accompaniment to fine food.

Another area for which Scotland is highly proud of is its dairy produce and **Scottish Pride** has the distinction of having won the Supreme Award for its new range of Cheeses at the 1996 Food for Scotland Excellence Awards.

Following deregulation of the milk industry in November 1994, Scottish Pride developed as a free-standing company, with the majority of the shareholders being dairy farmers. Since then Scottish Pride has emerged as Scotland's largest dairy company.

Scottish Pride currently offers a full range of milk and dairy produce including their fresh milk and cream range, the popular Fresh 'N' Lo semi-skimmed milk, a UHT milk and cream range, butter and a choice of fine quality cheddar cheeses.

The recently launched new range of connoisseur cheeses comprises five delicious cheeses designed to boost speciality cheese sales in major multiples, delicatessen outlets and restaurants throughout the country.

They are Highland, Mull of Kintyre, Arran, Isle of Bute and Drumleish. (For more detailed information see our article on Scotland's cheeses). These cheeses will also become available at selected Taste of Scotland establishments throughout the year.

No meal is complete without a fine choice of wines to enhance the enjoyment of the food so skilfully prepared. **Alexander Wines** is an independent, Glasgow based fine wine merchant established in 1981 by the proprietor, Fraser Alexander, and has an excellent reputation as suppliers to many of Scotland's best hotels and restaurants.

Importantly, and with few exceptions, Alexander Wines only stock wines not available in the High Street, sourced and imported directly from quality winemakers around the world, including Laurent-Perrier Champagne, Marques de

Riscal Rioja, Antonin Rodet Burgundies, Chateau Kirwan 3eme Cru Margaux, Simon Hackett from Australia and the renowned 'flying winemaker' Hugh Ryman. Specialists in personalised wine lists and 'own label', Alexander Wines are suppliers of the new Taste of Scotland House Wines.

Taste of Scotland is also proud to be associated with **ScottishPower**, suppliers of electricity and, more recently, gas to catering establishments throughout the country.

ScottishPower is committed to promoting Scottish business at all levels and their association with Taste of Scotland can only be of benefit to all our members.

Last but by no means least **British Airways, Regional (Scotland)**. British Airways have a commitment to Scottish producers and are working towards a strong Scottish presence of products on their flights out of and around Scotland.

A competition recently resulted in a Taste of Scotland member's recipe being adapted for in-flight use and Taste of Scotland is proud to have its name associated with this initiative.

If you, our reader, would like more information about any of these companies please do not hesitate to contact us – if we can help you we will and if not we will ensure you speak to someone who can.

ASSOCIATION OF
SCOTTISH
VISITOR
ATTRACTIONS

SCOTLAND'S FINEST VISITOR ATTRACTIONS

Whether you seek activity or leisurely strolls, a day out out with the family or a place of peace and contemplation, you will find enjoyable and educational experiences at a range of attractions listed in this booklet. Over 200 castles and historic houses, zoos, wildlife parks, sealife and marine centres, gardens, nature trails and country parks, abbeys and churches, activity and leisure centres, museums and galleries and many other attractions throughout Scotland welcome you to enjoy a further Taste of Scotland.

Pick up a leaflet at Tourist Information Centres or contact the Association of Scottish Visitor Attractions, Suite 6, Admiral House, 29/30 Maritime Street, Leith, Edinburgh EH6 6SE.

STB Quality Assurance

Since 1985 the Scottish Tourist Board has been inspecting hotels, guest houses, bed and breakfasts and self catering accommodation assessing the standards that visitors expect and helping owners and operators meet those standards.

In a two tier scheme, accommodation all over the country is visited annually and GRADED for quality and CLASSIFIED for facilities.

Grades are based on a wide ranging assessment of quality and service aspects. Each establishment is assessed on its own merits so that any type can achieve the highest grade.

DELUXE	–	*reflects an **excellent** overall standard*
HIGHLY COMMENDED	–	*reflects a **very good** overall standard*
COMMENDED	–	*reflects a **good** overall standard*
APPROVED	–	*reflects an **acceptable** overall standard*

These GRADES are awarded by the STB inspectors once they have checked all the important factors that contribute to quality in an establishment. Just as you would, they look for clean, attractive surroundings, well furnished and heated. They sample meals, sleep in the beds, and talk to the staff. Like you they know that quality should be assessed irrespective of the range of facilities on offer, they know the value of a warm and welcoming smile.

The CROWN CLASSIFICATION denotes the range of facilities on offer – things such as private bathrooms, lounges, meal provision and so on.

From a basic LISTED classification up to FIVE CROWNS can be added. So more crowns mean more facilities.

The distinctive Thistle plaques show the awards made by the STB inspectors as a result of their independent annual assessment.

For more information about grading and classification of accommodation in Scotland contact:

Scottish Tourist Board, Thistle House, Beechwood Park North, Inverness IV2 3ED.
Telephone: 01463 716996

After dinner
WHY NOT
round off the evening
WITH A VISIT TO THE
Highlands
& Islands?

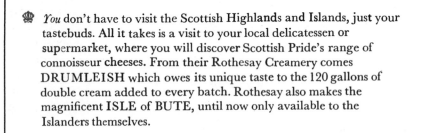

🜲 *You* don't have to visit the Scottish Highlands and Islands, just your tastebuds. All it takes is a visit to your local delicatessen or supermarket, where you will discover Scottish Pride's range of connoisseur cheeses. From their Rothesay Creamery comes DRUMLEISH which owes its unique taste to the 120 gallons of double cream added to every batch. Rothesay also makes the magnificent ISLE of BUTE, until now only available to the Islanders themselves.

🜲 From the Campbeltown Creamery on the Mull of Kintyre comes HIGHLAND (*the master cheesemaker swears you can taste the Atlantic wind, soft rain and morning dew in every wedge.*) The creamery was once a malt whisky distillery. Can you taste it in Scottish Pride's MULL of KINTYRE cheddar? There's only one way to find out.

🜲 In 1947, the opening of the Torrylinn Creamery on Arran was such a big event that it enticed the *whole* Royal Family to the Island. Try ARRAN for yourself and you will discover what the Windsors found so absolutely unmissable.

Whichever you choose you will experience a flavour of the Highlands and Islands.

CONNOISSEUR CHEESES FROM
THE HIGHLANDS AND ISLANDS

Scottish®
PRIDE

Local Tourist Information

For specific information on a particular part of Scotland, contact the following:

Aberdeen and Grampian Tourist Board
Tel: 01224 632727
Fax: 01224 639836

Angus and City of Dundee Tourist Board
Tel: 01382 434664
Fax: 01382 434665

Argyll, the Isles, Loch Lomond, Stirling, Trossachs Tourist Board
Tel: 01786 470945
Fax: 01786 471301

Ayrshire and Arran Tourist Board
Tel: 01292 262555
Fax: 01292 269555

Dumfries and Galloway Tourist Board
Tel: 01387 250434
Fax: 01387 250462

Edinburgh and Lothians Tourist Board
Tel: 0131 557 1700
Fax: 0131 557 5118

Greater Glasgow and Clyde Valley Tourist Board
Tel: 0141 204 4480
Fax: 0141 204 4772

The Highlands of Scotland Tourist Board
Tel: 01463 723024
Fax: 01463 717233

Kingdom of Fife Tourist Board
Tel: 01592 750066
Fax: 01592 611180

Orkney Tourist Board
Tel: 01856 872856
Fax: 01856 875056

Perthshire Tourist Board
Tel: 01738 627958
Fax: 01738 630416

Scottish Borders Tourist Board
Tel: 01750 20555
Fax: 01750 21886

Shetland Tourism
Tel: 01595 693434
Fax: 01595 695807

Western Isles Tourist Board
Tel: 01851 703088
Fax: 01851 705244

**For general enquiries please contact the
Scottish Tourist Board, 23 Ravelston Terrace, Edinburgh
Tel: 0131 332 2433 Fax: 0131 343 1513**

A sanctuary from the stress of urban living

BEN LOYAL HOTEL
Tongue Sutherland
Tel 01847 611216 Fax 01847 611212

The Ben Loyal provides the warmth of welcome, and comfortable, quality accommodation you deserve, and that is so rare in these parts.

The restaurant now has an AA Rosette and uses local fish, meats and game and our own grown organic salad leaves, vegetables and herbs.

Ideally situated in the middle of the North coast next to "the most northerly palm tree in the world", this Highland Oasis is perfect for either relaxing or active holiday. You can fish the hill lochs for wild brown trout or the Kyle for sea trout and some years sea bass. Walk the most northerly Munro, or do what many of our guests do, relax.

See entry Page 234

See entry Page 217

Conchra House Hotel

Skye & Lochalsh

Small Country House Hotel formerly a hunting lodge and seat of the McRae's of Eilean Donan. Centrally situated for exploring Western Highlands and Islands. Excellent comfortable accommodation in classic setting overlooking mountains and lochs. A warm welcome and good food assured. Table Licence. Reduced tariff for extended stays. "Taste of Scotland" and Johansens recommended

🦢🦢🦢

STB *Highly Commended*

Conference facilities and fully modernised self catering cottages also available.

• WALKING • TOURING • RETREATS
Conchra House Hotel, Ardelve, Kyle of Lochalsh, Ross-shire IV40 8DZ
Telephone/Fax 01599 555 233/433

See entry Page 85

See entry Page 228

CORSEMALZIE HOUSE HOTEL

PORT WILLIAM, NEWTON STEWART, WIGTOWNSHIRE

👑👑👑👑

AA ★★★ **RAC** STB *Commended*

EGON RONAY • TASTE OF SCOTLAND
• TASTE OF GALLOWAY FOOD

Country House Hotel set in 40 acres of gardens and woodland privately owned and personally run. Total seclusion and peace.

Excellent food and wines

Private Salmon/Trout fishing & shooting
Golfing arrangements on local courses

Write for brochure or

Telephone (0198) 8860254 Fax (0198) 8860213
Resident proprietors: Mr & Mrs P. McDougall

Coul House Hotel

Our views are breathtaking. The ancient 'Mackenzies of Coul' picked a wonderful situation for their lovely home. Today, Ann and Martyn will give you a warm Highland welcome. You'll enjoy the 'Taste of Scotland' food of chef Bentley, log fires, summer evening piper and 'Skye' and 'Hamish', the hotel's lovable labradors. Why not use our 'Highland Passport' to cruise on Loch Ness, visit Cawdor Castle, sail to the Summer Isles... or follow our 'Highland Heritage' trail to Glenfiddich Distillery, the Wildlife Park, Culloden Battlefield... for golfers, there's a 5-course holiday including championship Royal Dornoch... for anglers, we have our own salmon and trout fishing... there's pony trekking too.

Ring or write for our colour brochure.

Coul House Hotel
By Strathpeffer,
Ross-shire
Tel 01997-421487
Fax 01997-421945

Creebridge House Hotel

Galloway,
South West Scotland

Built in 1760 this former shooting lodge to the Earl of Galloway is now an elegant 20 bedroom Country Hotel set in Newton Stewart in 3 acres of private gardens and woodland. 18 hole Golf course 400 yards from the front door. Private Salmon and Trout fishing on the Cree & Bladnoch rivers.

Choose from either the Garden Restaurant or our friendly local Bar where renowned Chef Proprietor Chris Walker and his team cook some of their Taste of Scotland Award winning dishes using fresh local produce. All rooms en suite with colour TV, direct dial phone etc.

Prices from £27.50 bed and breakfast each
Phone or Fax for our brochure
Tel: 01671 402121 Fax: 01671 403258

See entry Page 197

See entry Page 199

Cullen Bay Hotel

BANFFSHIRE AB56 4XA
TEL.01542 840432 FAX.01542 840900

AA ★★

RAC★★ merit

Les Routiers
Highly Commended

♛♛♛♛
STB Commended

Arthur and Sheila Edwards are proud of their two restaurants' clifftop panorama of Cullen Bay's rocky crags with the sea in all her moods. This secret part of Scotland's coastline provides the perfect backdrop to the award winning cuisine of chef David McCallum.

Away from it all walks along shoreline and clifftop, old fishing villages to explore and whiskys' heartland to seek out.

In the evening, unwind beside our log fire and enjoy Scotland's finest produce and malts retiring to one of 14 newly refurbished en suite bedrooms, all with splendid sea or rural views.

Beside Cullen links, one of the 18 local courses – most are on inclusive ticket to uncrowded

See entry Page 81

See entry Page 230

Dungallan House Hotel

GALLANACH ROAD, OBAN, PA34 4PD
TEL: 01631 563799 FAX: 01631 566711

AA ★★ ❀   ♛♛♛
STB Commended

George and Janice Stewart look forward to welcoming you to their lovely Victorian Villa set high above Oban. Only half a mile away from the town centre with all its facilities yet far enough to be at peace amidst 5 acres of steep craggy tree-lined cliffs and lawns

MANSFIELD HOUSE HOTEL

At the Mansfield House Hotel we have all you need to help you enjoy your holiday... good food, friendly service and a lovely atmosphere... they're all to be found at the Mansfield. So whether you're touring or golfing, shooting or fishing, alone or with a small group, give us a call. We will tell you about our 18 rooms, several with jacuzzis, and about our special rates for weekends and week-long holidays. We can make your mouths water with the food in our restaurants and you can enjoy our more than 50 malt whiskies and our real ales. We will help book your tee-off times at Tain, Royal Dornoch and many other nearby courses and pass on discounts. We can suggest touring itineraries and we can arrange car hire. In short, we will do anything and everything to ensure that you enjoy your stay at the Mansfield House Hotel.

AA ★★★ Scotland's Commended
STB Highly Commended RAC★★★

SCOTSBURN ROAD, TAIN,
ROSS-SHIRE IV19 1PR
TEL. 01862-892052 FAX. 01862-892260

Promoting Scotland's Quality Cuisine

In recent years the term Scotland's Larder has become very user friendly and is frequently employed in references to the wonderful produce of Scotland. And if you think about it the natural larder of the country is unique in that it is able to produce such a variety of food from the land and from the sea.

Where else would you be able to sit down to lunch or dinner and choose from a menu with best Aberdeen Angus beef; with succulent venison fresh from the high tops of the highlands, grouse, hare and of course mutton and lamb – of the highest quality? The abundance of seafood dishes now gracing menus gives an indication of the wonderful harvest produced around our shores and from our lochs and rivers.

Wherever you travel in Scotland the opportunity exists to sample the local delicacies – Arbroath smokies, Lochfyne kippers, Forfar bridies, Selkirk bannocks, Orkney cheese, Islay cheese, Galloway cheese, Dundee cake, Moffat toffee etc. …

The culinary skills of the men and women of the country in producing home baked scones, pancakes, shortbread et al. is second to none. If you have ever been to one of the local country shows and observed the mountains of baking, jams and preserves on display you will know exactly what I mean.

Perhaps one of the most important ingredients of the Scottish larder is whisky – known as Uisge Beatha or the Water of Life. Whisky is without doubt Scotland's national drink, made in Scotland and consumed all over the world. Among the famous Highland malts are Glen Grant, Macallan, Glenfarclas, Knockando, Cardhu, Glenfiddich, Strathisla and Tamnavullin. Of course there are also island malts which have their own special appeal. These include Highland Park and Scapa on Orkney, Talisker from the misty Isle of Skye, Jura and the Islay malts which include Laphraoig, Bowmore and Bruichladdich.

Scottish Field magazine has featured several Taste of Scotland establishments and their innovative chefs and these articles have been enjoyed by readers both home and abroad and we enjoy this natural association with the best eating places and food in Scotland.

Archie Mackenzie,
Editor, Scottish Field

See entry Page 168

See entry Page 138   See entry Page 209

22

23

St Andrews • Bishop Kennedy • Strathkinness

Pentland • Howgate Brie • Camembert

Scotland's Cheeses

The climate and geography of Scotland are well suited to cheese-making. The short summer making season in Scotland meant that traditional cheeses usually required to be capable of being stored (matured) through the winter - hence the predominance of hard (pressed) cheese in Scotland and Britain. At one time most farmhouses or crofts made their own cheese, but there was little financial return. Improved transportation of milk changed the scene dramatically.

Today there are still more than two dozen cheesemakers across Scotland, ranging from large industrial Cheddar creameries to the handful of artisan and farmhouse cheese makers. Scottish Cheddar accounts for 70-80% of total output and the main creameries are located at Lockerbie, Stranraer and Campbeltown and on the islands of Bute, Arran, Islay, Mull (a peninsula), Gigha and Orkney. Often the creameries are open to visitors. The advent of modern temperature controlled facilities and refrigerated transport has revived artisan cheesemaking in small creameries and farms across the country.

Scottish Pride have created a range of five delicious connoisseur cheeses to awaken the palate to the delights of Scottish cheese. See under Highlands and Islands for more details. In recent years the main supermarkets have stocked a selection of local cheeses and specialist cheese shops in the main towns have extended their ranges. If you come across interesting local cheeses when you eat out, it may be worth enquiring where these can be bought.

Some of the cheeses to look out for are:

Bishop Kennedy: a 'trappist' cheese originating in the medieval monasteries of France but still relatively unknown in Scotland. Full fat soft cheese, rind washed in malt whisky to produce a distinctive orangey red crust and a strong creamy taste. Runny when ripe.

Bonchester: small coulommier-style cheese made with unpasteurised Jersey milk. Available mainly March to December.

Bonnet: mild, pressed goatsmilk cheese from small Ayrshire dairy. Similar to Inverloch (and Sanday).

Brie: Howgate Scottish Brie, traditionally made, matures to a runny sticky texture. Also Howgate Camembert.

Brodick Blue: ewes milk blue cheese from Brodick. Arran blue is the cows milk version.

Caboc: (see cream cheese)

Caithness: a new mild, Danish style wax coated cheese. Also available smoked.

Cream Cheese: several versions, mostly based on revived traditional Highland recipes and rolled in oatmeal, including Caboc (Ross-shire), Howgate (Perthshire) and Lochaber-smoked. Available plain or with peppercorns, garlic or herbs.

Crowdie: a soft fresh cheese, several versions, mainly available only locally. Originally made using milk left after the cream had separated naturally. Plain or flavoured with peppercorns, garlic or herbs. (Hramsa, Crannog, Gruth Dhu etc.).

Dunlop: resembles Scottish cheddar with soft texture. Mostly creamery-made in blocks on Arran and Islay but also traditionally in Ayrshire (Burns), near Dumfries and at Perth (Gowrie).

Dunsyre Blue: cows milk farmhouse blue cheese made on the same farm as Lanark Blue, with vegetarian rennet and unpasteurised milk.

Highlands and Islands: 'Drumleish' is produced on the Isle of Bute. A three month old mild cheese with a buttery flavour, uneven texture and piquant taste.
'Isle of Bute' (also produced on Bute) is a hard medium cheese with all the characteristics of a good cheddar.
'Mull of Kintyre', from the Cambeltown Creamery, is a mature cheddar with a nutty aroma and rounded taste.
'Highland', a mature cheese also from Campbeltown, has a unique, soft texture with a smooth flavour and strong aftertaste.
'Arran' cheddar, made by traditional methods, is a deliciously mellow medium to mature cheddar with a creamy soft texture.

Howgate: established artisan farmhouse cheesemaker, originally from Howgate near Edinburgh, now in Dundee, pioneered the making in Scotland of continental cheeses including Howgate Brie, Camembert and Pentland. Other cheeses include St Andrews, Bishop Kennedy, Strathkinness and Howgate Highland Cream Cheese.

Inverloch: pasteurised pressed goats cheese from Isle of Gigha. Coated in red wax. Also popular fruit shaped waxed cheeses.

Isle of Mull: traditional unpasteurised

farmhouse cheddar from Tobermory. Cloth-bound.

Kelsae: unpasteurised pressed cheese made near Kelso from Jersey milk. Like Wensleydale but creamier in texture and taste.

Lanark Blue: unpasteurised ewes milk cheese in the style of Roquefort.

Loch Arthur: traditional farmhouse organic cheddar from Loch Arthur near Dumfries.

Mull of Kintyre: small truckle of mature Scottish cheddar coated in black wax. A smoked version is also available.

The Orkney Isles: distinctive cheddar whose history goes back nearly two centuries, made in two creameries on Orkney. Several seasonal crofting cheeses sometimes available locally.

Pentland: white moulded soft cheese made in small quantities and not widely available.

St Andrews: award winning full fat, washed rind soft cheese, mild creamy, full flavoured with characteristic golden rind.

Scottish Cheddar: creamery produced cheddar now made in Galloway (Stranraer), Lockerbie, Rothesay and Campbeltown.

Stichill: unpasteurised creamy Jersey milk Cheshire style, from the Scottish Borders.

Strathkinness: award winning Scottish version of Gruyere, nearly 50 gallons of milk goes into a cheese! Matured 6–12 months. Limited availability.

Swinzie: pasteurised, pressed, ewes milk cheese from Ayrshire.

Teviotdate: vignotte style, white moulded unpasteurised cheese.

See entry Page 140

What did great-granpa's dram taste like?

Quality and consistency are the twin pillars upon which the Scotch whisky industry rests. Only when high quality products could be created and repeated batch after batch did it become possible to market them nationally and internationally. But, in spite of all the familiar claims about 'unchanging quality', 'the drink of your ancestors', 'the same as it ever was', and so on, one always wonders whether the whiskies enjoyed by our forebears tasted the same as today's dram.

Experts reckon that Highland malts were much more smoky, 150 years ago. Peat was the universal fuel in the Highlands, and barley malted over a peat fire takes on this smoky character. Many drinkers preferred it to the thinner, fierier whiskies produced by large distilleries in the Lowlands.

With the arrival of blended whisky – a mixture of full flavoured malts and lighter grain whiskies – in the 1860s and 70s popular taste began to favour the lighter bodied, less smoky dram. Many of the great blending houses – Johnnie Walker, Dewars, Bells, Ballantines, Teachers – made it big by producing whiskies which had the character and complexity of malt whisky, but the lightness of grain whisky. They sought less assertive malts for their blends; malts which would sing along in harmony with others rather than dominating the choir.

The arrival of the Strathspey branch line of the Great North of Scotland Railway in 1867 made it possible for distilleries in this, the heartland of malt whisky production, to import coal and coke for malting their barley, and thus achieve a less smoky spirit, while retaining all the sweet richness of flavour that the region is famous for. Such whiskies were known generically as the 'Glenlivets' – a description of style rather than place: only one distillery (out of the 18 which adopted the name) was actually in Glenlivet itself. They quickly became the darlings of the blenders.

But what did they taste like, these famous whiskies?

I had the pleasure of finding out recently, thanks to The Macallan distillers, who had bought a bottle of their wonderful whisky at auction. It had been made in 1874 and bottled in 1892.

The Macallan . The Malt.

When they got it back to the distillery, they couldn't resist drawing off a tiny sample with a syringe, to see what it was like. They were astonished and delighted to discover a) that it was in very good order and b) that it quite clearly had the character of The Macallan. In other words, in spite of all the technological changes that have taken place in making malt whisky, there has been very little change in the flavour of Macallan in 120 years.

This is perhaps less surprising than it seems, in the case of Macallan – a distillery which sticks scrupulously to 'the old ways of doing things'. They insist on using only Golden Promise barley, for example – a species with a low yield, difficult to grow and expensive to buy – in spite of the given wisdom that the species of barley makes no difference to the flavour. They use unusually small stills, and heat them directly from below. Just as they have always done. This not only makes distilling more difficult, it reduces the amount of spirit they can produce in each batch, but they maintain it is essential for the quality of that spirit.

And most of important of all for the flavour of The Macallan, they mature their malt only in ex-sherry casks – which cost over ten times as much as the ex-bourbon casks used by most distillers.

So close was the 1874 bottle to the present day Macallan, that the distiller's Director of Production, Frank Newlands, claimed that by carefully selecting individual casks he could create a whisky which, to all intents and purposes, was identical to the original.

At the launch of this new expression of Macallan, named simply "The 1874" the cork was drawn on the original and we were all invited to compare it with the new version. It was astonishingly similar – fresh and slightly orangey, with a trace of soft fudge. A comforting reminder that quality does not change, even in 120 years, so long as you do not compromise.

Charles MacLean
(Whisky correspondent for *Decanter*, and author of five books on Scotch)

FOOD FROM SCOTLAND

· 1996 WINNER ·

EXCELLENCE AWARD

SCOTTISH CHOICE

ESTABLISHED · 1864

MATTHEW ALGIE

Tea & Coffee Merchants

BLENDED IN SCOTLAND FOR SCOTLAND™

MATTHEW ALGIE

88 PREMIUM ROUND TEA BAGS

SCOTTISH CHOICE

**BLENDED IN SCOTLAND
FOR SCOTLAND™**

EXCLUSIVE OFFER

Subscribe to Scottish Field
12 issues - only £27.00 • 24 issues - only £50.00

And receive a Free gift of 3 Scottish Pride
Highlands and Islands Cheeses.
(R.R.P. £10.00)
- A cheese range for connoisseurs

Isle of Bute - a hard cheese from Scottish Pride's Rothesay Creamery with a rich mature cheddar taste.

The Mull of Kintyre - made by George McSporran cheesemaker at Campbeltown who attributes its rounded taste to the "Angels Share" of whisky fumes hovering from the Creamery's days as a malt whisky distillery.

Drumleish - using 120 gallons of Scottish double cream. Mild cheese with a piquant taste.

Offer applies to UK only.

Aberdeen 1

ARDOE HOUSE HOTEL

South Deeside Road, Aberdeen AB12 5YP
Tel: 01224 867355 Fax: 01224 861283

B9077, 3 miles west of Aberdeen.

Just outside Aberdeen this baronial style hotel provides very good accommodation and hospitality.

- Scottish baronial mansion converted to a comfortable country house hotel.
- Modern and traditional Scottish cuisine.
- "Scottish produce with friendly service."

Ardoe House is a classic Scots baronial granite mansion, with towers and corbelled bartizans, crow-stepped gables and crenellations. It was built in 1898 by a wealthy soap manufacturer, 'Soapie' Ogston, for his wife. As day turns to night Ardoe turns into a fairy castle and it is a delight to relax in the original palatial rooms. The bedrooms have private facilities and there are also function rooms available for conferences and weddings. Dining is à la carte or table d'hôte from an extensive menu of unusually treated dishes and imaginative combinations. Chef Peter McKenzie draws inspiration from classic French cooking, but gives every dish a spin of his own. The hotel has 1 AA Rosette. (*See advert Page 6.*)

Open all year
🏠 Rooms: 71 with private facilities
SP Special rates available
✗ Food served all day £££
✗ Lunch except Sat ££
✗ Dinner 4 course menu £££
Ⓥ Vegetarians welcome
🕭 Children welcome
♿ Facilities for disabled visitors
🚭 No smoking in dining room

Smoked salmon and oysters in Scottish wine jelly. Suprême of Grampian chicken stuffed with fruit pudding, wrapped in spiralled puff pastry with woodland mushrooms and fresh sage. White chocolate mousse wrapped in dark chocolate topped with cherries macerated in brandy.

STB Highly Commended 👑 👑 👑 👑 👑
💳 Credit cards: Access/Mastercard/Eurocard, American Express, Visa, Diners Club, Switch
👤 General Manager: Derek Walker

CALEDONIAN THISTLE HOTEL

Union Terrace
Aberdeen AB10 1WE
Tel: 01224 640233
Fax: 01224 641627

Follow signs to city centre, Union Terrace is located half-way along Union Street, Aberdeen's main thoroughfare.

Traditional city centre hotel.

- Town hotel in the heart of Aberdeen.
- Combination of traditional and Scottish cuisine.
- "A convenient central location offering genuine Scottish hospitality."

This large, imposing Victorian hotel overlooks Union Terrace Gardens and is very close to Union Street, the main shopping street of the Granite City. It is well-appointed and tastefully decorated in a style which complements the architectural features; bedrooms are traditionally furnished and very comfortable. The Restaurant on the Terrace is of a high standard offering a well-balanced table d'hôte menu which features local fish and seafood. For less formal eating there is Elrond's Cafe, a spacious bar and restaurant which serves drinks, snacks and a bistro menu. The Caledonian Thistle is a very conveniently located base to explore all that Aberdeen has to offer.

Open all year
🏠 Rooms: 80 with private facilities
SP Special rates available
✗ Food served all day ££
✗ Lunch except Sun Sat ££
✗ Dinner £££
Ⓥ Vegetarians welcome
🕭 Children welcome
♿ Limited facilities for disabled visitors – please enquire

Fine slices of smoked ham, marinated in whisky and wholegrain mustard presented on a compote of caramelised shallots. Breast of duck marinated in Bordeaux red wine, pot roasted with bay leaves and thyme. Coffee and orange bavarois.

STB Highly Commended 👑 👑 👑 👑 👑
💳 Credit cards: Access/Mastercard/Eurocard, American Express, Visa, Diners Club
👤 General Manager: Ewing Stewart

COURTYARD RESTAURANT
Alford Lane
Aberdeen AB1 1YD
Tel: 01224 213795
Fax: 01224 212961

In Aberdeen's West End, between Holburn Street and Albyn Place, just round the corner from Union Street.

A gourmet's paradise in central Aberdeen.

- City centre restaurant and bistro.
- Modern, creative Scottish cooking.
- "A first class establishment."

The Courtyard on the Lane is a small stone building in a cobbled lane in Aberdeen's commercial district. It is a sanctuary of good food and a great discovery. Martha's Bistro (downstairs) has an informal atmosphere. Upstairs, the Courtyard Restaurant is more formal and encourages you to linger over lunch or dinner. Glenn Lawson and his young kitchen team have created a fresh and innovative menu with daily selections of fish, game and poultry. The same menu is served in both dining areas. It is advisable to book. Winner of The Macallan Taste of Scotland Restaurant of the Year 1994.

Open all year except 1 + 2 Jan
Closed Sun Mon
✗ Lunch ££
✗ Dinner £££
Ⓥ Vegetarians welcome
✫ Children welcome
♿ Facilities for disabled visitors – bistro restaurant only
✍ No pipes or cigars in dining areas

Salad of lightly grilled goats cheese on toasted croûtons with a home-made chutney. Medley of fresh market fish on a bed of green vegetables with a saffron sauce. A light mint mousse in a milk chocolate cup with a light vanilla sauce.

💳 Credit cards: Access/Mastercard/Eurocard, American Express, Visa, Mastercharge, Switch, Delta
🅝 Manager: Richard Hood

THE CRAIGHAAR HOTEL
Waterton Road, Bankhead
Aberdeen AB21 9HS
Tel: 01224 712275
Fax: 01224 716362

Turn off A96 roundabout at Bankhead Avenue. Follow to end then turn left along Bankhead Road. Straight ahead at crossroads.

A comfortable user-friendly hotel with good restaurant and bar.

- A modern hotel in a residential part of Aberdeen, 10 minutes from the airport.
- Freshly made wholesome food served in pleasant surroundings.
- "Creative and interesting variations on traditional cooking."

Privately owned family-run hotel popular with business people and visitors alike. The traditional bar has a lively atmosphere, serves good bar food and has an open log fire. There are a number of attractive 'gallery suites', which have comfortable sitting rooms and bedrooms upstairs. There are also function rooms for conferences, seminars or private dinner parties. In the restaurant you will find friendly service and a wide ranging choice of modern and traditional dishes, which reflect the excellence of the produce available locally.

Open all year except Christmas Night, 1 + 2 Jan
🛏 Rooms: 55 with private facilities
🆂🅿 Special rates available
✗ Lunch except Sat: Carvery lunch Sun £
✗ Dinner ££
Ⓥ Vegetarians welcome
✫ Children welcome
♿ Facilities for disabled visitors

Finnan haddie fish cake with whisky and grain mustard sauce. Prime fillet of lamb grilled and topped with Dunsyre Blue cheese, served on red wine jus. Tayberry ice cream flavoured with The Macallan and served in heather honey tulip basket.

STB Highly Commended 👑 👑 👑
💳 Credit cards: Access/Mastercard/Eurocard, American Express, Visa, Diners Club, Mastercharge, Switch, Delta
🅝 General Manager: Helen Marshall

CRAIGLYNN HOTEL
36 Fonthill Road
Aberdeen AB11 6UJ
Tel: 01224 584050
Fax: 01224 584050

On corner of Fonthill Road and Bon Accord Street, midway between Union Street and King George VI Bridge. Car park access from Bon Accord Street.

An intimate and charming hotel, close to the centre of Aberdeen.

- An impressive Victorian family town house.
- Lovingly prepared Scottish cooking.
- "Comfortable accommodation, perfect food and genuine hospitality."

Craiglynn Hotel was once the home of a wealthy Aberdeen fish merchant and has attractive rooms with high moulded ceilings and carved fire surrounds. These features have been carefully preserved by the hotel's owners, Chris and Hazel Mann, as have the parquet flooring and rose-wood panelling in the dining room (which was originally the billiard room). Service is friendly and attentive, and guests are made to feel part of the family. In the handsome dining room menus are short, since everything is prepared from fresh produce (even home-grown), and the cooking homely. The bed-rooms are very comfortable and have unique en suite facilities.
e-mail 106053,1542 @ compuserve.com

Open all year except Christmas Day + Boxing Day
🏠 Rooms: 9, 7 with private facilities
♀ Restricted licence
✗ Dinner ££
Ⓥ Vegetarians welcome
☨ Children welcome
⊁ No smoking in dining room + bedrooms

Carrot and coriander soup. Lamb cobbler. Bramble and apple crumble.

STB Commended 👑 👑 👑
💳 Credit cards: Access/Mastercard/Eurocard, American Express, Visa, Diners Club, Mastercharge, Switch
ⵊ Partners: Hazel & Chris Mann

FARADAY'S RESTAURANT
2 Kirk Brae, Cults
Aberdeen AB15 9SQ
Tel: 01224 869666
Fax: 01224 869666

4 miles from Aberdeen on A96 to Cults.

Faraday's has a deserved reputation for the quality and originality of its cooking.

- Small, atmospheric restaurant in a tastefully converted Victorian electricity station.
- Traditional Scottish cooking, with European, Eastern and African influences.
- "John Inches is an inspired restaurateur."

Michael Faraday, after whom this restaurant is named, was 'The Father of Electricity'. The choice of name is appropriate for a building which was, in Victorian times, an electricity sub-station supplying the district of Cults. The room is long and inviting: its panelled walls decorated with tapestries and memorabilia; its tables of polished wood, with brass candlesticks and linen napery. Vases of cut flowers embellish the window embrasures, and there is a minstrel's gallery at one end. John Inches, Faraday's owner/chef, presents a short menu (five main courses, changing weekly) which he describes as 'Scottish traditional', but which draws inspiration from his extensive travels in France and makes intelligent use of Eastern flavourings and presentation.

Open all year except Boxing Day + New Year's Day
Closed Sun + Mon lunch
✗ Lunch except Sun Mon £-££
✗ Dinner except Sun ££
Ⓥ Vegetarians welcome
♿ Facilities for disabled visitors
⊁ No smoking before 2 pm + 10 pm

Italian garlic and rock salt roasted red peppers with leeks and bruschetti. Arbroath smokie and scallop terrine with spinach leaves and crab velouté. Blairgowrie raspberry and hazelnut biscuit with lemon posset.

💳 Credit cards: Access/Mastercard/Eurocard, Visa, Switch
ⵊ Director: John Inches

LAIRHILLOCK INN & RESTAURANT
Netherley
by Stonehaven
Aberdeenshire AB39 3QS
Tel: 01569 730001
Fax: 01569 731175

Take A90 south from Aberdeen, pass Portlethen then take right hand turn for Durris for 3 miles.

A charming old coaching inn between Stonehaven and Aberdeen.

- Atmospheric roadhouse with restaurant.
- Modern cooking, with continental influences.
- "A popular and long established traditional inn with lots of atmosphere."

Lairhillock is a traditional small coaching inn (originally a farmhouse). It stands on the old Stonehaven-Aberdeen road, and was certainly there when Bonnie Prince Charlie took this road north to ultimate defeat at Culloden in 1746. The place has been extensively refurbished by its current owners, Frank and Anne Budd, in a way which enhances the original rustic features (low ceilings, dark beams, carved oak bar front, large open hearth with real log fires). Friendly, helpful staff complete the picture to make a very welcoming inn. Beef comes from a local farm; daily fish from Gourdon; fruits from local suppliers. Sauces are interesting and appropriate, and the overall treatment of the food sensitive and unusually good. An interesting wine list features some unusual wines, and some first growths. No wonder Lairhillock is busy.

Open all year except 25, 26 Dec, 1 + 2 Jan
- ✕ Lunch £
- ✕ Dinner ££
- Ⅴ Vegetarians welcome
- ✸ Children welcome
- ♿ Facilities for disabled visitors

Gambas Creole juicy prawns with diced peppers, courgettes, shallots, Cajun spices, cream and garlic. Suprême of chicken Ecossais (with haggis and whisky sauce). Home-made sticky toffee pudding with cream.

- 💳 Credit cards: Access/Mastercard/Eurocard, American Express, Visa, Diners Club, Mastercharge, Switch, Delta
- 🅽 Proprietors: Frank & Anne Budd

THE MARCLIFFE AT PITFODELS
North Deeside Road
Aberdeen AB15 9YA
Tel: 01224 861000
Fax: 01224 868860

On A93 to Braemar. 1 mile from A92. 3 miles from city centre.

An outstanding country house hotel on the outskirts of Aberdeen with full facilities, en suite bedrooms and two restaurants.

- A large modern building tastefully in keeping with the older house it encompasses.
- Modern classic cooking with French influence and the best of Scottish ingredients.
- "The best of Scottish fare and hospitality in deluxe surroundings."

The Marcliffe at Pitfodels is a clever combination of old and new. During 1993 the original old house was restored and substantially added to, in a way which respected the style and feel of the older building. Its atmosphere is luxurious, and enhances modern design with antiques and baronial detailing – the spacious new foyer has a stone flagged floor, comfortable sofas and an open fire. The Marcliffe's proprietors, Sheila and Stewart Spence, are experienced hoteliers and this shows in the attention to detail and the high standard of service in every department. There are two restaurants: the Conservatory, and the Invery Room. Menus in both are well-balanced and extensive; and the cooking is accomplished. 100 malt whiskies and 300 wines available. e-mail – stewart@marcliff.win-uk.net

Open all year
- 🛏 Rooms: 42 with private facilities
- SP Special rates available
- ✕ Lunch ££
- ✕ Dinner £££
- Ⅴ Vegetarians welcome
- ✸ Children welcome
- ♿ Facilities for disabled visitors
- 🚭 No smoking in Invery Room Restaurant

Char-grilled gravadlax on a bed of creamed leeks. Roast rib of Aberdeenshire beef from the Carving Trolley. Apple clafoutis with calvados ice cream.

STB Highly Commended 👑 👑 👑 👑 👑
- 💳 Credit cards: Access/Mastercard/Eurocard, American Express, Visa, Diners Club, Mastercharge, Switch
- 🅽 Proprietors: Stewart & Sheila Spence

MARYCULTER HOUSE HOTEL

South Deeside Road, Aberdeen AB12 5GB
Tel: 01224 732124
Fax: 01224 733510

B9077 Banchory-Aberdeen (South Deeside Road)
c. 5 miles from Aberdeen, 1 mile west of B979 and
B9077 junction. Signposted.

An historic country hotel outside Aberdeen.

- Country hotel on the banks of the River Dee.
- Good hotel cooking with French influences.
- "Hospitable accommodation at the side of the Dee."

In the early 13th century a powerful Anglo-Norman noble founded a preceptory (college) of the Knights Templar on the south bank of the Dee. The remains of the preceptory are incorporated into Maryculter House – such as the vaulted ceiling in the cocktail bar and the huge open hearth fireplace above the old cellars (which date from 1255). The hotel has five acres of grounds on the banks of the river. The 23 bedrooms are all comfortable and tastefully decorated, as are the public rooms and bars. Food is served both in the bar, 'The Poacher's Pocket' and in the 'The Priory', a more formal dining room where the tables are charmingly dressed with linen and fresh orchids. The former's menu offers an interesting selection of well-priced bistro style food; the latter's is a solid table d'hôte menu (six main courses) with a broad choice of meat, poultry, fish and vegetarian dishes.

Open all year
- Rooms: 23 with private facilities
- SP Special rates available
- ✗ Food served all day £££
- ✗ Lunch ££
- ✗ Dinner £££
- V Vegetarians welcome
- ⚘ Children welcome
- ♿ Facilities for disabled visitors

Warm monkfish and woodland mushrooms salad with toasted pine kernels, crispy bacon and garlic dressing. Medallions of venison and pigeon breast with a celeriac rösti surrounded by a port and redcurrant jelly jus. Rich chocolate and brandy terrine set on a pool of sweet cinnamon cream with candied kumquats.

STB Commended ♔ ♔ ♔ ♔
- Credit cards: Access/Mastercard/Eurocard, American Express, Visa, Diners Club, Switch
- General Manager: Andrew Miller

THAINSTONE HOUSE HOTEL & COUNTRY CLUB

Inverurie, Aberdeenshire AB51 5NT
Tel: 01467 621643
Fax: 01467 625084

On A96 north of Aberdeen, 8 miles from airport – between Kintore and Inverurie.

A country house hotel and country club near Aberdeen, offering first class cooking and hospitality.

- Converted country mansion.
- Country house cooking.
- "Thainstone offers good quality food, imaginatively cooked in sumptuous surroundings."

This charming house has been modernised to become a comfortable hotel and country club. Behind its imposing facade the house has been radically altered to create a luxurious modern hotel and leisure centre. The Executive Chef Gordon Dochard (ex Gleneagles) offers both à la carte and table d'hôte menus in 'Simpsons' Restaurant. There is an ambitious and bold feeling about many of the dishes; the presentation is influenced by nouvelle cuisine, but portion sizes and the quality of the raw materials are influenced only by the rich farming country within which Thainstone stands. You can also eat in Cammie's Bar, where the food and atmosphere is more informal. The hotel has 2 AA Rosettes. *(See advert Page 23.)*

Open all year
- Rooms: 48 with private facilities
- SP Special rates available
- ✗ Food served all day ££-£££
- ✗ Lunch £££
- ✗ Dinner ££££
- V Vegetarians welcome
- ⚘ Children welcome
- ♿ Facilities for disabled visitors
- 🚭 No smoking in restaurant

Pan-fried gravadlax with pasta noodles and an Arran mustard and dill sauce. Roast loin of venison with a potato and celeriac gratin and spiced cabbage. Pavlova of local raspberries with pistachio cream.

STB Highly Commended ♔ ♔ ♔ ♔ ♔
- Credit cards: Access/Mastercard/Eurocard, American Express, Visa, Diners Club, Switch, Delta
- General Manager: M Jane Robertson

ABERDOUR

HAWKCRAIG HOUSE
Hawkcraig Point, Aberdour
Fife KY3 0TZ
Tel: 01383 860335

From centre of Aberdour, take Hawkcraig Road
(signed 'Silver Sands') through large car park,
then to right down very steep access to
Hawkcraig Point.

Enchanting old ferryman's house overlooking the harbour and Aberdour Bay.

- Whitewashed ferryman's house.
- Accomplished traditional cooking.
- "True Scottish hospitality with superb home cooking and fine views."

This charming old whitewashed ferryman's house
sits at the water's edge at Hawkcraig Point, next to
the old harbour with lovely views of Aberdour Bay
and Inchcolm Island's, 12th century abbey. Only
half an hour from Edinburgh by road or rail and a
pleasant hour's drive from Gleneagles, St Andrews
and the East Neuk of Fife. Elma Barrie is a superb
hostess whose accomplished cooking encourages
guests to return again and again to enjoy the
comfort and hospitality of Hawkcraig House. Not to
be missed – Hawkcraig House puddings!

....

Open mid Mar to late Oct
🛏 Rooms: 2 with private facilities
🍴 Open to non-residents – booked meals only
♀📺 Unlicensed – guests welcome to take own wine
✕ Dinner – booked meals only £££
Ⓥ Vegetarians welcome
🏃 Children over 8 years welcome
🚭 No smoking throughout

Home-made soups. Quality Assured Scottish beef and lamb. Pittenweem seafood in season. Scottish cheeses.

STB Deluxe 👑 👑 👑
💳 No credit cards
👤 Proprietors: Elma & Dougal Barrie

ABERFELDY

FARLEYER HOUSE HOTEL
Aberfeldy
Perthshire
PH15 2JE
Tel: 01887 820332
Fax: 01887 829430

Follow signs to the Castle Menzies and Weem on
the B846. The hotel is situated 1 mile past the
castle on right.

An award-winning country house hotel in beautiful surroundings.

- A small, formal and intimate hotel, rightly renowned.
- Elegant Scottish cuisine.
- "For food, comfort and hospitality – this ranks amongst the best."

In the heart of the old Castle Menzies estate,
Farleyer was built as a croft in the 16th century.
Enlarged twice since then Farleyer retains its air of
calm opulence. Thirty-four acres of grounds
enhance the house's tranquillity. Its Bistro offers
imaginative Scottish cooking in a relaxed and
informal atmosphere. The set menus in the
Menzies Restaurant make the most of the outstanding quality of local game, meat and fish.

....

Open all year
🛏 Rooms: 15 with private facilities
🆂🅿 Special rates available
✕ Food served all day £££
✕ Lunch ££
✕ Dinner ££££
Ⓥ Vegetarians welcome
🏃 Children welcome
♿ Facilities for disabled visitors
🚭 No smoking in Menzies Restaurant
🐄 Member of the Scotch Beef Club

Salad of seared Skye scallops and Glamis asparagus. Roast fillet of Angus beef and Aberfeldy malt sauce. Iced nougat with local raspberries and strawberries.

STB Deluxe 👑 👑 👑 👑
💳 Credit cards: Access/Mastercard/Eurocard, American Express, Visa, Diners Club, Switch, Delta
👤 General Manager: Andy Cole

GUINACH HOUSE
by The Birks, Aberfeldy
Perthshire PH15 2ET
Tel: 01887 820251
Fax: 01887 829607

On A826, south-west outskirts of Aberfeldy, on road to 'The Birks', Guinach is signposted from Urlar Road.

This small hotel is run by international Master Chef Bert MacKay and his wife, Marian.

- This Victorian house is set in three acres of secluded gardens and birch woods with stunning views across Perthshire.
- Sophisticated cuisine combining a range of national and international influences.
- "Bert and Marian MacKay offer the best Scottish hospitality and cuisine with professional standards."

Guinach House is a seven-roomed hotel immersed in the rolling countryside around Aberfeldy. It is an ideal location for those who simply wish to relax in tranquil surroundings and indulge in gastronomic inspiration. For those who prefer to build up an appetite more actively, there are nearby facilities for swimming, golf, fly fishing and riding. The MacKays are attentive and friendly hosts who run Guinach more like a home than a hotel. Bert's culinary expertise allows him to create rich and varied menus, while maximising on the availability of fresh local produce. Guinach has 2 AA Rosettes.

Open all year except Christmas Eve to 27 Dec
- Rooms: 7 with private facilities
- Dinner 4 course menu £££
- Vegetarians welcome
- Children welcome
- No smoking in dining room

Prawns cooked in Drambuie with capsicums and mushrooms finished with double cream. Medallions of Glen Lyon venison set on a rich port wine jus with tayberries and glazed chestnuts. Strawberry and almond meringue roulade.

STB Highly Commended 👑 👑 👑
- Credit cards: Access/Mastercard/Eurocard, Visa
- Proprietors: Mr & Mrs MacKay

Aberfoyle 4

BRAEVAL RESTAURANT
nr Aberfoyle, Stirling FK8 3UY
Tel: 01877 382 711 Fax: 01877 382 400

Situated on the A81, 1 mile outside Aberfoyle, next to the golf course.

A small restaurant which ranks among the best in Britain.

- A country restaurant with a formidable reputation.
- Outstanding modern Scottish cooking.
- "In a class of its own – a gourmet highlight."

Nick Nairn was the youngest Scottish chef ever to win a Michelin Star (in 1991, retained ever since). A former merchant seaman, he is self-taught (like so many leading chefs!) and opened Braeval with his wife, Fiona, in 1986 – until recently it was named 'Braeval Old Mill'. Since then he has won many awards. He presents a set four course menu (choice of desserts) at both lunch and dinner, and is happy to discuss special requirements (e.g. vegetarian) prior to arrival. The menus change daily according to the produce available – important, since Nick cooks in the straightforward modern manner which allows flavours to speak for themselves. He has evolved his own style: simple, but with flair and imagination. Nick also runs a cookery school at Braeval.

Open all year except 1 wk Feb, 1wk Jun + 2 wks Oct
Closed Mon
- Lunch Sun 4 course set menu ££: Wed to Sat 3 course set menu – bookings only ££
- Dinner Tue to Sat 4 course set menu £££
- Vegetarians welcome – prior notice required
- Facilities for disabled visitors
- Note: Guests are asked not to smoke pipes or cigars. Cigarettes permitted at coffee stage only
- Member of the Scotch Beef Club

Roast tomato and fennel soup with pesto oil. Roast fillet of turbot with saffron risotto and a chive butter sauce. Caramelised walnut and rum tart with Marscarpone.

- Credit cards: Access/Mastercard/Eurocard, Visa, Switch, Delta
- Proprietors: Nick & Fiona Nairn

THE SCOTTISH WOOL CENTRE
Riverside Car Park, Aberfoyle
Stirlingshire FK8 3UG
Tel: 01877 382850
Fax: 01877 382854

Adjacent to main car park in Aberfoyle, southern gateway to the Trossachs. 1 mile off A81 on A821.

Coffee shop, visitors centre and craft shop in the Trossachs.

- Coffee shop and restaurant.
- Home cooking.
- "An interesting family visitor centre, providing good refreshments all day long."

The visitors centre presents 'The Story of Scottish Wool' – a live theatre display spanning 2,000 years, 'where all the stars are on four legs'. Next door is a craft display area, where you can watch spinners and weavers, a knitwear and woollens shop and a gift shop. Outside there is a kiddie's farm, and, at the weekends, sheepdog trials and pipe bands. The restaurant which is part of all this activity is self-service and provides meals all day. The baking is especially good, and snacks and light meals are its forte. It has a stable feel, with pine furniture and old photographs.

Open all year except Christmas Day + New Year's Day
- Ⓤ Unlicensed
- ✗ Food served all day £
- ✗ Lunch £
- Ⓥ Vegetarians welcome
- ⚘ Children welcome
- ⚐ Facilities for disabled visitors

Home-made cock-a-leekie soup. Scotch lamb casserole with herb dumplings. Butterscotch sundae.

- 🕮 No credit cards
- ⚑ Catering Manager: Joan S Batison

Aboyne 5

HAZLEHURST LODGE
Ballater Road, Aboyne
Aberdeenshire AB34 5HY
Tel: 013398 86921
Fax: 013398 86660

On A93 on western side of Aboyne.

Traditional rose granite exterior with innovative design and artwork within.

- Victorian lodge to Aboyne Castle.
- Imaginative new Scottish cooking.
- "A visit to Hazlehurst is a memorable combination of food and art."

The traditional coach house exterior is charming but, in stunning contrast, it hides a wealth of modern art by internationally recognised Scottish artists, from the sculptures and paintings to the very furnishings around you – many specially commissioned. In a welcoming atmosphere, Anne Strachan combines traditional home cooking with an imaginative approach to sauces and accompaniments to create memorable dishes. Her wine list is selected from top growers, mainly French, and is very reasonably priced given the quality of the wines. There are three bedrooms, all individually designed, with full private facilities, plus a gallery and family accommodation in the adjoining cottage.
e-mail hazlehurst.lodge@nestorg.uk

Open Feb to Dec
- ⌂ Rooms: 5 with private facilities
- ✗ Lunch + special occasions by arrangement
- ✗ Dinner £££
- ⚐ No smoking in dining room

Crab soufflé set in crab soup. Rack of lamb with mushroom confit and ceps. Floating caramelised meringue on a custard cream accompanied by brandied peach.

STB Deluxe 👑 👑 👑
- 🕮 Credit cards: Access/Mastercard/Eurocard, American Express, Visa, Diners Club
- ⚑ Proprietors: Anne & Eddie Strachan

THE WHITE COTTAGE RESTAURANT
Dess, Aboyne
Aberdeenshire AB34 5BP
Tel: 013398 86265
Fax: 013398 86265

On main A93 Aberdeen-Braemar, 2½ miles east
of Aboyne.

**Award-winning restaurant in the heart of Royal
Deeside.**

- Pink granite 150 year old converted cottage.
- Creative Scottish cooking.
- "Enthusiasm, skill and the best fresh local
  produce combine to result in tasty imaginative
  dishes."

For over nine years Laurie and Josephine Mill have
built a strong reputation with local clientele for
their special style. Chef/proprietor Laurie Mill is
enthusiastic about the best raw materials he can
source and believes in allowing the intrinsic
flavours to emerge simply on the plate. Fish and
vegetables are minimally cooked, soup and stocks
are long in the making and sauces complement
rather than dominate. There is also a vegetarian
menu. The cottage is delightful, in the winter log
fires add to the intimacy and in the summer the
conservatory lends itself well to the relaxed
atmosphere that pervades. This commitment to the
food is also reflected in a short but carefully
compiled wine list with wines from the old and
new world and all reasonably priced. White
Cottage has 2 AA Rosettes.

Open most of the year except 24 Dec to 4 Jan
Closed Mon
🏠 Rooms: 1 with private facilities
♀ Restaurant licence
✕ Lunch except Mon £-££
✕ Dinner except Mon 4 course menu £££
Ⓥ Vegetarians welcome
♿ Facilities for disabled visitors
🚭 No smoking in restaurant

**Bourride of mussels and cod with aïoli. Roast Loin
of lamb with a fresh pear and rosemary sauce.
Crisp prune pie with crème fraîche.**

💳 Credit cards: Access/Mastercard/Eurocard,
  Visa, Switch
Ⓝ Proprietors: Laurie & Josephine Mill

Achiltibuie 6

SUMMER ISLES HOTEL
Achiltibuie
Ross-shire IV26 2YG
Tel: 01854 622282
Fax: 01854 622251

A835 to Ullapool and beyond – 10 miles North of
Ullapool turn left onto single track road to
Achiltibuie. Village is 15 miles on (i.e. 25 miles
from Ullapool).

**Award-winning country hotel in the West
Highlands.**

- A country hotel in a converted croft house.
- Innovative modern Scottish cooking.
- "Traditional fare of the highest calibre."

Achiltibuie is another world. The village itself is a
straggle of white cottages at the end of which you
find the hotel, facing out over the bay to the
Summer Isles and the Hebrides beyond. It is an
unlikely setting for an outpost of civilisation and fine
cooking. Proprietors Mark and Geraldine Irvine are
natural hosts, and create an undemanding
ambience in the hotel which ensures guests may
relax easily. Dinner is served promptly at 8pm from a
simple menu, prepared daily by the chef, dependant
upon fresh raw materials, and presented with skill
and flair. Everyone who goes there leaves
reluctantly, determined to return.

Open 26 Mar to 12 Oct
🏠 Rooms: 12 with private facilities
✕ Food served all day £
✕ Lunch £££
✕ Dinner ££££
Ⓥ Vegetarians welcome
👶 Children welcome
🚭 No smoking in restaurant + bedrooms

**Warm savoury cake of fresh local crab meat and
spiney lobster tails served with a dill and
cucumber relish. Roast saddle of Scotch lamb
with rosemary and caramelised garlic served
with stuffed baked aubergine. Hot steamed syrup
pudding with home-made vanilla custard.**

STB Highly Commended 👑 👑 👑
💳 Credit cards: Access/Mastercard/Eurocard,
  Visa, Switch
Ⓝ Proprietors: Mark & Gerry Irvine

ALLOA

GEAN HOUSE
Tullibody Road, Alloa
Clackmannanshire
FK10 2HS
Tel: 01259 219275
Fax: 01259 213827

A907 from Kincardine Bridge or Stirling. Park entrance on B9096 Tullibody, less than 5 minutes from Alloa Town Hall roundabout.

A delightful, richly decorated, family-run hotel.

- Country house hotel.
- Modern cooking, with many influences.
- "Edwardian country house offering Scottish hospitality with elegance."

Gean (the word is Scots for a wild cherry tree, and refers to the number of these which surround the house) is an unspoilt Edwardian mansion. Built in 1912, it is meticulously maintained by its owners, Paul and Sandra Frost. Head Chef Martin Russell has an excellent background and is energetic and excited about food using the best ingredients to work with. Friendly and well-run, very reasonably priced, imaginative food, Gean House is delightful. Twenty four hour service facility. Winner of Taste of Scotland Overall Excellence Award 1992.

....

Open all year
- 🏨 Rooms: 7 with private facilities
- 🆂🅿 Special rates available
- ✕ Food served all day £
- ✕ Lunch ££
- ✕ Dinner £££
- Ⓥ Vegetarians welcome
- 🕏 Children welcome
- ♿ Facilities for disabled visitors
- 🚭 No smoking in dining room

Tortellini of lobster and scallops with reduced lobster bisque and broad beans. Cutlet of 'Old Berkshire' pork with a tarragon mousse, red wine and lentil du puys. Guanaja chocolate and cinnamon mousse tart.

STB Deluxe 👑 👑 👑 👑
- 💳 Credit cards: Access/Mastercard/Eurocard, American Express, Visa, Diners Club, Delta, JCB
- 🅺 Reception: Debbie Millar

ALTNAHARRA

ALTNAHARRA HOTEL
Altnaharra
by Lairg
Sutherland IV27 4UE
Tel: 01549 411222
Fax: 01549 411222

A836, 21 miles north of Lairg.

An old coaching inn, recently refurbished, in a remote situation. The area's premier fishing hotel.

- Country hotel and restaurant.
- Imaginative traditional cooking.
- "A deservedly popular hotel with fishermen and 'other visitors'."

Anne Tüscher felt an immediate affinity with this isolated and beautiful part of central Sutherland so she bought the well-known hotel, which had been built as a coaching inn in the early 19th century and has catered for anglers for at least a century. It had been partly rebuilt in 1957, and during 1994/95 was completely overhauled. Fishing themes (prints and ornaments), are complemented by open fires and comfortable country house furniture. Anne is a warm and welcoming host, and the atmosphere is informal and friendly. The place is very popular with sportsmen and with locals. The short table d'hôte menus make good use of local fish and game.

....

Open 1 Mar to 1 Nov
- 🏨 Rooms: 16 with private facilities
- ✕ Lunch £
- ✕ Dinner 4 course menu £££
- Ⓥ Vegetarians welcome
- 🚭 No smoking in dining room

Roasted boneless quail with a compote of pickled vegetables. Leg of Scottish lamb slowly roasted with garlic and rosemary. Steamed golden fruit pudding coated with lemon custard.

- 💳 Credit cards: Access/Mastercard/Eurocard, Visa
- 🅺 Proprietor: Anne Tüscher

ALYTH

DRUMNACREE HOUSE
St Ninians Road, Alyth, Perthshire PH11 8AP
Tel: 01828 632194
Fax: 01828 632194

Turn off A926 Blairgowrie-Kirriemuir to Alyth.
Take first turning on left after Clydesdale
Bank – 300 yards on right.

**A small country hotel winner of the Glenturret
Perthshire Tourism Award 'Most Enjoyable
Restaurant Meal'.**

* Converted mansion.
* Modern Scottish and international cooking.
* "You know as soon as you go in through the
  front door that it's going to be good."

Drumnacree House is situated at the foot of
Glenisla in the old market town of Alyth, which has
a southern aspect and is surrounded by raspberry
fields. Allan and Eleanor Cull run their hotel most
efficiently and create a relaxing atmosphere. They
both do the cooking and draw from their years of
international travel to create unusual menus as
well as more traditional ones all of which are
accompanied by home-grown organic vegetables
and herbs from the kitchen garden; the dishes
express a national content while being inspired by
foreign impulses and are attractively described
and presented. Allan also cures his own fish and
game. Drumnacree has 2 AA Rosettes.

Open 1 Apr to 20 Dec
🏠 Rooms: 6 with private facilities
⑤⑨ Special rates available
♀ Restricted licence
✕ Dinner residents only Sun Mon: non-residents
   Tue to Sat ££
Ⓥ Vegetarians welcome – prior notice required
🕏 Children welcome
⚊ No smoking in dining room + bedrooms
🐄 Member of the Scotch Beef Club

**Arbroath smokie mousse with a tomato and basil
sauce. Fillet of venison on rösti with a wild
mushroom sauce. Steamed sticky gingerbread
pudding with crème anglaise.**

STB Highly Commended 👑 👑 👑
💳 Credit cards: Access/Mastercard/Eurocard,
   American Express, Visa
👤 Proprietors: Allan & Eleanor Cull

APPIN

INVERCRERAN COUNTRY HOUSE HOTEL
Glen Creran, Appin, Argyll PA38 4BJ
Tel: 01631 730 414 Fax: 01631 730 532

Just off A828 Oban-Fort William at head of Loch
Creran, 14 miles north of Connel Bridge.

**An idyllically positioned family-run hotel in the
wilds of Glen Creran.**

* Secluded country house with stylish appeal.
* Excellent quality Scottish cooking.
* "A very cultivated house in a wild glen setting."

The hotel commands stupendous mountain views,
built perched on a hillside enjoying uninterrupted
views over idyllic Glen Creran. The house itself is
strikingly different, cleverly designed to make the
most of its situation, yet not in the slightest out of
place in this secluded picturesque glen. Splendid
public rooms with spacious terraces, and large
comfortable bedrooms, contribute to the overall
feeling of luxury. The three generations of the
Kersley family who own and run the hotel do so with
unassuming charm and friendliness. The food lives
up to the high standards that mark this place featuring local meats and seafood in traditional recipes
presented to delight the eye and please the palate,
served within a delightful dining room. To fully
appreciate the excellent food here it is advisable to
book ahead – the morning of the same day will do.

Open 15 Mar to 15 Nov
🏠 Rooms: 9 with private facilities
⑤⑨ Special rates available
✕ Lunch ££ – booking essential
✕ Dinner ££££
Ⓥ Vegetarians welcome
🕏 Children over 5 years welcome
♿ Facilities for disabled visitors
⚊ No smoking in dining room
🐄 Member of the Scotch Beef Club

**Hot salmon soufflé served with a rich coriander
sauce. Pan-fried collops of Highland venison with
a fricassée of mushrooms and red Burgundy jus.
Oatmeal tulip basket filled with Scottish soft fruits
with Drambuie laced cream.**

STB Deluxe 👑 👑 👑 👑
💳 Credit cards: Access/Mastercard/Eurocard,
   Visa
👤 Manager: Tony Kersley

THE STEWART HOTEL
Glen Duror, Appin
Argyll PA38 4BW
Tel: 01631 740268
Fax: 01631 740328

A828 – Fort William 17 miles; Glencoe 10 miles;
Oban 30 miles.

A traditional Highland lodge in a historic setting.

- Small country hotel.
- Traditional Scottish cooking with innovative touches.
- "A delightful hotel where old and new combine harmoniously."

A classic Victorian hunting lodge which has retained many of its original features and thus combines the best of the old and the new. The hotel is set in its own grounds and overlooks Loch Linnhe, ten miles from Glencoe. The whole area is steeped in history, factual and fictional. It was the scene of the famous Appin Murder in 1751, and the setting for Robert Louis Stevenson's masterpiece, *Kidnapped*. The bedrooms are in a modern annexe and are comfortable and pleasantly furnished. The public rooms are in the older part of the house and are on a grander scale. Food is excellent, with a table d'hôte menu that changes daily, and distinctively Scottish menus, accompanied by an extensive and knowledgeable wine list. The gardens are a delight. The restaurant has 2 AA Rosettes.

Open 1 Apr to 15 Oct
🏠 Rooms: 19 with private facilities
SP Special rates available
✗ Lunch £
✗ Dinner 4 course menu £££
V Vegetarians welcome
🏃 Children welcome
🚭 No smoking in dining room

Loch Linnhe prawns served with garlic butter on a bed of samphire. Tail of monkfish encased in filo pastry served on a light spinach sauce. Fresh fruit brûlée.

STB Commended 👑 👑 👑 👑
💳 Credit cards: Access/Mastercard/Eurocard, American Express, Visa, Diners Club, Mastercharge
👤 Proprietors: The Lacy Family

Arbroath   11

LETHAM GRANGE RESORT
Colliston, Angus DD11 4RL
Tel: 01241 890373 Fax: 01241 890414

From A92, Arbroath, take A933 Brechin road and turn right at Colliston to Letham Grange.

A gracious and beautifully restored baronial mansion.

- A grand country house hotel preserving the best of the past.
- Modern/traditional Scottish cuisine.
- "A spacious, luxurious country house hotel with golf courses."

With its period features – original oak panelling, sculptured ceilings, period paintings – faithfully and carefully restored to their original splendour of 1884, its Victorian builders would recognise a great deal at Letham Grange. This is enhanced by modern comforts and a range of outdoor pursuits from golf on its rolling parkland estate, fishing, shooting, tennis and indoor curling rink. In its magnificent Rosehaugh Restaurant the hotel offers both à la carte and table d'hôte dishes that draw on fresh local produce, imaginatively cooked. Period conservatory open for lunch and light meals all day in summer months. The menus are well-balanced and reasonably priced. The wine list extensive. The hotel stocks over 90 single malt whiskies.

Open all year
🏠 Rooms: 41 with private facilities
SP Special rates available
✗ Food served all day ££
✗ Lunch £
✗ Dinner ££
V Vegetarians welcome
🏃 Children welcome
♿ Facilities for disabled visitors

Arbroath smokie – boned, smoked and sautéed in onions wrapped in a pancake and served with melted Orkney cheddar. Char-grilled Aberdeen Angus fillet with haggis croquettes and Drambuie cream sauce. Panacotta with fresh Tayside berry compote.

STB Commended 👑 👑 👑 👑
💳 Credit cards: Access/Mastercard/Eurocard, American Express, Visa, Diners Club, Switch, Delta
👤 General Manager: Alan T Wright

Ardentinny   12

THE ARDENTINNY HOTEL
Ardentinny
Argyll PA23 8TR
Tel: 01369 810 209
Fax: 01369 810 241

12 miles north of Dunoon. From Gourock-Dunoon ferry, take A815 then A880. Or scenic drive round Loch Lomond A82 and A83 then A815 through Strachur, and over hill to Ardentinny.

Rural family-run hotel.

- 18th century coaching inn.
- Traditional Scottish cooking.
- "Lively old hostelry in beautiful lochside position."

Now under new ownership – this delightful droving inn built in the 1700s lies on a small promontory on Loch Long and is surrounded by the glorious Argyll Forest Park. The hotel's gardens stretch down to the lochside and pier for those arriving by yacht (the hotel has its own moorings). Informal lunches and suppers can be eaten in the Buttery or patio garden, or guests may prefer a more formal dinner in the relaxed atmosphere of the dining room.

Open all year
- Rooms: 11 with private facilities
- Special rates available
- Food served all day £££
- Lunch £
- Dinner £££
- Vegetarians welcome
- Children welcome
- No smoking in dining room

Hot smoked salmon with chive and turmeric dressing. Best end of Argyll lamb with black pudding and a minted Madeira sauce. Glazed lemon tart with an orange crème anglaise.

STB Commended 🏰 🏰 🏰 🏰
- Credit cards: Access/Mastercard/Eurocard, Visa, Mastercharge, Switch, Delta
- Proprietors: Mr & Mrs P Webb
  Family-run by Bob & Anne Rennie

Ardnamurchan   13

FAR VIEW COTTAGE
Kilchoan, Acharacle
Argyll PH36 4LH
Tel: 01972 510357

Corran Ferry to Salen on A861 then B8007 to Kilchoan. A few hundred yards from the Tobermory-Kilchoan Ferry.

Spectacular sea views, glorious walking, wonderful hospitality.

- Extended keeper's cottage overlooking Sound of Mull.
- Imaginative home cooking.
- "Hospitality and serenity pervade this comfortable home in beautiful Ardnamurchan."

Rob and Joan Thompson own and run Far View, which takes its name from panoramic views to east, south and west, down the Sound of Mull, out to Tiree and across Kilchoan Bay. Originally a keeper's cottage it has been recently imaginatively extended with tasteful care which has successfully preserved the original character. Joan is an enthusiastic hostess who delights in producing appetising dishes, accompanied by the tastiest of sauces. Her home-made soups and desserts are delicious and seconds are often offered and accepted. Rob also cooks a substantial Scottish breakfast and his nutmeg potatoes and herbed sausage on a ring of apple are interesting and unusual. There is very much the feeling of staying in a friend's house here and a rare feeling of space and unhurried peace.

Open Apr to end Oct + Easter
- Rooms: 3 with private facilities
- Special rates available
- Packed lunches for residents £
- Dinner £-££
- Children over 12 years welcome
- No smoking throughout

Leek and pear soup. Pheasant breast cooked on a bed of onion served with a cream and redcurrant sauce. Captain Morgan's Revenge: bananas, chocolate, coffee, cream and rum.

STB Highly Commended 🏰 🏰 🏰
- No credit cards
- Proprietors: Rob & Joan Thompson

FEORAG HOUSE
Glenborrodale
Acharacle
Argyll PH36 4JP
Tel: 01972 500 248

Corran Ferry to Salen on A861. Then B8007 along Loch Sunart to Glenborrodale.

A handsome new house on the shores of Loch Sunart in Glenborrodale.

- A country house with wonderful views.
- Delightful home cooking.
- "Wonderful home cooking and the warmth of Scottish hospitality at its best."

Feorag House was designed and built by its present owners, Peter and Helen Stockdale, in 1994 on the wooded northern shore of Loch Sunart. It has a lovely situation, within yards of a rocky inlet and facing south. The view can best be appreciated from the large balcony attached to the sitting room, with open log fire, or in less clement weather, from the broad bay windows in the luxurious dining room. Altogether, the house has been sensitively designed, furnished and decorated to a high standard. The food is delicious: both Peter and Helen cook and bake on their Aga; everything is fresh and local. Their friendliness and hospitality is overwhelming. A real find!

Open all year
- Rooms: 3 with private facilities
- Special rates available
- Residents only
- Unlicensed – guests welcome to take own wine
- Dinner ££
- Vegetarians welcome – by arrangement
- Children over 10 years welcome
- No smoking in dining room + bedrooms

Queenie scallops flamed in a brandy sauce with fresh lime. Pan-fried breast of duck in orange and cranberry sauce. Home-made honey and ginger ice cream in brandy snap basket.

STB Deluxe ☆ ☆ ☆
- Credit cards: Access/Mastercard/Eurocard, Visa, Switch
- Proprietors: Peter & Helen Stockdale

MEALL MO CHRIDHE COUNTRY HOUSE
Kilchoan, West Ardnamurchan
Argyll PH36 4LH
Tel: 01972 510238
Fax: 01972 510238

From Corran Ferry by A861, then along B8007 by the side of Loch Sunart.

A beautiful shoreline Grade II Listed Georgian house.

- Country house built in 1790 - originally a manse.
- Good Scottish home cooking at its best.
- "Excellent Scottish home cooking in a comfortable and homely atmosphere reflecting great commitment and enthusiasm."

Meall mo Chridhe (pro. 'me-al-mo-cree') means 'little hill of my heart'. Standing within its own 45 acres, it has splendid views over Kilchoan and the Sound of Mull. Its resident owners, Roy and Janet Smith are committed to providing their guests with the very best, offering 'good food, peace and tranquillity'. Dinner is by candlelight, in what was originally the 'Marriage Room', sitting at a magnificently antique dining table. The four course set menu uses only fresh local produce; vegetables, fruits and herbs are grown in the walled garden. Janet uses her two Agas to great effect, producing home cooking and baking to tantalise every tastebud. Guests are made most welcome at Daisy Chain Crafts, an art studio with many of Janet's hand-produced goods. The adjoining farm shop has a selection of fresh home-grown fruits and vegetables, as well as locally supplied salmon, shellfish, cheeses and meats.

Open 1 Apr to 31 Oct
- Rooms: 3 with private facilities
- Special rates available
- Unlicensed – guests welcome to take own wine + spirits
- Dinner 4 course menu £££
- Vegetarians welcome
- Children over 12 years welcome
- No smoking throughout

Three cheese croustade served with a chilled tomato salsa. Locally dived king scallops with lime butter and fresh home-made pasta. Fruits from the garden served with elderflower and gooseberry ice cream.

STB Highly Commended ☆ ☆ ☆
- No credit cards
- Proprietors: Roy & Janet Smith

ARDUAINE

LOCH MELFORT HOTEL
Arduaine, by Oban
Argyll PA34 4XG
Tel: 01852 200233
Fax: 01852 200214

On A816, 19 miles south of Oban.

A country hotel in a splendid situation.

- Stylish and friendly hotel with the emphasis on welcome.
- Fresh, imaginative Scottish cuisine.
- "A great favourite with discerning clientele."

Under its owners Philip and Rosalind Lewis, the Loch Melfort Hotel deserves its growing reputation and such past awards as 'Hotel of the Year Scotland', 1992. It is dramatically situated with panoramic views across Asknish Bay to the islands. Originally the home of the Campbells of Arduaine, the hotel has been sensibly and tastefully extended to take maximum advantage of the magnificent land and seascape. The renowned Arduaine Gardens are adjacent to the hotel grounds. Both in its dining room and Chartroom Bar, the hotel offers the best of fresh local produce – particularly sea food and shellfish – and an imaginatively balanced wine list. The hotel has 1 AA Rosette.

Open all year except mid Jan to mid Feb
- ⊞ Rooms: 26 with private facilities
- SP Special rates available
- ✗ Food served all day from £
- ✗ Lunch (Chartroom Bar) from £
- ✗ Dinner £££
- Ⓥ Vegetarians welcome
- ⚘ Children welcome
- ⚿ Some facilities for disabled visitors
- ⚲ No smoking in dining room

A wee haggis parcel with a touch of the 'water of life' served with creamed leeks. Fillet of turbot with a light tomato and basil mousseline. The famous Loch Melfort rich chocolate cheesecake.

STB Highly Commended ♛ ♛ ♛ ♛
- ⊞ Credit cards: Access/Mastercard/Eurocard, Visa, Switch
- ⚿ Proprietors: Rosalind & Philip Lewis

ARISAIG

ARISAIG HOUSE
Beasdale, by Arisaig, Inverness-shire PH39 4NR
Tel: 01687 450622 Fax: 01687 450626

Just off A830 Fort William-Mallaig, 1 mile past Beasdale railway station.

One of the most distinguished hotels in the West Highlands.

- Scots baronial mansion luxuriously maintained.
- Innovative Scottish cooking.
- "Baronial splendour and an intriguing history make for a wonderful base to discover the area."

Arisaig House was built in 1864. The garden falls, in formal terraces, down to the beach from which Bonnie Prince Charlie escaped to France. Ruth, John and Andrew Smither, owners, have very capable managers in Alison and David Wilkinson (their daughter and son-in-law) who maintain the highest standards. Public and private rooms are tastefully furnished. Their priority is to provide 'peace and quiet and gentle luxury to the weary traveller'. Arisaig House's chef marries fresh local produce (notably, seafood from Mallaig) and personal inspiration, both table d'hôte and à la carte. Dinner in a formal way is a gourmet experience whilst lunch, equally delicious, can be anything from soup and sandwiches to more substantial fare served in the bar, garden terrace or dining room. Arisaig has 2 AA Rosettes.

Open 1 Apr to 31 Oct
- ⊞ Rooms: 14 with private facilities
- SP Special rates available
- ⚲ Residential licence
- ✗ Lunch £££
- ✗ Dinner ££££ 4 course menu – booking essential
- Ⓥ Vegetarians welcome
- ⚘ Children over 10 years welcome
- ⚲ No smoking in dining room

Tarte tatin of scallops with chive oil dressing. Medallions of local venison baked in a juniper and thyme crust. Steamed chocolate pudding with vanilla and chocolate sauces.

STB Deluxe ♛ ♛ ♛ ♛
- ⊞ Credit cards: Access/Mastercard/Eurocard, American Express, Visa, Switch
- ⚿ Partner: Ruth Smither

THE OLD LIBRARY LODGE & RESTAURANT
High Street, Arisaig
Inverness-shire PH39 4NH
Tel: 01687 450651
Fax: 01687 450219

In centre of village on waterfront.

Little restaurant in a village setting.

- Small restaurant with rooms.
- Good, fresh natural Scottish cooking.
- "The kind of 'little find' people are always looking for – essential to book at night especially."

The Old Library Lodge and Restaurant enjoys an attractive situation on the waterfront in Arisaig with fine views out over the small Hebridean isles. The building itself is a 200 year old stone built stable converted into a restaurant of character with accommodation attached. A cheerful and welcoming atmosphere prevails not least in the dining room where guests choose from a table d'hôte menu with a choice of five of everything – starters, main courses and puddings. The menu is fresh, simple and well-balanced featuring, naturally enough, a wealth of locally caught fish and seafood attractively cooked and presented. The comfortable accommodation is in a wing of terraced bedrooms with balconies overlooking the terraced garden. Breakfast is something to look forward to.

Open 24 Mar to end Oct
Closed Tue lunch
🏠 Rooms: 6 with private facilities
SP Special rates available
♀ Table licence
✗ Lunch except Tue
✗ Dinner £££
Ⓥ Vegetarians welcome – prior notice required

Mussel and fennel soup with home-made bread. Grilled duck breast marinated in honey and soy sauce. Rhubarb fudge crumble with cream or ice cream.

STB Highly Commended 👑 👑 👑
💳 Credit cards: Access/Mastercard/Eurocard, American Express, Visa, Switch, Delta
🍴 Proprietors: Alan & Angela Broadhurst

Auchencairn 16

BALCARY BAY HOTEL
Shore Road, Auchencairn
Dumfries & Galloway
DG7 1QZ
Tel: 01556 640217/640311
Fax: 01556 640272

A711 Dalbeattie-Kirkcudbright to Auchencairn. Then take 'no through road' signposted Balcary (single track) for 2 miles.

An idyllically situated country house hotel in an area of rare natural beauty.

- Superb country house dating back from 1625 set standing close to the beach of Balcary Bay.
- Modern Scottish cooking.
- "Exquisite restaurant food, served with precision and cooked with great skill."

This house stands in a splendidly exposed position by the Solway Firth, in three acres of grounds. Under the personal care of resident managers Graeme and Clare Lamb the service is friendly and efficient, and the hotel is maintained to accommodate guests in considerable comfort. Most of the en suite bedrooms have spectacular views. A short table d'hôte menu is offered in the restaurant, featuring fresh local specialities as well as an extensive à la carte menu. The conservatory extension to the bar is delightful for meals.

Open Mar to mid Nov
🏠 Rooms: 17 with private facilities
SP Special rates available
✗ Lunch Mon to Sat – by prior reservation only £££: Sun – booking advisable £
✗ Dinner £££
Ⓥ Vegetarians welcome
☈ Children welcome
♿ Facilities for non-resident disabled visitors
🚭 Smoking discouraged

Mousse of Arbroath smokies served with a sherry and grain mustard sauce. Noisettes of lamb with a gin and juniper berry sauce. Strawberry shortcake decorated with an apricot coulis.

STB Highly Commended 👑 👑 👑 👑
💳 Credit cards: Access/Mastercard/Eurocard, American Express, Visa, Switch, Delta
🍴 Proprietors: The Lamb Family

Auchterarder 17

AUCHTERARDER HOUSE
Hunter Street, Auchterarder, Perthshire PH3 1DZ
Tel: 01764 663646 Fax: 01764 662939

Off B8062 Auchterarder-Crieff, 1 mile from village.

A majestic country house hotel.

- Baronial style 19th century mansion.
- Country house cooking, with modernist overtones.
- "Pampering and luxury redolent of a bygone age."

Ian and Audrey Brown, the proprietors of this sumptuously appointed red sandstone mansion, make every effort to create the atmosphere of a country house. The magnificent public rooms retain a strong period style and have many echoes of past elegance in the furnishings and decor. The house itself is surrounded by 17½ acres of manicured lawns and mature woodland, making it a peaceful refuge from the outside world. The food served in the dining room has a refined country house feel, with elements of surf and turf; plenty of seafood and game cooked with pleasing and enhancing sauces and accompaniments. Head Chef Keirnan Darnell has been awarded Master Chef of Great Britain. Auchterarder House has 2 AA Rosettes. *(See advert Page 27.)*

Open all year
⊞ Rooms: 15 with private facilities
SP Special rates available
✗ Non-residents – by reservation
✗ Food served all day – by reservation ££
✗ Lunch – by reservation ££
✗ Dinner – by reservation ££££
Ⓥ Vegetarians welcome
⚥ Children over 12 years welcome
♿ Facilities for disabled visitors
🐂 Member of the Scotch Beef Club

Goats cheese soufflé with caramelised red onions complemented by a tomato and sweet roasted pepper chutney. Roast rack of Perthshire lamb with a wild rabbit sausage and cabbage tattie scone. Hot cherry and bakewell tart with a Drambuie sabayon.

STB Highly Commended 👑 👑 👑 👑 👑
💳 Credit cards: Access/Mastercard/Eurocard, American Express, Visa, Diners Club, Switch, Delta
👤 Proprietors: Mr & Mrs I M Brown

DUCHALLY HOUSE HOTEL
nr Auchterarder
Perth PH3 1PN
Tel: 01764 663071
Fax: 01764 662464

Take A823 junction off A9 Gleneagles/Crieff/ Dunfermline sign. Hotel is 2 miles along and well-signposted.

A comfortable country hotel.

- Granite Victorian country house.
- Good hotel cooking .
- "Warm hospitality and well-cooked food."

This hotel is hybrid of original 19th century architecture and modern extensions, standing in 28 acres. Inside it retains some of the Victorian features, including a fine staircase, some attractive fireplaces (there are open log fires in all the public rooms) and a panelled billiards room. The restaurant is attractively decorated and furnished, and both table d'hôte and à la carte menus are presented; dishes are traditional and familiar, but are cooked to order and well-presented. The hotel has 1 AA Rosette.

Open all year except 24 to 27 Dec
⊞ Rooms: 13 with private facilities
SP Special rates available
✗ Food served all day £
✗ Lunch ££
✗ Dinner £££
Ⓥ Vegetarians welcome
⚥ Children welcome
♿ Facilities for disabled visitors

Terrine of oak-smoked Tay salmon with dressed crab, with a basil bree. Roast saddle of Perthshire lamb with aubergine tartlet and a rosemary jus. Sugar glazed lemon tart with chantilly cream.

STB Highly Commended 👑 👑 👑 👑
💳 Credit cards: Access/Mastercard/Eurocard, American Express, Visa, Diners Club
👤 Proprietor: Arne Raeder

THE GLENEAGLES HOTEL
Auchterarder, Perthshire PH3 1NF
Tel: 01764 662231 Fax: 01764 662134

½ mile west of A9, 10 miles north of Dunblane,
1 mile south of Auchterarder.

A luxury resort hotel.

- Palatial Edwardian resort hotel.
- Several restaurants and styles of cooking.
- "One of the most famous hotels which lives up to its name."

When Gleneagles, the first 'resort hotel' opened in 1924, the Morning Post's headline ran 'The Scottish Palace in the Glens; The Playground of the Gods'. This is no exaggeration. The effect is awesome, Gleneagles has 4 restaurants of one kind or another – from brasseries (in the Clubhouse) to afternoon tea and light lunch. Gourmets seek out the Strathearn – glittering with silver, crystal, chandeliers and fine china. À la carte and daily changing table d'hôte menus are presented for lunch and dinner. The style of cooking might be described as 'modernised-classical, in the grand hotel tradition'. The new Bar – opened in May '96 now offers a circular bar in the centre of the room where guests may watch the cocktails being prepared. Recent refurbishments have been tastefully done.

Open all year
🏨 Rooms: 234 with private facilities
🆂🅿 Special rates available
✕ Food available all day £
✕ Lunch (Strathearn) Sun only £££
✕ Lunch (The Bar) from ££
✕ Dinner (Clubhouse) except Sat from ££
✕ Dinner (Strathearn) except Sat ££££
🍽 Note: please telephone in advance for non-residential dining in Strathearn Restaurant, Clubhouse and Equestrian Centre
Ⓥ Vegetarians welcome
🧒 Children welcome
🚭 No smoking area in restaurants
🐄 Member of the Scotch Beef Club

Haddock tartare with avocado and dill sauce. Loin of Tayside new season lamb. Chocolate piano with redcurrant and raspberries.

STB Deluxe 👑 👑 👑 👑 👑
💳 Credit cards: Access/Mastercard/Eurocard, American Express, Diners Club, Mastercharge, Switch
👤 Managing Director: Mr Peter J Lederer

Nr Auchtermuchty   18

ARDCHOILLE FARM GUEST HOUSE
Dunshalt, Auchtermuchty, Fife KY14 7EY
Tel: 01337 828414 Fax: 01337 828414

On B936 just outside Dunshalt village, 1½ miles south of Auchtermuchty. 1 hour's drive from Edinburgh, 20 minutes from St Andrews or Perth.

A spacious, well-appointed guest house with views over the Lomond Hills.

- A farmhouse built in 1957 where guests' comfort is a priority.
- Traditional, good home cooking, using only fresh ingredients.
- "A guest house with true Scottish welcome and food."

From the embroidered linen napkins you can tell that attention to detail is the aim of proprietors Donald and Isobel Steven. They succeed in making you feel like a guest in their own elegantly furnished home. Wonderful home-made shortbread is available in the bedrooms. Freshly prepared meals of local produce are served at a long mahogany table set with fine china and crystal in the comfortable dining room, husband Donald serves the food that Isobel cooks. Breakfasts are "the best we've ever had". Home-made soups, vegetables from the garden, home baking, preserves and home-made ice cream – a speciality – can all be enjoyed here. The personal touch is evident throughout. Ardchoille's location makes it an excellent base for touring, golf or just relaxing.

Open all year except Christmas/New Year
🏨 Rooms: 3 with private facilities (2 en suite)
🍷 Unlicensed – guests welcome to take own wine
✕ Dinner 4 course menu ££
🍽 Dinner for non-residents – by prior arrangement only
Ⓥ Vegetarians welcome – prior notice required
🧒 Children welcome
🚭 No smoking throughout

Fresh Tay salmon fillet on crispy lettuce with cucumber mayonnaise. Roast loin of free range Scottish pork on a hot bramley apple sauce. Chilled 'garden' rhubarb fool with a ginger meringue.

STB Highly Commended 👑 👑 👑
💳 Credit cards: Access/Mastercard/Eurocard, Visa
👤 Proprietors: Donald & Isobel Steven

Auldgirth by Dumfries 19

AULDGIRTH BY DUMFRIES

LOW KIRKBRIDE FARMHOUSE
Auldgirth
Dumfries DG2 0SP
Tel: 01387 820258

From Dumfries take A76 Kilmarnock for 2 miles, then B729 to Dunscore. Beyond Dunscore at crossroads go right. After 1½ miles take first left. Farm first on left.

Farmhouse bed and breakfast set amidst rolling Dumfries pastures.

- Farmhouse family-bed and breakfast.
- Good home cooking.
- "Unpretentious home cooking with the stamp of an accomplished cook."

This is a working farm with a prize-winning herd of Friesian cattle and lots of sheep, so there is much to entertain those who love the countryside and farming life. It is located in remote rolling countryside just north of Dumfries. The traditional farmhouse has beautiful views and has a lovingly tended garden to the front. The guest rooms are comfortable with a domestic appeal about them. Dinner is provided for residents with substantial helpings of wholesome home-made dishes using home-grown produce wherever possible. You will be joined by Zan Kirk and her family, who cook, serve and entertain you in their friendly and happy home.

Open all year except Christmas Day
Rooms: 2
Special rates available
Residents only
Unlicensed
Dinner ££
Vegetarians welcome
Children welcome
No smoking in bedrooms

Carrot and ginger soup. Roast breast of pigeon with cabbage, bacon and a game sauce. Dunscore Delight: ice cream, meringue, chocolate sauce liqueur and cream.

STB Commended Listed
No credit cards
Proprietors: Joe & Zan Kirk

Aviemore 20

AVIEMORE

LYNWILG HOUSE
Aviemore, Inverness-shire PH22 1PZ
Tel: 01479 811685
Fax: 01479 811685

A9 Perth-Inverness, take Lynwilg road 1 mile south of Aviemore.

A beautiful country house built in the 1930s.

- Country house overlooking the Cairngorms.
- Traditional Scottish cooking.
- "A delightful experience – and Marjory Cleary's lemon tart was a fitting flourish to an excellent meal."

Lynwilg is an impressive country house, built by the Duke of Richmond, standing on high ground looking out over the Cairngorms. The house is set in four acres of attractively landscaped gardens with a well-planned kitchen garden providing much of the fruit, vegetables and herbs used in the daily changing menus. Marjorie Cleary presents a set menu each evening; her inventiveness and flair in the kitchen mean that every meal is special. Comfortable, well-furnished bedrooms (3 of which are en suite), roaring log fires, croquet on the lawn and fishing on a private loch are all indications of a relaxed country house style. A private self-catering cottage in the grounds sleeps four. Winner of The Macallan Taste of Scotland Special Merit Award for Outstanding Hospitality 1994.

Open New Year to 31 Oct
Rooms: 4 with private facilities
Special rates available
Non-residents welcome subject to availability
Unlicensed – guests welcome to take own wine
Dinner 4 course menu £££
Vegetarians welcome
Children welcome
No smoking in restaurant

Smoked duck breast with crispy green salad and honey dressing. Collops of monkfish, pan-fried on a sweet red pepper sauce. Warm lemon tart with vanilla and sweet geranium ice cream.

STB Highly Commended 👑👑👑
Credit cards: Access/Mastercard/Eurocard, Visa
Proprietors/Owners: Alan & Marjory Cleary

THE OLD BRIDGE INN

Dalfaber Road
Aviemore PH22 1PU
Tel: 01479 811137
Fax: 01479 810270

At south end of Aviemore, take B970 ski road (Cairngorms) for 300 yards then take turning on left for another 300 yards.

A cosy Highland pub nestling beside the river Spey.

- A friendly informal place of great hospitality.
- Good pub food.
- "A friendly pub to relax in."

Only minutes on foot from the centre of Aviemore, the Old Bridge Inn has the air of a country pub. This quaint and unpretentious building offers pub food as it should be – freshly prepared and cooked. Proprietor Nigel Reid and Chef Norma Hutton concentrate on fresh local produce for their extensive and imaginative menu. Rightly popular, they even make their own ice cream. There is a special children's menu. In the evenings, the menu is based on food cooked on a large chargrill. In the summer the inn hosts regular Highland ceilidhs, with pipers and Scottish dancing.

Open all year
✘ Lunch £
✘ Dinner ££
Ⓥ Vegetarians welcome
🕇 Children welcome
♿ Facilities for disabled visitors

Hot smoked salmon with dill relish. Salmon and sole roulade with a dill sauce. Lemon poached pears and strawberry coulis.

💷 No credit cards
🕅 Owner: Nigel Reid

THE ROWAN TREE RESTAURANT & GUEST HOUSE

Loch Alvie, by Aviemore
Inverness-shire PH22 1QB
Tel: 01479 810207
Fax: 01479 810207

1½ miles south of Aviemore on old A9 (B9152) overlooking Loch Alvie.

Restaurant and guest house, with horn carving visitor attraction and all day tea-room.

- A small restaurant and guest house on Speyside.
- Traditional Scottish fare.
- "Fresh honest to goodness cooking served in a relaxing atmosphere."

One of the oldest hotels in Strathspey, The Rowan Tree is fast establishing a reputation as a place to find traditional quality Scottish food. A four course table d'hôte dinner menu offers generous portions of dishes with a distinctly Scottish theme and there is a comfortable lounge to enjoy a pre-dinner drink and peruse the wine list. George and Gillian have added a tea-room offering delicious home baking, sandwiches and salads to complement the Speyside Horn and Country Crafts – visitor attraction where guests can see the traditional craft of horn carving and visit the craft shop.

Open 27 Dec to 1 Nov
Note: Jan to Mar open Fri Sat nights only
Closed Sun
🛏 Rooms: 10, 8 with private facilities
🆂🅿 Special rates available
✘ Food served all day except Sun £
✘ Dinner except Sun – 4 course menu ££
Ⓥ Vegetarians welcome
🕇 Children welcome
🚭 No smoking in dining room

Parcels of smoked Scottish salmon wrapped around a mousse of fresh salmon, cream and chives. Badenoch venison casserole cooked in a red wine and home-made rowanberry gravy. Summer fruits, puff pastry hearts and ice cream in a pool of fresh cream.

STB Commended 👑 👑 👑
💷 Credit cards: Access/Mastercard/Eurocard, Visa, Mastercharge
🕅 Proprietors: George & Gillian Orr

Ayr 21

FOUTERS BISTRO RESTAURANT
2A Academy Street, Ayr
Ayrshire KA7 1HS
Tel: 01292 261391
Fax: 01292 619323

Town centre, opposite Town Hall.

Historic basement restaurant in Ayr.

- Converted bank vaults.
- Modern Scottish cooking.
- "A real jewel in the heart of Ayr."

Situated in a converted basement of the 18th century British Linen Bank building, in an old cobbled lane opposite the Town Hall in Ayr, Fouters has been a restaurant since 1973, and is one of the best places to eat in South-west Scotland. Laurie and Fran Black create a bright and cheerful atmosphere; white walls and stencils give a casual, continental feel to this underground sanctuary. It has been one of the most popular restaurants in Ayr since it opened. The style of cooking is inspired by the traditional French kitchen, and makes good use of the fish and shell-fish from Ayr Fish Market, game in season from local estates and top quality Ayrshire beef and dairy products. Menus are supplemented by daily 'chef's specials'. Fouters has 2 AA Rosettes. Member of the Scotch Beef Club.

Open all year except 25 to 27 Dec + 1 to 3 Jan
Closed Sun lunch + Mon
✗ Lunch except Sun Mon ££
✗ Dinner except Mon £££
Ⓥ Vegetarians welcome
Special diets catered for
✶ Children welcome
🐄 Member of the Scotch Beef Club

Taste of Scotland Platter. Salmon in pastry with almond and ginger butter, and wine cream sauce. Crème brûlée.

💳 Credit cards: Access/Mastercard/Eurocard, American Express, Visa, Diners Club, Mastercharge, Switch
Ⓜ Owners: Laurie & Fran Black

THE HUNNY POT
Beresford Terrace
Ayr KA7 2EU
Tel: 01292 263239

In the town centre of Ayr, first left off Burns' Statue Square.

Coffee shop in Ayr.

- Wholefood coffee shop and licensed restaurant.
- Home baking/cooking.
- "A well-established rendezvous for locals and visitors alike."

Felicity Thomson runs this quaint coffee shop in Ayr which has the theme of Winnie the Pooh – thus accounting for the curious spelling in its name! There are teddy bears everywhere and the motif reigns on the menu with references to the characters of Milne's books. The food is simple plain fare, with masses of home baking and light snacks available all day. In Poohspeak a Hunny Pot is his favourite place for 'a little smackerel of something' – what more need one say?

Open all year except Christmas Day, Boxing Day, 1 + 2 Jan
♀ Licensed
✗ Food served all day £-££
✗ Lunch £
✗ Dinner £
Ⓥ Vegetarians welcome
✶ Children welcome
♿ Facilities for disabled visitors
⌇ Majority of tables non-smoking

Parsnip soup. Leek and cheese flan. Pear and walnut crumble.

💳 No credit cards
Ⓜ Proprietor: Felicity Thomson

MONTGREENAN MANSION HOUSE HOTEL
Montgreenan Estate
nr Kilwinning
Ayrshire KA13 7QZ
Tel: 01294 557733
Fax: 01294 850395

On A736, 4 miles north of Irvine.

A luxury country house hotel in its own grounds.

- An impeccably restored and maintained Georgian mansion.
- Fine modern/traditional Scottish cuisine.
- "One of the most tranquil and relaxing houses I have ever stayed in."

Built in 1817 by a wealthy tobacco baron, and set in 50 acres of secluded parklands and beautiful gardens, Montgreenan still retains the impressive architecture and decorative features of the period – down to white-aproned helpful staff. Yet the hotel offers every possible modern comfort: it even has a heliport. Based on the finest raw materials, the hotel offers excellent and imaginative cuisine. Its wine list is unusually comprehensive, and will satisfy the most demanding connoisseur. Guests can also enjoy horse-riding, clay pigeon shooting and fishing. The hotel has 1 AA Rosette.

Open all year
🏠 Rooms: 21 with private facilities
✕ Lunch ££
✕ Dinner £££
Ⓥ Vegetarians welcome
🧒 Children welcome
🚭 No smoking in restaurant

Smoked haddock mousse. Oak-smoked salmon with watercress, pine kernels and dill dressing. French fruit flan.

STB Highly Commended 👑 👑 👑 👑
💳 Credit cards: Access/Mastercard/Eurocard, American Express, Visa, Diners Club, Mastercharge
🔑 Proprietor: Darren Dobson

NORTHPARK HOUSE HOTEL
Alloway Village, Ayr
Ayrshire KA7 4NL
Tel: 01292 442336
Fax: 01292 445572

Alloway Village, near Burns' cottage, 2 miles from Ayr town centre.

A charming, well-restored small country house hotel and restaurant in the heart of Burns country.

- An award-winning, family-run establishment of excellent reputation.
- Outstanding and varied traditional cuisine.
- "A beautiful house to stay and relax and enjoy good food."

Robert Burns was born almost next door to Northpark, an early 18th century farmhouse that has been sympathetically extended and converted. Surrounded by Belleisle's two fine golf courses, it stands in its own grounds. Although the hotel has five well-appointed bedrooms, it is best known for its four unique restaurants, grouped around a central conservatory which serves light meals and snacks. In each of the restaurants, both table d'hôte and à la carte menus offer the best of local produce cooked with flair but without pretension. With 95 bins, the wine list befits the cuisine.

Open all year
🏠 Rooms : 5 with private facilities
🅢🅟 Special rates available
✕ Food served all day
✕ Lunch ££
✕ Dinner £££
Ⓥ Vegetarians welcome
🧒 Children welcome
♿ Facilities for disabled visitors
🚭 Two dining rooms non-smoking

Warm mousseline of pike filled with a ragoût of creamed chives and prawns. Pan-fried fillet of lamb set on a warm shallot salad with a blackcurrant and capsicum essence. Home-made vanilla ice cream with poached seasonal fruits and berries.

STB Highly Commended 👑 👑 👑 👑
💳 Credit cards: Access/Mastercard/Eurocard, American Express, Visa, Diners Club, Mastercharge, Switch
🔑 Proprietors: Rosamond & Graeme Rennie

THE STABLES COFFEE HOUSE
Queen's Court, 41 Sandgate
Ayr KA7 1BD
Tel: 01292 283704

To the rear of the old courtyard at the corner of
Sandgate and Newmarket Street.

A small, charming town centre restaurant and tea-room with garden dating back to the 18th century.

* Unmistakably Scottish fare and atmosphere in a charming corner of Ayr.
* Ethnic Scottish cooking.
* "Well researched old recipes presented in historic atmosphere."

Proprietor Ed Baines is a man of firm opinions. At the Stables, a converted block built of local stone in the 1760s, he caters for those who wish distinctively Scottish fare, from tea and a scone to a full meal. You will find neither burgers nor chips in his restaurant. The cakes, scones and iced cream are excellent and made on the premises, the family smokehouse at Craigrossie always produces something interesting. Enjoy a glass of Silver Birch wine with farm-made cheeses and fresh oatcakes or one of the traditional dishes listed below. This is an iconoclastic establishment, but what Ed Baines does, he does well. Children's toys and books available.

Open all year except 25, 26 Dec, 1 + 2 Jan
Note: Open Sun during summer only
✕ Food served all day £
✕ Lunch £
Ⓥ Vegetarians welcome
⚐ Children welcome
⚐ Main dining room non-smoking + separate non-smoking dining room

Cullen skink. Tweed Kettle: casserole of salmon, mushrooms, celery and onions spiced with mace and cooked in white wine. Brown bread ice cream.

⊞ No credit cards
Ⓝ Proprietor: Edward J T Baines

Ballachulish 22

BALLACHULISH HOUSE
Ballachulish, Argyll PA39 4JX
Tel: 01855 811 266
Fax: 01855 811 498

From roundabout south of Ballachulish Bridge take A828 Oban. Signed on left, 200 yards beyond Ballachulish Hotel.

A charming guest house in Argyllshire with a family atmosphere.

* An 18th century country house, immersed in history and beautiful countryside in a remote corner of Scotland's west coast.
* Home cooking; local fish a speciality.
* "Full of old world charm and ambience."

Ballachulish House is steeped in history. It has been the seat of the Stewarts of Ballachulish since the 16th century, indeed the final order for the massacre of Glencoe was signed here. Today Ballachulish House offers quiet, peace and comfort to the traveller. The rooms are spacious and elegantly furnished with antiques; log fires throughout the year ensure a warm and relaxed ambience; the en suite bedrooms have spectacular views over Loch Linnhe and the Morven Hills and in keeping with the rest of the house are comfortable and well-decorated. The owners, Liz and John Grey, treat visitors to their home as personal guests. The dining room is situated in the oldest part of the house, has a low ceiling and looks out to the garden. A simple but elegant table d'hôte menu is presented, the food is carefully presented and well-balanced.

Open all Feb to Nov
🛏 Rooms: 5 with private facilities
⚐ Restricted hotel licence
✕ Dinner 4 course menu £££
Ⓥ Vegetarians welcome
⚐ Children welcome
⚐ No smoking in dining room + bedrooms

Mussels and mushrooms in puff pastry baskets. Fillet of pork with ginger and spring onions. Crêpes with Cointreau and orange butter.

STB Deluxe 👑 👑 👑
⊞ Credit cards: Access/Mastercard/Eurocard, Visa, Switch, Delta, JVC
Ⓝ Owners: Liz & John Grey

COSSES COUNTRY HOUSE

Ballantrae
Ayrshire KA26 0LR
Tel: 01465 831 363
Fax: 01465 831 598

From A77 at southern end of Ballantrae, take inland road signed to Laggan. Cosses is c. 2 miles on right.

Luxury bed and breakfast to the highest standards with superb cooking and hospitality to match.

- Converted farmhouse full of character.
- Gourmet country house cooking.
- "Every comfort and stylish convenience in the heart of beautiful Ayrshire countryside."

Now a country house, dating from 1606, standing in 12 acres of glorious gardens and woodland in a fold in the hills, Cosses was built as a shooting lodge and became the home farm for nearby Glenapp Estate. It is the home of Robin and Susan Crosthwaite, and guests are made to feel they are part of the family. They grow their own vegetables, herbs and some fruit, and Susan – a Cordon Bleu Chef – presents delicious, four course, table d'hôte menus which feature local seafood and game, Scottish cheeses and home-made petit fours (the menus are often discussed with guests beforehand). Two cottage suites are provided within the courtyard and there is a double bedroom en suite within the house itself.

Open 17 Jan to 23 Dec
- 🛏 Rooms: 3 with private facilities
- SP Special rates available
- ✕ Dinner £££
- ✕ Dinner for non-residents – by reservation only
- Ⓥ Vegetarians welcome
- 大 Children welcome
- ⌖ No smoking in dining room

Monkfish tails, queenies and Ballantrae prawns in a light saffron sauce with a Cosses spinach feuillete. Crailoch pheasant roast with whisky, cream bay and thyme. Cosses fresh blackcurrant brûlée.

STB Deluxe 👑 👑 👑
- 💳 No credit cards
- Ⓜ Proprietors: Susan & Robin Crosthwaite

BALGONIE COUNTRY HOUSE HOTEL

Braemar Place, Ballater AB35 5NQ
Tel: 013397 55482
Fax: 013397 55482

Off A93 Aberdeen-Perth, on outskirts of village of Ballater.

A country house hotel in the heart of Deeside.

- Tranquil Edwardian mansion in four acres of mature gardens with views towards hills of Glen Muick.
- Traditional and innovative recipes using fresh local produce.
- "First class cooking from fresh Scottish produce, served in elegant surroundings."

Balgonie is five minutes' walk from Ballater on Royal Deeside, set in spacious gardens overlooking Ballater Golf Course. The resident proprietors, John and Priscilla Finnie, pride themselves on maintaining a friendly but unobtrusive service. The nine en suite bedrooms are very comfortable and tastefully furnished. The dining room is the heart of Balgonie providing an inviting cuisine using locally sourced fish and game. When in season, herbs and soft fruits from the garden are always found on the menu. French and German is spoken. The hotel has 2 AA Rosettes. Winner of Taste of Scotland Country House Hotel of the Year Award 1993.

Open 12 Feb to 5 Jan
- 🛏 Rooms: 9 with private facilities
- SP Special rates available
- ✕ Lunch – by reservation only ££
- 🍴 Dinner 4 course menu non-residents – by reservation £££
- Ⓥ Vegetarians welcome – prior notice required
- 大 Children over 5 years welcome at dinner
- ⌖ No smoking in dining room

A filo pastry parcel filled with Finnan Haddock and sole served with a smoked fish cream. Fillet of Scotch lamb garnished with a ragoût of mushrooms, asparagus and kidneys, with a rosemary-scented jus. Rhubarb crumble served with Deeside heather honey parfait.

STB Deluxe 👑 👑 👑 👑
- 💳 Credit cards: Access/Mastercard/Eurocard, American Express, Visa, Switch, Delta
- Ⓜ Proprietor: John G Finnie

DARROCH LEARG HOTEL
Braemar Road, Ballater
Aberdeenshire AB35 5UX
Tel: 013397 55443
Fax: 013397 55252

½ mile from centre of village of Ballater, off A93.

Country house hotel on Royal Deeside with views of Cairngorms.

* Victorian period house overlooking Ballater and Royal Deeside.
* Modern Scottish cooking.
* "Excellent – a very high quality, family-run hotel."

Darroch Learg was built in 1888 as a country residence when Royal Deeside was at its most fashionable. The hotel enjoys a wonderful situation, high up on a rocky hillside, with excellent views. The house has period charm and has retained the comfortable atmosphere of the family home it once was, with two drawing rooms (smoking and non-smoking). The dining room and spacious conservatory allow diners to enjoy the wonderful outlook south to the hills of Glen Muick. The short table d'hôte menu (two main courses) offers top quality local meat from the excellent local dealers confidently and expertly prepared in unusual combinations and sauces. The hotel has 2 AA Rosettes.

Open Feb to Dec closed Christmas
🏢 Rooms: 18 with private facilities
✗ Food served all day £££
✗ Lunch £££
✗ Dinner ££££
Ⓥ Vegetarians welcome – prior notice required
🕏 Children welcome
♿ Facilities for disabled visitors – ground floor
🚭 No smoking in dining room

Pan-fried trout with buttered asparagus ravioli of lobster and courgette cream sauce. Saddle of Deeside roe deer with an envée of garden green, spinach, cous-cous and a morel sauce. William pear in puff pastry with a warm ginger and butterscotch sauce and a lime custard.

STB Highly Commended 👑 👑 👑 👑
💳 Credit cards: Access/Mastercard/Eurocard, American Express, Visa, Diners Club, Switch
🗝 Proprietors: Nigel & Fiona Franks

DEESIDE HOTEL
Braemar Road, Ballater
Aberdeenshire AB35 5RQ
Tel: 013397 55420
Fax: 013397 55357

On west side of Ballater, set back from A93 Braemar road.

A comfortable family hotel with a relaxed atmosphere.

* Pink granite town house.
* Traditional Scottish cooking.
* "Honest, tasty and wholesome food."

The Deeside is an attractive pink granite building, set back from the main road with an informal well-maintained garden. It is a family-run establishment with nine en suite bedrooms, two of which are situated on the ground floor. The house is welcoming and in the sitting room there is an impressive painted frieze of wild animals; the original Victorian mantelpiece and tiled fireplace has been retained. Through an open archway from the lounge bar is the dining room with its varnished wooden floor and oil paintings of mountain scenery on the walls. In the evening meals are available in both the restaurant and bar where you can also sample a good selection of Scottish real ales and malt whiskies. Caithness Glass 'Taste of Royal Deeside' Best Value for Money Award 1995.

Open 10 Feb to 2 Jan except Christmas Day + Boxing Day
🏢 Rooms: 9 with private facilities
SP Special rates available
✗ Lunch Sun ££
✗ Dinner ££
Ⓥ Vegetarians welcome
🕏 Children welcome
♿ Facilities for disabled visitors
🚭 No smoking in restaurant

Fish soups and chowders. Roast rack of lamb with garlic and rosemary. Cloutie dumpling.

STB Commended 👑 👑 👑
💳 Credit cards: Access/Mastercard/Eurocard, Visa, Switch
🗝 Directors: Donald & Alison Brooker

GLEN LUI HOTEL

Invercauld Road, Ballater
Aberdeenshire AB35 5RP
Tel: 013397 55402 Fax: 013397 55545

Off A93 at western end of Ballater.

A town hotel with a country house appeal overlooking the golf course and Lochnagar.

- A country house style hotel standing in two acres of grounds.
- Modern Scottish cooking, with some French influences.
- "A combination of good food and a well-chosen wine cellar."

A house which has been much added to, most recently by the addition of a wrap-around conservatory/restaurant overlooking the golf course. Accommodation is comfortable; service polite, friendly and well-trained. The courses of the table d'hôte menu (four starters, four main courses) are titled in French – 'votre plat principal', etc – but you forgive all when you discover that the owner is himself French, and that the cooking is sublime. The plain menu descriptions do not do justice to the confidence and artistry each dish demonstrates. A family style 'bistro menu' is also offered. There is a very comprehensive wine list with vintage wines.

Open all year
Note: Possible renovation Jan/Feb – please telephone
🏠 Rooms: 19 with private facilities
SP Special rates available
✕ Lunch £
✕ Dinner £-££
Ⓥ Vegetarians welcome
☆ Children welcome
⅍ Facilities for disabled visitors
⊬ No smoking in restaurant + bedrooms

Seared queen scallops served on a fine julienne of vegetables with a lemon and coriander dressing. Pan-fried noisette of venison served with a parfait of black pudding on a bed of red cabbage, edged with a juniper and port essence. Home-made cranachan ice cream served in a lacy biscuit on a pool of raspberry coulis garnished with fresh raspberries.

STB Highly Commended 🏅 🏅 🏅 🏅
💳 Credit cards: Access/Mastercard/Eurocard, American Express, Visa, Mastercharge, Switch
🅰 Proprietors: Serge & Lorraine Geraud

THE GREEN INN RESTAURANT WITH ROOM

9 Victoria Road, Ballater
Aberdeenshire AB35 5QQ
Tel: 013397 55701
Fax: 013397 55701

In centre of Ballater on village green.

A quality restaurant with rooms; Jeffrey and Carol Purves both have a justified reputation for delicious food in intimate and comfortable surroundings.

- A two-storey granite building, once a temperance hotel.
- Modern regional Scottish cooking, with good use of international influences.
- "Skilful combination of textures."

Jeff Purves' reputation is well-deserved: his cooking is innovative and imaginative, draws inspiration from other traditions (Oriental, for example) and applies this to the excellent local produce available on Deeside. Chef specials change daily, often treat classic Scottish dishes in an unusual way and combine flavours with assured confidence. An outstanding selection of Scottish cheeses is always available. Jeff's cooking adopts a 'healthy' approach – using cream only when necessary, replacing sugar with honey, and so on – and he is also delighted by the challenge of vegetarian cooking, but requests advance warning to do it justice. Service from Carol is friendly and helpful in the intimate dining room. The Green Inn has 2 AA Rosettes. Winner of The Macallan Taste of Scotland Restaurant of the Year Award 1995.

Open all year except 2 wks Nov,
Christmas Day + 26 to 28 Dec
Closed Sun Oct to Mar
🏠 Rooms: 3 with private facilities
SP Special rates available
✕ Lunch Sun ££
✕ Dinner £££
Ⓥ Vegetarians welcome
☆ Children welcome
⅍ Disabled access only
⊬ Smoking permitted at coffee stage only

A confit of gigot of rabbit with butter beans with garlic sauce. Inky Pinky. Iced cranachan parfait with raspberry sauce and seasonal berries.

STB Highly Commended 🏅 🏅 🏅
💳 Credit cards: Access/Mastercard/Eurocard, American Express, Visa Mastercharge
🅰 Proprietors: J J & C A Purves

HAYLOFT RESTAURANT

Bridge Square, Ballater
Aberdeenshire AB35 5QJ
Tel: 013397 55999
Fax: 013397 55999

Central Ballater, close to the bridge.

A highly atmospheric restaurant by the River Dee.

- Converted 19th century stables.
- Home cooking and fresh light meals.
- "Traditional cooking to suit most tastes."

The old stable building stands beside the river in the centre of town and has been converted into a licensed restaurant. The interior makes a theme of its former function, retaining many of the original features, with hay bales and items of riding tack decorating the room. The restaurant has a high wooden ceiling and has been set out on two levels with a long gallery running along one side. Pine tables and chairs, horse brasses and other paraphernalia add to the peculiar rustic atmosphere here. The varied menus offer both daily specials and traditional dishes (plus pizzas, pastas and children's specials), cooked simply with attention to presentation. The service is cheerful and there is a delicious range of home baking available during the day.

Open mid Jan to end Nov + Christmas period
Note: Please book ahead if possible
Closed 1½ days during winter – please telephone

- ✗ Lunch £-££
- ✗ Dinner £-£££
- Ⓥ Vegetarians welcome
- ⚹ Children welcome
- ♿ Facilities for disabled visitors
- ⚞ No pipes or cigars

Marinated herrings. Escalope of venison. Grilled local salmon with parsley butter. Steaks.

- ⊞ Credit cards: Access/Mastercard/Eurocard, American Express, Visa, Diners Club, Mastercharge, Switch, Delta
- ꗞ Proprietors: Brodie & Winnie Hepburn

RAVENSWOOD HOTEL

Braemar Road, Ballater
Aberdeenshire AB3 5RQ
Tel: 013397 55539
Fax: 013397 55539

On the A93, western end of Ballater – a 10 minute walk from centre of village.

Small friendly hotel.

- Converted Victorian villa.
- Traditional Scottish hotel cooking.
- "Relaxing atmosphere with good service and food."

Ravenswood Hotel is a small friendly family-owned Victorian hotel in the pretty village of Ballater which is already renowned as home to some of the best eating places in Scotland. The hotel is a splendid period building which retains many of its original features. The Fyfes offer simple good food, local produce well-cooked. Family service meals are offered in the dining room and the lounge bar (with fireplace) offers a selection of alternative dishes. Ravenswood is unpretentious, good value and a lovely place from which to explore Royal Deeside.

Open all year except 10 Nov to 5 Dec

- ⌸ Rooms: 8, 5 with private facilities
- ⒮ᴾ Special rates available
- ✗ Lunch ££
- ✗ Dinner ££
- Ⓥ Vegetarians welcome
- ⚹ Children welcome
- ⚞ No smoking in dining room

Cream of carrot soup. Pan-fried Deeside venison steak with a creamy whisky sauce. Fan of Ogen melon with bramble sorbet.

STB Approved 👑 👑 👑

- ⊞ Credit cards: Access/Mastercard/Eurocard, American Express, Visa
- ꗞ Owners: Fraser & Cathy Fyfe

STAKIS ROYAL DEESIDE
(formerly Craigendarroch Hotel
& Country Club)
Braemar Road, Ballater
Royal Deeside AB35 5XA
Tel: 013397 55858
Fax: 013397 55447

On A93 western end of Ballater, near Balmoral.

**A resort hotel with full leisure and sports
facilities.**

- Victorian country house.
- Modern grand hotel with fine dining and
  bistro cooking.
- "Excellent for that special occasion."

This house was built in the 19th century for the
Keiller family (the inventors of marmalade) and has
been converted into a modern resort hotel with
time-ownership lodges and every imaginable
facility. The food on offer has all the feel of a large
hotel with a brigade of chefs working busily to
support the restaurants. The Oaks is a classy
formal restaurant, serving interesting and
imaginative dishes prepared by Executive Chef,
Paul Moran, both continental and classic
influences are detectable is his beautifully
presented dishes. In The Clubhouse Restaurant,
which adjoins the pool area in the Leisure Club, the
bistro style food is fast, comprehensive and
unsophisticated – good grub for all the family, and
some dishes may be taken away.

Open all year
🏠 Rooms: 44 with private facilities
ⓢⓟ Special rates available
✕ Lunch (Clubhouse Restaurant) ££
✕ Dinner (Clubhouse Restaurant) ££
✕ Dinner (The Oaks) ££-£££
Ⓥ Vegetarians welcome
ⓚ Children welcome
✄ No smoking in The Oaks

**Terrine of Deeside game. Pan-fried roulade of
salmon on a bed of buttered spinach. Crêpes
suzette.**

STB Highly Commended 👑 👑 👑 👑 👑
🗄 Credit cards: Access/Mastercard/Eurocard,
   American Express, Visa, Diners Club, Switch,
   Delta
ⓜ General Manager: Eric H Brown

Ballindalloch   25

THE DELNASHAUGH INN
Ballindalloch
Banffshire AB37 9AS
Tel: 01807 500255
Fax: 01807 500389

From A9 Aviemore, take A95 via Grantown-on-
Spey, or A941 from Elgin, to Ballindalloch.

A stylishly refurbished country inn on Speyside.

- Old drovers inn with a lovely situation.
- Home cooking.
- "Creative country cuisine."

The Delnashaugh Inn dates back to the 16th
century, when it provided rest and food for the
drovers as they took their cattle to the markets in
the south. Today it is popular with sportsmen,
particularly fishermen: it stands within the
Ballindalloch Estate and overlooks the valley of the
River Avon, which joins the Spey not far from the
hotel; fishing, shooting and stalking can be
arranged. It was completely refurbished recently,
in a way which respects the original atmosphere
and character of the old inn. The inn's proprietors,
David and Marion Ogden, present a simple table
d'hôte menu (three starters, three main courses),
often featuring salmon and game from the estate.
The cooking is traditional and tempting.

Open mid Mar to end Oct
🏠 Rooms: 9 with private facilities
✕ Lunch £
✕ Dinner £££
Ⓥ Vegetarians welcome – prior notice required
ⓚ Children welcome
♿ Facilities for disabled visitors

**Smoked trout mousse wrapped in smoked salmon.
Roast loin of lamb with apricot and hazelnut
stuffing. Meringue with chocolate sauce.**

STB Highly Commended 👑 👑 👑 👑
🗄 Credit cards: Access/Mastercard/Eurocard,
   Visa
ⓜ Proprietors: David & Marion Ogden

BALQUHIDDER

MONACHYLE MHOR
Balquhidder, Lochearnhead, Perthshire FK19 8PQ
Tel: 01877 384 622
Fax: 01877 384 305

11 miles north of Callander on A84. Turn right at Kingshouse Hotel – 6 miles straight along glen road.

A small, award-winning farmhouse hotel in the Perthshire hills.

- Family-run establishment of great character .
- Elegant Scottish/traditional cooking.
- "Relaxing hideaway set in glorious Scottish scenery."

In Rob Roy country of mountains and lochs, Monachyle Mhor sits in its own 2,000 acres in the heart of the Braes o' Balquhidder. The hotel's views over Lochs Voil and Doine are breathtaking. Proprietors Rob and Jean Lewis fully deserve their reputation for hospitality. All rooms are comfortable and have bathrooms en suite. Both the restaurant and cosy bar serve imaginative, good food that makes the best of fresh, local produce – offering game from the estate, fish from the West Coast and the finest Scottish meat cooked with a French influence by chef, Tom. Interesting, discerning wine list. Monachyle has 2 AA Rosettes. There are also three self-catering cottages, equipped and appointed to the same high standards as the hotel. *(See advert Page 265.)*

Open all year
Rooms: 10 with private facilities
✘ Food served all day £-£££
✘ Lunch ££
✘ Dinner £££
Ⓥ Vegetarians welcome
✌ No smoking in restaurant

Hot soufflé of smoked trout and horseradish with a tapenade sauce. Slice of pork loin with fresh dates stuffed with apricot purée wrapped in spinach and roasted, served with a mild curry sauce. White peaches lightly poached in a clove and tea syrup served with home-made ice cream and fresh cream.

STB Commended 🏅 🏅 🏅
▣ Credit cards: Access/Mastercard/Eurocard, Visa, Switch
Ⓜ Proprietor: Jean Lewis

BANKFOOT

PERTHSHIRE VISITOR CENTRE
Bankfoot
Perth
PH1 4EB
Tel: 01738 787696
Fax: 01738 787120

8 miles north of Perth on A9. Follow signs for Bankfoot.

Just off the A9, this is a good place to break a journey.

- Waitress service restaurant, plus shop and 'Macbeth Experience'.
- Country kitchen restaurant with good home cooking.
- "An excellent stop for A9 travellers."

'The Macbeth Experience', which is the focus of this visitor centre, is a multi-media exploration of Scotland's mis-judged 11th century warrior king. Next door is a well-stocked shop (knitwear, glass, books, foods and whisky, gifts and souvenirs) and a comfortable friendly restaurant, offering freshly made soups, desserts and a varied selection of home baking as well as a selection of freshly cooked meals listed on a blackboard. There is a large car park adjacent, and a children's play area.

Open all year except Christmas Day + New Year's Day
✘ Food served all day £
♀ Table Licence
Ⓥ Vegetarians welcome
♿ Facilities for disabled visitors

Home-made soups and home baking. Haggis, neeps and tatties. Perthshire beef. Cloutie dumpling.

▣ Credit cards: Access/Mastercard/Eurocard, Visa
Ⓜ Proprietors: Wilson & Catriona Girvan

Beauly 28

CHRIALDON HOUSE HOTEL
Station Road
Beauly
Inverness-shire IV4 7EH
Tel: 01463 782336

On A862 main road through Beauly, close to the square. 12 miles from Inverness.

A small hotel just off the main street in the centre of Beauly; an ideal touring base for the Highlands.

- Red sandstone Victorian detached town house.
- Scottish home cooking.
- "Freshly prepared quality food."

Surrounded by a very well-tended garden in the town of Beauly, the Chrialdon is elegant yet informal with spacious rooms in a homely environment. The hotel is run by new owners Nicoll and Valerie Reid, who are welcoming and helpful hosts and who pay attention to the small details and needs which make for a memorable stay. They offer short but well-balanced menus, using only such fresh produce as is seasonally available; the cooking is simple, creative and tasty – and extremely good value for money. The Chrialdon has such a good local reputation which it retains under its new, caring proprietors.

Open all year except Christmas Day
🏠 Rooms: 9, 6 with private facilities
SP Special rates available
✗ Residents only
✗ Dinner ££
V Vegetarians welcome
⚘ Children welcome
⚯ No smoking in dining room

Home-made soups. Cushions of venison in port wine and juniper berry sauce. Meringue and fresh cream blended with Glayva.

STB Commended 👑 👑 👑
💳 Credit cards: Access/Mastercard/Eurocard, Visa
👤 Proprietors: Nicoll & Valerie Reid

LOVAT ARMS HOTEL
Beauly
Inverness-shire IV4 7BS
Tel: 01463 782313
Fax: 01463 782862

On A862, 11 miles from Inverness in Beauly centre.

Superior small town hotel.

- Elegant town hotel.
- Modern Scottish cooking.
- "Delightful hotel in picturesque town."

The name Beauly derives its name from 'beau lieu' or beautiful place. The Lovat Arms is a stylish family-owned hotel in the centre of a picturesque small market town. The remains of Beauly Priory, built around 1230 and visited by Mary Queen of Scots, makes an ideal picnic location. The food is very well-cooked and presented by Head Chef Donald Munro who uses his skills to present local produce in innovative ways for good value for money. The hotel is an ideal place from which to explore Beauly or Moray Firth with their natural beauty and wide variety of wild life.

Open all year
🏠 Rooms: 22 with private facilities
SP Special rates available
✗ Food served all day ££
✗ Lunch ££
✗ Dinner £££
V Vegetarians welcome
⚘ Children welcome
⚬ Facilities for disabled visitors – please telephone
⚯ No smoking in dining room

Sautéd asparagus spears in clarified butter, glazed with melted Caithness smoked cheese. Pan-fried saddle of Torachilty lamb covered in crushed peppercorns and finished with natural yoghurt and freshly chopped herbs.

STB Commended 👑 👑 👑 👑
💳 Credit cards: Access/Mastercard/Eurocard, Visa
👤 Proprietor: William Fraser

`BETTYHILL`

BORGIE LODGE HOTEL
Skerray, Bettyhill, Sutherland KW14 7TH
Tel: 01641 521 332 Fax: 01641 521 332

Take A836 for 7 miles from Tongue, turn left at the Torrisdale Road. Borgie Lodge is ½ mile along on the right.

A traditional hunting and fishing lodge in pleasant gardens on Scotland's northern seaboard.

- Spacious country house hotel.
- Home cooking – local fish is a speciality.
- "A comfortable hotel providing very good food in the heart of the most renowned fishing area in Scotland."

Quiet and secluded, Borgie Lodge has been the home of Peter and Jacqui MacGregor for three years. In this time the hunting and fishing lodge has been tastefully upgraded to provide comfortable accommodation while keeping its traditional Highland image by way of Clan Sutherland tartan carpets, sporting prints and crackling log fires. A self-taught cook, Jacqui makes excellent use of the Caithness beef and lamb available to her, and the daily changing choice dinner menu will often feature the salmon and brown trout caught by the guests! Should you decide to contribute to the dinner menu, Borgie Lodge has salmon fishing rights on the Rivers Borgie and Halladale and boats for wild brown trout on the hotel's 20 hill lochs! Shooting and stalking on the 12,600 acre Tongue Estate. Peter can supply all the necessary ghillies, equipment and tuition.

Open all year except 24 Dec to 3 Jan
- ⌂ Rooms: 6 with private facilities
- ✕ Lunch £
- ✕ Dinner £££
- Ⓥ Vegetarians welcome
- ✶ Children welcome
- ⊭ No smoking in dining room + bedrooms

Lasagne of seared salmon with asparagus, tomato and a frothy herb sauce. Roast saddle of Borgie Glen venison. Iced cranachan parfait with a fresh raspberry sauce.

STB Highly Commended 👑 👑 👑
- ⊞ Credit cards: Access/Mastercard/Eurocard, Visa
- Ⓝ Proprietors: Peter & Jacqui MacGregor

`BIGGAR`

HARTREE COUNTRY HOUSE HOTEL
Biggar
Lanarkshire ML12 6JJ
Tel: 01899 221027
Fax: 01899 221259

Just off A702 on western outskirts of Biggar.

Country house hotel in its own grounds on the Lanarkshire/Peeblesshire border.

- Old sandstone baronial mansion.
- Good Scottish cooking.
- "Good Scottish cooking served by friendly hosts in a homely and elegant atmosphere."

Hartree is an historic country house with parts dating from the 15th century, although it is mainly Victorian and set in seven acres of peaceful wooded countryside. It is not far from Biggar, and offers a good base from which to tour this part of the Borders. The house is charming and has retained many baronial features in its interior – heavy mouldings and panelling, a marble floor in the lobby, and carved fireplaces. The grand dining room offers an interesting menu with daily changing 'specials' and many Scottish specialities. Almost equidistant from Edinburgh and Glasgow. Over 100 whiskies.

Open Mar to Dec
- ⌂ Rooms: 12 with private facilities
- ⌷ Special rates available
- ✕ Dinner £-££
- Ⓥ Vegetarians welcome
- ✶ Children welcome

Home-made soups. Barbary duck with port and raspberry coulis. Rum and chocolate mousse.

STB Commended 👑 👑 👑 👑
- ⊞ Credit cards: Access/Mastercard/Eurocard, American Express, Visa, Diners Club, Mastercharge, Switch, Delta
- Ⓝ Proprietors: John & Anne Charlton Robert & Susan Reed

SKIRLING HOUSE
Skirling
Biggar
Lanarkshire
ML12 6HD
Tel: 01899 860274
Fax: 01899 860255

In Skirling village overlooking the village green.
2 miles from Biggar on A72.

Architecturally unique, this splendid house is also wonderfully hospitable.

- Small deluxe guest house overlooking the village green in Skirling.
- Good home cooking.
- "A little haven of peace and tranquillity where every effort is made to make guests welcome."

Private houses in the Arts and Crafts style are not common in Scotland, and to find one which retains so many of its original features is a great joy. The house was built in 1908 for Lord Gibson Carmichael and is now the home of Bob and Isobel Hunter, for whom nothing is too much trouble if it makes your stay more enjoyable. Bob presents a four course set menu each evening (guests preferences are sought in advance), based upon the fresh produce available locally that day; he cooks with a light touch and his dishes are very well-executed. Everything is home-made, including breads, ice cream and preserves. "This place is a real gem."

Open 1 Mar to 31 Dec
- 🏠 Rooms : 3 with private facilities
- ♀ Restricted hotel licence
- ✗ Lunch – by arrangement only
- ✗ Dinner 4 course menu ££
- Ⓥ Vegetarians welcome
- ♿ Restricted access
- 🚭 No smoking throughout

Warm salad with smoked venison. Rack of Borders lamb with a pecan and herb crust. Calvados soufflé.

STB Deluxe 👑 👑 👑
- 💳 No credit cards
- Ⓜ Proprietors: Bob & Isobel Hunter

Blair Atholl 31

ATHOLL ARMS HOTEL
Blair Atholl
Perthshire
PH18 5SG
Tel: 01796 481205
Fax: 01796 481550

1 mile from A9. Opposite Blair Castle.

Traditional Highland hotel steeped in history.

- Baronial style hotel.
- Modern British cooking.
- "The best of Scottish innovative cuisine served in traditional surroundings."

The Atholl Arms built in 1832 is a traditional hotel which has built up a reputation for good food, comfort and friendly service over many years. Bar style meals are available at lunchtime and in the evening dinner is served in the grand dining room. An excellent stopping point for travellers close to the busy A9.

Open all year
- 🏠 Rooms: 26 with private facilities
- 🆂🅿 Special rates available
- ✗ Lunch £-££
- ✗ Dinner ££
- Ⓥ Vegetarians welcome
- ♿ Facilities for disabled visitors
- 🚭 No smoking in dining room
- 🐄 Member of the Scotch Beef Club

Rolled breast of pheasant with an orange, sage and horseradish filling served on a whisky and orange caramel sauce. Seared escalopes of salmon with lemon chutney. Drambuie and cooked oatmeal parfait with raspberries and glazed sabayon sauce.

STB Commended 👑 👑 👑 👑
- 💳 Credit cards: Access/Mastercard/Eurocard, Visa

THE HOUSE OF BRUAR LTD
by Blair Atholl
Perthshire PH18 5TW
Tel: 01796 483236
Fax: 01796 483218

7 miles north of Pitlochry on the side of A9 at Bruar. Restaurant services A9.

An astonishing new emporium of the 'best of Scottish'.

- Self-service restaurant.
- Home cooking and baking.
- "A good quality centre for Scottish goods with food of the same standard."

The House of Bruar is a large, splendidly designed (inspired by Victorian hunting lodges) and expensively built (dressed stone, slate roof, astragal windows, etc) 'emporium' selling the very best of Scottish country products. It includes a cashmere hall, a cloth room, a wildflower nursery, country wear hall, food hall and 200 seater cafe/restaurant. Play and picnic areas are also provided. The lengthy blackboard menus offer snacks and full meals, with many classic Scottish dishes; the cooking is fresh and accomplished; breads, cakes and scones are freshly baked. A cheerful place for the whole family to break a journey.

....

Open all year except Christmas Day + New Year's Day
✗ Food served all day
Ⓥ Vegetarians welcome
✶ Children welcome
♿ Facilities for disabled visitors
✔ No smoking throughout

Home-baked cakes and scones. Fresh salmon. Aberdeen Angus beef.

💷 Credit cards: Access/Mastercard/Eurocard, American Express, Visa, Mastercharge, Switch, Delta
🅽 Restaurant Manager: Susan Booth

WOODLANDS
St Andrews Crescent, Blair Atholl
Perthshire PH18 5SX
Tel: 01796 481 403

A9, 7 miles north of Pitlochry. 100 yards down left turn in centre of Blair Atholl.

A charming guest house in Blair Atholl.

- Attractive town house.
- Good home cooking.
- "Dolina is a wonderful cook and accomplished hostess."

Sheltered in its own gardens down a small lane off the main Blair Atholl thoroughfare, Woodlands is a warm and welcoming home. And no ordinary home either for owner and hostess Dolina MacLennan is an enchanting character and a well-known Gaelic singer and actress. Her idiosyncratic home has all the charm of an old Scottish family house, with creaking floorboards and over-excited plumbing! Dolina's guests return again and again, revelling in her delightful company and generous hospitality. Sherry is offered in the sitting room in the early evening before dinner is served. Dolina seeks out the finest fresh foods, from Hebridean seafood to Highland venison and game, all cooked simply and carefully in the best tradition of home cooking. Gaelic spoken.

....

N.B. Opening times variable, depending on filming commitments
🛏 Rooms: 3
🆄 ⚲ Unlicensed – guests welcome to take own wine
✗ Dinner ££
✗ Dinner for non-residents by arrangement
Ⓥ Vegetarians welcome

Cream of spinach soup. Baked salmon fillets with smoked salmon crust with dill. Lemon soufflé.

💷 No credit cards
🅽 Proprietor: Dolina MacLennan

Blairgowrie 32

ALTAMOUNT HOUSE HOTEL
Coupar Angus Road
Blairgowrie
Perthshire PH10 6JN
Tel: 01250 873512/876814
Fax: 01250 876200

Take A923 to Coupar Angus from centre of the town. The hotel is 500 yards on right hand side and is well-signed.

A comfortable family-run hotel offering good food.

- A stone built house within lovely grounds.
- Traditional Scottish cooking.
- "A warm welcome and friendly hospitality."

Altamount Hotel is a lovely old Georgian house built in 1806 and set in six acres of its own well-tended gardens. The hotel has all the tranquillity of a country house hotel but is located only 500 yards from the centre of the town. Run by Alastair Campbell and his wife Rosie, the atmosphere is 'easy' and one has the feeling of being welcomed to a caring family-run hotel. Menus change daily and produce is sourced locally wherever possible and dishes are traditional and well-cooked.

Open all year except Christmas Day
- ⌂ Rooms: 7 with private facilities
- SP Special rates available
- ✗ Food served all day £
- ✗ Lunch £
- ✗ Dinner ££
- Ⅴ Vegetarians welcome
- ⋏ Children welcome
- ⌘ Wheelchair access
- ⌇ No smoking in dining room

Quenelles of choux pastry flavoured with cheese and chives. Loin of lamb sandwiched with a wild mushroom and tarragon farce. Varied choice of home-made desserts and ice creams.

STB Commended 👑 👑 👑 👑
- ⊞ Credit cards: Access/Mastercard/Eurocard, American Express, Visa, Switch, Delta
- ⍟ Proprietor: Alastair Campbell

CARGILLS RESTAURANT & BISTRO
Lower Mill Street
Blairgowrie
Perthshire PH10 6AQ
Tel: 01250 876735

At the Square in the centre of Blairgowrie, turn left off A93 Perth-Braemar road into Mill Street. Cargills is behind the car park, 200 yards down on the left.

An attractive bistro in a converted grain store.

- Converted mill store of old stone.
- Modern Scottish cooking with some European influence.
- "A newly opened bistro/restaurant offering excellent food."

The old grain store with original stone exterior has been attractively converted into a modern bistro/restaurant with some original fittings such as metal pillars left as a feature. The arched door leads into a spacious area with polished wooden floor and attractive dark green wooden tables and chairs. There is a bar in the corner and a blackboard shows daily choices in addition to the menu. The menu offers an impressive selection of dishes all reasonably priced and a short wine list complements this. An ideal venue for an informal lunch or dinner which could be followed by a riverside stroll to Cargills Leap – a few hundred yards away!

Open all year except 13 to 27 Jan
Closed Sun after 7pm + Mon
- ✗ Lunch ££
- ✗ Dinner ££
- Ⅴ Vegetarians welcome
- ⋏ Children welcome
- ⌘ Facilities for disabled visitors

Salmon hash served with soured cream. Lamb fillets roasted in peanut butter and served on grain mustard fruits. Blairgowrie summer pudding with vanilla sauce.

- ⊞ Credit cards: Access/Mastercard/Eurocard, American Express, Visa, Switch, Delta
- ⍟ Chef/Proprietor: Willie Little

Boat of Garten 33

THE BOAT HOTEL
Boat of Garten
Inverness-shire PH24 3BH
Tel: 01479 831258
Fax: 01479 831414

Leave A9 north of Aviemore, take A95 then turn off for Boat of Garten. 4½ miles from A9.

A comfortable village hotel close to angling and golfing.

- Neat country hotel in an attractive village.
- Traditional Scottish cooking.
- "Well-cooked local produce."

Boat of Garten takes its name from the ferry which crossed the Spey at this point: the hotel is an excellent base from which to explore the many attractions of Upper Speyside. The hotel is privately owned by Bruce and Jean Wilson – attentive and experienced hosts who are supported by a professional and friendly staff. Although it has 30 bedrooms and a large airy restaurant, The Boat manages to retain the atmosphere of a small, personal hotel. Guests have compared it to a country house. The food, chosen from a four course table d'hôte menu, is well-conceived, with interesting combinations of flavour. The service is excellent. The hotel is extremely popular with golfers, birdwatchers, hill walkers and groups.

....

	Open 21 Dec to 10 Nov
⌂	Rooms: 30 with private facilities
SP	Special rates available
✕	Lunch £
✕	Dinner £££
V	Vegetarians welcome
☨	Children welcome
⌇	No smoking in restaurant

Warm salad of tossed leaves with slivers of calf liver and lardons of smoked bacon dressed with olive oil infused with sage. Pot-roasted loin of venison. Rhubarb and ginger fool with orange shortbread.

STB Commended ♕ ♕ ♕ ♕
- 💳 Credit cards: Access/Mastercard/Eurocard, American Express, Visa, Diners Club, Mastercharge, Switch, Delta, JCB
- ⋈ Proprietors: Bruce and Jean Wilson

HEATHBANK – THE VICTORIAN HOUSE
Boat of Garten
Inverness-shire PH24 3BD
Tel: 01479 831 234

Situated in village of Boat of Garten.

Country house set in heather and herb gardens run by Graham and Lindsay Burge.

- Victorian house with painstakingly designed interiors.
- Imaginative cooking using freshest local produce.
- "Friendly, courteous, professional and fun!"

Built at the turn-of-the-century, Heathbank retains much of its period charm: etched glass, cast-iron fireplaces and fine staircase. Bedrooms, including two with four-poster beds, are beautiful and filled with Victoriana – fans, lace, tapestries and mirrors – one even has a sunken bathroom. Each is individually designed by Lindsay Burge, the joint-owner. Her skills are particularly apparent in the new conservatory dining room, which has a Rennie Mackintosh theme with furniture tailor-made by local craftsmen. In the kitchen Graham Burge, a member of the Association Culinaire Française, is an experienced and professional chef. A set menu is presented in the evening from local produce. Heathbank has an AA Rosette.

....

	Open 26 Dec to 31 Oct
⌂	Rooms: 7 with private facilities
♀	Restricted licence
⌸	Packed lunches available £
✕	Dinner 4 course menu ££
⋈	Non-residents – booking essential
V	Vegetarians welcome
☨	Children over 10 years welcome
⌇	No smoking throughout

Wild duck sausage with juniper berries and raisins with home-made bread. Steamed River Spey salmon escalope with orange stuffing served with light sage sauce. Ice cream eclair with hot butterscotch sauce.

STB Highly Commended ♕ ♕ ♕
- 💳 No credit cards
- ⋈ Proprietors: Lindsay Burge & Graham Burge AHCIMA

Bothwell 34

THE GRAPE VINE RESTAURANT & CAFE BAR
27 Main Street, Bothwell
Lanarkshire G71 8RD
Tel: 01698 852014
Fax: 01698 854405

On main street in Bothwell, ½ mile off M74 (East Kilbride exit).

Informal restaurant/coffee shop/pub.

- Village pub with restaurant.
- Good standard cooking.
- "'Specials' menu offering fresh Scottish produce."

The Grape Vine is in the centre of the picturesque conservation village of Bothwell. Whether for informal dining – a light meal or snack in the bar – or a more leisurely experience in the restaurant, both are available all day. Menus are creatively prepared to include a wide selection of familiar choices, including burgers and grills, pizzas and pasta, to smoked salmon, lamb and duck.

    Open all year except Christmas Day, Boxing Day, 1 + 2 Jan
✗ Food served all day ££
✗ Lunch £
✗ Dinner ££

Gâteau of haggis with Drambuie. Roast loin of lamb with cous-cous and wild berries. Tart Tatin with cheesecake cream.

▦ Credit cards: Access/Mastercard/Eurocard, American Express, Visa, Diners Club, Switch
▨ Proprietor: Colin Morrison

Braemar 35

BRAEMAR LODGE HOTEL
Glenshee Road
Braemar
Aberdeenshire AB35 5YQ
Tel: 013397 41627
Fax: 013397 41627

On main A93 Perth-Aberdeen road, on the edge of Braemar.

A neat Victorian shooting lodge at the head of Glen Clunie.

- Small country house hotel.
- Creative country house cooking.
- "Comfortable country house providing genuine hospitality and good food."

Wood panelling, log fires, antique furniture, lovely grounds – all the attributes one would expect of a Victorian shooting lodge. Edna and Sarah Coyne bought Braemar Lodge in October 1994, and have upheld the lodge's gastronomic reputation, which included an AA Rosette. Edna presents a three course table d'hôte menu cooked with imagination and flair and well-presented in a tastefully decorated candlelit dining room. Both she and her daughter, Sarah (who waits and assists in front of house), are friendly and attentive hosts. It is not surprising that Braemar Lodge is so popular.

    Open 29 Dec to 31 Oct
▥ Rooms: 7, 6 with private facilities
ⓢⓟ Special rates available
✗ Dinner – 3 course menu £££
ⓥ Vegetarians welcome
ⅈ Children welcome
⊬ No smoking in dining room

Scottish smoked salmon enveloped in a crêpe and accompanied by an Orkney cheese sauce. Breast of duck pan-fried with an apricot, blueberry and white wine sauce. Atholl Brose pavlova with Scottish raspberries.

STB Highly Commended 👑 👑 👑
▦ Credit cards: Access/Mastercard/Eurocard, Visa, Mastercharge
▨ Proprietors: Sarah & Edna Coyne

BROUGHTY FERRY

SOUTH KINGENNIE HOUSE
Kellas, by Broughty Ferry
Dundee DD5 3PA
Tel: 01382 350 562

From A92 Dundee-Arbroath, take B978 to Kellas
then road to Drumsturdy to signpost for South
Kingennie, 2 miles.

Converted farmhouse.

• A quiet and formal restaurant in a tranquil
  country setting.
• Traditional British cooking.
• "A pleasant formal dining room offering very
  good meals."

Originally a farmhouse, South Kingennie deserves
its excellent local reputation. Owned and run by
Peter and Jill Robinson, it serves inexpensive and
imaginative table d'hôte meals in a long, elegant
dining room. Peter's stylish and imaginative
cooking is matched by Jill's supervision of the
front of the house. Atmosphere and service are
relaxed and friendly. The wine list is
comprehensive. Tasting notes are clear and
helpful.

Open all year except Boxing Day, 1 Jan,
last wk Jan + first wk Feb
Closed Sun evening + Mon
✕ Lunch except Mon £-££
✕ Dinner except Sun Mon £££-££££
Ⓥ Vegetarians welcome
⚘ Children welcome
⚹ Facilities for disabled visitors
⚐ No smoking in restaurant

**Medley of seafood poached in a white wine and
basil sauce. Warm salad of avocado and pigeon
breast with mustard dressing. Vanilla bavois and
citrus sauce.**

⊞ Credit cards: Access/Mastercard/Eurocard,
  Visa, Mastercharge, Switch, Delta
⊠ Proprietors: Peter & Jill Robinson

CAIRNDOW

LOCH FYNE OYSTER BAR
Cairndow
Argyll PA26 8BH
Tel: 01499 600217/600264
Fax: 01499 600234

A83 Glasgow-Oban-Campbeltown, at head of Loch
Fyne near Cairndow.

Renowned seafood restaurant.

• Converted farm steading.
• Fresh seafood.
• "Has earned a justifiable reputation for superb
  seafoods enjoyed by local and international
  clientele."

In 1978 John Noble and Andrew Lane started a
business which sets out to make the best possible
use of the wonderful fish and shellfish of Loch
Fyne, historically the most famous fishing loch on
the West Coast (during the mid-19th century 670
boats were based here, and its oyster-beds
supplied all Edinburgh). Their plan was to
re-establish the oyster beds and, as well as
offering them for sale generally, to establish an
oyster bar on the loch where people could sample
them, and other seafood – cooked, cured, or
simply served for the purist on ice. The restaurant
eschews 'haute cuisine'; dishes are very simply
prepared, so the fresh natural flavour of the
seafood can be enjoyed. Meals served throughout
the day, and the adjacent shop (and tree nursery)
permits 'carry-outs'. Winner of The Macallan
Taste of Scotland Special Merit Award for
Achievement 1995.

Open all year except Christmas Day +
New Year's Day
✕ Food served all day
Ⓥ Vegetarians welcome

**Queen scallops roasted with bacon. Shellfish
platter – fresh oysters, langoustines, queen
scallops, brown crab and clams. Lemon pavlova.**

⊞ Credit cards: Access/Mastercard/Eurocard,
  Visa, Diners Club, Switch, Delta
⊠ Proprietors: Loch Fyne Oysters Ltd

Callander 38

HIGHLAND HOUSE HOTEL
South Church Street, Callander
Perthshire FK17 8BN
Tel: 01877 330269

Just off A84 (main street through town centre).

Family-run town hotel, winner of 'Best Place to Stay' in area tourism awards.

- Georgian townhouse.
- Good home cooking.
- "Mrs Shirley personally cooks an excellent dinner for her guests."

The inviting appearance of this neat Georgian house with roses round the door is matched by the warm and welcoming haven within. In the small dining room overlooking the street you will enjoy the home-cooked offerings of the enthusiastic Dee Shirley who creates interesting dishes, presented on table d'hôte menus, using the freshest produce she can obtain. Dee and her husband David have earned a strong local reputation for their high standards and cheerful hospitality.

....

Open 1 Mar to 5 Nov
- ⌂ Rooms: 9, 8 with private facilities
- SP Special rates available
- ✗ Dinner ££
- Ⓥ Vegetarians welcome and special diets catered for
- ✗ No smoking in dining room + bedrooms

Peppered mackerel. Scottish venison with whisky and cream sauce. Chocolate nut sundae.

STB Commended ♛ ♛ ♛
- ⊞ Credit cards: Access/Mastercard/Eurocard, American Express, Visa
- Ⅺ Proprietors: David & Dee Shirley

ROMAN CAMP HOTEL
Off Main Street, Callander
Perthshire FK17 8BG
Tel: 01877 330003
Fax: 01877 331533

At the east end of Callander main street from Stirling, turn left down 300 yard drive to hotel.

A renowned country house hotel of dignity and charm.

- Close to the town, yet set on the banks of the River Teith.
- Outstanding Scottish cuisine.
- "A sumptuous country house built as a shooting lodge for royalty."

Designed and built for the Dukes of Perth in 1625, the Roman Camp has been a hotel since 1939. Under the guidance of Eric and Marion Brown, it maintains its atmosphere of elegance. With its 20 acres of beautiful gardens, old library and secret chapel, the hotel offers the peace of the past alongside every possible modern convenience. The dining room, hung with tapestries and lit by candles, boasts a particularly fine painted ceiling. The best of fresh local produce is imaginatively used to create the finest Scottish cuisine, complemented by an excellent wine list. Service is unhurried and impeccable. Roman Camp has 2 AA Rosettes. One of 12 establishments shortlisted for The Macallan Taste of Scotland Awards 1996. *(See advert Page 23.)*

....

Open all year
- ⌂ Rooms: 14 with private facilities
- SP Special rates available
- ✗ Lunch ££
- ✗ Dinner 4 course menu ££££
- Ⓥ Vegetarians welcome
- ⚲ Children welcome
- ♿ Facilities for disabled visitors
- ✗ No smoking in dining room

Gâteau of scallops with freshwater crayfish, fresh pasta and pearls of vegetables. Fillet of lamb wrapped in a wild mushroom farci with compote of plum tomatoes and a basil jus. Hot rice pudding soufflé with a compote of raspberries and strawberries.

STB Highly Commended ♛ ♛ ♛ ♛
- ⊞ Credit cards: Access/Mastercard/Eurocard, American Express, Visa, Diners Club, Mastercharge, Switch, Delta
- Ⅺ Proprietors: Eric & Marion Brown

`CAMPBELTOWN`

BALEGREGGAN COUNTRY HOUSE

Balegreggan Road
Campbeltown
Argyll PA28 6NN
Tel: 01586 552062
Fax: 01586 552062

Off A83 from outskirts of Campbeltown, follow farm road for ½ mile. Go through farmyard to top of hill.

A Victorian villa with careful home cooking.

- Substantial stone villa.
- Careful home cooking.
- "A comfortable base just outside the town."

The history of Balegreggan House dates back to mid 1800s when it was built and named after the Gaelic 'Bhaile Ghriogan' meaning 'Place of the Rocks'. Since then the house has been tastefully extended and passed through the hands of several caring owners. Now it is in the safe hands of Sarah Urquhart, Chef/Proprietor, and her husband who both work very hard to offer excellent Scottish hospitality. Bruce is an attentive host and Sarah's good home cooking will ensure first time visitors find their way back.

Open all year
🏠 Rooms: 4 with private facilities
SP Special rates available
♀ Restricted licence
✗ Dinner £££
V Vegetarians welcome
⚹ Children welcome
♿ Facilities for disabled visitors – residents only
✗ No smoking throughout

Seared local scallops with a spaghetti of carrots and a Moscato del Piemonte sauce. Pan-fried pheasant breast with caramelised apples, chestnuts and a cider and parsley sauce. Bramble cranachan in a brandy snap basket.

STB Highly Commended 👑 👑 👑
💳 Credit cards: Access/Mastercard/Eurocard, Visa
👤 Proprietors: Sarah Urquhart

`CARDROSS`

KIRKTON HOUSE

Darleith Road, Cardross, Dunbartonshire G82 5EZ
Tel: 01389 841 951
Fax: 01389 841 868

Cardross is mid way between Helensburgh and Dumbarton on the north bank of the Clyde. At west end of Cardross village turn north off A814 up Darleith Road. Kirkton House drive ½ mile on right.

Pleasant family-run accommodation in tranquil location by the River Clyde.

- Old farm guest house.
- Home cooking.
- "A most comfortable family home which gives a warm welcome to all guests."

Kirkton House is a converted, late 18th century farmhouse built around a courtyard – described by its owners, Stewart and Gillian Macdonald, as a residential farmstead hotel. It sits above Cardross village, looking over the River Clyde towards Greenock – a good base from which to explore Glasgow, if you are looking for rural tranquillity. Stewart and Gillian are relaxed and friendly, and set out to make your stay as pleasant as possible. The public rooms have their original stone walls and rustic fireplaces – the fire in the lounge is lit on chilly evenings. Kirkton has all the facilities of a small hotel, serves a homely dinner and a wonderful breakfast.

Open all year except 20 Dec to 13 Jan
🏠 Rooms: 6 with private facilities
SP Special rates available
✗ Residents + friends of residents only
♀ Restricted licence
✗ Snacks served throughout day – residents only
✗ Dinner 4 course menu ££
V Vegetarians welcome
⚹ Children welcome
♿ Facilities for disabled visitors – downstairs rooms only
✗ No smoking in dining room

Avocado and king prawn salad. Home-made venison pie. Cherry and almond tart.

STB Highly Commended 👑 👑 👑
💳 Credit cards: Access/Mastercard/Eurocard, American Express, Visa, Delta
👤 Proprietors: Stewart & Gillian Macdonald

Carnoustie 41

11 PARK AVENUE
11 Park Avenue
Carnoustie
Angus DD7 7JA
Tel: 01241 853336
Fax: 01241 878453

Park Avenue runs from the main street in Carnoustie towards the railway and beach. Follow signs for free parking.

An excellent small town restaurant.

- Converted Victorian masonic hall.
- Modern Scottish cooking.
- "A dedicated chef offering elegant and quality cuisine."

Described by our Inspector as the "jewel in Carnoustie's crown" – 11 Park Avenue offers a most pleasurable eating experience. The restaurant is small, situated in the centre of Carnoustie and is pleasingly decorated and thoughtfully laid out. All food served here is home-made from the brown rolls to start – to the ice cream at the finish. Chef/Proprietor Stephen Collinson is a highly decorated chef and runs a fine restaurant. This is one place that deserves a long successful life.

Open all year except 25, 26 Dec + first wk Jan
Closed Sun Mon + Sat lunch
✕ Dinner except Sun Mon ££
Ⅴ Vegetarians welcome
ᴊ Children welcome
⅄ Smoking area in restaurant

Fresh West Coast mussels cooked in white wine with shallots and parsley. Pan-fried fillet of lamb on a basil, tomato and port wine jus. Classic glazed baked lemon tart with home-made vanilla ice cream.

⊞ Credit cards: Access/Mastercard/Eurocard, American Express, Visa, Diners Club
ᴎ Chef/Proprietor: Stephen Collinson

Carradale 42

CARRADALE HOTEL
Carradale, Argyll PA28 6RY
Tel: 01583 431 223
Fax: 01583 431 223

From Tarbert (Loch Fyne) 26 miles via A83, B8001 and B842. From Campbeltown about 17 miles on B842.

A country hotel in a pretty garden setting.

- Country hotel in its own grounds.
- Innovative/traditional cooking.
- "Wide choice of local produce – well-cooked."

Quite the most prominent feature of the village, the Carradale Hotel occupies a splendid location above the harbour in its own grounds and gardens. You will be kindly received by Marcus and Morag Adams who have been steadily improving the hotel's facilities over the past few years. The menus present local fish and meat with unusual and accomplished coulis and sauces. The cooking has a delightful freshness about it and each dish is well-balanced. Carradale offers pleasant beach and forest walks. The hotel has squash courts, sauna, solarium, mountain bikes, game fishing and an adjacent 9-hole golf course.

Open all year except 23 to 26 Dec
🛏 Rooms: 14 with private facilities, 3 children's rooms (adjacent to parents' rooms) + 1 family suite
SP Special rates available
✕ Food served all day ££
✕ Lunch £
✕ Dinner ££
Ⅴ Vegetarians welcome
ᴊ Children welcome
⅄ No smoking in restaurant

Gravadlax: Loch Fyne salmon cured in whisky and served with home-made brown bread. Rack of Argyll hill lamb with an Arran mustard and tarragon crust served with a redcurrant and port reduction. Home-made banana and butterscotch ice cream served in a brandy snap basket with a fresh raspberry coulis.

STB Commended ♔ ♔ ♔
⊞ Credit cards: Access/Mastercard/Eurocard, Visa
ᴎ Proprietors: Marcus & Morag Adams

Carrbridge 43

DALRACHNEY LODGE HOTEL

Carrbridge, Inverness-shire PH23 3AT
Tel: 01479 841252 Fax: 01479 841382

Leave A9 at Carrbridge junction and follow A938 for 1½ miles, continue through village for 20 yards – Dalrachney is on right.

Victorian shooting lodge in peaceful setting.

- Country hotel, formerly a hunting lodge of the Countess of Seafield.
- Traditional Scottish cooking: extensive bar meal menu.
- "Popular local venue with comfortable accommodation."

Dalrachney Lodge is a traditionally built Highland shooting lodge standing in 16 acres of peaceful grounds on the banks of the River Dulnain. Decor throughout the hotel is of a high standard with comfortable, spacious bedrooms and well-maintained public rooms. There are also two self-contained houses within the grounds which are available on a self-catering or serviced basis. The Lodge Restaurant is a typical period dining room with a bright, open outlook. At lunch a wide-ranging bar menu is presented, augmented by a dish of the day – this can be eaten in the restaurant or in the bar. For dinner, both à la carte and table d'hôte menus are offered. Provision is made for anyone with food allergies and special needs and there is always a good vegetarian choice.

Open all year
🏠 Rooms: 16 with private facilities
✗ Lunch ££
✗ Dinner 5 course menu £££
Ⓥ Vegetarians welcome
🕏 Children welcome
🚭 No smoking in restaurant

Mussels with a garlic, butter, spinach, Parmesan and parsley topping. Fillet of salmon with fresh ginger, asparagus tips, butter, garlic and a hint of Drambuie, wrapped in pastry. Cloutie dumpling with Glayva cream.

STB Highly Commended 👑 👑 👑 👑
💳 Credit cards: Access/Mastercard/Eurocard, American Express, Visa, Mastercharge, Switch, Delta
👤 Proprietor: Helen Swanney

Chirnside nr Duns 44

CHIRNSIDE HALL COUNTRY HOUSE HOTEL

Chirnside, nr Duns
Berwickshire TD11 3LD
Tel: 01890 818 219
Fax: 01890 818 231

Between Chirnside and Foulden on A6105. 1 mile east of Chirnside.

Classical country house hotel.

- Sandstone Victorian mansion house.
- Imaginative Scottish cuisine with strong French emphasis.
- "Sumptuous comfort, elegant food – this place is a real treat."

Opened in October 1995, this classical country house is set in rolling open countryside overlooking the Cheviot Hills to the south in Northumberland. Everything at Chirnside Hall is on a grand scale – from massive mahogany doors – to the carpeted, carved stone staircase. The food is described by our inspector as refined, innovative and skilful with a good choice of quality ingredients. Interesting and contemporary combinations alongside more traditional dishes given an innovative touch. Chirnside has 1 AA Rosette.

Open all year
🏠 Rooms: 10 with private facilities
SP Special rates available
✗ Food served all day £
✗ Lunch ££ – booking essential
✗ Dinner ££ – booking essential
Ⓥ Vegetarians welcome
🕏 Children welcome
🚭 No smoking in dining room

Ravioli of langoustines on a bed of courgette ribbons with tomato and basil. Noisettes of Border lamb with a confit of shallots on a port and thyme sauce. Diamonds of white chocolate mousse on a Grand Marnier crème anglaise.

STB Highly Commended 👑 👑 👑 👑
💳 Credit cards: Access/Mastercard/Eurocard, American Express, Visa, Switch, Delta, JCB
👤 Proprietors: Alan & Karla White

Cleish nr Kinross 45

NIVINGSTON HOUSE
Cleish, Kinross-shire KY13 7LS
Tel: 01577 850216
Fax: 01577 850238

From M90, junction 5, take B9097 towards Crook of Devon. Hotel is 2 miles from junction 5.

A Victorian mansion standing in 12 acres of gardens.

- Country house hotel.
- Good country-house cooking.
- "An attractive country house hotel with atmosphere, offering good Scottish cuisine."

Nivingston House is a tranquil place, standing as it does in 12 acres of gardens, with fine views over the rolling countryside, yet it is only a couple of miles from the M90. The building is a pleasing example of an old Scottish country house which has been extended with care, using different styles of architecture. Its location is ideal for reaching Edinburgh and Glasgow, not to mention St Andrews and the north. The atmosphere is comfortable and welcoming, with log fires and broad armchairs. In the pleasant, candlelit dining room, you will enjoy good quality country house cuisine, with interesting sauces. Nivingston has 1 AA Rosette.

Open all year
- Rooms: 17 with private facilities
- Special rates available
- Lunch ££
- Dinner £££
- Vegetarians welcome
- Children welcome
- Facilities for disabled visitors
- Smoking discouraged
- Member of the Scotch Beef Club

Fresh West Coast scallops grilled with bacon served with a light curry-flavoured mayonnaise. Roast half Perthshire pheasant with a prune and whisky sauce. Home-made traditional cloutie dumpling.

STB Highly Commended 👑 👑 👑 👑
- Credit cards: Access/Mastercard/Eurocard, American Express, Visa, Mastercharge, Switch, Delta
- Proprietor: A Deeson

Coldingham 46

DUNLAVEROCK HOUSE
Coldingham Bay
Coldingham
Berwickshire TD14 5PA
Tel: 018907 71450
Fax: 018907 71450

Take A1107 to Coldingham and then follow signs to Coldingham Bay.

Small deluxe country house hotel overlooking the sea-topped sands of Coldingham Bay.

- Late Victorian villa.
- Innovative home cooking.
- "One's cares of the week wash away on arriving at this wonderfully relaxing, hospitable home."

Leslie and Donald Brown travelled all over Scotland to find this little haven which opened three years ago. The house has six spacious individually decorated, en suite bedrooms and every effort has been taken to make guests as comfortable as possible. Leslie and a small dedicated team prepare meals to a very high standard using the very best of local produce. Menus are compiled daily, depending upon availability and guests' preference. The Browns are superb hosts, the good food, warmth and hospitality encourages guests to re-visit time after time.

Open 1 Feb to 2 Jan except 22 to 26 Dec
- Rooms: 6 with private facilities
- Special rates available
- Dinner ££
- Vegetarians welcome
- Children over 9 years welcome
- Facilities for disabled visitors
- No smoking in dining room

Camembert and caramelised onions in a filo purse. Honey-glazed noisettes of Border lamb stuffed with apricots. Dunlaverock whisky and maple torte with a pecan praline topping.

STB Highly Commended 👑 👑 👑
- Credit cards: Access/Mastercard/Eurocard, Visa, JVC
- Proprietors: Donald & Leslie Brown

Comrie 47

THE DEIL'S CAULDRON
27 Dundas Street, Comrie
Perthshire PH6 2LN
Tel: 01764 670352

On A85 west end of Comrie.

Lounge bar/restaurant in Comrie.

- 18th Century town building.
- Auld Alliance cooking.
- "Popular lounge bar and restaurant with individual charm."

The Deil's Cauldron is an attractive bar and restaurant which has been created from a 200 year old Listed building in the village. There is a rugged charm about the interior, with its exposed stone walls lined with prints and old photographs. Two dining rooms (one for non-smokers) offer intimate and comfortable surroundings in which to enjoy fresh local produce interestingly and skillfully prepared. Lunch may be taken in the garden on fair days. There is a choice of home-cooked dishes which will accommodate all tastes, appetites and pockets. The restaurant is popular amongst locals and visitors. Watch out for excellent daily specials – our inspector was most impressed with a salad of sea bass. Winner of 'Glenturret Tourism Award For Most Enjoyable Restaurant Meal in Perthshire'.

> Open all year except Christmas Day +
> 31 Dec to 2 Jan
> Note: Nov to Mar advisable to check
> opening times
> Closed Tue
> ✗ Lunch except Tue £ – booking preferred
> ✗ Dinner except Tue ££ – booking preferred
> Ⓥ Vegetarians welcome
> ⚲ Children welcome – by arrangement
> ⚟ Separate dining room for non-smokers

Warm salad of char-grilled scallops with sesame dressing. Dover sole grilled on the bone with herb butter. Fillet of Aberdeen Angus steak with mushrooms and a light tomato and garlic sauce.

▦ Credit cards: Access/Mastercard/Eurocard, American Express, Visa, Switch, Delta
▨ Proprietors: Robert & Judith Shepherd

THE GRANARY
Drummond Street, Comrie
Perthshire PH6 2DW
Tel: 01764 670838

On main street of Comrie (A85 west of Crieff) – opposite garage.

A small, welcoming coffee shop on the main street of Comrie.

- A charming little tea-room/coffee shop with the comfortable air of an Edwardian coffee shop.
- Good home baking.
- "A welcoming coffee shop offering a wide selection of home baking."

The Granary is an old fashioned building in the centre of the bustling village of Comrie. The large windows with sunny flowered curtains look towards the Perthshire hills and the antique mahogany counter is laden with a mouth-watering display of home baking. Local watercolours decorate the walls, and a rich collection of home-made jams and chutneys crowd the shelves. Proprietors Liz and Mark Grieve have made The Granary a special place with a warm and welcoming atmosphere, tempting customers with a delicious choice of food. There is a good selection of ground coffees and teas (including fruit and herbal infusions). The full menu is available all day and visitors can purchase cakes and scones, breads and preserves to carry out.

> Open 28 Feb to 28 Oct
> Closed Mon except Bank Holiday Mondays
> ⓤ Unlicensed
> ✗ Food served all day Tue to Sat:
> afternoon Sun £
> ✗ Lunch £
> Ⓥ Vegetarians welcome
> ⚲ Children welcome
> ♿ Facilities for disabled visitors
> ⚟ No smoking throughout

Home-made soups. Open sandwich salad platter served on home-made soda bread. Home baking and home-made ice creams.

▦ No credit cards
▨ Proprietors: Mark & Elizabeth Grieve

TULLYBANNOCHER FARM FOOD BAR
Comrie
Perthshire PH6 2JY
Tel: 01764 670827

½ mile west of Comrie on A85.

A popular, informal bistro/restaurant on the banks of the river Earn.

- A self-service, relaxed and ideal place to break your journey.
- The best of farmhouse cooking.
- "Good quality food in lovely surroundings. Carrot cake to die for."

Just outside the picturesque village of Comrie, Tullybannocher is ideally placed for those enjoying a drive along Loch Earn. It stands in beautiful woodland, is easy to pull in to and offers ample car parking. The decor of this large log cabin is simple. It offers a wide range of inexpensive and freshly-prepared meats, fish and quiches and simple but good salads. The smell of home baking is refreshing and real. In fine weather, the rustic tables on the restaurant's rolling lawn are understandably popular. Self-service during the day. Table service for diners in the evening (6pm – 9pm).

Open 1 Apr to 14 Oct
♀ Restaurant licence
✗ Food served all day £
✗ Lunch £
✗ Dinner ££
Ⓥ Vegetarians welcome
⚡ Children welcome
🚭 Smoking area in restaurant

Home-made pork pâté with sherry. Venison casserole with red wine. Cloutie dumpling

⊞ Credit cards: Access/Mastercard/Eurocard, Visa, Switch
Ⓝ Proprietor: Peter Davenport

Craigellachie **48**

CRAIGELLACHIE HOTEL
Victoria Street, Craigellachie, Moray AB38 9SR
Tel: 01340 881204 Fax: 01340 881253

On A941, 12 miles south of Elgin.

An imposing hotel in its own grounds just off the main square of the village, with the River Spey at the foot of the garden.

- A large 19th century country hotel, refurbished in 1995.
- Country hotel cooking.
- "Very welcoming, very comfortable, good cooking."

Located at the heart of Whisky Country, within the attractive Speyside village of Craigellachie, this imposing hotel is decorated to a high standard and in excellent taste. Comfortable and well-run, its elegant interior is matched by attentive and unobtrusive service. The bedrooms, some with four-poster beds and all with private facilities, have lovely views over the river and countryside beyond. The kitchen uses fresh produce as far as practicable, and carefully sources delicacies from all around Scotland – from Ayrshire smoked bacon to Sheildaig shellfish. The hotel has recently introduced two new restaurants; for fine dining the Ben Aigan which offers a set menu using only the freshest and best ingredients available on the day; and a Rib Room where the speciality is a 32oz single rib steak! The hotel also has modern leisure facilities. Craigellachie has 1 AA Rosette.

Open all year
🛏 Rooms: 30 with private facilities
SP Special rates available
✗ Lunch ££
✗ Dinner 4 course menu £-££££
Ⓥ Vegetarians welcome
⚡ Children welcome
🚭 No smoking in Ben Aigan restaurant

Turbot fillet with samphire and sweet pepper coulis. Venison loin with root vegetables, prune and a malt whisky jus. Teardrops of white chocolate mousse and strawberries.

STB Highly Commended 👑 👑 👑 👑
⊞ Credit cards: Access/Mastercard/Eurocard, American Express, Visa, Diners Club, Mastercharge, Switch, Delta
Ⓝ Resident Director: Nick White

CRAIL

HAZELTON GUEST HOUSE
29 Marketgate, Crail
Fife KY10 3TH
Tel: 01333 450250

In town centre opposite tourist office and Tolbooth.

A town guest house in Crail.

- Victorian terraced house.
- Creative Scottish cooking using fresh local produce.
- "Small friendly establishment offering good value for money."

Hazelton is situated in the centre of Crail opposite the famous 16th century Tolbooth in Marketgate. Owners Alan and Rita Brown extend a warm welcome to their guests whom they accommodate in seven warm comfortably furnished bedrooms. The dining room overlooking Marketgate is airy and well-appointed. Breakfast, is chosen from a well-balanced traditional menu. The dinner menu changes daily and is imaginative and interesting, always including fresh fish or seafood and red and white meat dishes, home-smoked specialities appear frequently. The Browns' attention to detail combined with the relaxed and friendly atmosphere and the high standard of Rita's award-winning culinary skills ensure that guests return time and again. National winner of 'New Covent Garden Soup Co. and Scotland on Sunday 1996 Recipe Competition'.

Open mid Feb to end Oct
- 🏠 Rooms: 7
- SP Special rates available
- ✕ Residents only
- ✕ Dinner except Mon Tue – unless by prior arrangement ££
- ✕ It is requested that guests select their menu by 4 pm
- V Vegetarians welcome
- ⚕ Dinner menu not suitable for children

Chicken, tomato and basil pancake. Baked Crail crab with cream, white wine and fresh herbs. Chocolate and orange marmalade cake.

STB Commended Listed
- 💳 No credit cards
- Ⓝ Proprietors: Alan & Rita Brown

CRIANLARICH

ALLT-CHAORAIN HOUSE
Crianlarich
Perthshire FK20 8RU
Tel: 01838 300283
Fax: 01838 300238

Off A82, 1 mile north of Crianlarich on Tyndrum road.

Small country hotel with glorious well-tended gardens.

- Informal country house.
- Home cooking.
- "Traditional Scottish food served in a welcoming and homely atmosphere."

This house is perched on a hill in its own grounds overlooking the scenic countryside of Benmore and Strathfillan. Its owner, Roger McDonald, runs the hotel personally and takes pride in maintaining an unobtrusive, homely atmosphere. Each evening he presents a different dinner menu for guests in the charming wood-panelled dining room where you will share one of three large tables with others staying in the hotel. The dishes are interesting, with a strong traditional Scottish theme; the cooking is much appreciated by guests. A 'trust' bar is available in the attractive drawing room where a log fire burns throughout the year. *(See advert Page 6.)*

Open 17 Mar to 1 Nov
- 🏠 Rooms: 7 with private facilities
- SP Special rates available
- ✕ Residents only
- ✕ Dinner ££
- V Vegetarians welcome
- ⚕ Facilities for disabled visitors
- ⚕ Smoking in sun lounge only

Scottish minestrone soup. Beef olives with haggis stuffing served with braised celery and leek, mashed parsnip and carrot. Hot bananarama surprise.

STB Commended 👑 👑 👑
- 💳 Credit cards: Access/Mastercard/Eurocard, American Express, Visa, Switch, Delta
- Ⓝ Proprietor: Roger McDonald

Crieff 51

CRIEFF VISITORS CENTRE
Muthill Road, Crieff
Perthshire PH7 4HQ
Tel: 01764 654014
Fax: 01764 652903

On A822 leading out of Crieff to the south. 15 miles from Gleneagles Hotel by road and less than 1 hour from Edinburgh or Glasgow.

A visitors centre with a number of attractions.

- Self-service, cafeteria style restaurant.
- Home baking and light meals.
- "A wide choice of dishes to suit everyone in the family."

This self-service, 180 seat, restaurant is part of a visitor complex of showroom, shops, audio-visual display and garden centre beside two rural factories producing thistle pattern Buchan pottery and paper-weights. The restaurant itself is a large, light and airy building, with glass, brick and pine being used most successfully in its design and construction. It is a very busy establishment and is self-service. The range of food on offer goes from familiar starters, to soups, hot main courses, fresh salads and ending with an impressive array of home baking. It is good value and the produce used is all local and fresh, ideal for the family as there are special children's meals on the menu.

Open all year except 25, 26 Dec, 1 + 2 Jan
✗ Food served all day £
✗ Lunch £
Ⓥ Vegetarians welcome
⚹ Children welcome
♿ Facilities for disabled visitors

Home-made soups. Haggis, neeps and tatties. Daily dishes. Fresh home baking.

⊞ Credit cards – showroom only
▧ Managing Director: Neil Drysdale

SMUGGLERS RESTAURANT
Glenturret Distillery Ltd, The Hosh
Crieff, Perthshire PH7 4HA
Tel: 01764 656565 Fax: 01764 654366

A85 Crieff to Comrie road. Just over 1 hour from Edinburgh (M9) and Glasgow (M8).

Two restaurants in a converted distillery building, offering a range of good quality food for both formal and informal occasions.

- An 18th century bonded warehouse in the grounds of Scotland's oldest distillery.
- Traditional Scottish fare.
- "Good food in a high quality self-service restaurant at the converted distillery – run by true professionals."

Glenturret makes a strong claim to being Scotland's oldest distillery. It was established in 1775 although the site was used by illicit distillers and smugglers long before then. The first distillery to encourage visitors, it now attracts over 220,000 people per annum with a heritage centre, exhibition museum and shop as well as these two restaurants. Smugglers, on the first floor of the warehouse is self service but has high standards of cooking. The Pagoda Room which extends from Smugglers and is a smaller more formal setting, offers efficient and friendly waitress service. In good weather visitors can sit at tables on the balcony. The menus feature Highland venison, beef and salmon. Coffee, afternoon tea and home baking are also available during the day. Dinners and parties are welcome at Glenturret by prior arrangement.

Open all year except 25, 26 Dec, 1 + 2 Jan
✗ Food served all day £
✗ Lunch ££
▯ Dinner – by private arrangement only ££££
Ⓥ Vegetarians welcome
⚹ Children welcome
♿ Facilities for disabled visitors
⚹ Complete facilities are no smoking but a smoking area is provided in Smugglers Restaurant

Smoked salmon specially cured in demerara sugar and The Glenturret Single Highland Malt Scotch Whisky. Venison in illicit whisky sauce. Cranachan: oatmeal, cream and raspberries flavoured with The Glenturret Original Malt Liqueur.

STB Highly Commended Visitor Attraction
⊞ Credit cards: Access/Mastercard/Eurocard, American Express, Visa, Switch
▧ Director of Tourism: Derek Brown

Crinan 52

CRINAN HOTEL
Crinan, Lochgilphead, Argyll PA31 8SR
Tel: 01546 830261 Fax: 01546 830292

A82 Glasgow-Inveraray, then A83 to Lochgilphead.
Follow A816 (Oban) for c. 5 miles, then B841 to Crinan.

**One of Scotland's most famous hotels,
consistently good.**

- Country hotel with a spectacular location.
- Classical Scottish cooking with French influence.
- "Style and finesse are words that best suit."

The tiny village of Crinan lies at the north end of the
Crinan Canal which connects the Firth of Clyde (via
Loch Fyne) to the Atlantic. The white family-owned
hotel rises conspicuously above the holding basin
and has stupendous views over a pattern of islands
to the north and west. The hotel's small and
exclusive Lock 16 Restaurant is in the top storey of
the building and its picture windows enjoy the view
to the full. Seafood is the speciality here. It is freshly
landed daily below the hotel. Indeed so much does
the chef rely on the catch of the day that he will
often not know until 5 pm what his menu will be. The
hotel's main restaurant, the Westward, offers a
delicious table d'hôte menu (prefaced by the local
shipping forecast!) which features prime beef, wild
venison and hill lamb, as well as fish. The
celebrated Lock 16 Restaurant has a newly
re-designed bar alongside it, and displayed here are
paintings by Frances Macdonald (Mrs Ryan).

Open all year except Christmas
🏠 Rooms: 22 with private facilities
SP Special winter rates available
✗ Lunch £
✗ Dinner (Westward Restaurant) £££
✗ Dinner (Lock 16 mid Apr to end Sep only)
  except Sun Mon booking essential ££££
Ⓥ Vegetarians welcome
🧒 Children welcome
♿ Facilities for disabled visitors

**Mussels marinière. A selection of local seafood
with cheese and fruit. Profiteroles with a
butterscotch sauce.**

STB Highly Commended 👑 👑 👑 👑
💳 Credit cards: Access/Mastercard/Eurocard,
  American Express, Visa, Switch
👤 Proprietors: Nick & Frances Ryan

SEALGAIR
c/o Castlecary Castle
Walton Road
Bonnybridge
Stirlingshire
FK4 2HP
Tel: 01546 606230
Fax: 01546 606230

**Classic cruising yacht based at Bellanoch, by
Crinan, Argyll.**

- Charter yacht.
- Home cooking.
- "A delightful and unique eating experience with
  superb home cooking."

This magnificent 46 foot wooden ketch is equipped
to the highest standards for comfort, performance
and safety and is maintained in top condition.
Sealgair was the first cruising yacht to be invited
to join Taste of Scotland and the high standard of
food served on board continues to delight her
guests. Crewed by an experienced and
professional crew dedicated to ensuring guests
have a relaxing holiday enhanced by tasty and
imaginative meals. Normally cruising the West
Coast of Scotland. Sealgair is also available for
longer more adventurous trips. Six guest berths
available. Group booking only. Category 1 Safety
Code. Fully Bonded. Yacht Charter Association
members. Internet site is at:
http://www-edin. easynet.co.uk/scotyacht/
or e-mail at bobhunter@easynet.co.uk

Open 1 May to mid Sep
⚓ Cabins: 3 (2 double + 1 twin) + separate
  crew cabin
UL Ⓨ Unlicensed – wine provided with evening meal
Ⓥ Vegetarians welcome
🧒 Children over 12 years welcome with prior
  approval of the Skipper
🚭 No smoking below deck

**Avocado and grapefruit with raspberry
vinaigrette. Parcels of trout with ginger and
spring onions. Chocolate fondue with
strawberries, starfruit and mango.**

💳 No credit cards
👤 Skipper: Bob Hunter

CROMARTY

THE ROYAL HOTEL CROMARTY

Marine Terrace, Cromarty
Ross-shire IV11 8YN
Tel: 01381 600217
Fax: 01381 600217

A9 past Inverness, Kessock Bridge 2 miles
turn right.

Traditional family-owned Scottish country house hotel.

- Seafront hotel with verandah.
- Traditional Scottish cooking.
- "A friendly family-owned hotel."

This traditional hotel has been around for over 150 years and overlooks the beach and harbour of the ancient and historic village of Cromarty (all bedrooms share this splendid view – watch out for the bottle-nosed dolphins which live in the Cromarty Firth). The public rooms are pleasantly furnished and the dining room is bright and sunny. Friendly, well-trained staff offer a table d'hôte menu which features classic Scottish dishes. The food is simply presented but of a high standard. Children's selection on menu.

Open all year
🏨 Rooms: 10 with private facilities
SP Special rates available
✕ Lunch ££
✕ Dinner ££
Ⓥ Vegetarians welcome
⚘ Children welcome
♿ Facilities for disabled visitors – ground floor only

Mushroom and nutmeg soup. Nairn smoked salmon and asparagus rolls. Mandarin charlotte.

STB Commended ♛ ♛ ♛
💳 Credit cards: Access/Mastercard/Eurocard, American Express, Visa, Mastercharge
🗝 Proprietors: John & Brenda Shearer

CULLEN

THE BAYVIEW HOTEL & RESTAURANT

Seafield Street, Cullen
Banffshire AB56 4SU
Tel: 01542 841031
Fax: 01542 841731

A98 between Banff and Fochabers – overlooking Cullen Harbour.

A really charming hotel in a picturesque fishing village on the Moray Firth.

- A small town hotel converted from a quayside house commanding magnificent views over the harbour and the bay beyond.
- Imaginative and honest cooking.
- "All freshly prepared and flavoursome."

A delightful typical West Coast townhouse, close to the harbour at Cullen with lovely views over the Moray Firth. This is a pleasant haven from which to explore the surrounding countryside and historic local fishing villages. New proprietors Malcolm and Patricia Watt are 'hands on' in the Bayview with a keen understanding of what it takes to make a pleasurable stay for their guests. Their chef makes full use of the hotel's location by maximising on the excellent choice of fresh fish available daily, and the à la carte menus feature an excellent variety of fresh produce, imaginatively presented.

Open all year except Christmas Day
🏨 Rooms: 6 with private facilities
SP Special rates available
✕ Food served all day £-£££
✕ Lunch £-££
✕ Dinner ££-£££
Ⓥ Vegetarians welcome
⚘ Children welcome
🚭 No smoking in restaurant

Smoked North Sea haddock in pastry shells with a sherry and cream sauce served on a chervil and cucumber salad. Baked Mediterranean sea bass with West Coast scallops in a whisky and carrot sauce. Sticky toffee pudding.

STB Commended ♛ ♛ ♛ ♛
💳 Credit cards: Access/Mastercard/Eurocard, American Express, Visa, Switch
🗝 Owners: Malcolm & Patricia Watt

CULLEN BAY HOTEL
Cullen
Banffshire AB56 4XA
Tel: 01542 840 432
Fax: 01542 840 900

On main A98, Fraserburgh to Inverness road,
¼ mile west of Cullen.

An attractive hotel with a commanding view.

- Extended clifftop house.
- A combination of modern and traditional cooking.
- "Fresh food and friendly service on a superb clifftop location."

The Cullen Bay Hotel was built in 1924 adjacent to Cullen Golf Links on the remains of Farskane House, a residence of the Lairds of Gordon dating from 1677, and the site of an even older mysterious baronial castle. The garden walls of Farskane House are now all that remain. The hotel is run by Arthur and Sheila Edwards who, with their Head Chef David McCallum, ensure that guests may enjoy the best local produce. The menus are well-written with descriptions of dishes and origins of food giving strong reference to Scottishness and local produce. *(See advert Page 19.)*

....

Open all year except Christmas Day evening, Boxing Day morning + 6 to 10 Jan
- 🏠 Rooms: 14 with private facilities
- 🆂🅿 Special rates available
- ✖ Food served all day ££
- ✖ Lunch £
- ✖ Dinner ££
- Ⓥ Vegetarians welcome
- ⚥ Children welcome
- ♿ Facilities for disabled visitors
- 🚭 Smoking area in dining room

Cullen skink. Chicken stuffed with a light haggis mousseline coated in oatmeal and served on a bed of chive-flavoured potato purée. Heather honey parfait served on a bed of strawberries flavoured with black pepper and surrounded with a light Drambuie sabayon, garnished with a marbled tuile thistle.

STB Commended 👑 👑 👑 👑
- 💳 Credit cards: Access/Mastercard/Eurocard, Visa, Mastercharge, Switch, Delta,
- 🏢 Proprietors: Arthur & Sheila Edwards

THE SEAFIELD ARMS HOTEL
19 Seafield Street, Cullen
Banffshire AB56 4SG
Tel: 01542 840791
Fax: 01542 840736

Situated on A98 (main road through Cullen) up from town square.

A charming and well-appointed old town hotel offering comfort and relaxation.

- A 17th century coaching inn in the heart of Cullen.
- Traditional Scottish cooking.
- "An attractive hotel with pleasant and friendly staff."

The Seafield Arms is an impressive former coaching inn, built by the Earl of Seaforth in 1822. The statistical Account of Scotland in 1845 stated: "The Seafield Arms... has no superior between Aberdeen and Inverness." The character and hospitality of this hostelry are still evident. The staff are smart, polite and attentive; the accommodation comfortable and traditional. All the 23 bedrooms were refurbished in 1995. The place is popular with local people and the bar offers a range of over 100 whiskies to enjoy before a roaring fire. A wide ranging menu caters for all ages and preferences.

....

Open all year
- 🏠 Rooms: 23, 22 with private facilities
- ✖ Lunch £
- ✖ Dinner £££
- Ⓥ Vegetarians welcome
- ⚥ Children welcome
- ♿ Facilities for disabled visitors
- 🚭 No smoking in dining room

Smoked haddock and prawn gratin. Select prawns in a tomato, onion and garlic sauce finished with cream and tagliatelle. Home-made meringue nest with fresh fruit and fresh cream.

STB Highly Commended 👑 👑 👑 👑
- 💳 Credit cards: Access/Mastercard/Eurocard, American Express, Visa, Switch, Delta
- 🏢 Proprietors: Herbert & Alison Cox

Cupar 55

EDEN HOUSE HOTEL
2 Pitscottie Road, Cupar
St Andrews
Fife KY15 4HF
Tel: 01334 652 510
Fax: 01334 652 277

Overlooking Haugh Park, Cupar. On A91 road to St Andrews, 8 miles west of St Andrews.

Scottish food served with charm.

- Country house hotel.
- Traditional Scottish cuisine with a classical influence.
- "Dining in the conservatory – for that special occasion – by candlelight."

Eden House Hotel has style. The house itself is Victorian – built for a merchant and reflecting the pompous grandeur favoured by the period. It has been very well refurbished, in a way which respects the original but allows for modern comforts. The house overlooks the Haugh Park, on the outskirts of the town, and a large conservatory has been built on to accommodate the restaurant. It also has an 'annexe' in the road-side gate-house. The Vizan family run the hotel with enthusiasm and attention to detail. The cooking makes use of local meat and fish and favours interesting and richly flavoured sauces.

Open all year
Closed Sun morning
🏠 Rooms: 11 with private facilities
SP Special rates available
✗ Lunch £-££
✗ Dinner ££
Ⓥ Vegetarians welcome
⅄ Children welcome
♿ Facilities for disabled visitors
⅄ Smoking area in restaurant

Prawn and salmon roulade. Salmon fillet with wild mushroom, cayenne pepper, sherry and creamy cheese sauce. Passion fruit cheesecake.

STB Commended 👑 👑 👑
💷 Credit cards: American Express, Visa
🗡 Proprietors: Laurence & Mary Vizan

OSTLERS CLOSE RESTAURANT
Bonnygate, Cupar
Fife KY15 4BU
Tel: 01334 655574

Small lane directly off A91 main road through town.

An award-winning, cottage-like town centre restaurant of distinction and charm.

- A cosy and comfortable establishment in a narrow Cupar lane.
- Elegant Scottish cuisine.
- "Excellent Scottish cuisine enjoyed in relaxed and charming surroundings."

Nestling in a lane or 'close' just off the market town of Cupar's main street, Ostlers is a simply and unpretentiously decorated small restaurant. Chef/proprietor Jimmy Graham deserves the excellent reputation he has earned for his imaginative cooking over the past 15 years. His treatment of fish and shellfish is outstanding, but he applies the same flair to Scottish meat and game. Jimmy has a particular passion for wild mushrooms and these are to be sought after if on the menu. Given such quality, a meal here – complemented by a good wine list – is excellent value for money. Amanda Graham looks after guests with courtesy and charm. Ostlers has 3 AA Rosettes.

Open all year except Christmas Day, Boxing Day, 1 Jan + first 2 wks June
Closed Sun Mon
✗ Lunch except Sun Mon ££ – booking advised
✗ Dinner except Sun Mon £££
Ⓥ Vegetarians welcome
⅄ Children welcome
⅄ Smoking restricted until all diners at coffee stage

Roast fillet of cod with a pesto-flavoured sauce. Roast roe venison and breast of woodpigeon with skirlie in game sauce. Apricot and almond tart with cream custard.

💷 Credit cards: Access/Mastercard/Eurocard, American Express, Visa, Mastercharge, Switch, Delta
🗡 Proprietors: Jimmy & Amanda Graham

DALMALLY

CRUACHAN GUEST HOUSE
Dalmally
Argyll PA33 1AA
Tel: 01838 200 496

Situated in Monument Lane, 50 yards from village Post Office. Follow signs to railway station and Dalmally Village. Cruachan is first house on the left over the old bridge.

A quiet villa in a small Highland village.

- Stone built Victorian villa.
- Careful home cooking.
- "A kindly household in a sheltered corner."

A charming couple both linguists who lived in France for a while and where Maureen learned her cooking skills and practised for many years. The Victorian house has all the mellow charm and grace of its period, standing in a lovely old garden on a quiet country lane. Maureen and Mike Borrett, the proprietors, let three bedrooms, two of which are on the ground floor, en suite and fully suitable for wheelchair-bound guests. Guests have free access to the pretty garden (with wheelchair ramp) and downstairs lounge and dining room. A great base for touring this lovely part of the West Coast – these thoughtful hosts even provide a light supper menu for guests or non-residents wishing a change from full dinner menu. A great find.

....

Open all year except Christmas Day + Boxing Day
🏠 Rooms: 3 with private facilities
SP Special rates available
UL ⨂ Unlicensed – guests welcome to take own wine
✕ Lunch £-££
✕ Dinner ££
V Vegetarians welcome
⚹ Children welcome
♿ Facilities for disabled visitors
⚮ No smoking throughout

Home-made soups and pâtés. Lamb Tagine. Lemon mousse with home-made shortbread.

STB Commended 👑 👑
💳 No credit cards
⚅ Proprietors: Mike & Maureen Borrett

NR DALRY

BRAIDWOOD'S RESTAURANT
1 Mile, nr Dalry, North Ayrshire KA24 4LN
Tel: 01294 833544

A737 Kilwinning-Dalry. On southern outskirts of Dalry, take road to Saltcoats for 1 mile and follow signs.

An outstanding restaurant deep in the Ayrshire countryside.

- A converted 18th century miller's cottage surrounded by rolling farmland.
- Innovative modern Scottish cooking.
- "Prepared by two of Scotland's best chefs, the food here is outstanding."

This restaurant was converted in 1994 from two long and low cottages by Keith and Nicola Braidwood into a tasteful contemporary restaurant. The owners have been described simply as 'two of Scotland's best younger chefs'. They are both highly qualified, with impressive track records (Shieldhill, Murrayshall, Peat Inn, Inverlochy Castle, etc.) and demonstrate their skills daily in wonderfully original combinations of flavour, textures and unusual ingredients. Their table d'hôte menus give an unexpected, and wholly successful, twist to classic dishes. Raw materials are carefully sourced locally. A truly gourmet experience. Braidwood's has 2 AA Rosettes. Winner of The Macallan Taste of Scotland Special Merit Award for Newcomers 1995.

....

Open last wk Jan to last wk Sep + second wk Oct to 31 Dec except Christmas Day
Closed Sun pm, Mon + Tue lunch
⨂ Table licence
✕ Lunch except Mon Tue ££
✕ Dinner except Sun Mon £££
V Vegetarians welcome – prior notice required
⚹ Children over 12 years welcome
⚮ No smoking throughout
🐄 Member of the Scotch Beef Club

Breast of pigeon carved on its own charlotte. Baked fillet of turbot with tapenade on a shellfish stew. An iced caramelised pecan nut parfait with raspberry coulis.

💳 Credit cards: Access/Mastercard/Eurocard, American Express, Visa, Switch, Delta
⚅ Owners: Keith & Nicola Braidwood

Daviot nr Inverness 58

DAVIOT MAINS FARM
Daviot
Inverness IV1 2ER
Tel: 01463 772215
Fax: 01463 772215

On B851 (B9006) to Culloden/Croy, 5 miles south
of Inverness.

Category B Listed farmhouse on a working farm.

- Early 19th century Highland farmhouse.
- Home cooking.
- "Peaceful rural guest house offering substantial home cooking."

Daviot Mains is a lovely and most unusual farm-house in that it is almost completely square and built around a courtyard. One of only three of its type in Scotland, this is the warm and friendly home of Margaret and Alex Hutcheson, with log fires in the public rooms. Newly licensed, guests can now enjoy wine with Margaret's excellent home cooking. Ingredients are meticulously sourced to provide only the best of Highland meat and fish. Portions, as one might expect on a working farm, are generous. At 10pm guests are offered a supper of tea and the day's home baking such as scones, shortbread or sponges.

Open all year except Christmas Eve, Christmas Day, 31 Dec + New Year's Day
Note: Dinner not served Sun Sat 12 Apr to 21 Sep incl.
🏠 Rooms: 3, 2 with private facilities
SP Special rates available
♀ Licensed
✗ Dinner except Sun ££
Ⓥ Vegetarians welcome – prior notice required Special diets on request
⚹ Children welcome
✗ No smoking throughout

According to season – home-made soups, fresh local salmon and trout, Scottish meats, vegetables and cheeses. Local fruits and home-made puddings.

STB Highly Commended 👑 👑
🆔 Credit cards: Access/Mastercard/Eurocard, Visa
🅽 Proprietors: Margaret & Alex Hutcheson

Dingwall 59

KINKELL HOUSE
Easter Kinkell, by Conon Bridge
Dingwall, Ross-shire IV7 8HY
Tel: 01349 861270
Fax: 01349 865902

1 mile from A9 on B9169, 10 miles north
of Inverness.

A well-appointed hotel with a reputation for high class cooking.

- Small country house hotel.
- Country house cooking.
- "There is a most relaxing atmosphere in this lovely house which makes dining here a very enjoyable experience."

Once a large farmhouse, Kinkell stands in its own grounds on the Black Isle, overlooking the Cromarty Firth, towards Ben Wyvis and the hills of Wester Ross. It is the home of Marsha and Steve Fraser, and retains the atmosphere of a private house, with appropriate period furnishings and log fires. The excellence of Marsha's cooking has won Kinkell an AA Rosette, which is presented in interesting and well-balanced à la carte menus for lunch and dinner (five main courses; changing daily) featuring fresh local produce with both classic and innovative treatments. The restaurant is popular, and non-residents are asked to book in advance.

Open all year
🏠 Rooms: 7 with private facilities
SP Special rates available
✗ Lunch – by reservation ££
✗ Dinner – by reservation ££
Ⓥ Vegetarians welcome
⚹ Children welcome
♿ Facilities for disabled visitors
✗ No smoking in dining room + bedrooms

Baked salmon and dill custard with tossed mixed salad leaves. Duo fillets of venison and pigeon served with a ragoût of red cabbage and a sauce of sloe gin and raisins. Brioche bread and butter pudding with apricots marinated in Glayva.

STB Highly Commended 👑 👑 👑
🆔 Credit cards: Access/Mastercard/Eurocard, Visa
🅽 Proprietors: Marsha & Steve Fraser

DIRLETON

THE OPEN ARMS HOTEL
The Green, Dirleton
East Lothian EH39 5EG
Tel: 01620 850 241
Fax: 01620 850 570

From Edinburgh take coast road to Gullane and
North Berwick. Dirleton is 2 miles between them.

A small country hotel and restaurant in the 'time-locked' hamlet of Dirleton.

- Late 1800s sandstone building – originally farmhouse.
- Modern Scottish.
- "Choice traditional Scottish fayre embracing the 'taste of Scotland' ideal."

The Open Arms is set in the sleepy hamlet of
Dirleton, opposite Dirleton Castle and village
green. Long a favourite of its Edinburgh neighbours
the Open Arms offers a warm friendly atmosphere
in surroundings reminiscent of a country home in a
renovated farmhouse. A founder member of the
Taste of Scotland Scheme, the Open Arms
embraces the ideals of Taste of Scotland offering
the best Scottish produce with typical Scottish
influences. There is a good accompanying wine
list, with thoughtfully selected vintages and fairly
priced. Awarded 2 AA Rosettes.

Open all year
- 🏠 Rooms: 10 with private facilities
- 🆂🅿 Special rates available
- ✗ Lunch ££
- ✗ Dinner £££
- Ⓥ Vegetarians welcome
- ⚡ Children welcome
- ♿ Limited facilities for disabled visitors
- ✝ Smoking discouraged: Cigars + pipes not permitted

**Timbale of salmon and sole with a light crayfish
sauce. Roast loin of venison nested on a tattie
scone with bramble and claret fumet. Banana
parfait with caramelised bananas enhanced with
a Glenkinchie malt whisky sauce.**

STB Highly Commended 👑 👑 👑 👑
- 💳 Credit cards: Access/Mastercard/Eurocard, Visa, Mastercharge, Switch, Delta
- 🅺 Proprietors: Tom & Emma Hill

DORNIE

CONCHRA HOUSE HOTEL
Sallachy Road/Killilan Road
Ardelve
Ross-shire IV40 8DZ
Tel: 01599 555233
Fax: 01599 555433

From south continue westwards on A87 past
Dornie/Eilean Donan Castle. Follow hotel signposts
turning right for ¾ mile (Sallachy/Killilan Road).

An historic 18th century hunting lodge.

- A family-run country house hotel.
- Home cooking.
- "Comfort and care in a peaceful setting."

Conchra House was built in the 1760s to house the
government's agent in Kintail, following the seizure
of Jacobite estates after the '45 Rising. The house
is most attractive, fits into the landscape well and
enjoys a lovely situation overlooking Loch Long. It
is full of interesting antiques and period details.
Conchra means 'a fold' or 'haven', and the stated
aim of Colin and Mary Deans, the hotel's resident
owners, is to provide just this for their guests. They
succeed in full measure. The place is wonderfully
peaceful; guests are made to feel very much at
home; the food is simple but intelligently cooked
and appetising. A gem of a place. *(See advert
Page 18.)*

Open all year except 24, 25, 31 Dec + 2 Jan
- 🏠 Rooms: 6, 3 with private facilities
- 🆂🅿 Special rates available
- ✗ Open to non-residents – by arrangement
- ♀ Restricted licence
- 🅟 Lunch – by prior arrangement ££
- Ⓥ Vegetarians welcome
- ⚡ Children welcome
- ✝ No smoking throughout

**Avocado pear, grape and local goats cheese.
Venison medallions marinaded in red wine and
herbs. Spiced apple sponge.**

STB Highly Commended 👑 👑 👑
- 💳 Credit cards: Access/Mastercard/Eurocard, Visa, Switch
- 🅺 Proprietor: Colin & Mary Deans

DORNIE HOTEL
Francis Street
Dornie, by Kyle of Lochalsh
Ross-shire IV40 8DT
Tel: 01599 555 205
Fax: 01599 555 429

A87 past Eilean Donan Castle. Turn right into village of Dornie and hotel is on right-hand side.

A long established village inn in a delightful situation.

- Whitewashed inn.
- Good use of local produce well-cooked.
- "Ian Robin's cooking is very good – and great care is taken in all areas.

This is a family-run hotel, situated in the picturesque village of Dornie. Dornie Hotel is a small hotel that grew and great care has been taken to maintain and restore the premises. Chef/proprietor Ian Robin produces imaginative and interesting dishes using excellent local produce. Menus change regularly and offer excellent value for money. The dining room is very attractive with a pleasant outlook and enclosed patio to the loch. Bar meals are also served.

Open all year except Christmas Day
🛏 Rooms: 12, 6 with private facilities
SP Special rates available
✕ Food served all day £££
✕ Lunch ££
✕ Dinner £££
Ⓥ Vegetarians welcome
ᚴ Children welcome
ᚦ Facilities for disabled visitors

Home-made soups served with granary bread. Breast of Barbary duck in red wine and black cherry sauce. Home-made apple pie.

STB Commended 👑 👑 👑
💳 Credit cards: Access/Mastercard/Eurocard, Visa, Switch, Delta
𝕏 Proprietors: Ian & Olive Robin

Dornoch   **62**

MALLIN HOUSE HOTEL
Church Street, Dornoch
Sutherland IV25 3LP
Tel: 01862 810335
Fax: 01862 810810

Down to centre of town, turn right.

Comfortable town hotel popular with golfers.

- Family-run hotel close to historic golf course.
- Traditional Scottish hotel cooking.
- "Relaxed and friendly establishment, offering substantial pub and restaurant food."

The hotel is a mere 200 yards from the Royal Dornoch Golf Course, one of the finest and oldest links courses in the world. As you would expect, it is very popular with golfers: its bar, in particular, is a refuge from the rigours of the course, with an exceptionally good range of bar meals including lobster and a special 'malt of the month' promotion. An extensive à la carte menu offers a good choice of local produce with superb, locally caught seafood as something of a speciality. Food is imaginatively prepared with unusual sauces and accompaniments. The restaurant itself has magnificent views of the Dornoch Firth and the Struie Hills. Accommodation is very comfortable with recent new additions and improvements including a residents' lounge.
e-mail address mallin.house.hotel@2etnet.co.uk

Open all year
🛏 Rooms: 10 with private facilities
✕ Lunch ££
✕ Dinner £-££
Ⓥ Vegetarians welcome
ᚴ Children welcome
ᚦ Facilities for disabled visitors

King scallops and crab claws with ginger, spring onion, sliced peppers and a suspicion of garlic. Breast of duck oven-roasted and topped with sauce of brambles, ginger, double cream and malt whisky. Crème caramel.

STB Commended 👑 👑 👑
💳 Credit cards: Access/Mastercard/Eurocard, American Express, Visa, Switch, Delta
𝕏 Proprietors: Malcolm & Linda Holden

THE ROYAL GOLF HOTEL
The First Tee
Dornoch
Sutherland IV25 3LG
Tel: 01862 810283
Fax: 01862 810923

From A9, 2 miles into Dornoch town square, straight across crossroads, 200 yards on right.

The hotel is appropriately named, being adjacent to the first tee.

- Seaside golfing hotel.
- Innovative Scottish cooking.
- "A friendly hotel with golfing traditions."

The Royal Golf is a traditional Scottish hotel, within yards of the first tee of the famous golf course of the same name, and having a broad, picture-windowed modern extension overlooking the course and the sandy beaches of the Dornoch Firth beyond. The restaurant also benefits from this splendid view. Here Chef Martyn Woodward – who came 2nd in the 1995 Scottish Chef of the Year Competition – presents a well-priced table d'hôte menu featuring local fish, poultry, beef and lamb. The cooking is first rate and presentation attractive.

Open 1 Mar to 31 Dec
- 🏠 Rooms: 24 with private facilities
- SP Special rates available
- ✗ Lunch £
- ✗ Dinner 4 course menu £££
- Ⓥ Vegetarians welcome
- ⅄ Children welcome

Dornoch Firth seafood chowder. Medallions of Aberdeen Angus beef. Fresh raspberry shortbread.

STB Commended 🦀 🦀 🦀 🦀
- 💳 Credit cards: Access/Mastercard/Eurocard, American Express, Visa, Diners Club, Mastercharge
- 🗓 General Manager: Donald MacLeod

Drybridge 63

THE OLD MONASTERY RESTAURANT
Drybridge, Buckie
Banff AB56 5JB
Tel: 01542 832660
Fax: 01542 832660

Turn off A98 at Buckie Junction onto Drybridge Road. Follow road for 3 miles – do not turn right into Drybridge village.

Converted Benedictine monastery with stunning views and exquisite food.

- A lovingly converted monastery within its own grounds.
- A blend of classical French and Scottish.
- "An award-winning team assure the very best of Scottish hospitality."

Originally built in 1904 as a holiday retreat for the Benedictine monks from Fort Augustus Abbey – The Old Monastery Restaurant was converted by Maureen and Douglas Gray in 1987 and has acquired an excellent reputation both locally and abroad for its exquisite food. The views overlook the western mountains and Moray Firth, and stepping into the monastery you enter a world where the eating experience is the harmonisation of body and soul in an atmosphere of comfort and relaxation. Menus change seasonally and feature locally sourced Scottish produce. Two AA Rosettes and gold medal-winning chefs make this a very special place indeed.

Open all year except 2 wks Nov + 3 wks Jan
Closed Sun Mon
- ✗ Lunch except Sun Mon ££
- ✗ Dinner except Sun Mon ££££
- Ⓥ Vegetarians welcome
- ⅄ Children over 8 years welcome
- 🚭 No smoking in restaurant

Pan-fried escalopes of monkfish tail served with red pepper relish. Medallions of west Highland venison served with mulberry and mead sauce. Caramel nut tart.

- 💳 Credit cards: Access/Mastercard/Eurocard, American Express, Visa, Mastercharge, Switch
- 🗓 Partners: Maureen & Douglas Gray

DUFFTOWN

A TASTE OF SPEYSIDE
10 Balvenie Street, Dufftown
Banffshire AB55 4AB
Tel: 01340 820860
Fax: 01340 820860

50 yards from the Clock Tower on the road to Elgin.

Popular restaurant on the whisky trail.

- Informal town restaurant.
- Good wholesome Scottish fare.
- "A hearty combination of good food and good service."

The restaurant is situated in malt whisky heartland and was originally set up as a whisky tasting centre and restaurant. To this day one of its major attractions is the superb selection of malt whiskies on offer. Situated close to the centre of Dufftown the restaurant revels in its Scottishness, evident in its tartan inspired decor and style of cuisine, but in a tasteful, rather than a mawkish way. You will find simple fare that makes the most of local ingredients, cooked and presented with style. This is home cooking at its best, enhanced by a well-chosen wine list with a predominance of reasonably priced New World wines. Awarded 1 AA Rosette.

Open 1 Mar to 14 Nov
- ✗ Food served all day £
- ✗ Lunch £
- ✗ Dinner ££
- Ⓥ Vegetarians welcome
- ⚹ Children welcome

Smoked breast of woodpigeon with horseradish cream. Venison casserole. Heather honey and malt whisky cheesecake.

- Credit cards: Access/Mastercard/Eurocard, American Express, Visa
- Partners: Joseph Thompson, Raymond McLean & Peter Thompson

DULNAIN BRIDGE

AUCHENDEAN LODGE HOTEL
Dulnain Bridge, Inverness-shire PH26 3LU
Tel: 01479 851 347
Fax: 01479 851 347

On A95, 1 mile south of Dulnain Bridge.

A charming Highland country hotel.

- Edwardian hunting lodge, with a great view over the Spey.
- Original, talented, eclectic cooking.
- "Dining here is quite an occasion."

Auchendean was built just after the turn of the century as a sporting lodge and has architectural details from the Arts and Crafts Movements. The present owners, Eric Hart and Ian Kirk, are convivial professionals dedicated to giving their guests a full dining experience. Before dinner you are served drinks in the drawing room and meet the other diners. Both Ian and Eric share the cooking; Eric is a keen mycologist and over 20 varieties of edible wild mushrooms locally; the hotel's garden also provides vegetables (including six varieties of potato!), salads, herbs and honey. Eggs are supplied by the hotel's own hens. Wild berries, mountain hare, rabbit, pigeon, mallard, pheasant and home-cured gravadlax are specialities. The menu changes every night but always balances a simple main course with something more exotic. As a New Zealander Ian has created an extensive cellar including over 30 special wines from his home country. French spoken.

Open all year except 4 Apr to 28 Apr
- Rooms: 8, 5 with private facilities
- ⓢ Special rates available
- Pre-booked packed lunch £
- ✗ Dinner £££
- Ⓥ Vegetarians welcome – prior notice required
- ⚹ Children welcome
- ⅙ Facilities for non-residents only
- No smoking in dining room + one lounge

Home-made gravadlax with mustard and dill sauce. Roast loin of pork with garlic and rosemary. Soufflé omelette with Amaretto and almonds.

STB Highly Commended 👑 👑 👑
- Credit cards: Access/Mastercard/Eurocard, American Express, Visa, Diners Club
- Proprietors: Eric Hart & Ian Kirk

DUNBAR

ARABESQUE
Woodbush Brae
Dunbar
East Lothian EH42 1HB
Tel: 01368 864169
Fax: 01368 864169

From A1 take A1087 to Dunbar at south end of High Street, take road towards seashore.

A French restaurant set in courtyard within a conservation area.

- Restaurant set in courtyard.
- Modern French cooking.
- "Intimate restaurant overlooking the sea serving seasonal fresh food."

New chef/proprietor René Gaté and proprietor Marguerita Apps have recently taken over this popular restaurant and have already made their impression on the place. The best and freshest ingredients are used by René – who has a natural genius for fine cuisine. As you would perhaps expect – all wines all French and carefully chosen.

....

Open all year except Christmas Day + Boxing Day
SP Special rates available
✕ Lunch £££
✕ Dinner £££
V Vegetarians welcome
⚲ Children welcome
⚲ No smoking throughout

Tempura of local Scottish langoustines, salad of fresh garden herbs. Turbot roasted on the bone with glazed baby onions and mushrooms. Bavarois of carrots and passion fruit with saffron ice cream.

⊞ Credit cards: Access/Mastercard/Eurocard, American Express, Visa, Switch, Delta
⋈ Chef/Proprietor: Réne Gaté
⋈ Proprietor: Marguerita Apps

DUNDEE

OLD MANSION HOUSE HOTEL
by Dundee DD3 0QN
Tel: 01382 320366
Fax: 01382 320400

Take A923 (Coupar Angus) road out of Dundee – cross the Kingsway and fork right at Muirhead. Hotel is left a further 3 miles from there.

A small, luxury country house hotel beautifully situated in the Sidlaw hills.

- A formal and elegant establishment of old fashioned virtues.
- Fine Scottish/modern cuisine.
- "The consistent high standards here has won renown and popularity."

This 16th century baronial mansion has been care-fully and lovingly converted by its present owners, Nigel and Eva Bell. Magnificent plaster-work and fine vaulted ceilings are matched by fine furnishings to retain all the graciousness of the past. All rooms are well-appointed. Outside, the hotel's ten acres of grounds offer squash and tennis courts, a croquet lawn and a heated swimming pool. In the splendid dining room, with its fine Jacobean fireplace, Chef Campbell Bruce offers outstanding and reasonably-priced cuisine that combines imagination and style with the best of local produce. Service is attentive, formal and impeccable. The hotel has 1 AA Rosette.

....

Open 4 Jan to 24 Dec
⌂ Rooms: 6 with private facilities
SP Special rates available
✕ Lunch £
✕ Dinner £££
V Vegetarians welcome
⚲ Children welcome
⚲ No smoking in restaurant

Warm Arbroath smokie salad with tarragon dressing. Escalope of venison with local wild mushrooms and red wine sauce. Tayberry crème brûlée.

STB Highly Commended 👑 👑 👑 👑
⊞ Credit cards: Access/Mastercard/Eurocard, American Express, Visa, Diners Club, Mastercharge, Switch
⋈ Owners/Proprietors: Nigel & Eva Bell
⋈ General Manager: Norman Preedy

THE SANDFORD COUNTRY HOUSE HOTEL

Newton Hill, Wormit
Fife DD6 8RG
Tel: 01382 541802
Fax: 01382 542136

4 miles south of Dundee at the A914/B946 junction to Wormit.

An historic 20th century building on the Tay.

- Country house hotel.
- Traditional, Scottish and European cooking.
- "Very attractive building offering high quality food and service."

A Listed building designed by Baillie Scott at the turn of the century for the Valentine (post-card manufacturers) family of Dundee. It stands in five acres of gardens and policies, part of which is given over to Newton Hill Country Sports, where you can shoot a few clays, try your hand at 4 x 4 off-road driving or fly fish for trout at Newton Farm Loch. Al fresco dining during the summer months in the open-air courtyard with wishing well is popular. The Garden Room Restaurant offers a range of Scottish and European dishes changed seasonally. German, Italian and some Japanese spoken. *(See advert Page 265.)*

Open all year
🏠 Rooms: 17 with private facilities
SP Special rates available
✕ Lunch £
✕ Dinner £££
Ⓥ Vegetarians welcome
† Children welcome
⚸ No smoking in restaurant + 3 bedrooms

Terrine of baby leeks and Loch Fyne smoked haddock with sauce vierge. Baked saddle of Perthshire lamb in a pastry with woodland mushroom duxelle, fresh tarragon and Madeira jus. Vanilla panacota, tuile wafers and passion fruit sorbet with blackcurrant coulis.

STB Highly Commended 👑 👑 👑 👑
⊞ Credit cards: Access/Mastercard/Eurocard, American Express, Visa, Diners Club, Mastercharge, Switch
Ⅺ General Manager: Stephen Kelly

Dunfermline 68

DAVAAR HOUSE HOTEL

126 Grieve Street, Dunfermline
Fife KY12 8DW
Tel: 01383 721886/736463
Fax: 01383 623633

From M90 Junction 3 to Dunfermline, follow A907 Kincardine into Carnegie Drive. Right into Chalmers Street, then second left to Grieve Street.

Small, family-run town hotel and restaurant.

- Victorian townhouse.
- Home cooking.
- "High quality home cooking with creativity and style."

Davaar House was built at the turn of the century and retains such features as a splendid oak staircase, marble fireplaces and elaborate cornices. It is centrally situated in a residential area of Dunfermline. There is an appealing, chintzy, appearance to the hotel which stands in lovely gardens. The food is cooked by Doreen Jarvis and her daughter Karen who create traditional dishes with intuitive flair and, using the best fresh vegetables, supplied by Jim and their son Kyle who have their own fruit and vegetable business.

Open all year except 23 Dec to 6 Jan
Closed Sun
🏠 Rooms: 8 with private facilities
SP Special rates available
♀ Restricted Licence
✕ Lunch (Dec only) except Sun ££
✕ Dinner except Sun £££
Ⓥ Vegetarians welcome
† Children welcome
♿ Facilities for disabled visitors
⚸ No smoking in restaurant + 1st floor bedrooms

Grilled mushrooms stuffed with Davaar House pâté served with warm oatcakes. East Neuk basket of seafood of fresh haddock, scampi and prawns in a creamy white wine sauce served in a filo pastry basket. Crème brûlée with fresh raspberries poached in Drambuie.

STB Commended 👑 👑 👑
⊞ Credit cards: Access/Mastercard/Eurocard
Ⅺ Proprietors: Doreen & Jim Jarvis

KEAVIL HOUSE HOTEL
Main Street, Crossford
nr Dunfermline
Fife KY12 8QW
Tel: 01383 736258
Fax: 01383 621600

Junction 3, M90, 7 miles from Forth Road Bridge. Take A985 then right after bridge. From Dunfermline take A994.

An attractive country house near Dunfermline.

- Country house hotel.
- Traditional Scottish cooking.
- "A warm friendly welcome in very pleasant surroundings."

Crossford village is just outside Dunfermline, and Keavil House is on the Main Street, standing in 12 acres of gardens and woods. As well as having two restaurants to choose from, the hotel also has a swimming pool, gym and sauna/solarium, etc. Staff are smart and well-trained; rooms are very comfortable. There is a choice of à la carte or table d'hôte menus which offer both traditional and more adventurous dishes, all of them well-cooked and presented. Keavil is part of the Best Western group of hotels, but is much, much better than the average. Keavil has 1 AA Rosette.

- Open all year
- Rooms: 33 with private facilities
- Special rates available
- Food served all day
- Lunch £
- Dinner £££
- Vegetarians welcome
- Children welcome
- Facilities for disabled visitors
- No smoking throughout

Jellied smoked eel and Ayrshire bacon terrine with a root vegetable vinaigrette. Sautéed king scallops and red mullet fillet. Home-made Dalmore single malt and heather honey ice cream topped with tay berry compote.

STB Commended 👑 👑 👑 👑
- Credit cards: Access/Mastercard/Eurocard, American Express, Visa, Diners Club, Switch
- Manager: Mark Simpkins

Dunkeld 69

STAKIS DUNKELD HOUSE RESORT HOTEL
Dunkeld, Perthshire PH8 0HX
Tel: 01350 727771 Fax: 01350 728924

A9 to Dunkeld, hotel lies c. 1 mile east of village.

A popular country house hotel set in idyllic surroundings.

- Highly regarded as offering the best of the old and the new.
- Outstanding Scottish cuisine with flair.
- "An idyllic setting, a good centre from which to explore Perthshire."

Built originally for the Seventh Duke of Atholl, this Edwardian house has been sympathetically extended and restored to form a rare combination of country house and luxury hotel. The hotel sits within its own 280 acre estate on the banks of the River Tay and has a private 2-mile salmon beat. An excellent leisure centre includes an indoor pool. Outdoors, the hotel offers all-weather tennis courts, a croquet lawn and clay-pigeon shooting. Menus in the dining room are intended to satisfy the most discerning of palates. The table d'hôte menu offers four choices for each course. It should be noted that during the quiet season the dining room is not always available at lunchtime. Dishes are well-balanced and use fresh, local ingredients. Presentation and service round off a pleasurable experience.

- Open all year
- Rooms: 86 with private facilities
- Special rates available
- Food served all day £
- Lunch ££
- Dinner £££
- Vegetarians welcome
- Children welcome
- Facilities for disabled visitors

Tartlet of Elie crab with a small leaf salad and lemon yoghurt sauce. Pan-seared lamb fillets with grain mustard sauce and parsley dumpling. Warm apple and ginger pudding with vanilla sauce and ice cream.

STB Commended 👑 👑 👑 👑 👑
- Credit cards: Access/Mastercard/Eurocard, American Express, Visa, Diners Club, Mastercharge, Switch
- Hotel Manager: Dick Beach
- Executive Chef: George McIvor

Dunoon 70

THE ANCHORAGE HOTEL & RESTAURANT
Shore Road, Ardnadam
Holy Loch, Dunoon, Argyll PA23 8QG
Tel: 01369 705108 Fax: 01369 705108

3 miles out of Dunoon on A815 heading north.

A recently refurbished lochside hotel.

- Very pretty whitewashed Victorian house.
- Scottish food imaginatively cooked.
- "A fresh, alive and enthusiastic approach by an ambitious young couple who will merit success."

On the banks of the Holy Loch sits this white Victorian house which was bought by Dee and Tony Hancock four years ago. Since then they have both worked hard to renovate and refurbish and Tony recently completed the building of a charming conservatory/dining room which overlooks a well-laid out and most attractive garden. The decor is attractive and their attention to detail has resulted in a delightful, tasteful and comfortable place to stay. This dedication also extends to their well-planned menus which offer dishes carefully selected to make use of a wide range of local produce including shellfish, venison and game. The Anchorage is an enjoyable place to stay with its panoramic views across the loch and attentive professional hosts.

Open all year
- Rooms: 5 with private facilities
- ✕ Lunch £
- ✕ Dinner £££
- Ⓥ Vegetarians welcome
- ☆ Children welcome
- ♿ Facilities for disabled visitors
- ⚊ No smoking throughout

Roast Isle of Arran king scallops served on a bed of courgette ribbons with a warm orange, ginger and dill sauce, topped with aubergine crisps. Perthshire pork filet wrapped in Parma ham and sage sautéed and served with a Marsala wine and pineapple sauce on a pasta ribbon bed. White chocolate and kahlua sponge.

STB Highly Commended 🏅 🏅 🏅
- Credit cards: Access/Mastercard/Eurocard, Visa, Delta
- Owners: Dee & Tony Hancock

ARDFILLAYNE HOUSE
West Bay, Dunoon
Argyll PA23 7QJ
Tel: 01369 702267
Fax: 01369 702501

1 mile from Dunoon centre on Innellan road at end of promenade.

Country house on the outskirts of Dunoon.

- Country house.
- Scottish/French cooking.
- "Bill McCaffrey is an attentive host, Master Chef, and wine buff – you will be in good hands."

A traditional country house situated in a 16 acre wooded estate on an elevated position overlooking the Firth of Clyde on the outskirts of Dunoon, the hotel retains the atmosphere of a bygone era. The interior of the house is crammed with antique furniture, Victoriana, bric-a-brac and an interesting collection of clocks. Beverley's Restaurant is decorated with lace, crystal and silverware with an extensive à la carte menu. Service is formal and the cooking applies classical French techniques to traditional Scottish recipes. Bill McCaffrey, the owner, buys his wine by his own careful selection at wine auctions. Ardfillayne has 1 AA Rosette.

Open all year
- Rooms: 7 with private facilities
- Ⓢ Special rates available
- Open for dinner – advance booking requested £££
- Ⓥ Vegetarians welcome – prior notice required
- ⚊ No smoking in restaurant

Sliced smoked chicken breast in a lime cassis. Roast haunch of hill venison. Dark chocolate and brandy gâteau.

STB Deluxe 🏅 🏅 🏅 🏅
- Credit cards: Access/Mastercard/Eurocard, American Express, Visa, Diners Club
- Proprietor: Bill McCaffrey

CHATTERS
58 John Street, Dunoon
Argyll PA23 8BJ
Tel: 01369 706402

On John Street, Dunoon, opposite the cinema.

Charming, award-winning small restaurant in popular seaside resort.

- Town restaurant in converted traditional cottage.
- Traditional French influenced Scottish cooking.
- "Talented, happy cooking from chef David Craig – no wonder it's so popular!"

Now in its sixth year of operation in the capable hands of Rosemary MacInnes this restaurant has picked up several awards. The young chefs are very enthusiastic, original and extremely competent. Credible and well-balanced à la carte menus are presented for lunch and dinner (six starters, six main courses); every dish is an unusual and successful combination of flavours and textures, and each demonstrates considerable talent. There is also a lounge extension opening out onto a small garden, used for pre-lunch/dinner drinks and coffee. In spite of its excellence and distinction, Chatters has a friendly, informal atmosphere and is very popular with locals for coffee and afternoon tea, with home baking. Winner of The Macallan Taste of Scotland Special Merit Award for Enterprise 1994.

Open 17 Feb to 31 Dec except Christmas Day
Closed Sun
♀ Table licence
✗ Lunch ££
✗ Dinner ££
⚞ Smoking discouraged

Terrine of four cheeses served with apricot and spiced orange chutney. Warm salad of local seafood garnished with quail's eggs. A wide selection of home-made puddings.

⊞ Credit cards: Access/Mastercard/Eurocard, Visa
⋈ Proprietor: Rosemary Anne MacInnes

ENMORE HOTEL
Marine Parade, Dunoon
Argyll PA23 8HH
Tel: 01369 702230
Fax: 01369 702148

On seafront near Hunters Quay Ferry, approx 1 mile from town centre.

Very comfortable small hotel in its own grounds facing the sea.

- 18th century villa.
- Modern Scottish cooking.
- "Great care and a very sure touch in the kitchen ensures food of a high standard, with hospitality to match."

Originally built in 1785 as a country retreat for a wealthy Glasgow businessman, the house has been enlarged over the years into a luxurious small hotel. It has ten en suite bedrooms, and the public rooms are attractively furnished with reproduction period pieces. There is a colourful garden, a squash court, a private beach and golf and fishing are within easy reach. The limited choice menu guarantees the freshness of the produce – 'creel caught crayfish' and Loch Fyne scallops – and the hotel's own garden provides herbs and vegetables. Chef/proprietor, David Wilson, has an AA Rosette, and is always looking for new ways to produce and present great ingredients. His wife, Angela, puts as much care into making sure your stay is happy as he does into his menus.

Open all year except 22 to 29 Dec
🛏 Rooms: 10 with private facilities
SP Special rates available
✗ Food served all day £-£££
✗ Lunch ££-£££
✗ Dinner £££
Ⓥ Vegetarians welcome
⚸ Children welcome
♿ Facilities for disabled visitors – non-residents only
⚞ No smoking in dining room

Hot smoked salmon with a warm Sauterne sauce. Breast of pheasant with a rhubarb confit served with potato and chive pancake. Chocolate Marquise with raspberry sauce.

STB Highly Commended 👑 👑 👑 👑
⊞ Credit cards: Access/Mastercard/Eurocard, American Express, Visa, Mastercharge, Switch, Delta
⋈ Proprietors: Angela & David Wilson

36

36 Great King Street
Edinburgh EH3 6QH
Tel: 0131 556 3636
Fax: 0131 556 3663

Great King Street is off Dundas Street, the continuation of Hanover Street – 5 minutes from Princes Street.

Modern new restaurant within elegant Georgian building.

- Contemporary interior design within New Town elegance.
- Modern Scottish cooking.
- "Inspired dishes, friendly staff and a great addition to the Edinburgh scene."

36 is an exciting newcomer to the Edinburgh scene. Located in a basement of Edinburgh's New Town one has the feeling of light and air despite the location. Clever use has been made of modern lighting and the decor is fresh and contemporary without being intimidating. The staff are all well-trained, professional but with an extra friendly quality which removes any pretentiousness often found in 'better' restaurants. They are rightly proud of their new restaurant and this is conveyed in their manner. The cooking is skilful, by Chef Malcolm Warham who uses the best fresh ingredients and his imagination to come up with inspired dishes. It is described as intrinsically Scottish with worldly influences.

Open all year
✕ Lunch £-££
✕ Dinner ££
Ⓥ Vegetarians welcome
⚬ No smoking in restaurant

A pastry tartlet of sweet onion marmalade and warm goats cheese set on a tomato and black pepper salad. Seared West Coast scallops with an avocado and mangetout salsa. Iced orange fudge parfait with macerated strawberries.

💳 Credit cards: Access/Mastercard/Eurocard, American Express, Visa, Diners Club, Mastercharge, Switch, Delta
Ⓜ Restaurant Manager: Ishbel Moffat

ATRIUM

10 Cambridge Street
Edinburgh EH1 2ED
Tel: 0131 228 8882
Fax: 0131 228 8808

Within Saltire Court, at entrance to Traverse Theatre, adjacent to Usher Hall.

A flagship modern restaurant with an enviable reputation.

- Stylish and much lauded city restaurant.
- Outstanding modern Scottish cooking.
- "Inspirational and imaginative modern Scottish cooking. Andrew Radford never fails to please."

From its specially-designed oil-lamps to its overall decor, the Atrium is a striking example of modern Scottish design. Appropriately, the imaginative cooking here is as distinctive as the restaurant it serves. The restaurant's talented Chef/proprietor, Andrew Radford, has seen his success recognised informally by a devoted clientele. He has won a number of awards, including The Macallan Personality of the Year Award 1994. The restaurant he started offers an à la carte menu that is based on fresh local produce and changes twice daily. The Atrium also offers a snack menu available at lunchtime and in the evening for pre-theatre meals. Both menus are inspired, creative and well balanced, as befits the Atrium's deserved reputation: one of Edinburgh's foremost restaurants.

Open all year except 1 wk Christmas
Closed Sun
✕ Lunch except Sun Sat ££
✕ Dinner except Sun £££
Ⓥ Vegetarians welcome
⚼ Children welcome

Shellfish samosa with garlic, leek and fine herbs. Roast loin of venison with charterelles and shallots. Baked apple with cinnamon ice cream.

💳 Credit cards: Credit cards: Access/Mastercard/ Eurocard, American Express, Visa, Switch, Delta
Ⓜ Proprietors: Andrew & Lisa Radford

THE BALMORAL HOTEL

1 Princes Street, Edinburgh EH2 2EQ
Tel: 0131 556 2414 Fax: 0131 557 3747

Princes Street at the corner of North Bridge.

A grand and impressive city hotel that has long been an important Edinburgh landmark.

- Sumptuous, elegant and distinguished hotel
- Variety of impeccable cuisines
- "The height of elegance, sumptuous cuisine."

Since its opening as the North British Hotel in 1902, The Balmoral has maintained its reputation as the embodiment of hospitality and ease. Under Executive Chef Billy Campbell, the hotel's principal restaurant – the spacious and elegant No. 1 Princes St. – offers outstanding classically-orientated cooking which is exquisitely presented and served. Alternatively, the hotel's Brasserie is designed along continental lines, with an all day service of light meals and snacks. Bar lunches are available in NB's Bar and the Palm Court affords somewhere to sit and drink coffee or tea whilst a harpist plays. For food, ambience and service, this hotel deserves its reputation for all round excellence. The Balmoral has 2 AA Rosettes. Winner of The Macallan Taste of Scotland Hotel of the Year Award 1995.

Open all year
- ⏣ Rooms: 189 with private facilities
- ⬛ Special rates available
- ✕ Food served all day £££
- ✕ Lunch £-££££
- ✕ Dinner ££-££££
- Ⓥ Vegetarians welcome
- ⬤ Children welcome
- ⬤ Facilities for disabled visitors
- ⬤ No smoking area in restaurants
- ⬤ Member of the Scotch Beef Club

Pan-seared Oban scallops in a light puff pastry case with prime young vegetables and a pineapple butter sauce. Loin of spring Sutherland lamb enrobed with tapenade, spinach and crépinette served with a rich rosemary jus. Glayva ice cream on a bed of marinated seasonal fruits and berries.

STB Deluxe 👑 👑 👑 👑 👑
- ⊞ Credit cards: Access/Mastercard/Eurocard, American Express, Visa, Diners Club, Mastercharge, Switch, Delta
- ⬛ General Manager: Jacques Ligné
- ⬛ Sales & Marketing Manager: Sarah Reid
- ⬛ Food & Beverage Manager: Jonathan Walker

CALEDONIAN HOTEL

Princes Street
Edinburgh EH1 2AB
Tel: 0131 459 9988
Fax: 0131 225 6632

West end of Princes Street

One of Scotland's best hotels.

- City centre grand hotel
- Traditional and modern cooking with French influences.
- "A grand hotel of charm and character which offers excellent cuisine that is both imaginative and inspirational."

The 'Caley' has been a landmark and an Edinburgh institution since it opened its doors in 1903. La Pompadour Restaurant is situated immediately above the hotel's front door, and affords engaging views over the busy West End of Princes Street. Chef de Cuisine Tony Binks has combed old manuscripts and investigated how Scottish cooks applied and adapted classic methods in order to compose a menu which he describes as 'Legends of the Scottish Table'. Service is state-of-the-art; the wine list is exceptional; and the flavours are out of this world. Downstairs there is the Carriages Restaurant. La Pompadour was awarded The Taste of Scotland Restaurant Of The Year Award 1992. *(See advert Page 6.)*

Open all year
- ⏣ Rooms: 236 with private facilities
- ⬛ Special rates available
- ✕ Lunch (Carriages) ££
- ✕ Dinner (Carriages) ££
- ✕ Dinner (La Pompadour) ££££
- Ⓥ Vegetarians welcome
- ⬤ Children welcome
- ⬤ Facilities for disabled visitors
- ⬤ Smoking areas in restaurants
- ⬤ Member of the Scotch Beef Club

Woodland mushrooms and Roquefort salad with fried polenta. Pan-fried fillet of turbot with char-grilled courgette in a lime and basil sauce. Delicate summer pudding with a medley of ripe berries.

STB Highly Commended 👑 👑 👑 👑 👑
- ⊞ Credit cards: Access/Mastercard/Eurocard, American Express, Visa, Diners Club, Switch, Delta
- ⬛ General Manager: Stephen Carter

CARLTON HIGHLAND HOTEL
North Bridge
Edinburgh
EH1 1SD
Tel: 0131 556 7277
Fax: 0131 556 2691

City centre – North Bridge links the east end of Princes Street with the Royal Mile.

Standing on the North Bridge and High Street, with fine views across the New Town to the Forth.

- Large city centre hotel.
- Traditional cooking with European influences.
- "A very friendly city centre hotel."

The Carlton Highland rises massively above the North Bridge, a ponderously articulated Edwardian building, which nevertheless commands wonderful views. The decoration is tasteful and the furnishings comfortable throughout; the hotel has a leisure club, gift shop, beauty/hair salon, patisserie and even a nightclub. It also has two restaurants: Carlton Court – an informal bistro and carvery; Quills – which has the theme of a country house library with professional service. The cooking gives an imaginative modern twist to classic dishes. The Carlton Highland has 1 AA Rosette.

Open all year
- 🏨 Rooms: 197 with private facilities
- ✗ Food served all day
- ✗ Lunch (Carlton Court) £
- ✗ Lunch (Quills) ££
- ✗ Dinner (Carlton Court) ££
- ✗ Dinner (Quills) £££
- Ⓥ Vegetarians welcome
- ☩ Children welcome
- ♿ Facilities for disabled visitors
- 🚭 Smoking only in Carlton Court restaurant

Slivers of smoked salmon served on a salad with potatoes, anchovies and quail eggs. Loin of lamb with a herb crust served with mint. Drambuie flavoured crème brûlée.

STB Highly Commended 👑 👑 👑 👑 👑
- 💳 Credit cards: Access/Mastercard/Eurocard, American Express, Visa, Diners Club, Mastercharge, Switch, Delta
- 🛎 Operations Manager: William Gorol

CHANNINGS BRASSERIE
South Learmonth Gardens
Edinburgh
EH4 1EZ
Tel: 0131 315 2225/6
Fax: 0131 332 9631

South Learmonth Gardens is parallel to Queensferry Road, a few minutes walk from the west end of Edinburgh city centre.

A private hotel and brasserie in a quiet residential street.

- Townhouse hotel.
- Innovative Scottish cooking.
- "A cosmopolitan blend of dishes using fresh Scottish ingredients."

Originally five terraced townhouses in a smart Edwardian terrace, Channings is a privately owned hotel with the atmosphere of a gentleman's club. The attractive features of the buildings have been retained in the conversion, and furniture and fabrics are tasteful; bedrooms are individually designed. In the Brasserie, the interesting menus change with the seasons and draw inspiration from old classic European dishes. The ingredients are fresh, and the house 'specials' are original and delicious. Appropriate wines are suggested for each dish. The atmosphere of the Brasserie is relaxed and pleasant, and the garden adjacent to it is used in the summer. The bar offers a wide range of malt whiskies. Channings has 1 AA Rosette.

Open all year except 24, 26 + 27 Dec
- 🏨 Rooms: 56 with private facilities
- 🆂🅿 Special rates available
- ✗ Lunch £
- ✗ Dinner ££
- Ⓥ Vegetarians welcome
- ☩ Children welcome
- 🚭 No smoking in brasserie

Dunbar fish cakes garnished with a crayfish bisque. Gingered pork steaks garnished with braised chorizo sausage and country style lentils. Iced lemon and vodka parfait with mango sauce.

STB Highly Commended 👑 👑 👑 👑
- 💳 Credit cards: Access/Mastercard/Eurocard, American Express, Visa, Diners Club, Mastercharge, Switch, Delta
- 🛎 Proprietor: Peter Taylor

CRAMOND GALLERY BISTRO

4 Riverside Cramond, Cramond Village
Edinburgh
EH4 6NY
Tel: 0131 312 6555

Follow Cramond Glebe Road down to harbour front.

A small restaurant by the sea.

- Village restaurant with apartments.
- Simple fresh cooking.
- "Good use of local produce, cooked fresh in a lovely situation."

Cramond Gallery Bistro overlooks Cramond Harbour, at the mouth of the River Almond, where it joins the Forth. It is a 16th century cottage, built on the site of a second century Roman boatshed (Cramond was an important Roman base: there are the remains of a fort alongside the church). A small low dining room with timber beams, astragal windows and a pleasant atmosphere. Changing exhibitions of pictures (for sale) decorate the walls of the restaurant – hence its name. Fish is something of a speciality, but game and other meats also feature on the short menus. The cooking is straightforward and well-priced. Four luxury self-catering cottage apartments are available, awarded STB Highly Commended 3 Crowns.

Open all year except Christmas Day
Note: closed Mon Tue from Oct to Jun
Ⓤ Ⓛ ♀ Unlicensed – guests welcome to take own wine
✗ Lunch £-££
✗ Dinner £££
Ⓥ Vegetarians welcome
✄ No smoking in restaurant

Haddock and salmon fishcakes. Scotch lamb medallions with red wine and mint. Hot chocolate cake with chocolate ice cream.

💷 No credit cards
Ⓝ Proprietors: Alan & Evelyn Bogue

CREELERS SEAFOOD BISTRO BAR & RESTAURANT

3 Hunter Square
Edinburgh
EH1 1QW
Tel: 0131 220 4447/4448
Fax: 0131 220 4149

The Square surrounds the back of the Tron Kirk on the Royal Mile.

Seafood bistro bar and restaurant.

- Informal style in the heart of the Old Town.
- Bistro cooking.
- "Creelers Arran's origins are reflected in the menu and the delightful decor."

A sister establishment to Creelers in Brodick (Isle of Arran – see entry), Tim and Fran James bring fresh fish and home smoked products from the island to their restaurant in the heart of Edinburgh, just off the High Street. The bistro bar has an informal atmosphere, with quiet decor and murals of Arran; the restaurant is more formal and exhibits the work of local and Arran artists (for sale) – an excellent feature here. Downstairs is a private room, seating 12–15 people. Head Chef Stuart Allan presents a lightweight table d'hôte menu and a lengthy à la carte menu, for lunch and dinner, featuring game and vegetarian dishes as well as Scottish seafood.

Open all year except Christmas Day,
Boxing Day, New Year's Day +
second wk in Jan
Closed Sun Oct to Apr
✗ Food served all day £
✗ Lunch £
✗ Dinner ££-£££
Ⓥ Vegetarians welcome
🅿 No parking

Smoked chicken and orange salad. Timbale of marinaded seafood with pickled vegetables. Whole lemon sole stuffed with crab meat on an orange butter sauce.

💷 Credit cards: Access/Mastercard/Eurocard, Visa, Switch
Ⓝ Proprietors: Fran & Tim James & Co Ltd

DRUM & MONKEY

80 Queen Street
Edinburgh
EH2 4NF
Tel: 0131 538 8111
Fax: 0131 220 5077

Corner site in the heart of Edinburgh's New Town at west end of Queen Street.

Sophisticated city bistro.

- Georgian ground floor and basement restaurant.
- Innovative bistro cooking.
- "Prime ingredients interestingly prepared with style."

The Drum and Monkey has become a local institution where customers may choose between the more informal bar setting of ground floor or the more formal seating in the basement. Both offer good value dishes that can be part of a memorable meal or a brief, yet top quality, working lunch. There is a pleasant ambience in wooden panelling decor with pew seating with old wine bottles and memorabilia lining the walls. The house motto is 'the odd libation for the over-worked'.

Open all year except 25, 26 Dec, 1 + 2 Jan
Closed Sun evening
✗ Food served all day ££
✗ Lunch except Sun Sat ££
✗ Dinner except Sun ££
Ⓥ Vegetarians welcome
✶ Children welcome
♿ Facilities for disabled visitors – limited

Scottish black pudding with baked apple and Calvados jus. Baked fillet of salmon en croûte, stuffed with tapenade and spinach and served with bashed new potatoes and home-dried tomato pesto sauce. Cranachan cheesecake with fresh berry compote.

▣ Credit cards: Access/Mastercard/Eurocard, American Express, Visa, Diners Club, Switch
▨ Manager: Grant Cullen

DUBH PRAIS RESTAURANT

123b High Street
Edinburgh EH1 1SG
Tel: 0131 557 5732
Fax: 0131 557 5263

Edinburgh Royal Mile, opposite Holiday Inn Crowne Plaza.

Small basement restaurant.

- City centre restaurant.
- Traditional Scottish cooking.
- "Scottish dishes cooked with flair."

Walking down the Royal Mile which leads from Edinburgh Castle to Holyrood Palace, look out for the sign of the black pot (in Gaelic 'dubh prais') down a few steps on the left in the High Street. Its imaginative chef/owner, James McWilliams, presents a well-balanced à la carte menu which devotes itself entirely to Scottish seasonal produce and regional recipes. The restaurant is popular with locals and tourists alike, and the dishes offered are described with patriotic fervour and are cooked using simple methods as the freshest produce requires.

Open all year except 2 wks Christmas + 2 wks Easter
Closed Sun Mon
✗ Lunch except Sun Mon £
✗ Dinner except Sun Mon £££
Ⓥ Vegetarians welcome
✶ Children welcome
✍ Guests are asked not to smoke cigars or pipes

Wild mushrooms with lemon sauce served on a potato scone. Suprême of chicken stuffed with smoked pheasant coated with a sherry sauce. Atholl Brose parfait served on a blackcurrant sauce.

▣ Credit cards: Access/Mastercard/Eurocard, American Express, Visa, Mastercharge, Switch, Delta, JCB
▨ Chef/Proprietor: James McWilliams
▨ Proprietor: Heather McWilliams

DUCK'S AT LE MARCHÉ NOIR
2/4 Eyre Place
Edinburgh EH3 5EP
Tel: 0131 558 1608
Fax: 0131 556 0798

Eyre Place is at northern end of Dundas Street (continuation of Hanover Street, north of Princes Street).

An excellent small Franco/Scottish restaurant.

* Highly regarded, cosy and intimate.
* Excellent modern French/Scottish cuisine.
* "A relaxed restaurant with an attentive host."

Proprietor Malcolm Duck established this friendly restaurant in what had been a shop. Now recently refurbished the restaurant has the feel of a small, typically French restaurant. Tucked away in a quiet corner of the New Town, Duck's at Le Marché Noir's ambience is relaxed and restful. Staff are cheerful, efficient and welcoming. The kitchen produces innovative and excellent French/Scottish à la carte cuisine that is always well-presented. Malcolm Duck takes justifiable pride in his extensive and interesting wine list. The restaurant has 2 AA Rosettes.

....

Open all year except 25 + 26 Dec
* ✗ Lunch ££
* ✗ Dinner £££
* Ⓥ Vegetarians welcome
* ✦ Children welcome
* ♿ Facilities for disabled visitors
* 🚭 No smoking room in restaurant

Haggis dumplings served on a bed of creamed leeks. Escalopes of venison on a bed of celeriac purée with a juniper-scented sauce topped with a julienne of deep-fried vegetables. Home-made lemon and sultana steamed pudding with crème anglaise.

* 💳 Credit cards: Access/Mastercard/Eurocard, American Express, Visa, Diners Club, Switch, Delta, JCB
* Ⓜ Proprietor: Malcolm Duck

(fitz)HENRY
19 Shore Place
Edinburgh
EH6 6SW
Tel: 0131 555 6625

City end of 'the shore' in Leith.

In Leith, just behind 'the shore' running along the Water of Leith.

* Exceptionally fine brasserie.
* Atmospheric converted old town warehouse.
* "A joy to eat in – an experienced not to be missed."

David Ramsden and Ros McKnight, the charismatic owners of (fitz)Henry, had a bistro in William Street ten years ago called 'Hoora Henry's'. Hence the name. He is a man of considerable panache, and this shows in this venture. The venue is a beautifully restored old warehouse just off the shore in Leith: spacious, simply furnished, subtly lit. Chefs: No 1, Hugue Borelly, and No 2, Herve Vareille, offer exceptional cuisine of the highest standard with considerable flair. Presentation is well considered and service attentive and friendly. The relaxed ambience of (fitz)Henry communicates style, good taste and high standards. This restaurant deserves to do very well.

....

Open all year except 25 Dec + 1 Jan
Closed Sun
* ✗ Lunch except Sun ££
* ✗ Dinner except Sun £££
* Ⓥ Vegetarians welcome – prior notice required
* ✦ Children welcome
* ♿ Facilities for disabled visitors

Spinach orzotto with Chinese sausage. Pan-fried cod fillet with olive oil mash and beetroot vinaigrette. Pistachio and carob délice.

* 💳 Credit cards: Access/Mastercard/Eurocard, American Express, Visa, Switch, Delta
* Ⓜ Proprietors: David H Ramsden & Ros McKnight

THE GRANGE

8 Whitehouse Terrace
Edinburgh
EH9 2EU
Tel: 0131 667 5681
Fax: 0131 668 3300

1½ miles from Princes Street, up Lothian Road – at Tollcross follow signs for Jedburgh then turn right into Marchmont Road. Continue to traffic lights straight across Kilgraston Road – Whitehouse Terrace is third right.

19th century Scottish baronial home.

- Small country house hotel in leafy residential part of Edinburgh.
- Traditional Scottish cooking.
- "Relaxing and comfortable with good food and wine."

This beautiful Scottish baronial home was originally built for a wealthy Glasgow accountant called Jackson. It was later bought and extended by the famous Edinburgh brewing family of Usher in 1903. The Grange has now been renovated and restored and offers good food and wine with easy access to the city centre whilst enjoying comfortable surroundings in residential Edinburgh. The cooking is traditional Scottish with French influences and daily changing menus offer good choices for discerning diners. Food is served in the restaurant, bar and the conservatory.

Open all year
🛏 Rooms: 13 with private facilities
ⓢ Special rates available
Note: (Conservatory £) (Restaurant ££)
✖ Food served all day £-££
✖ Lunch £-££
✖ Dinner £-££
Ⓥ Vegetarians welcome
⚲ Children welcome

Quenelles of haggis in a cream Drambuie sauce. Fillet of beef in filo pastry with smoked Orkney cheese. Selection of home-made desserts.

STB Commended 🏵 🏵 🏵
💳 Credit cards: Access/Mastercard/Eurocard, American Express, Visa, Mastercharge, Switch, Delta
👤 Owner: Mrs Liz Woodrow

HENDERSON'S SALAD TABLE

94 Hanover Street
Edinburgh EH2 1DR
Tel: 0131 225 2131
Fax: 0131 220 3542

2 minutes from Princes Street under Henderson's wholefood shop.

A popular city centre wholefood eating and meeting place.

- Lively, informal, cosmopolitan basement bistro in New Town.
- Innovative and interesting vegetarian cuisine.
- "Wholefood cuisine at its best."

Henderson's was an established institution long before wholefoods became popular and its enviable reputation for excellent and inexpensive fare is as well deserved now as in Janet Henderson's day. The atmosphere here is always congenial and the counter-served helpings generous. Vegetarian salads, savouries, quiches and puddings are freshly prepared and eagerly consumed throughout the day with an unusual selection of real ales and wines, some Scottish and many organic also on offer. Henderson's still actively run by the family, appeals to all ages proving that wholefoods can be fun, especially Monday to Saturday nights when 'real' musicians enliven the wine bar.

Open all year except Christmas Day, Boxing Day, 1 + 2 Jan
Closed Sun except during Edinburgh Festival
✖ Food served all day except Sun £
✖ Lunch except Sun £
✖ Dinner except Sun £
Ⓥ Vegans welcome
⚲ Children welcome
⚞ No smoking in main restaurant + wine bar areas

Apricot and lentil soup with nutty malt bread. Aubergine and smoked cheese pie topped with filo pastry served with mixed salad or baby potatoes. Dried and fresh fruits with soured cream and ginger.

💳 Credit cards: Access/Mastercard/Eurocard, American Express, Visa, Switch, Delta, JCB
👤 Proprietors: The Henderson Family

HOLIDAY INN CROWNE PLAZA
(formerly Scandic Crown Hotel)
80 High Street, The Royal Mile, Edinburgh EH1 1TH
Tel: 0131 557 9797
Fax: 0131 557 9789

Centre of the Royal Mile tourist area.

A new building designed to look old on Edinburgh's High Street.

- Large city centre hotel.
- Modern/British cooking with Scandinavian overtones.
- "City hotel offering good food in pleasant surroundings."

The Holiday Inn Crowne Plaza has been heralded 'the finest example of Scottish medieval architecture built in recent times'. Halfway between Edinburgh Castle and Holyrood Palace on the world famous Royal Mile, the building has been sympathetically designed to blend perfectly with its ancient neighbours and incorporates four original Royal Mile Closes. The hotel has two restaurants named after such Royal Mile Closes: Carrubber's bistro, which has a medieval theme with its simulated eaves and murals, serves a selection of dishes in a relaxed informal atmosphere – the ideal place to meet friends; Advocates' is a stylish à la carte restaurant incorporating a striking turret feature looking out onto the Royal Mile. The tranquil elegant surroundings are ideal for enjoying a sumptuous speciality menu accompanied by a fine selection of wines. Under the guidance of Jean-Michel Gauffre, one of Scotland's top chefs, both restaurants are achieving an excellent reputation for fine food and convivial atmosphere.

Open all year except 24 to 27 Dec
🏠 Rooms: 238 with private facilities
✕ Food served all day ££
✕ Lunch ££
✕ Dinner £££
Ⓥ Vegetarians welcome
⚘ Children welcome
⚲ Facilities for disabled visitors

Parcel of Tay salmon and lobster in a mango and watercress cream. Medallions of venison with parsnips croquant and horseradish sauce. Raspberry and Drambuie crumble.

STB Highly Commended 👑 👑 👑 👑 👑
💳 Credit cards: Access/Mastercard/Eurocard, American Express, Visa, Diners Club, Mastercharge, Switch, Delta, JCB

HOWIES RESTAURANT
208 Bruntsfield Place
Edinburgh
EH10 4DE
Tel: 0131 221 1777

1½ miles from Princes Street.

A popular lively bistro offering modern Scottish cooking with French influences.

- Converted bank offering spacious premises.
- Modern Scottish with French influences.
- "A friendly and lively atmospheric bistro in which to enjoy good food."

Opened in 1995, Howies at Bruntsfield was formerly a banking hall dating back to 1853. Original features have been exposed including marble tiles and the high corniced ceiling is home to an old church chandelier. The bar/servery was constructed from the original banking counter. The atmosphere is relaxed and informal and the place buzzes with a mix of clientele. Cooking is Scottish with interesting French bistro influences and offers good value for money. Whilst the restaurant is licensed – diners are welcome to take their own wine (no corkage charge). The walls are hung with rotating Scottish art exhibits which are for sale.

Open all year except 25, 26 Dec, 1 + 2 Jan
✕ Lunch £
✕ Dinner ££
Ⓥ Vegetarians welcome
⚘ Children welcome
⚲ Facilities for disabled visitors
🚭 Please consider others when you consider smoking

Whole Scottish button mushrooms sautéd in garlic, white wine and cream. Breast of duck pan-fried and presented on a bed of black cherry, port and game reduction. Howies infamous banoffi pie.

💳 Credit cards: Access/Mastercard/Eurocard, American Express, Visa, Switch, Delta

HOWIES RESTAURANT
63 Dalry Road
Edinburgh
EH11 2BZ
Tel: 0131 313 3334

2 minutes walk from Haymarket Station, up Dalry Road.

Popular city bistro.

- Bistro within old commercial and residential buildings.
- Modern Scottish with French influences.
- "Budget food with flair."

One of three restaurants, Howies has successfully gained a niche in the market with its appetising fare at reasonable prices. Much of its success lies in its idiosyncratic nature: off-beat location, eclectic selection of tables, chairs and even cutlery! Great care, however, is taken over the daily changing menus to create appealing choices. In keeping with its slightly spartan bistro character, customers may bring their own wine if they wish (no corkage charge).

Open all year except 25, 26 Dec, 1 + 2 Jan
Closed Mon lunch only
✕ Lunch except Mon £
✕ Dinner ££
Ⓥ Vegetarians welcome
⚘ Children welcome
♿ Facilities for disabled visitors
🚭 No smoking area in restaurant

Smoked salmon and avocado roulade served with a pink peppercorn mayonnaise. Roast rib of Aberdeen Angus beef presented with a wholegrain mustard, mushroom and whisky jus. Blueberry and apple tart served hot with cream.

💳 Credit cards: Access/Mastercard/Eurocard, American Express, Visa, Switch, Delta

HOWIES RESTAURANT
75 St Leonards Street
Edinburgh
EH8 9QR
Tel: 0131 668 2917

½ mile south of the Royal Mile following South Bridge/Nicolson Street. Turn left at Rankeillor Street – Howies is 20m on right.

Bistro style restaurant close to city centre.

- Relaxed and informal bistro.
- Good value Scottish produce with French influences.
- "One of three popular bistro restaurants offering good value in attractive surroundings for all ages."

The original 'Howies' this restaurant opened over six years ago. It is a small restaurant (with only nine tables) with a relaxed atmosphere. The Art Nouveau light fittings and high ceiling give the place a true French bistro/cafe feel. Howies was originally unlicensed but now operates a licence whilst still welcoming diners to bring their own wine (there is no corkage charge). The cooking is Scottish with strong French bistro style influences and certainly offers excellent value for money.

Open all year except 25, 26 Dec, 1 + 2 Jan
Closed Mon lunch
✕ Lunch except Mon £
✕ Dinner ££
Ⓥ Vegetarians welcome
⚘ Children welcome

Pan-fried breast of woodpigeon presented with a grain mustard vinaigrette and fresh plums. Délice of wild salmon gently poached and served with fresh mussels and a dill and white wine bisque. Chocolate and almond terrine served with a raspberry coulis.

💳 Credit cards: Access/Mastercard/Eurocard, American Express, Visa, Switch, Delta

IGG'S RESTAURANT
15 Jeffrey Street
Edinburgh EH1 1DR
Tel: 0131 557 8184
Fax: 0131 441 7111

Edinburgh's Old Town – just off Royal Mile.

An attractive small restaurant off the Canongate.

- Elegant L-shaped restaurant with a continental style.
- Spanish and Scottish cuisine.
- "A delightful melange of Scottish produce and Spanish cuisine."

A small friendly owner-run restaurant in the heart of Edinburgh's Old Town – Igg's has nothing to do with Spanish donkeys at all! Indeed, it is difficult to know whether to describe it as a Scottish restaurant with Spanish influences or vice versa. Its decoration, pictures and furnishing are elegant and tasteful; tables are attractively dressed with linen and flowers; lighting is subtle. Iggy Campos, is enthusiastic, generous and laid back – an excellent host who sets a relaxed tone in his stylish little restaurant. At lunchtime a tapas menu is available as well as a good priced three/four course table d'hôte and à la carte menus. Igg's has 1 AA Rosette.

Open all year except 1 to 3 Jan
Closed Sun
✗ Lunch ££
✗ Dinner £££
Ⓥ Vegetarians welcome
⚲ Children welcome
♿ Wheelchair access

Tapas. Mousseline of smoked trout. Loin of Border lamb with stuffed duxelle of wild mushrooms and pine kernels. Choux pastry buns filled with white chocolate and hazelnut praline ice cream coated in a rich dark chocolate sauce.

💳 Credit cards: Access/Mastercard/Eurocard, American Express, Visa, Diners Club, Switch, Delta, JCB
Ⓜ Owner: Iggy Campos

JACKSON'S RESTAURANT
209-213 High Street
Royal Mile, Edinburgh
EH1 1PL
Tel: 0131 225 1793
Fax: 0131 220 0620

Halfway down the Royal Mile.

A restaurant in the heart of Edinburgh's Old Town.

- Cellar restaurant with more formal dining upstairs.
- Modern Scottish cooking.
- "Tastefully Scottish – unique atmosphere, creative menus."

Jackson's is on the High Street, the original thoroughfare and market place of the ancient city of Edinburgh. The cellar restaurant is open for both lunch and dinner, offering table d'hôte and à la carte menus (à la carte only in the evenings during the Festival) and its location attracts many tourists in this busy area. There is a bistro style feel to the cellar with alcoves, stone walls, pine tables, tapestries and discreet lighting. Upstairs there is a more formal dining room which can also be hired for private dinners. The table d'hôte 'business' lunch is creative and very well-priced; the à la carte majors on Scottish dishes, treated in unusual and original ways.

Open all year except Christmas Day + Boxing Day
✗ Lunch £
✗ Dinner ££££
✿ Extended hours during Edinburgh Festival
Ⓥ Vegetarians welcome

Half dozen fresh Orkney oysters gently grilled in their shells with raspberry scented olive oil. Noisettes of prime lamb wrapped in spinach and proscuitto presented on a thyme and berry reduction. Hot chocolate steamed sponge, dripping in chocolate sauce with fresh whipped cream.

💳 Credit cards: Access/Mastercard/Eurocard, American Express, Visa, Switch, Delta
Ⓜ Proprietor: Lyn MacKinnon

KEEPERS RESTAURANT
13B Dundas Street
Edinburgh EH3 6QG
Tel: 0131 556 5707
Fax: 0131 556 5707

Dundas Street (continuation of Hanover Street) is to north of Princes Street.

A cellar restaurant in the heart of the Georgian New Town.

- City centre restaurant.
- Traditional Scottish cooking.
- "Original stone walls and the hints of tartan combine to create an authentic setting for fine Scottish fare."

As its name suggests, this well-established restaurant specialises in game – supported by fish, shellfish and prime meat. The cooking is traditional, with good sauces and rich jus; the menus are both table d'hôte (four starters, four main courses) and à la carte and the dishes are naturally presented. Although centrally located, just down the hill from George Street, Keepers has an attractive intimacy. The wine list is well-chosen and reasonably priced. The restaurant serves lunch and dinner on a table d'hôte and à la carte basis. Individual rooms (or, indeed, the entire place) can be booked for private or business functions.

Open all year
Closed Sun, Mon lunch + Sat lunch unless by prior arrangement
- ℍ Note: Parties by prior arrangement
- ✗ Lunch except Sun Mon Sat £
- ✗ Dinner except Sun £££
- Ⓥ Vegetarians welcome
- ⚹ Children welcome
- ⚗ Non-smoking area by request

Mussels with a creamy saffron sauce and a hint of garlic. Duet of game with pine kernels and a port reduction. White chocolate and raspberry cheesecake on a bed of fruit coulis.

- ⊞ Credit cards: Access/Mastercard/Eurocard, American Express, Visa, Switch
- ℍ Proprietors: Keith & Mairi Cowie

LE CAFÉ SAINT-HONORE
34 North West Thistle Street Lane
Edinburgh
EH2 1EA
Tel: 0131 226 2211

Centre of Edinburgh, just off Frederick Street, 3 minutes from Princes Street.

A small French bistro, serving excellent Scottish food.

- Traditional Parisian café style.
- Modern Scottish cooking, with French influences.
- "Excellent Scottish food reflecting the Auld Alliance."

Café St Honore is located in a service street parallel to George Street. It was formerly an authentic French restaurant, was decorated accordingly and still has a Gallic charm. Its owners favour a more Scottish style of cooking, making good use of the produce available, although there are French influences in the preparation. The lunch and dinner menus change daily and are à la carte – realistically limited to about half a dozen starters and the same number of main courses, and very reasonably priced. The cooking is adventurous and highly professional; interesting combinations and fresh, innovative sauces appear regularly. Chef Chris Colverson is an outstanding vegetarian cook, and is delighted to prepare vegetarian dishes if given notice (they don't generally appear on the menu).

Open all year except Christmas Day, Boxing Day, 2 wks Easter and 1 wk Oct
Closed Sun except during Edinburgh Festival
- ✗ Lunch ££
- ✗ Dinner £££
- Ⓥ Vegetarians welcome
- ⚹ Children welcome
- 🅿 No parking
- ⚗ No smoking area in restaurant

Potted crab with lemon and capers. Breast of Barbary duck with cabbage, honey and thyme. Tarte tatin.

- ⊞ Credit cards: Access/Mastercard/Eurocard, American Express, Visa, Diners Club, Mastercharge, Switch, Delta
- ℍ Proprietors: Jerry Mallet & Chris Colverson

LE CHAMBERTIN RESTAURANT
21 George Street
Edinburgh EH2 2PB
Tel: 0131 459 2306
Fax: 0131 226 5644

City centre of Edinburgh.

A restaurant of distinction within one of Edinburgh's finest hotels.

- An elegant, gourmet restaurant with a relaxed ambience.
- Modern/traditional Scottish cuisine with French influence.
- "Unusual award-winning dinner menu offering the choice to sample many of the wines from Le Chambertin's excellent wine list."

Although within the highly regarded George Inter-Continental Hotel, Le Chambertin is fast developing a formidable reputation of its own, not least for its excellent and fairly priced business lunches. Restaurant Manager Barnaby Hawkes makes the most of the restaurant's grand and gracious ethos. Tables are well spaced out amid a splendid blue decor. The atmosphere is unhurried, calm. Menus are creative and well-balanced, with a good selection of game, fish, beef and lamb. Le Chambertin is also now fully air-conditioned. The excellent value wine list reflects the range of such gourmet cuisine. Chef de Cuisine, Klaus Knust, is a member of the prestigious Confrerie de Chaine des Rotisseurs. Le Chambertin has 1 AA Rosette.

Open all year except Boxing Day, 1 + 2 Jan
Closed Sun + Sat lunch
✗ Lunch except Sun Sat £££
✗ Dinner except Sun £££
Ⓥ Vegetarians welcome
⚐ Children welcome
♿ Facilities for disabled visitors
🚭 No smoking area in restaurant

Smoked Tobermory scallop ravioli with pearl barley risotto on a roast tomato and oregano coulis. Home cured venison with wild berries and fig and whisky chutney. Cramond basket with Drambuie and heather honey ice cream with logan berry compote and toasted oatmeal.

💳 Credit cards: Access/Mastercard/Eurocard, American Express, Visa, Diners Club, Mastercharge, Switch, Delta
Ⓚ Restaurant Manager: Barnaby Hawkes

MARTINS RESTAURANT
70 Rose Street North Lane
Edinburgh EH2 3DX
Tel: 0131 225 3106

In the north lane off Rose Street between Frederick Street and Castle Street.

A first class restaurant tucked away in a back street.

- Small city centre restaurant.
- Creative contemporary Scottish cooking.
- "Innovative combination of ingredients, and excellent selection of cheeses."

Generally regarded as one of the best places to eat in Edinburgh, Martin and Gay Irons established their restaurant in 1983. It is small and discreet, tucked away in a cobbled service lane parallel to Princes Street, in the very heart of the city. Its modest exterior gives no clue to the excellence within: the interior is bright, fresh and pastel-hued, decorated with fresh flowers and good contemporary pictures, and cleverly lit; the dining room is a pleasure to behold. Chefs Forbes Stott and Peter Banks create innovative dishes which allow the true flavours of the essential ingredients to come through (Martins buys its produce carefully, mainly from small producers). His menus are healthy and well-balanced, his style light; organic and wild foods are favoured. Service is good. Martins sets out to provide a 'total gourmet experience' – and succeeds.

Open all year except 23 Dec to 16 Jan, 26 May to 3 Jun + 28 Sep to 7 Oct
Closed Sun Mon
✗ Lunch except Sun Mon Sat ££-££££
✗ Dinner except Sun Mon £££-££££
Ⓥ Vegetarians welcome – prior notice required
🚭 No smoking in dining areas

Home-made bread served with a daily changing fresh herb vinaigrette. Grilled saddle of venison with beetroot and Puy lentils. Award-winning cheeseboard.

💳 Credit cards: Access/Mastercard/Eurocard, American Express, Visa, Diners Club, Mastercharge, Switch, Delta
Ⓚ Proprietors: Martin & Gay Irons

ROCK CAFE RESTAURANT
18 Howe Street
Edinburgh EH3 6TG
Tel: 0131 225 7225

Howe Street (continuation of Frederick Street) is to north of Princes Street.

Situated in trendy Stockbridge the Rock Cafe is popular with all ages.

- Informal restaurant with American diner theme.
- American style cooking with modern Scottish influence.
- "Something for everyone, best burger I've tasted for a long time!"

The Rock Cafe's decor is a real talking point for guests over a meal in this fashionable informal restaurant. Huge murals of rock stars dominate the room and there is a relaxed, laid back atmosphere. As well as excellent steaks and burgers the menu features fish and shellfish and good local vegetables. The dishes of the day are listed on a blackboard and there is no shortage of choice. When the food arrives, it does not disappoint. There is a small selection of wines. An interesting venue which promises excellent food.

Open all year except 24 Dec to 4 Jan incl
Closed Sun Mon
✗ Dinner except Sun Mon £-£££
Ⓥ Vegetarians welcome

Smoked salmon. Aberdeen Angus beef steaks and burgers. Char-grilled Scottish salmon with basil butter. Fish of the day.

▣ Credit cards: Access/Mastercard/Eurocard, American Express, Visa, Switch
Ⓝ Proprietor: John Mackay

THE ROUND TABLE
31 Jeffrey Street
Edinburgh EH1 1DH
Tel: 0131 557 3032

Off the Royal Mile and less than 5 minutes walk from Waverley Station.

An ideally located city centre restaurant-bistro.

- Unpretentious, no frills, inexpensive eating.
- Good traditional cooking.
- "Traditional Scottish fayre prepared by a chef who is clearly passionate about his home grown produce."

With its fine views over the city to the north, The Round Table takes its name from the shape of the tables on which it serves its simple, good fare. The ambience is informal and fun. No money has been wasted on creating a theme or pseudo-atmosphere: what you see is what you get. The cooking is based on fresh Scottish meats and fish. The lunch menu offers a fixed price option of outstanding value. The simple, two page wine list is well-chosen and fairly priced. Downstairs is a small private, non-smoking room available for private parties of up to 14.

Open all year except Christmas Day,
Boxing Day + 1 Jan
ᛉ Closed Sun except during Edinburgh Festival
✗ Lunch except Sun £
✗ Dinner except Sun ££
Ⓥ Vegetarians welcome
ᚲ Children welcome

Norwegian style herring salad. Fillets of beef with shallots and red wine sauce. Scottish cheese plate.

▣ Credit cards: Access/Mastercard/Eurocard, Visa, Mastercharge
Ⓝ Proprietors: Anne & Robert Winter

SHERATON GRAND HOTEL

1 Festival Square, Edinburgh EH3 9SR
Tel: 0131 229 9131 Fax: 0131 229 6254

Entrance off Festival Square. 500 yards from junction of Princes Street and Lothian Road.

A luxury city centre hotel.

- The Sheraton Grand Hotel embodies the best of Scottish style.
- Imaginative French/Scottish cuisine.
- "A superbly trained restaurant staff led by a very talented chef, presents meals which are a gastronomic delight."

The Sheraton Grand Hotel is a modern hotel; and no expense has been spared in its furnishing and decoration; there is a 'Leisure Club' with pool, sauna, solarium and gym. The staff are extremely professional and well-trained, but they are also helpful and friendly. The hotel has two restaurants; The Grill Room and The Terrace. The latter overlooks Festival Square (and its fountain) and offers a sophisticated brasserie style menu. The former is formal and intimate: Executive Chef, Nicolas Laurent, is ex Waldorf, London, and brings international expertise to the finest raw ingredients available. The Grill Room has 2 AA Rosettes. Winner of The Taste of Scotland Hotel of the Year Award 1993.

Open all year
- 🏠 Rooms: 261 with private facilities
- ✕ Lunch (The Terrace) ££ (The Grill Room) ££
- ✕ Dinner (The Terrace) ££ (The Grill Room) ££££
- Ⓥ Vegetarian menus available in both restaurants
- ⚘ Children welcome with special menu available
- ♿ Facilities for disabled visitors
- ⚰ Pipes and cigars after 9pm in The Grill Room
- ⚰ No smoking area in The Grill Room
- ⚰ Smoking is discouraged in The Terrace
- 🐄 Member of the Scotch Beef Club

Pan-fried West Coast langoustine tail served with roquette salad and garnished with Parmesan and saffron vinaigrette. Fillet of Ayrshire spring lamb served with sautéd potatoes, forest mushrooms and rosemary jus. Apple and mango tatin served with cinnamon ice cream and Glayva sauce.

STB Deluxe 👑 👑 👑 👑 👑
- 💳 Credit cards: Access/Mastercard/Eurocard, American Express, Visa, Diners Club, Mastercharge, Switch
- 👤 Executive Chef: Nicolas Laurent
- 👤 Restaurant Manager: Jean-Philippe Maurer

STAC POLLY

8-10 Grindlay Street
Edinburgh
EH3 9AS
Tel: 0131 229 5405
Fax: 0131 556 5331

Opposite Sheraton Hotel off Lothian Road, 100 yards from Usher Hall and Lyceum Theatre.

A small and friendly city centre restaurant of character.

- Informal and distinctively Scottish.
- Modern/Scottish cuisine.
- "Delightfully and distinctively Scottish with unusual and imaginative use of Scottish produce."

Stac Polly, from which this restaurant takes its name, is a magnificent mountain on Scotland's West Coast. Proprietor Roger Coulthard, who also runs the established restaurant of the same name in Dublin Street, has tastefully decorated Stac Polly to reflect the heather-clad hills, with tartan curtains to make for an air of cosiness. The strength of Stac Polly's menu is its originality. Chef Steven Harvey compiles menus which take full advantage of Scotland's glorious larder to provide exciting interpretations of modern and traditional Scottish cuisine. From a full to a light meal, choice and service are excellent. The wine list is small but selective and moderately priced and is complemented by a comprehensive malt whisky and Scottish beer list.

Open all year
- ✕ Lunch £
- ✕ Dinner ££
- Ⓥ Vegetarians welcome
- ⚰ Smoking area in restaurant

Baked filo pastry parcels of haggis set on a sweet plum sauce. Saddle of venison with a herb crust set on pickled red cabbage with an orange and basil sauce. Bread and butter pudding with vanilla custard.

- 💳 Credit cards: Access/Mastercard/Eurocard, American Express, Visa, Mastercharge
- 👤 Proprietor: Roger Coulthard

THE WITCHERY BY THE CASTLE
Castlehill, Royal Mile
Edinburgh EH1 1NE
Tel: 0131 225 5613
Fax: 0131 220 4392

Situated at the entrance to Edinburgh Castle.

Unusual atmospheric restaurant in the historic Old Town.

- Formal restaurant.
- Innovative Scottish cooking.
- "Modern Scottish cooking using the freshest of produce."

The Witchery is situated right by the entrance to Edinburgh Castle on a site that was once the centre of witchcraft in the Old Town. It has been decorated with immense style and taste and The Secret Garden, converted from a former school playground, is one of the most romantic dining spots in the city. Lunch and dinner are table d'hôte and à la carte with a choice of stylish and interesting dishes. James Thomson's wine list is spectacular with a large selection of excellent wines from all the wine-growing countries. The Inner Sanctum suite has its own private dining room.

Open all year except Christmas Day
- 🏨 Rooms: 1 suite with private facilities
- ✕ Lunch ££
- ✕ Dinner £££
- 🎗 Reservations advisable

Flaked salmon and shredded mange tout salad. Char-grilled chicken with julienne vegetables. Plum and almond tart with a caramel ice cream.

- 💳 Credit cards: Access/Mastercard/Eurocard, American Express, Visa, Diners Club, Switch
- 🗲 Proprietor: James Thomson

Edinburgh (Outskirts)　71

DALHOUSIE CASTLE
Bonnyrigg, nr Edinburgh
Midlothian EH19 3JB
Tel: 01875 820153
Fax: 01875 821936

A7, 7 miles south from Edinburgh or north from Galashiels. Turn right/left at B704 Junction − ½ mile journey.

Elegant castle hotel.

- Historical building with some superb features.
- Traditional Scottish cooking.
- "An enjoyable and unique dining experience in the castle's ancient dungeons."

Splendour and history surrounds this 13th century castle which was built over 700 years ago by the Ramsays of Dalhousie. Situated amongst acres of forest, parkland and pasture yet close to Edinburgh and gateway to the north. Dalhousie is a memorable place to visit. In a unique dungeon setting the cooking is traditional Scottish with French influences serving fresh local produce at its best.

Open all year except except 3 wks Jan
- 🏨 Rooms: 28 with private facilities
- 🆂🅿 Special rates available
- ✕ Food served all day ££
- ✕ Lunch ££
- ✕ Dinner £££
- Ⓥ Vegetarians welcome
- ⚹ Children welcome
- 🚭 No smoking in dining room

Timbale of East Coast scallops and Bresse chicken set on an Armagnac and tarragon essence. Pan-fried rack of Border lamb with a spicy crust on a base of saladise potato on a basil and redcurrant sauce with caramelised shallots. Poached Williams pear stuffed with Crowdie cheese and walnuts accompanied by a warm chocolate sauce.

STB Highly Commended 👑 👑 👑 👑
- 💳 Credit cards: Access/Mastercard/Eurocard, American Express, Visa, Diners Club, Switch, Delta
- 🗲 Director & General Manager: Neville S Petts

THE HAWES INN

Newhalls Road, South Queensferry
Edinburgh EH30 9TA
Tel: 0131 331 1990
Fax: 0131 319 1120

At east end of the village, under the Forth Rail
Bridge.

A quaint and charming 16th century inn.

- A village inn of rare character.
- High quality pub food.
- "Charming 16th century inn steeped in
  Scottish history."

Splendidly situated, with fine views across the
Forth and an outlook onto the Forth Railway
Bridge, this is a justly popular establishment, much
loved by both Sir Walter Scott and R L Stevenson.
Among others, the novel *Kidnapped* was
conceived here. As well as serving home-made,
no-nonsense bar meals in generous portions, the
inn has a traditional, fairly priced Scottish
restaurant and a large beer garden with a
children's play area.

Open all year
🏠 Rooms: 8
SP Special rates available
✗ Food served all day £££
✗ Lunch £
✗ Dinner £££
Ⅴ Vegetarians welcome
🕇 Children welcome

**Mussels poached in white wine, orange cream,
leeks and herbs. Salmon and sole chequers
served on a bed of prawns with tomato and
saffron sauce. Strawberry shortcake.**

STB Approved ♔
💳 Credit cards: Access/Mastercard/Eurocard,
American Express, Visa, Diners Club, Switch
🙎 Manager: Glen Mills

HOUSTOUN HOUSE HOTEL

Uphall, West Lothian EH52 6JS
Tel: 01506 853831 Fax: 01506 854220

Just off A89 Edinburgh-Bathgate at Uphall.

**A 17th century tower house, with additions, in an
ancient garden.**

- Country house hotel.
- Modern Scottish, with continental influences.
- "Friendly relaxing atmosphere – good freshly
  cooked food."

The core of the house is a substantial, early 16th
century tower, built for Sir John Shairp, advocate
to Mary Queen of Scots, and lived in by his
descendants for 350 years. Its gardens were laid
out in the 18th century, and include a 20 foot high
yew hedge planted in 1722 and a cedar tree which
is even older. Extensions and additions to the house
– including the Houstoun Suite for banqueting and
conferences – have been done sympathetically.
The restaurant is situated in the former drawing
room, library and great hall on the first floor – each
of them delightful rooms, with 17th and 18th century
panelling and plasterwork, beautifully furnished with
antiques and pictures. Vegetables and herbs for the
kitchen are grown in the garden, and Houstoun
House's talented Chef, Joe Queen, presents a
sophisticated and well-balanced table d'hôte menu
at lunch and dinner. His cooking is first class, and
this is complemented by an award-winning wine list.

Open all year
🏠 Rooms: 42 with private facilities
SP Special rates available
✗ Lunch except Sat ££
✗ Dinner 4 course menu £££
Ⅴ Vegetarians welcome
🕇 Children welcome
♿ Facilities for disabled visitors
🚭 No smoking dining room available

**Poached lobster and spinach ravioli scented in a
crayfish sauce with a brioche glaze. Tournedos of
beef resting on a potato and shallot rosti served
with a Madeira, rosemary and truffle essence.
Delicate orange chocolate Marquise coated with
a white chocolate ganache nestled on fillets of
citrus fruits.**

STB Highly Commended ♔ ♔ ♔ ♔ ♔
💳 Credit cards: Access/Mastercard/Eurocard,
American Express, Visa, Diners Club,
Mastercharge, Switch
🙎 General Manager: Irene Tilley

JOHNSTOUNBURN HOUSE HOTEL
Humbie, nr Edinburgh
East Lothian EH36 5PL
Tel: 01875 833696
Fax: 01875 833626

From A68 Edinburgh-Jedburgh 2 miles south of Pathhead, turn at Fala (hotel is signposted) – 2 miles on right.

A peaceful, charming country house hotel only 15 miles from Edinburgh.

- A beautifully restored and maintained Scottish baronial mansion
- Scottish cuisine.
- "Scottish hospitality in a beautiful setting."

Built below the rolling Lammermuir Hills in 1625, Johnstounburn House stands in its own extensive, lovely grounds. The staff are welcoming and friendly, as is the ambience – open log fires, panelled and comfortable rooms. The hotel is a Thistle Country House Hotel. The table d'hôte dishes are excellent, making the most of good, local produce. The wine list is large – 70 bins – and concentrates on French and European wines.

Open all year
- ₤ Rooms: 20 with private facilities
- SP Special rates available
- ✗ Lunch – reservation required ££
- ✗ Dinner – reservation required £££
- Ⅴ Vegetarians welcome
- ✵ Children welcome
- ✕ No smoking in dining room

Crayfish tails with a spicy tomato mayonnaise. Roast Border duck in an orange and Grand Marnier sauce. Drambuie syllabub.

STB Commended 👑 👑 👑 👑
- 💳 Credit cards: Access/Mastercard/Eurocard, American Express, Visa, Diners Club, Mastercharge
- ☒ General Manager: Ken Chernoff

MARRIOTT DALMAHOY HOTEL & COUNTRY CLUB RESORT?
Kirknewton
Midlothian EH27 8EB
Tel: 0131 333 1845
Fax: 0131 333 1433

7 miles west of Edinburgh along A71.

A large hotel and country club with two golf courses, sophisticated leisure facilities and comfortable accommodation.

- Restored Georgian country house in well-landscaped grounds just outside Edinburgh.
- International hotel cuisine.
- "An interesting and imaginative range of dishes prepared with enthusiasm."

Dalmahoy is the family home of the Earl of Morton, who converted it into a luxurious hotel about five years ago. The building is a stately Georgian mansion, standing in its own park, contains two internationally acclaimed golf courses and a state-of-the-art leisure complex. The formal Pentland Restaurant is an elegant Regency style room, beautifully furnished, with splendid views towards the Pentland Hills. The menu is extensive, well-balanced and beautifully presented. Last year the hotel was awarded 2 Rosettes by the AA. Dalmahoy also has a bistro style restaurant in the Leisure Centre.

Open all year
- ₤ Rooms: 151 with private facilities
- SP Special rates available
- ✗ Food served all day ££££
- ✗ Lunch except Sat £££
- ✗ Dinner except Sat £££
- Ⅴ Vegetarians welcome
- ✵ Children welcome
- ♿ Facilities for disabled visitors
- ✕ No smoking in restaurants
- 🐂 Member of the Scotch Beef Club

Pressed terrine of chicken with oyster mushrooms and artichokes. Roast Guinea fowl set on a tian of Mediterranean vegetables with a lime an ginger sauce. Home-made classic tiramisu with light sponge fingers.

STB Highly Commended 👑 👑 👑 👑 👑
- 💳 Credit cards: Access/Mastercard/Eurocard, American Express, Visa, Diners Club, Switch, Delta
- ☒ Executive Chef Gary Bates

NORTON HOUSE HOTEL
Ingliston, Edinburgh, Midlothian EH28 8LX
Tel: 0131 333 1275
Fax: 0131 333 5305

Just off A8, 6 miles from Edinburgh city centre,
2 miles from airport, on the road to Glasgow.

A country house hotel just outside Edinburgh.

- Victorian mansion set in its own park.
- Gourmet/Scottish cooking.
- "A stylish country house hotel set in beautiful parkland."

Recently refurbished in luxurious style, this 19th century country house is a Listed building. The hotel is part of Richard Branson's Virgin Group. The hotel has two restaurants: The Gathering Bar and Bistro which offers a high quality family menu in a walled garden with a barbeque area, and the Conservatory Restaurant. This is an extremely elegant, flower filled glass-house, which has been awarded two AA Rosettes for the excellence of its cooking. An experienced team of chefs cook the food for both venues and in the Conservatory you will be treated to an extensive à la carte menu, a lunch/dinner table d'hôte menu and a short Taste of Scotland menu. The dishes are imaginative – a combination of the unusual and the traditional, but even the latter are given a creative twist.

Open all year
🏠 Rooms: 47 with private facilities
SP Special rates available
✗ Food served all day £££
✗ Lunch except Saturday ££
✗ Dinner £££
Ⓥ Vegetarians welcome
🖈 Children welcome
♿ Facilities for disabled visitors
🚭 No smoking area in restaurant

Slices of marinated tuna loin with tapenade and a lime and shallot vinaigrette. Ragoût of artichokes and asparagus in a white wine and herb sauce served in a flaky pastry case with a warm green salad. Iced banana parfait with a chocolate sorbet and glazed bananas.

STB Highly Commended 👑 👑 👑 👑 👑
💳 Credit cards: Access/Mastercard/Eurocard, American Express, Visa, Diners Club, Mastercharge, Switch
👤 General Manager: Alan P Campbell
👤 Head Chef: Ivor Clark
👤 Restaurant Manager: Pascal Kurth

Elgin   72

MANSEFIELD HOUSE HOTEL
Mayne Road, Elgin
Moray IV30 1NY
Tel: 01343 540883
Fax: 01343 552491

Just off A96 in Elgin. From Inverness, drive towards town centre and turn right at first roundabout. At mini-roundabout, hotel on right.

A popular family-run hotel and restaurant.

- Town house hotel in country setting.
- Traditional Scottish cooking, with some French influences.
- "The best of Moray's produce, well-cooked and presented."

Close to the centre of Elgin, this completely refurbished and restored former manse provides a comfortable retreat. It has excellent facilities to suit the commercial and private guest and the restaurant is especially popular with the local business community. The Head Chef, Scott Hood, presents a well-priced à la carte menu made up of classic Scottish dishes, using market available fish, meat and vegetables. The quality of his cooking has been recognised by an AA Rosette. *(See advert Page 111.)*

Open all year
🏠 Rooms: 20 with private facilities
SP Special rates available
✗ Lunch £
✗ Dinner £££
Ⓥ Vegetarians welcome
🖈 Children welcome
♿ Facilities for disabled visitors
🚭 No smoking in restaurant

Trio of smoked salmon, North Sea prawns and melon. Darne of Lossiemouth halibut with jumbo scampi tails steamed and presented on a lemon cream sauce. White and dark chocolate mousse.

STB Highly Commended 👑 👑 👑 👑
💳 Credit cards: Access/Mastercard/Eurocard, American Express, Visa, Switch
👤 Owners: Mr & Mrs T R Murray

MANSION HOUSE HOTEL & COUNTRY CLUB

The Haugh, Elgin
Moray IV30 1AW
Tel: 01343 548811
Fax: 01343 547916

Turn off main A96 in Elgin into Haugh Road.

An imposing baronial house set in a rural location and bordered by the River Lossie.

- Country house hotel.
- Classical cooking.
- "An extensive range of good quality local produce prepared and cooked with care."

The baronial house was built by the Bibby Shipping Line and stands in beautifully landscaped grounds overlooking the River Lossie, only minutes from the centre of Elgin. The interior is opulent and High Victorian – with sumptuous detailing and individually styled four poster bedrooms. It also has a fully equipped Country Club (with swimming pool and gymnasium). Chef John Alexander presents daily changing table d'hôte and à la carte menus: the latter is comprehensive, the former combines fresh produce with unusual sauces and liaisons. The hotel also has a well-priced wine list and an AA Rosette.

Open all year
- Rooms: 23 with private facilities
- Special rates available
- Lunch £££
- Dinner ££££
- Vegetarians welcome
- Children welcome
- No smoking in restaurant

Warm salmon mousse with a caper vinaigrette. Loin of roe deer with smoked bacon and wild mushrooms. Whisky and honey parfait served with marinated prunes and almond fingers.

STB Highly Commended 👑 👑 👑 👑 👑
- Credit cards: Access/Mastercard/Eurocard, American Express, Visa, Diners Club, Switch
- Owners: Joan & James Stirrat

Erbusaig 73

THE OLD SCHOOLHOUSE RESTAURANT

"Tigh Fasgaidh," Erbusaig, Kyle
Ross-shire IV40 8BB
Tel: 01599 534369
Fax: 01599 534369

Outskirts of Erbusaig on Kyle-Plockton road.

A small restaurant with three bedrooms.

- A charming 19th century schoolhouse in its own grounds on the picturesque road between Kyle and Plockton.
- Imaginative modern cooking.
- "The schoolhouse is called 'Tigh Fasgaidh' meaning sheltered house, and in every way it is. A delightful place to find."

This old school has been tastefully converted by the owners Calum and Joanne Cumine into a small restaurant with three bedrooms, each of which is restfully decorated and en suite. The conversion has been sensitively done, and retains the character of the place, and the feel of the past, while providing the level of comfort required by today's guests. The cooking is imaginative and versatile, and makes good use of the wonderful fish, shellfish, meat and game so readily available in this unspoiled corner of the West Highlands. The menu is reasonably priced and the owners are delighted to cater for vegetarians. It is no wonder that this small restaurant has such a big reputation locally.

Open Easter to end Oct
- Rooms: 3 with private facilities
- Special rates available
- Dinner ££-£££
- Vegetarians welcome
- Children welcome
- Facilities for disabled visitors – restaurant only
- No smoking in restaurant

Selection of smoked meats: venison, duck, lamb, ham and boar served with fresh melon jelly. Monkfish braised with vegetables and white wine finished with cream and fresh basil. Raspberry pavlova.

STB Commended 👑 👑 👑
- Credit cards: Access/Mastercard/Eurocard, American Express, Visa, Switch, Delta
- Proprietors: Calum & Joanne Cumine

`FALKIRK`

INCHYRA GRANGE HOTEL
Grange Road, Polmont
Falkirk FK2 0YB
Tel: 01324 711911
Fax: 01324 716134

Take B9143, junction 5, M9 motorway. Situated on border of Polmont/Grangemouth.

A country house hotel with gardens and full leisure facilities.

- Fully modernised and extended country house.
- Good hotel cooking.
- "Good quality food at affordable prices."

Inchyra Grange traces its origins to the 12th century, but its internal lay-out and furnishings are modern. It stands in five acres of garden and park, and has a popular leisure club with swimming pool, sauna and steam baths, multi-gym, solarium and resident beautician. Twenty five bedrooms have been added in the past year and more are planned. There are two restaurants: the first is in the Leisure Club, and features 'healthy meals and snacks'; the main restaurant specialises in classic Scottish cooking and offers extensive à la carte and table d'hôte menus. The hotel's central situation near Falkirk makes it popular as a business venue, for meetings and conferences, not to mention business lunches, and it also does a good trade in functions.

Open all year
🏠 Rooms: 73 with private facilities
✗ Food served all day £££
✗ Lunch except Sat ££
✗ Dinner £££
Ⓥ Vegetarians welcome
⚘ Children welcome
♿ Facilities for disabled visitors
🚭 No smoking in restaurant

Home-made soup of the day. Grilled salmon with tikka and coriander butter. Brandy basket with black cherries and kirsch ice cream.

STB Commended 👑 👑 👑 👑
▣ Credit cards: Access/Mastercard/Eurocard, American Express, Visa, Diners Club, Mastercharge, Switch
Ⓝ General Manager: Mr Andy Burgess

`FALKLAND`

KIND KYTTOCK'S KITCHEN
Cross Wynd, Falkland
Fife KY15 7BE
Tel: 01337 857477

A912 to Falkland. Centre of Falkland near the Palace, turn up at the Square into Cross Wynd.

An outstanding tea-room in an historic setting.

- Traditional Scottish tea-room.
- Home cooking; home baking; home-made preserves.
- "Very good – traditional style with high standards – the ideal 'tea-room'."

Kind Kyttock's is situated in a charming 17th century terraced cottage overlooking the cobbled square in one of Scotland's most picturesque villages. Its two rooms are most attractive – comfortable, informal and cheerful, with a 'country tea-room' feel. And this is precisely what Kind Kyttock's is, a tea-room of outstanding quality, which has frequently won the Tea Council's Award for Excellence. Bert Dalrymple is its owner/cook, his baking is divine – including scones, oatcakes, pancakes and other Scottish delicacies – and as well as this he preserves his own fruits, jams, pickles and chutneys, roasts his own meats for sandwiches, makes his own soups, etc. No wonder the place is so popular with locals, and you can buy baking to take away when it is available.

Open all year except Christmas Eve to 5 Jan
Closed Mon
✗ Food served all day except Mon £
Ⓥ Vegetarians welcome
⚘ Children welcome
🚭 No smoking throughout

Home-baked pancakes, scones, fruit squares, shortbread, wholemeal bread, stovies, cloutie dumpling. Locally grown vegetables used in Scotch broth and at salad table. Selection of teas available.

▣ Credit cards: Access/Mastercard/Eurocard, Visa
Ⓝ Owner: Bert Dalrymple

FOCHABERS

BAXTERS VISITOR CENTRE
Fochabers
Moray IV32 7LD
Tel: 01343 820666
Fax: 01343 821790

1 mile west of Fochabers on the main A96.

A quality and unique 'visitor experience' on the Spey.

* A well-laid out and interesting visitor centre.
* Home cooking and baking.
* "The Baxters Story is fascinating and the restaurant provides a good variety of food for any customer."

At Baxter's you can see exactly how their famous preserves and tinned foods are prepared. The self-service Spey Restaurant there is spacious and attractive, furnished with pine. It features their own products, but also home baking (pancakes made to order are a speciality!) and daily changing hot lunch dishes. Baxters Visitors Centre is adjacent to the Baxters factory. It has recently been extended and furnished to a very high standard. Within the complex are three shops, Ena Baxter's Kitchen, pottery and gift shops. There is also the newly opened Gordon Restaurant where themed dinners take place every week.

Open all year except 25, 26 Dec, 1 + 2 Jan
♀ Licensed
✘ Food served all day £
✘ Lunch £
✘ Dinner ££-£££
Ⅴ Vegetarians welcome
⃰ Children welcome
⅄ Facilities for disabled visitors
⅃ Smoking area in restaurant

Home-baked breads, Danish and sandwiches. Daily carvery. Wide selection of home-produced desserts.

⊞ Credit cards: Access/Mastercard/Eurocard, Visa, Mastercharge, Switch, Delta
Ⅺ Executive Chef: Alan N Coxon

FORFAR

CHAPELBANK HOUSE HOTEL
69 East High Street, Forfar
Angus DD8 2EP
Tel: 01307 463151
Fax: 01307 461922

Town centre – Forfar. 15 miles north of Dundee on A90.

A family-run hotel with an emphasis on service.

* Small, town centre hotel.
* Good, traditional home cooking.
* "Scottish hospitality at its best with excellent accommodation."

Built in 1865 on the main road leading through the market town of Forfar, Chapelbank was once the home of the town's doctor. The present owners, Duthie and Edith Douglas, have converted and furnished it well. Standards of fittings are high throughout and the Douglas' take a special pride in their cuisine. Calm and spacious, the dining room is popular with local non-residents as a place where fair prices and fresh, straightforward produce meet in both a table d'hôte and an extensive à la carte menu. A large dining room window overlooks the small but attractive front garden. Landscapes by local artists adorn the walls. From a warm welcome to a simple but varied wine list, from freshly prepared porridge and cream among other things for breakfast, to service that is friendly and capable, Duthie and Edith know what they are doing and do it well.

Open 21 Jan to 4 Oct + 14 Oct to 31 Dec
Closed Sun evening + Mon
🛏 Rooms: 4 with private facilities
♀ Restricted hotel licence
✘ Lunch except Mon £
✘ Dinner except Sun Mon ££
Ⅴ Vegetarians welcome
⃰ Children welcome
⅄ Facilities for disabled visitors
⅃ No smoking in dining room

Smoked haddock soup. Fillet of Angus beef. Ginger brûlée.

STB Highly Commended 👑 👑 👑 👑
⊞ Credit cards: Access/Mastercard/Eurocard, Visa, Switch, Delta, JCB
Ⅺ Owners: Duthie & Edith Douglas

Forres 78

FORRES

BRODIE COUNTRYFARE
Brodie, by Forres
Moray IV36 0TD
Tel: 01309 641 555
Fax: 01309 641 499

On A96 between Forres and Nairn.

Popular self-service restaurant.

- Cafeteria within a shopping complex.
- Home baking and traditional meals.
- "Good choice of traditional and snack items."

This is a country style theme restaurant within the Brodie Countryfare complex. Excellence is the hallmark here from the quality products sold to the food presented. Ideal for a rainy day when you can browse through all the lovely gifts on sale and then eat a meal (at any time of the day), either outside in the garden or inside in the eating area which has a conservatory. The à la carte menu offers freshly made soups and baking, salads and a long list of snacks and desserts; the 'chef's specials' are more substantial.

Open all year except Christmas Day, Boxing Day, 1 + 2 Jan
Licensed
Food served all day £
Lunch £
Vegetarians welcome
Children welcome
Facilities for disabled visitors
Restaurant is non-smoking with small smoking area

Soup of the day. Country lamb casserole. Eve's pudding and custard.

Credit cards: Access/Mastercard/Eurocard, Visa, Switch
Proprietor: Kathleen Duncan

FORRES

KNOCKOMIE HOTEL
Grantown Road, Forres
Moray IV36 0SG
Tel: 01309 673146
Fax: 01309 673290

1 mile south of Forres on A940. 26 miles east of Inverness.

A timeless and elegant hotel overlooking the Royal Burgh of Forres.

- A rare example of Arts and Crafts Movement architecture – an elegant villa built in 1914 around an earlier building.
- The best of Scottish cooking with French influences.
- "Great comfort, relaxed atmosphere, terrific food!"

Ideally placed for visiting the castles, stately homes and distilleries of the north-east, this gracious country house offers guests first-rate accommodation and dining facilities. Part of the hotel's landscaped gardens are set aside to supply herbs and salad leaves; vegetables are grown locally, to order. Knockomie's resident director is Gavin Ellis, who is knowledgeable, courteous and hospitable, and his staff are smart and well-trained. The daily changing table d'hôte menu is carefully selected; the food is all local and fresh; cooking is 'modern classic'. The wine list is of especial interest – very well-priced, with some wonderful rarities; over 80 whiskies are also listed. Knockomie has 2 AA Rosettes.

Open all year except Christmas Day
Rooms: 14 with private facilities
Special rates available
Lunch £
Dinner 5 course menu £££
Vegetarians welcome
Children welcome
No smoking in dining room
Facilities for disabled visitors

Leek and potato soup. Fresh salmon topped with herb crust. White chocolate and Malibu bavarois with marinated oranges.

STB Highly Commended 👑👑👑👑
Credit cards: Access/Mastercard/Eurocard, American Express, Visa, Diners Club, Mastercharge, Switch, Delta, JCB
Resident Director: Gavin Ellis

RAMNEE HOTEL
Victoria Road, Forres, Moray IV36 0BN
Tel: 01309 672410 Fax: 01309 673392

A96 Inverness-Aberdeen, off bypass at roundabout at eastern side of Forres – 500 yards on right.

An attractive small hotel in the centre of Forres.

- Turn of the century Edwardian private house.
- Modern cooking, well-served.
- "A high standard of accommodation and hospitality."

The Ramnee Hotel was built in 1907 as a private residence for Richard Hamblin returning to Scotland after a long career in the Indian Civil Service. Set in two acres of carefully landscaped gardens, the hotel enjoys a central location in Forres, a charming Victorian spa town on the Morayshire and Nairnshire border. Each of the hotel's 20 bedrooms is individually furnished and fitted with all the extras you would expect in a first rate establishment. Food in Hamblin's Restaurant is characterised by generous portions imaginatively presented. A table d'hôte menu is available at lunchtime and there is a choice of excellent value table d'hôte and à la carte menus at dinner. The accompanying wine list is extensive and well-chosen. Lighter, more informal meals are available in Tippling's cocktail lounge. Ramnee has 1 AA Rosette.

....

Open all year except Christmas Day + 1 to 3 Jan
- 🏠 Rooms: 20 with private facilities
- 🆂🅿 Special rates available
- ✕ Lunch £
- ✕ Dinner £££
- Ⓥ Vegetarians welcome
- 🕭 Children welcome
- 🚭 No smoking in restaurant

Fresh home-made ravioli filled with mature cheddar and hazelnuts and surrounded with a tomato and basil coulis. Roast saddle of fallow deer garnished with a potato and creamed spinach gâteau and a rich blackcurrant vinegar sauce. White chocolate leaves layered with a dark chocolate and Cointreau mousse set on a passion fruit coulis.

STB Highly Commended 👑 👑 👑 👑
- 💳 Credit cards: Access/Mastercard/Eurocard, American Express, Visa, Diners Club, Switch, Delta
- 🅺 Director: Garry W Dinnes

BRAE HOTEL
Bunoich Brae, Fort Augustus
Inverness-shire PH32 4DG
Tel: 01320 366289
Fax: 01320 366702

300 metres off A82. Turn left to Bunoich Brae just before leaving Fort Augustus heading north to Inverness on A82.

In an elevated position overlooking Fort Augustus this is a family-run hotel with a period atmosphere and a warm welcome.

- A Victorian manse with fine views.
- International modern cooking.
- "Most enjoyable meal with truly excellent home-made bread and skilled use of fresh produce."

This restored Victorian building stands in its own pretty grounds, looking out over Fort Augustus and the Great Glen, with spectacular views of the Caledonian Canal, River Oich and Loch Ness. The resident owners, Andrew and Mari Reive want their hotel to be a 'home from home' and go to great lengths to put their guests at ease. An enclosed verandah has been added recently in which to lounge away wet days with a good book and the dining room is light and airy. Mari Reive does all the cooking, including the preserves and marmalades which are served for breakfast, and heavenly after-dinner chocolates. She describes her style of cooking as 'international' and her eclectic menus feature fresh fish, seafood and game from nearby Loch Lochy. The Brae Hotel has 1 AA Rosette.

....

Open Mar to Oct
- 🏠 Rooms: 7 with private facilities
- 🅼 Non-residents – prior booking recommended
- ✕ Dinner £££
- Ⓥ Vegetarians welcome – prior notice required
- 🕭 Children over 7 years welcome
- 🚭 No smoking in dining room

Warm salad of scallops and bacon. Guinea fowl wrapped in bacon and roasted with caramelised shallots and apples. Home-made ice creams.

STB Highly Commended 👑 👑 👑
- 💳 Credit cards: Access/Mastercard/Eurocard, American Express, Visa, Switch, Delta, JCB
- 🅺 Owners: Andrew & Mari Reive

LOVAT ARMS HOTEL
Fort William Road, Fort Augustus
Inverness-shire PH32 4DU
Tel: 01320 366206/4
Fax: 01320 366677

A82 Fort William-Inverness.

A small and informal country hotel in an excellent location.

- Friendly, unhurried and relaxed Highland hospitality.
- Traditional home cooking.
- "One of the best fish dishes I have tasted this year."

This spacious Victorian building stands in two acres of well-kept grounds overlooking the village of Fort Augustus. Proprietors Hector and Mary MacLean are welcoming hosts. High ceilinged and wood-panelled, the dining room offers good home cooking using a wide range of West Coast fish and shellfish together with local game and beef. Chef Eric MacDonald ensures that a very high standard of food and quality cooking is offered at this busy Highland hotel. There is also a bar meal menu served in the spacious lounge bar.

Open all year
🏠 Rooms: 21 with private facilities
SP Special rates available
✕ Lunch (Restaurant lunch – by arrangement groups only) £-££
✕ Dinner ££
Ⓥ Vegetarians welcome
🏃 Children welcome

Warm smoked haddock mousse with chive butter sauce. Pan-fried fillet of halibut with beetroot, sorrel and spring onions. Steamed marmalade pudding with whisky custard.

STB Commended 👑 👑 👑
💳 Credit cards: Access/Mastercard/Eurocard, American Express, Visa
📋 Proprietors: Hector & Mary MacLean

Fort William   80

AN CRANN
Seangan Bridge, Banavie
Fort William PH33 7PB
Tel: 01397 772 077

From A830 at Banavie, take B8004 for 2½ miles. From A82 at Commando Memorial take B8004 for 8 miles.

Original and interesting 30 seater restaurant.

- Converted steading.
- Imaginative Scottish cookery.
- "Imaginative, skilled cooking achieved by someone who loves her craft."

This little restaurant has been beautifully converted from an old farm steading which was built for one of Sine Ross's forebears in 1896. This was done three years ago, retaining the original stone work and adding large arched windows to allow in the light. Home-made snacks and baking are available throughout the day, as well as daily specials, soups and vegetarian dishes. Sine is an original cook, preferring to adapt her sauces and techniques to the food she has available. Venison, lamb and salmon are all readily obtainable locally and she tends to concentrate her energies on creating interesting combinations of flavours and textures according to her mood and the seasonal produce. There is a delightful honesty about the food at An Crann; there are no aspirations to grandeur but the dishes are the work of a dedicated and inspired cook.

Open Apr to Oct
♀ Table licence
✕ Lunch except Sat £
✕ Dinner ££
Ⓥ Vegetarians welcome
🏃 Children welcome
♿ Facilities for disabled visitors

Local prawns served on a bed of rice with a sherry, garlic and cream sauce. Scottish lamb with rosemary and Madeira. Home-made cloutie dumpling with whisky cream.

💳 Credit cards: Access/Mastercard/Eurocard, Visa
📋 Proprietor/Chef: Sine Ross

CRANNOG SEAFOOD RESTAURANT

Town Pier, Fort William
PH33 7NG
Tel: 01397 705589
Fax: 01397 705026

Fort William town pier – off A82 Fort William town centre bypass.

An award-winning seafood restaurant, established by fishermen.

- Seafood restaurant.
- Fresh seafood, cooked simply.
- "The perfect location to enjoy freshest caught seafood."

The Fort William branch of Crannog is a small, octagonal, red-roofed building on the pier at Fort William. The decor is simple – white walls, blue carpet, comfortable chairs – and the room has splendid views over Loch Linnhe. When they are not admiring the view, diners can sometimes watch the catch being landed direct into the kitchen – and soon afterwards enjoy the freshest imaginable seafood. This is Crannog's philosophy: very fresh seafood in friendly surroundings. It works, and the restaurant is very popular, so it is advisable to book.

Open all year except Christmas Day + 1 Jan
✗ Lunch £
✗ Dinner ££
Ⓥ Vegetarians welcome
Ⓚ Children welcome
♿ Facilities for disabled visitors
Ⓚ Smoking area in restaurant

Crannog bouillabaisse made from a variety of finfish and shellfish. Wing of skate in foamed lemon butter with capers. Walnut tart and cream.

🆔 Credit cards: Access/Mastercard/Eurocard, Visa, Switch
🅜 Managing Director: Finlay Finlayson

MOORINGS HOTEL

Banavie, Fort William, Inverness-shire PH33 7LY
Tel: 01397 772797
Fax: 01397 772441

Situated off A830, 3 miles from Fort William at Banavie.

A Highland hotel on the banks of the Caledonian Canal.

- A family-run hotel with a nautical theme.
- Modern Scottish cooking with flair.
- "There is a happy atmosphere here and good choice of place to eat, drink and relax."

Set against a backdrop of dramatic Highland scenery The Moorings Hotel deserves its Scottish Tourist Board's 4 Crowns status. Bedrooms are well-appointed and comfortable with colour TV and satellite. Much of the charm of the public rooms derives from faithfulness to the hotel's nautical imagery and you can enjoy splendid views of Ben Nevis and Aonach Mhor while sipping a pre-dinner drink in the Upper Deck Lounge Bar. The highlight of a visit however is dinner in the hotel's Jacobean Restaurant with its cheerful and colourful atmosphere. Here you find modern Scottish cooking at its best with beautifully cooked food presented with an interesting choice of accompaniments and garnishes, which coincides with a wine list with just the right balance between price and choice. The hotel has 2 AA Rosettes.

Open all year except 2 wks Christmas but open New Year
🛏 Rooms: 24 with private facilities
Ⓢ Special rates available
✗ Lunch ££ (only restaurant lunch by arrangement)
✗ Dinner £££
Ⓥ Vegetarians welcome
Ⓚ Children welcome
♿ Facilities for disabled visitors
Ⓚ No smoking in restaurant

Seared Mallaig scallops with a julienne of leeks and ginger set on a green herb and star aniseed cream. Pan-fried loin of Scottish spring lamb set around home-grown rhubarb chutney with a fresh rosemary glaze. Iced cream parfait flavoured with Scottish raspberries and served with a rich raspberry coulis.

STB Highly Commended 👑 👑 👑 👑
🆔 Credit cards: Access/Mastercard/Eurocard, American Express, Visa, Diners Club
🅜 Managing Director: Mr Norman J A Sinclair

THE PRINCE'S HOUSE
Glenfinnan
Inverness-shire PH37 4LT
Tel: 01397 722 246
Fax: 01397 722 307

15 miles west of Fort William on A830 'Road to the Isles' ½ mile on right past Glenfinnan Monument.

A charming, small family-run hotel and restaurant set in a beautiful and historic location.

- A former 17th century coaching inn on the 'Road to the Isles' in Glenfinnan.
- Modern and traditional Scottish menu.
- "A warm welcome and good food awaits guests at this friendly hotel."

Once known as the Stage House, this former inn was providing hospitality even before Bonnie Prince Charlie raised his standard – just down the road in 1745. It has now been completely modernised as a hotel and restaurant, with a change of name to suit. The evening à la carte menu and Sunday lunches in 'Flora's' Restaurant have earned Chef Carole a justifiable reputation by using the natural larder of the local mountains and lochs. Robert's interesting wine list complements the cuisine, and the log fire enhances the atmosphere of the hotel in winter. A blackboard lists specialities of the day.

Open 1 Mar to 2 Jan except Christmas
- 🏨 Rooms: 8 with private facilities
- ✗ Lunch £
- ✗ Dinner £££
- Ⅴ Vegetarians welcome
- ✁ No smoking in restaurant + bedrooms

Whole boned quail with a hazelnut and herb stuffing presented on an apricot and horseradish coulis. Local wild rabbit braised in cider and served with a lentil and carrot purée. Individual round of home-made shortbread topped with fresh Scottish strawberries on whipped Drambuie cream.

STB Commended 👑 👑 👑 👑
- ▣ Credit cards: Access/Mastercard/Eurocard, American Express, Visa, Switch, Delta
- 𝕹 Partners: Robert & Carole Hawkes
  Suzanne Buxton

TORBEAG HOUSE
Muirshearlich, Banavie
Fort William
Inverness-shire
PH33 7PB
Tel: 01397 772412
Fax: 01397 772412

Take A830 Mallaig road from Fort William. After 1 mile turn right into Banavie on B8004. Follow for 2½ miles.

A modern country house converted into an outstanding guest house.

- Stylish modern guest house, with spectacular mountain views.
- Excellent home cooking.
- "The excellent Scottish food tastes so good in this peaceful, attractive and friendly place."

Ken and Gladys Whyte bought Torbeag House in late 1992, and opened their doors in early 1994, with the intention of offering 'top quality accommodation and food in agreeable surroundings at sensible prices'. A well-designed 1960s building with large picture windows giving stunning views of the north face of Ben Nevis and Aonach Mor. The owners are warm and welcoming, and have decorated and appointed their home tastefully, with a mixture of modern and traditional furniture and some fine paintings. Ken was a farmer and is a self-taught chef; he serves a set four course menu for dinner (consulting guests about preferences). Baking, preserves, after-dinner fudge and breakfast muesli are all made in-house.

Open all year except Christmas
- 🏨 Rooms: 3 with private facilities
- ⓢⓟ Special rates available
- ✗ Residents only
- ⓤⓛ ♀ Unlicensed – guests welcome to take own wine
- ✗ Dinner ££
- Ⅴ Vegetarians welcome
- ✁ No smoking throughout

Broccoli and Dunsyre soup. Baked salmon with lemon and chive sauce. Torbeag bread and butter pudding.

STB Deluxe 👑 👑 👑
- ▣ Credit cards: Access/Mastercard/Eurocard, Visa
- 𝕹 Owners: Gladys & Ken Whyte

Gairloch 81

LITTLE LODGE
Special Merit Award for Hospitality 1996

North Erradale, Gairloch
Wester Ross IV21 2DS
Tel: 01445 771237

Take B8021 from Gairloch towards Melvaig for 6 miles, situated ¼ mile beyond turning to North Erradale.

A charming converted crofthouse.

- Whitewashed crofthouse.
- Traditional Scottish and innovative cooking.
- "For the most heartening welcome, comfortable surroundings and exquisite food, the Little Lodge would be hard to surpass."

Little Lodge stands on a heather-clad peninsula with splendid views towards the Torridon mountains and Skye. Di Johnson and Inge Ford are charming and welcoming hosts, and have restored their home in a way which best displays its original features. All bedrooms are en suite. Outside, their own hens, sheep and goats roam; their garden provides vegetables and herbs. Di's imaginative marinades and sauces enhance the excellent seasonal local produce (especially freshly-landed fish from Gairloch itself), while Inge's home-made bread, oatcakes, yoghurt and preserves make breakfast a special treat. Little Lodge is an idyllic retreat with superb cuisine which has earned Di and Inge much praise.

Open Apr to Oct
🏠 Rooms: 3 with private facilities
SP Special rates available
✗ Residents only
🍷♀ Unlicensed – guests welcome to take own wine + spirits
✗ Dinner ££
Ⓥ Vegetarians welcome – by prior arrangement
⚘ No children
⚞ No smoking throughout

Local prawn tails and scallops stir-fried and delicately flavoured with fresh root ginger, scallions and coriander leaves. Noisettes of home-reared lamb flambéd with brandy and served with rosemary and redcurrant sauce. Strawberry crème patissiere.

STB Highly Commended 👑 👑 👑
⊞ No credit cards
🅗 Proprietors: Di Johnson & Inge Ford

MYRTLE BANK HOTEL
Low Road, Gairloch
Ross-shire IV21 2BS
Tel: 01445 712004
Fax: 01445 712214

Close to the centre of Gairloch, just off B2081.

Seafront hotel in spectacular setting.

- Modern village hotel.
- Traditional Scottish cooking.
- "Cleverly garnished dishes."

Myrtle Bank Hotel is a modern village hotel set amongst spectacular scenery in the centre of Gairloch in a quiet cul de sac. Its location makes it an ideal exploring base. The hotel has been run by local proprietors for ten years and is popular with both locals and visitors to the area. The cooking is good and provides popular dishes in a simple, traditional style. Seafood is particularly tasty given the local catch!

Open all year except New Year's Day
🏠 Rooms: 12 with private facilities
SP Special rates available
✗ Lunch £
✗ Dinner £££
Ⓥ Vegetarians welcome
⚘ Children welcome
⚒ Facilities for disabled visitors
⚞ No smoking in dining room

Loch Ewe scallops poached in a Stilton cheese sauce, presented on a bed of tagliatelle. Suprême of Highland chicken stuffed with haggis, wrapped in bacon, served on a sweet pepper and sherry sauce. Grannie's caramel fruit pudding.

STB Commended 👑 👑 👑 👑
⊞ Credit cards: Access/Mastercard/Eurocard, American Express, Visa, Switch
🅗 Proprietors: Iain & Dorothy MacLean

GARVE

INCHBAE LODGE HOTEL
by Garve
Ross-shire IV23 2PH
Tel: 01997 455269
Fax: 01997 455207

Situated on A835 Inverness-Ullapool road. 6 miles north west of Garve.

A small family-run hotel with a panoramic view of Ben Wyvis.

- Small country hotel.
- Modern Scottish cooking.
- "Arriving late, cold and wet, I opted for the bar supper dish of the day and was presented with a pot-roasted pigeon, salad and potato – stunning!"

A former Victorian hunting lodge. It stands in seven acres of lovely wild garden, including its own island with free trout fishing in the River Blackwater and clay pigeon shooting available, by arrangement. The lodge has an intimate cottage feel with bags of character. The 12 rooms are divided between the lodge itself and a cedar wood chalet nearby. The owners, Patrick and Judy Price, go to great lengths to make their guests comfortable: children are accommodated free of charge. Patrick's menus are inventive with a choice of two starters, main course and pudding and table d'hôte; produce is all fresh and imaginatively cooked.

Open all year except 24 to 30 Dec
🏨 Rooms: 12 with private facilities
SP Special rates available
✕ Lunch £
✕ Dinner 4 course menu £££
Ⓥ Vegetarians welcome
🏃 Children welcome
🚭 No smoking in dining room + bedrooms

Hot smoked salmon in anchovy sauce. Fillet of roast Highland lamb lightly rolled in crushed peppercorns served with a red wine and rowan jelly sauce. Amaretto and praline syllabub.

STB Commended 👑 👑 👑
💳 Credit cards: Access/Mastercard/Eurocard, Visa
🊭 Proprietors: Patrick & Judy Price

GATEHOUSE-OF-FLEET

CALLY PALACE HOTEL
Gatehouse-of-Fleet
Dumfries & Galloway DG7 2DL
Tel: 01557 814341
Fax: 01557 814522

1 mile from Gatehouse-of-Fleet exit off A75 Dumfries-Stranraer, 30 miles west of Dumfries.

Grand and imposing country house hotel.

- Palatial hotel overlooking its own loch and golf course.
- Fine traditional Scottish cooking.
- "Traditional and comfortable with many 'little extras'."

Approached by a long, sweeping drive through beautiful woodland, this mansion stands in its own 150 acres of grounds. Its marble pillars, floors and tables combine with gilt and fine plasterwork to recall the grandeur of the 18th century. The hotel's public rooms are elegant and grand, with fine views over the landscaped grounds. The traditional dining room offers flowers, candles and music from the grand piano. Menus concentrate on selecting and presenting good, fresh, local produce with style. A snack menu is available all day and a popular high tea is available for 'tiny guests'. Both menus change daily. here is putting, tennis and croquet outside and a swimming pool sauna and jacuzzi inside.

Open 7 Mar to 3 Jan
🏨 Rooms: 56 with private facilities
SP Special rates available
✕ Food served all day £
✕ Lunch ££
✕ Dinner £££
Ⓥ Vegetarians welcome
🏃 Children welcome
♿ Facilities for disabled visitors
🚭 No smoking in dining room

Deep-fried cream cheese and herbs tortellini and fresh tomato sauce. West Coast king scallops wrapped in filleted Dover sole. Crisp almond parcel filled with apricot brandy mousse.

STB Deluxe 👑 👑 👑 👑
💳 Credit cards: Access/Mastercard/Eurocard, Visa, Switch
🊭 General Manager: Jennifer Adams

GIRVAN

BALKISSOCK LODGE
Balkissock, by Ballantrae
nr Girvan, Ayrshire KA26 0LP
Tel: 01465 831537 Fax: 01465 831537

Take first inland road off A77, south of River
Stinchar at Ballantrae and follow for 2¼ miles. Turn
right at T-junction and continue along single track
'no through road' to its end, c. 1½ miles.

**A quiet country guest house, run by Adrian and
Janet Beale.**

- An early 19th century shooting lodge.
- Innovative Scottish cooking with international
  influences.
- "Good cooking in friendly, intimate surroundings."

Just south of the picturesque fishing village of
Ballantrae, deep in rural Ayrshire you will find
Balkissock Lodge, a relaxed and atmospheric small
guest house. The owners are considerate and
attentive hosts, and Janet spends most of her long
days in the kitchen, preparing her imaginative
meals. Menus are table d'hôte and à la carte and
guests are asked to make their dinner choices in
the afternoon, so that everything can be freshly
prepared. Janet is an experienced cook, and this is
reflected in the excellent standards evident in all
the meals she prepares. In particular her breakfast
menus show flair and imagination offering everything from the usual to the unusual.

Open all year
🏠 Rooms: 3 with private facilities
SP Special rates available
✗ Non-residents by prior arrangement
🍷 Unlicensed – guests welcome to take own
wine
✗ Lunch – special circumstances ££
✗ Dinner £££
Ⓥ Vegetarians welcome
ૠ Children welcome
⚘ No smoking throughout

**Bonchester cheese in a crumb and herb crust.
Stir-fried fillet of venison perfumed with rosemary
and flavoured with Madeira plumped vine fruits.
Raspberry pudding.**

💳 Credit cards: Access/Mastercard/Eurocard,
Visa
🅜 Owner: Janet Beale

GLAMIS

CASTLETON HOUSE HOTEL
by Glamis, Forfar
Angus DD8 1SJ
Tel: 01307 840340
Fax: 01307 840506

On A94 – Coupar Angus to Forfar. Approx 3 miles
west of Glamis Castle.

**A distinctive country house hotel in peaceful
surroundings.**

- Well-appointed Victorian house.
- Modern Scottish cooking.
- "Excellent accommodation and cuisine in an
  informal country atmosphere."

Castleton House Hotel is an ideal retreat for those
who appreciate good food and the best of comfort
in a relaxing environment. Run by Willie and
Maureen Little the house is very comfortable and
tastefully furnished with good use of antique and
quality reproduction furniture and subtle colour
schemes appropriate to the style. Willie Little has
excellent local sources of the best and freshest
ingredients and uses them well in his cooking
which is modern, innovative but clearly Scottish.
There are two dining rooms at Castleton – the
small homely restaurant or light airy conservatory
with a choice of table d'hôte or à la carte menus.
Castleton has 1 AA Rosette.

Open all year
🏠 Rooms: 6 with private facilities
SP Special rates available
✗ Lunch ££
✗ Dinner £££-££££
Ⓥ Vegetarians welcome
ૠ Children welcome
⚐ Facilities for disabled visitors – non-residential
only
⚘ No smoking in restaurant only

**Monkfish tails on bulb fennel glazed with
hollandaise. Pan-fried rump of venison with
mousseline of potato and black cherry sauce.
Terrine of layered chocolate mousse with orange
anglaise.**

STB Deluxe 👑 👑 👑 👑
💳 Credit cards: Access/Mastercard/Eurocard,
American Express, Visa
🅜 Proprietors: Willie & Maureen Little

GLAMIS CASTLE
Estates Office
Glamis, by Forfar
Angus DD8 1RJ
Tel: 01307 840 393
Fax: 01307 840 733

6 miles west of Forfar on A94. From Edinburgh
81 miles, from Glasgow 93 miles.

**A self-service restaurant in the old kitchens
of the castle.**

- Picturesque historic castle.
- Traditional Scottish cooking.
- "Good freshly cooked food in atmospheric
  surroundings."

Glamis Castle is the family home of the Earls of
Strathmore and Kinghorne and has been a royal
residence since 1372. The building is a five storey
L-shaped tower block which was re-modelled in
the 17th century and contains magnificent rooms
with a wide range of historic items. The restaurant
is on the ground floor in the converted old kitchens
and has retained many of the original fixtures and
fittings. It is a self-service operation with a blackboard featuring 'daily specials' and excellent
home-cooked and baked dishes.

Open 28 Mar to 26 Oct – otherwise by
appointment only
✗   Food served all day £
✗   Lunch £
Ⓥ   Vegetarians welcome
⚘   Children welcome
♿   Facilities for disabled visitors

**Home-made pâté. Salmon and spring onion
quiches. Home baking.**

💳   No credit cards
👤   Castle Administrator: Lt Col P J Cardwell
     Moore

Glasgow   86

78 ST VINCENT
78 St Vincent Street
Glasgow G2 5UB
Tel: 0141 221 7710
Fax: 0141 221 8304

On the corner of West Nile Street and St Vincent
Street. Only a few minutes walk from both Queen
Street and Central Stations.

**Contemporary styled city restaurant in carefully
restored historic building.**

- Spacious dining in adapted Phoenix
  Assurance building.
- Modern cosmopolitan cooking.
- "Using the best of Scotland's produce to
  combine excellent flavour with a hint of
  the unusual."

Located in the well-known 'Phoenix Building'
this cosmopolitan restaurant is predominantly
French with a Scottish flavour. However there are
also influences from Japan and the Middle East
which combine to offer an eclectic menu. The
carefully restored interior features an original
marble staircase, some amazing metal work and a
stunning mural by Glasgow artist Donald
McLeod. 78 St Vincent is a new addition to the
Glasgow scene (only opened in June 1996) and a
welcome addition to Taste of Scotland offering
excellent food, wine and ambience at very
reasonable prices.

Open all year except Christmas Day, 1 + 2 Jan
Closed Sun lunch
✗   Lunch except Sun £
✗   Dinner ££
Ⓥ   Vegetarians welcome
⚘   Children welcome
♿   Facilities for disabled visitors
🚭   Separate smoking area

**Oban landed lobster bisque. Breast of duck with
root vegetables and mushroom and tarragon
essence. Fruits of the forest parfait.**

💳   Credit cards: Access/Mastercard/Eurocard,
     American Express, Visa, Diners Club, Switch,
     Delta
👤   Director: Mike Conyers
👤   Manager: Caron Jardine

ARGYLL HOTEL
FEATURING SUTHERLANDS RESTAURANT
973 Sauchiehall Street
Glasgow
G3 7TQ
Tel: 0141 337 3313
Fax: 0141 337 3283

½ mile west of city centre.

An authentic Scottish hotel restaurant.

- Terraced hotel.
- Modern Scottish cooking.
- "Native dishes from Scotland rarely seen outside the home."

Sutherlands is one of Glasgow's most recent additions to the numerous hotel restaurants on offer in the city. Located in the basement of the Argyll Hotel the theme is based on the Argyll and Sutherland Highlanders, and although Scottish throughout it is discrete and subtle in influence. There is a large bar area with dance floor (often live entertainment a feature) with the restaurant adjacent. Staff are professional and friendly and Chef John Baxter offers the finest of food served in traditional ways. Ideal for business occasions and visitors to the city.

Open all year
Closed Sun Sat lunch
🏠 Rooms: 38 with private facilities
✗ Food served all day except Sun Sat lunch £££
✗ Lunch except Sun Sat £
✗ Dinner ££
Ⓥ Vegetarians welcome
🕇 Children welcome

Smoked salmon kedgeree with a light whisky cream. Escalope of venison with redcurrant and rosemary sauce. Atholl Brose cheesecake.

STB Commended 👑 👑 👑
💳 Credit cards: Access/Mastercard/Eurocard, American Express, Visa, Switch, Delta
𝄡 Manager: Donna McVey
𝄡 Head Chef: John Baxter

BABBITY BOWSTER
16-18 Blackfriars Street
Glasgow G1 1PE
Tel: 0141 552 5055
Fax: 0141 552 7774

In the heart of Glasgow's merchant city – at the East End of city centre.

An atmospheric hotel with good Scottish fayre.

- An Adam building c. 1790.
- Scottish cooking.
- "A busy vibrant establishment full of buzz and laughter."

Babbity Bowster is a splendid building on the site of what was originally a monastery. It takes its unusual name from a dance 'The Babbity Bowster' from the late 18th century 'babbity' meaning 'bob at the' and 'bowster' being a bolster or large pillow. Babbity Bowster is described as a cafe/bar/hotel/restaurant and it performs all of these functions with an atmosphere of excitement and is known as one of the 'in places' in Glasgow's city centre. Though casual in appearance Babbity Bowster provides good quality meals all day, both in the Schottische Restaurant and in the bar and garden area. Quality food, good drink and intellectual conversation is the key to the success of this place together with Fraser Laurie's personal supervision.

Open all year except Christmas Day + New Year's Day
Note: Restaurant closed Sun
🏠 Rooms: 6 with private facilities
✗ Food served all day ££
✗ Lunch £
✗ Dinner £££
Ⓥ Vegetarians welcome
🕇 Children welcome

Asparagus and tomato salad with pine nuts and a raspberry vinaigrette. Roast haunch of venison with a thyme and rosemary jus. Traditional cloutie dumpling with sticky toffee sauce and ice cream.

💳 Credit cards: Access/Mastercard/Eurocard, American Express, Visa
𝄡 Owner: Fraser Laurie

THE BRASSERIE
176 West Regent Street
Glasgow G2 4RL
Tel: 0141 248 3801
Fax: 0141 248 8197

Approach via Bath Street from city centre; turn left into Blythswood Street then left into West Regent Street. From outwith city, follow one way systems via Blythswood Square to West Regent Street.

City centre restaurant and brasserie.

- Restaurant in the heart of Glasgow.
- Modern Scottish cooking.
- "Lots of good choices here in a particularly friendly atmosphere."

This elegant brasserie lies close to both Glasgow's theatreland and its mercantile centre and is popular both with businessmen at lunchtime and theatre goers in the evening (they suggest a delicious 'after theatre supper' of warm duck salad or scrambled eggs with smoked salmon). The Brasserie has an impressive pillared facade, and inside there is a horseshoe bar and dining area with a Victorian atmosphere. It has an air of restrained elegance and the à la carte menu reflects this, with a good choice of freshly cooked dishes, both brasserie-style and more substantial. A daily changing plat du jour is also available. Flair, continental influences and modern cooking styles are evident, and the service is excellent.

Open all year except Christmas Day,
Boxing Day, New Year's Day + 2 Jan
Closed Sun
✘ Food served all day except Sun ££
✘ Lunch except Sun ££
✘ Dinner except Sun ££
Ⓥ Vegetarians welcome
⚤ Children welcome

Filo parcel of baked Brie with Cumberland sauce. Brochette of monkfish and scallops with basil, tomato and saffron vinaigrette. Crème brûlée.

💳 Credit cards: Access/Mastercard/Eurocard, American Express, Visa, Diners Club, Switch
Ⓜ Manager: Ryan James

THE BUTTERY
652 Argyle Street, Glasgow G3 8UF
Tel: 0141 221 8188
Fax: 0141 204 4639

Junction 19, M8 – approach by St Vincent Street and Elderslie Street.

Gourmet restaurant – in old tenement style.

- Converted tenement building.
- Innovative Scottish cooking.
- "Established as one of Glasgow's finest, an institution of excellence."

The Buttery is a perennial favourite and continues to be one of Glasgow's premier restaurants. The outside of this old tenement building gives no clues to the interior, which has a unique character, with bits of church furniture and Victoriana lending the whole of the restaurant an air of comfort and charm. Polite, well-informed and unobtrusive service characterises The Buttery, which is efficiently run by Jim Wilson, a man with a reputation for high standards. Chef Steven Johnson's à la carte menus are an appetising balance of traditional Scottish dishes treated in a novel way and with unusual combinations, exquisitely presented with lots of interesting textures and flavours. He also presents outstanding vegetarian and dessert menus. The luncheon menu is also excellent value. The Buttery has 2 AA Rosettes. One of 12 establishments shortlisted for The Macallan Taste of Scotland Awards 1996.

Open all year except Christmas Day +
New Year's Day
Closed Sun
✘ Lunch except Sun Sat ££
✘ Dinner except Sun £££
Ⓥ Vegetarians welcome
⚬ Smoking of pipes + cigars is preferred in the bar

Trio of salmon (gravadlax, tartare and smoked) with a lemon creamed pepper root sauce. Highland venison layered with vegetarian haggis on a rich Madeira-flavoured jus. Buttery Grand Dessert – a small taste of all desserts on the menu.

💳 Credit cards: Access/Mastercard/Eurocard, American Express, Visa, Diners Club, Switch, Delta
Ⓜ Manager: Jim Wilson

THE CABIN RESTAURANT
996-998 Dumbarton Road
Whiteinch
Glasgow G14 9RR
Tel: 0141 569 1036

From Glasgow city take Clyde expressway, pass Scottish Exhibition & Conference Centre to Thornwood Roundabout. Follow sign to Whiteinch (½ mile). Restaurant on right-hand side.

A Victorian 'front room' on Dumbarton Road.

- Small city restaurant.
- Modern Scottish, with continental influences.
- "Fascinating owners, Wilma – singer, and exceptional cuisine make this restaurant outstanding – but very different."

The restaurant opened three years ago. It is the original front room of an Edwardian tenement building, and is decorated accordingly, with original Art Deco features, a sideboard with china ornaments, old pictures and mirrors. The atmosphere is informal and cheerful. Dishes from the table d'hôte menu (five starters, seven main courses) are cooked to order; the cooking technique is creative, confident and to a very high standard; menus change daily, according to what is available in the market. About 9 pm, Wilma arrives to hostess and to sing one hour later. She is larger than life, first visited the restaurant shortly after it opened, and now returns nightly to encourage guests to sing along and let their hair down. The BBC made a half hour TV programme about her in Las Vegas! Head Chef Kenny Wilson is co-presenting STV's Square Meals programme.

Open all year except 1 to 14 Jan + 15 to 30 Jul
Closed Sun Mon
✗ Lunch except Sun Mon Sat £
✗ Dinner except Sun Mon £££
Ⓥ Vegetarians welcome
✶ Children welcome
♿ Facilities for disabled visitors
⚞ Pipes and cigars not permitted

Arbroath smokie mousse with lime-flavoured bannocks. Duck and wild mushroom croustade. Heather honey bavarois with poached figs and plums.

💳 No credit cards
Ⓜ Proprietors: Mohammad Abdulla & Denis Dwyer

THE CITY MERCHANT RESTAURANT
97 Candleriggs
Glasgow G1 1NP
Tel: 0141 553 1577

Facing City Halls in Candleriggs, in Glasgow's Merchant City. Candleriggs on right going east along Ingram Street.

Post office converted into seafood restaurant.

- City centre restaurant.
- Modern Scottish.
- "A Victorian styled restaurant serving the freshest of Scottish produce using modern techniques."

Candleriggs has been upgraded, the City Halls renovated and now opposite the City Merchant Restaurant has expanded, doubling its capacity to cope with demand. This restaurant is not only popular with the business community but also shoppers and visitors. The restaurant specialises in seafood, but also offers game, prime Scottish steaks and vegetarian dishes. Daily fish market 'extras' are offered on the blackboard: Isle of Seil oysters Loch Sween mussels, king scallops, lobster and turbot as well as exotics such as red snapper. Lots of other fish and shellfish on offer on any day. The wine list is extensive with a choice of over 60 bins, but a 'bin-end' blackboard offers excellent value.

Open all year except Christmas Day, 1 + 2 Jan
✗ Food served all day ££
✗ Lunch ££
✗ Dinner ££
♨ Bookings advisable
Ⓥ Vegetarians welcome
✶ Children over 6 years welcome
♿ Facilities for disabled visitors
⚞ No smoking area in restaurant

A juxtaposition of Scottish fin fish and shellfish, marinaded in Speyside malt grain mustard, heather honey, sea salt and coriander. Collops of pheasant and venison on a reduction of port wine, juniper and redcurrant jus, served with a skirlie tart. Mixed berry brose – berries, toasted oats folded into Highland liqueur flavoured whipped cream with shortbread.

💳 Credit cards: Access/Mastercard/Eurocard, American Express, Visa, Diners Club, Mastercharge, Switch
Ⓜ Proprietors: Tony & Linda Matteo

THE DRUM AND MONKEY
93-95 St Vincent Street
Glasgow
G2 5TL
Tel: 0141 221 6636
Fax: 0141 204 4278

On corner of St Vincent and Renfield Street –
approx 100 yards from Central Station.

This bar was named 'Pub of the Universe' in 1995.

* Bank building.
* Very atmospheric.
* "A meeting place for the business community in
  the centre of Glasgow."

The Drum and Monkey was originally a downtown
bank but today it has a warm and comfortable
ambience where shoppers rest on wicker chairs
and leather couches. A fine selection of beers
especially real ales and continental lagers is readily
available. Bar food is available, with a simpler
menu thereafter of freshly prepared to order filled
sandwiches and wholesome salads. But for the
real food experience the adjoining bistro provides
more elaborate lunches and dinners in the most
intimate of settings, combining modern dishes with
the more traditional Scottish classics.

Open all year except 25, 26 Dec, 1 + 2 Jan
✖ Food served all day £££
✖ Lunch except Sun ££
✖ Dinner ££
Ⓥ Vegetarians welcome
⚘ Children welcome
♿ Facilities for disabled visitors

**Haggis with clapshot (neeps and tatties). Herb-
crusted confit of duck with braised red cabbage
and potato gratin. Cranachan.**

💳 Credit cards: Access/Mastercard/Eurocard,
American Express, Visa, Diners Club, Switch,
Delta
Ⓝ General Manager: Stewart Moran
Ⓝ Bistro Manager: Lucie Moran

FROGGIES
53 West Regent Street
Glasgow
G2 2AE
Tel: 0141 332 8790
Fax: 0141 353 1117

From George Square take St Vincent Street, turn
third right into Hope Street, then first right into
West Regent Street.

A French restaurant in the heart of Glasgow.

* A spacious, city centre bistro/restaurant.
* First class cuisine.
* "An authentic French restaurant serving
  traditional regional cooking."

Froggies has the unforced style and vibrant
atmosphere of a cafe/restaurant in Lyons – 'more
friendly than Paris'! It first opened in 1990 and is so
well supported by the local business community
that it was substantially expanded in late 1992.
Jean-Louis Turpin, its Toulouse-born proprietor,
says that his goal is "to de-mystify the forbidding
atmosphere of some French restaurants, and to
produce authentic French dishes, using fresh
Scottish produce." His chef, Philippe Avril (from
Marseilles) presents a distinguished à la carte
menu, a table d'hôte menu and a 'Repas d'Affaire'.
All are very well-priced.

Open all year except Christmas Day,
Boxing Day, 1 + 2 Jan
✖ Lunch £
✖ Dinner ££
Ⓥ Vegetarians welcome
⚘ Children welcome
🚭 Smoking area in restaurant

**Thinly sliced side of fresh salmon marinated in
olive oil, tarragon and coriander. Honey glazed
fillet of pork on a wholegrain mustard jus with
baby roast potatoes and seasonal vegetables.
White chocolate cheesecake on a rick dark
chocolate sauce.**

💳 Credit cards: Access/Mastercard/Eurocard,
American Express, Visa, Switch
Ⓝ Owner: Mr Jean-Louis Turpin

GLASGOW HILTON INTERNATIONAL
Camerons Restaurant
1 William Street
Glasgow G3 8HT
Tel: 0141 204 5555
Fax: 0141 204 5004

Access from M8 to hotel, or via Waterloo Street and Bishop Street from city centre.

20-storey landmark in central Glasgow.

- International luxury hotel.
- Grand hotel cooking.
- "Having been built and opened in 1992, this hotel has now settled into its luxury city centre style of hotel niche."

This very luxurious city centre hotel lives up to its international reputation in Glasgow. In the four years since its opening the 'rough' edges are now disappearing as it settles into its niche as one of Glasgow's best. Camerons Restaurant provides relaxed high quality dining in a traditional restaurant now mellowing with the years. Concentrating on the best and freshest Scottish produce Chef Mizzen cooks seafood and game to exceptional standards developing the flavours of the produce and complementing them with interesting jus, sauces, and accompaniments, all beautifully presented and served by accomplished tartan-clad staff. Facilities of the hotel include a leisure centre, shopping mall and beauty salon as well as Minsky's Deli and Restaurant offering light meals and snacks all day.

Open all year
- 🏠 Rooms: 319 with private facilities
- ✘ Lunch except Sun Sat £££
- ✘ Dinner £££-££££
- Ⓥ Vegetarians welcome
- ✸ Children welcome
- ♿ Facilities for disabled visitors
- 🚭 No smoking area in restaurant
- 🐄 Member of the Scotch Beef Club

Carpaccio of lamb in curry sauce. Medley of Scottish game with rich port sauce. Praline mousse with chestnut and redcurrant sauce.

STB Deluxe 👑 👑 👑 👑 👑
- 💳 Credit cards: Access/Mastercard/Eurocard, American Express, Visa, Mastercharge, Switch
- 🗓 Restaurant Manager: Michael Deary

GLASGOW MOAT HOUSE
Congress Road
Glasgow G3 8QT
Tel: 0141 306 9988
Fax: 0141 221 2022

Situated on the banks of the River Clyde, next to the SECC.

A luxurious ultra-modern skyscraper hotel in city centre, on banks of the River Clyde.

- Large, modern skyscraper hotel in the heart of Glasgow.
- Modern international cuisine.
- "Built in 1990 this luxury hotel provides comfort in an opulent atmosphere, with good Scottish food and service."

The Glasgow Moat House takes its theme from its splendid position on a former wharf, on the banks of the River Clyde: its fully equipped leisure area, its principal restaurant 'The Mariner', its carvery 'The Pointhouse', its cocktail bar the 'Quarter Deck'. Both of the hotel's award-winning restaurants provide standards not often encountered in large 'international' hotels. The Pointhouse is brasserie style, The Mariner (which has two AA Rosettes) fine dining. The style of cooking is modern, fresh and elegant: Scottish produce and international techniques. Winner of The Taste of Scotland Hotel of the Year Award 1992.

Open all year
- 🏠 Rooms: 283 with private facilities
- ✘ Food served all day (Pointhouse) ££
- ✘ Note: Buffet also available
- ✘ Lunch (Mariner) except Sun Sat ££-£££
- ✘ Dinner (Mariner) except Sun £££
- Ⓥ Vegetarians welcome
- ✸ Children welcome
- ♿ Facilities for disabled visitors
- 🚭 No smoking areas in restaurants

Lobster bisque. Baked fillet of seabass with shrimp tortellini and sweet pepper dressing. Blueberry and coconut tart.

STB Highly Commended 👑 👑 👑 👑 👑
- 💳 Credit cards: Access/Mastercard/Eurocard, American Express, Visa, Mastercharge
- 🗓 General Manager: Mrs Jela Stewart

PAPINGO RESTAURANT
104 Bath Street
Glasgow
G2 2EN
Tel: 0141 332 6678
Fax: 0141 332 6549

City centre, parallel to Sauchiehall Street and next block to shopping centre.

A city centre restaurant with a tremendous buzz.

- Basement of office building.
- Modern Scottish cooking.
- "I loved eating in this restaurant with a busy but unhurried atmosphere."

Situated in the basement of an old office building this restaurant celebrates its seventh anniversary this year, proving it is one which is here to stay. The decor is fresh and clean-cut with clever use of mirrors to give the illusion of more space. Papingo is the old Scots word for parrot and these abound in various styles and unusual places. The menu offers good value for money, lots of alternatives and is nicely balanced with lovely Scottish concoctions of fish, game, poultry lamb and vegetarian dishes. All in all – first class.

Open all year except 1 + 2 Jan
✗ Food served all day £-££
✗ Lunch except Sun £
✗ Dinner ££
Ⓥ Vegetarians welcome
大 Children welcome before 8pm
⊭ Separate no smoking area

Timbale of Highland haggis wrapped in carrots and leeks on a rich cream sauce scented with fine Scotch whisky. Baked saddle of venison roasted in pine nuts and filled with shallots, sweet basil and black pudding stuffing. Home-made tiramisu.

⊞ Credit cards: Access/Mastercard/Eurocard, American Express, Visa, Diners Club, Mastercharge, Switch, Delta
Ⅺ Owner: Alan C Tomkins

THE PUPPET THEATRE
Ruthven Lane
Glasgow, Hillhead
G12 9BG
Tel: 0141 339 8444
Fax: 0141 339 7666

In Ruthven Lane – off Byres Road in Glasgow's West End. Ruthven Lane opposite Hillhead underground station.

A luxurious restaurant offering excellent conservatory dining.

- Converted mews house.
- Modern Scottish cooking.
- "A welcome newcomer to Taste of Scotland – wonderful food, atmosphere and design."

In converted mews premises behind Byres Road, this little restaurant is made up of little rooms providing intimate dining in a Victorian setting with the modern addition of a stylistic conservatory bringing the restaurant into the 1990s. The furnishings in the 'old' room are Victorian whilst the conservatory is 'modern' with a 'designer' feel to it. Opened in 1994 the Puppet Theatre has become one of the best restaurants in Glasgow with booking required weeks in advance for the weekends. The cooking is described by our Inspector as "first class" with best Scottish produce presented in modern Scottish style which looks great and with tastes that match expectation!

Open all year except Christmas Day, Boxing Day, New Year's Day + 2 Jan
Closed Mon
✗ Lunch except Mon Sat £-££
✗ Dinner except Mon £££
Ⓥ Vegetarians welcome
大 Children 12 years and over welcome
♿ Facilities for disabled visitors
⊭ Smoking area, if requested

Baked Ayrshire potatoes with smoked salmon, caviar and sour cream. Duo of game, purée of celeriac and blackberry sauce. Hot raspberry soufflé in butter pastry with white chocolate ice cream.

⊞ Credit cards: Access/Mastercard/Eurocard, American Express, Visa, Mastercharge, Switch, Delta
Ⅺ Manager: Andrew Jukes

ROGANO

11 Exchange Place
Glasgow G1 3AN
Tel: 0141 248 4055
Fax: 0141 248 2608

Glasgow city centre, near/off Buchanan Street precinct and Queen Street/George Square.

Glasgow's most famous restaurant.

- Art Deco seafood restaurant.
- Classic cooking, specialising in fish.
- "Built in the 1930s and still the same in style, atmosphere and quality."

Really good restaurants survive, and Rogano has been around for generations. In 1935, as the great floating palace the 'Queen Mary' took shape on the Clyde, a restaurant was re-fitted in the same Art Deco style – and a Glasgow legend was born. It was painstakingly restored in 1983. The atmosphere is authentically of that period and service is stylish. The restaurant's reputation was built on seafood – and this is still a feature – although vegetarian and meat alternatives are offered on the marvellous à la carte menu. The style of cooking in the restaurant is modern with classical influences. The wine list imaginative. Downstairs is Cafe Rogano, less expensive and the cooking is simpler – but as delicious. Rogano has 2 AA Rosettes.

Open all year except Christmas Day, Boxing Day, 1, 2 + 3 Jan
✗ Food served all day (Cafe Rogano) £-££
✗ Lunch (Restaurant) ££-££££
✗ Dinner (Restaurant) ££££
Ⓥ Vegetarians welcome
⅄ Children welcome
⅄ Smoking discouraged before 2pm (Lunch) + 9pm (Dinner)

Rogano fish soup. Seared scallops with spring onion and ginger. White and dark chocolate mousse with a mandarin syrup.

⊞ Credit cards: Access/Mastercard/Eurocard, American Express, Visa, Diners Club, Switch, Delta
Ⓜ Manager: Gordon James Yuill

TWO FAT LADIES RESTAURANT

88 Dumbarton Road
Glasgow
Strathclyde
G11 6NX
Tel: 0141 339 1944

In the heart of Glasgow's west end, 500 metres from Kelvingrove Museum/Park towards Byres Road.

An unpretentious fish restaurant in Glasgow's West End.

- Contemporary restaurant.
- Fish a speciality, but offers meat and vegetarian as well.
- "Market fresh produce, individually cooked to order."

A small, busy, modern restaurant at 88 Dumbarton Road (hence the name), in the contemporary 'spartan/post-punk' style. The atmosphere is intimate, informal and cheerful. Chef/patron Calum Matheson's cooking is also very contemporary – 'Riverside Cafe-ish' – relying on utterly fresh ingredients, a searingly hot grill and the skilful use of fresh herbs. The results are extremely successful, the flavours of the fresh fish coming through well. The menu is table d'hôte (six starters, six main courses) and includes poultry, meat and vegetarian dishes. Pre-theatre supper Monday to Saturday.

Open all year except 1 to 12 Jan + Bank Holidays
Closed Sun
♀ Table licence
✗ Lunch Fri Sat only ££-£££
Ⓟ Private Lunch Parties – by arrangement
✗ Dinner except Sun £££
Ⓥ Vegetarians welcome
⅄ Children welcome
♿ Facilities for disabled visitors
⅄ No cigars

Saffron fish and leek broth. Steamed salmon and spinach with orange, mustard and chive sauce. Light and dark marbled chocolate terrine with mango coulis.

⊞ Credit cards: Access/Mastercard/Eurocard, Visa, Switch
Ⓜ Proprietor: Calum Matheson

UBIQUITOUS CHIP

12 Ashton Lane
Glasgow G12 8SJ
Tel: 0141 334 5007
Fax: 0141 337 1302

Behind Hillhead underground station, in a secluded lane off Byres Road in the heart of Glasgow's West End.

An exceptionally busy Scottish restaurant in Glasgow's West End.

- A restaurant of character.
- Modern Scottish cooking.
- "This restaurant has become a Glasgow institution, particularly patronised by members of the media."

The Ubiquitous Chip, known affectionately by its regulars as 'The Chip', was established in 1971 by Ronnie Clydesdale – it has been described as a 'legend in its own lunchtime'. It has also received a Michelin Red M, an award never before bestowed upon a Glasgow restaurant. The chip is situated in a cobbled mews in Glasgow's West End. It has a spectacularly green and vinous courtyard area with a trickling pool and a more traditional dining room. The cuisine marries the traditional and original in innovative recipes and this variety is complemented by a wine list rated among the top 10 in Britain for quality and value.

Open all year except Christmas Day, 31 Dec + 1 Jan
✗ Food served all day
✗ Lunch ££
✗ Dinner £££
Ⓥ Vegetarians welcome
⚱ Children welcome
♿ Facilities for disabled visitors

Air-dried beef served with extra virgin oil. Howtowdie chicken with candied shallots and a quail's egg. Scotch malt whisky tart.

💳 Credit cards: Access/Mastercard/Eurocard, American Express, Visa, Diners Club, Masthercharge, Delta
Ⓜ Proprietor: Ronnie Clydesdale

YES BAR & RESTAURANT

22 West Nile Street, Glasgow G1 2PW
Tel: 0141 221 8044
Fax: 0141 248 9159

City centre between Gordon Street and St Vincent Street. 2 minutes from Central and Queen Street Stations.

Spacious, stylish and first-class city centre restaurant.

- Restaurant with public and private dining room, bar and brasserie.
- Modern Scottish cooking.
- "One of our Scottish Master Chefs puts perfection on a plate."

Among his many accolades including Master Chef, Ferrier Richardson has led both the Scottish and British national culinary teams to international success in prestigious events. This restaurant in Glasgow's fashionable city centre bears his stamp both in the high standards of the food and wine served and the venue's stylishness and originality. As you would expect, food is outstandingly good, embodying the distinctive approach and innovative techniques that have established Ferrier Richardson as a master. The finest of Scottish dishes emerge beautifully presented to delight the taste buds. His wine list complements the menu with a balance and choice of wines to suit varied budgets. Given the quality of what is on offer here, prices are more than reasonable. One of 12 establishments shortlisted for The Macallan Taste of Scotland Awards 1996.

Note: Bar + Brasserie closed Christmas Day, Boxing Day, 1 + 2 Jan
Restaurant closed all public holidays
Closed Sun
Restaurant + Brasserie closed Sun
✗ Food served all day (Brasserie) except Sun £
✗ Lunch (Restaurant) except Sun ££
✗ Dinner (Restaurant) except Sun £££
Ⓥ Vegetarians welcome
⚱ Children welcome
♿ Facilities for disabled visitors in Brasserie

Hot smoked Otter Ferry salmon and Mull of Kintyre soufflé, hollandaise sauce. Suprême of turbot with a mussel and vegetable chowder. Coconut parfait with grilled pineapple and a mint syrup.

💳 Credit cards: Access/Mastercard/Eurocard, American Express, Visa, Diners Club, Switch
Ⓜ Managing Director: Ferrier Richardson

BEARDMORE HOTEL
Restaurant of the Year 1996
Beardmore Street, Clydebank
Glasgow G81 4SA
Tel: 0141 951 6000 Fax: 0141 951 6018

Between Glasgow and Loch Lomond. Off A82, 8 miles from M8 junction 19.

A modern, international hotel in an attractive setting (adjacent to HCI Medical Centre).

- Newly built within its own grounds, with views over the River Clyde.
- Award-winning, imaginative, international cuisine.
- "A unique hotel serving both business and leisure guests."

The Beardmore Hotel is an ultra-modern red brick building with striking green roofs. A leisure club, purpose-built conference centre and 168 air-conditioned bedrooms complete its range of facilities. Executive Chef James Murphy trained with Anton Mossiman at the Dorchester and at Maxim's in Paris. This is reflected in a cuisine that is creative and distinct, extending over a well-stocked buffet in the hotel's spacious Brasserie as well as an à la carte menu. The Macallan Award-winning Symphony Room restaurant has the atmosphere of a private dinner party at home. The service is efficient, friendly and relaxed. The Beardmore has 1 AA Rosette.

Open all year
- 🛏 Rooms: 168 with private facilities
- 🆂🅿 Special rates available
- ✗ Food served all day ££
- ✗ Lunch ££
- ✗ Dinner ££
- Ⓥ Vegetarians welcome
- ⚘ Children welcome
- ♿ Facilities for disabled visitors
- 🚭 Smoking area in restaurant

Tortellini of woodland mushrooms with tarragon essence. Fillet of Borders lamb with basil butter and seared tomato. Mille feuille of chocolate.

STB De Luxe 👑 👑 👑 👑 👑
- 💳 Credit cards: Access/Mastercard/Eurocard, American Express, Visa, Diners Club, Mastercharge, Switch
- 🅺 Director & General Manager: David Clarke

FIFTY FIVE BC
128 Drymen Road
Bearsden
Glasgow G61 3RB
Tel: 0141 942 7272
Fax: 0141 942 9650

On the main Drymen Road at Bearsden Cross.

A well-established bar and restaurant popular with locals.

- Small restaurant attached to a large wine bar.
- Modern Scottish cooking, with French influences.
- "Lighter meals or gourmet dinners, informally served at reasonable prices."

Fifty Five BC was, of course, the date that Julius Caesar first arrived in Britain: the restaurant has adopted this date as its name on account of the Roman remains that have been found nearby. Gary Fletcher, has recently been appointed Head Chef and has continued to maintain the high standards for which Fifty Five BC has become known. His short à la carte menus are imaginative; his creations make ingenious use of fresh local produce and are beautifully presented and delicious. Robust bar meals (potato skins, burgers, pasta) are served Monday to Saturday. The style of the place is modern, light and airy. Service is casual. Fifty Five BC is particularly popular locally and deserves to be better known.

Open all year except New Year's Day
- ✗ Lunch £-££
- ✗ Dinner £££
- Ⓥ Vegetarians welcome
- ⚘ Children welcome
- ♿ Facilities for disabled visitors
- 🚭 No smoking area – bar food only

Medallions of hare salad with oriental spices. Seared fillet of sea bass served with French beans, smoked bacon and tomato concasse with a light tomato and black olive dressing. Brandy basket of pecan-toasted brioche.

- 💳 Credit cards: Access/Mastercard/Eurocard, American Express, Visa, Diners Club, Mastercharge, Switch, Delta, JCB
- 🅺 Proprietor: Hamish McLean

GLEN CANNICH

MULLARDOCH HOUSE HOTEL
Glen Cannich, By Beauly, Inverness-shire IV4 7LX
Tel: 01456 415460
Fax: 01456 415460

Take A831 from Beauly or Drumnadrochit to
Cannich. 8 miles west of Cannich on single track
road toward Loch Mullardoch.

A country house hotel in a stunning location.

- Edwardian hunting lodge whose character has
  been carefully preserved.
- Traditional Scottish cooking.
- "Wholesome menu with interesting dishes
  served within beautiful surroundings."

Converted from a hunting lodge originally built for
Chisholm of Chisholm in 1912, Mullardoch House
Hotel has recently undergone major refurbishment
to a very high standard. The hotel looks out over
Loch Sealbanach to the Affric mountains beyond
and is the perfect base for those wishing to enjoy
countryside pursuits such as walking, climbing,
fishing and boating. The area is one of great
unspoilt beauty and is extremely rich in wildlife –
early risers have even spotted otters playing at the
lochside. Accommodation at the hotel is spacious
and comfortable and great care is taken to make
guests feel at home hence an abundance of books,
magazines and games in the public rooms. The
hotel's chef specialises in traditional Scottish
cooking using fresh produce, no mean
achievement given the remote location.
Mullardoch has 1 AA Rosette.

    Open all year
    Rooms: 6 with private facilities
⚥ Restricted licence
✗ Food served all day £
✗ Lunch ££
✗ Dinner 4 course menu ££
Ⓥ Vegetarians welcome
⊥ Children welcome
─ No smoking in dining room

**Asparagus tartlets. Monkfish fillet with tarragon
hollandaise. Crème brûlée with exotic fruits.**

STB Highly Commended ♛ ♛ ♛
⊒ Credit cards: Access/Mastercard/Eurocard,
    American Express, Visa
ᴐ Owners: Andrew & Helen Johnston

GLENISLA

THE GLENISLA HOTEL
Kirkton of Glenisla
by Blairgowrie
Perthshire PH11 8PH
Tel: 01575 582223
Fax: 01575 582223

From south take A93 to Blairgowrie then A926 to
Alyth (4 miles). By-pass Alyth to roundabout follow
signs to Glenisla (12 miles). From north take B951
off A93 – follow signs to Glenisla (5 miles).

A 17th century coaching inn in a pretty glen.

- Historic old stone country inn.
- Imaginative home cooking.
- "Very friendly, very informal – the atmosphere
  of a village pub."

Kirkton of Glenisla is two-thirds of the way up the
glen, on the old Perth-Braemar coach route. The
current inn buildings have been standing since at
least 1750, and the inn itself may be older. Today it
is a friendly local with an excellent pub – and
adding to the atmosphere – open log fires and oak
beams. There is also a tastefully decorated small
restaurant, with Georgian windows overlooking
the glen. Simon and Lyndy Blake are justifiably
proud hosts and welcome their guests warmly. The
cooking reflects a degree of flair and style which
has won the hotel an enviable local reputation. The
menu changes daily with excellent use of local
produce a feature – watch out for wicked
puddings!

    Open all year except Christmas Day +
    Boxing Day
🏠 Rooms : 6 with private facilities
Ⓢ Special rates available
✗ Lunch £
✗ Dinner ££
Ⓥ Vegetarians welcome
⊥ Children welcome
♿ Limited facilities for disabled visitors
─ No smoking in dining room + bedrooms

**Wild brown trout from local lochs. Game casserole.
Various desserts with fruits from the Glen.**

STB Commended ♛ ♛ ♛
⊒ Credit cards: Access/Mastercard/Eurocard,
    Visa
ᴐ Proprietors: Simon & Lyndy Blake

Glenlivet   89

MINMORE HOUSE
Glenlivet, Banffshire AB37 9DB
Tel: 01807 590 378
Fax: 01807 590 472

Take A95 from Grantown-on-Spey. Right after 15 miles B9008 -follow signs to The Glenlivet Distillery.

A country house hotel in the heart of whisky country.

- Converted Scottish country house with fine views over the River Livet.
- Imaginative country house cooking.
- "A perfect setting for rest and relaxation."

The original home of the founder of The Glenlivet Distillery and standing adjacent to it, Minmore House lies in its own grounds close by the River Livet. The house retains very much the feel of a Scottish country house thanks to period furnishings and atmospheric decor. Roaring log fires and comfortable armchairs are welcoming features of the hotel's public rooms. Owner, Belinda Luxmoore, has earned a well-deserved reputation for the quality of her cooking. She draws her inspiration from the abundance of fresh locally produced ingredients and serves a set menu that is changed daily. The cheeseboard is something of a speciality with a wide selection of Scottish cheeses attractively presented. To finish the evening, guests have the pleasure of choosing a night-cap from over 100 malt whiskies stocked at the bar. Weekly terms and short breaks available.

Open 1 May to mid Oct
- 🏨 Rooms: 10 with private facilities
- 🆂🅿 Special rates available
- 🍺 Bar + picnic lunches can be arranged for residents £
- ✘ Dinner 5 course menu £££
- Ⅴ Vegetarians welcome
- 🧍 Children welcome
- 🚭 No smoking in dining room

Fresh Lossiemouth Langoustine. Escalope of venison with Cassis. Raspberry pavlova roulade.

STB Highly Commended 👑 👑 👑 👑
- 💳 Credit cards: Access/Mastercard/Eurocard, Visa
- 🅽 Owner: Belinda Luxmoore

Glenrothes   90

BALBIRNIE HOUSE HOTEL
Hotel of the Year 1996
Balbirnie Park, Markinch Village
by Glenrothes, Fife KY7 6NE
Tel: 01592 610066 Fax: 01592 610529

½ hour equidistant from Edinburgh and St Andrews. Just off A92 on B9130. Follow directions to Markinch village then Balbirnie Park.

Award-winning country house hotel in the grand manner.

- Georgian country house, converted to a splendid small luxury hotel.
- Elegant Scottish cooking, with strong French and continental influences.
- "Luxury building in beautiful grounds with justified award-winning cuisine."

Built in 1777 and standing in a beautiful estate of 400 acres, Balbirnie is a Grade A Listed building of great architectural and historic importance. Now owned and run by the Russell family, the house and grounds have been immaculately and lovingly restored. The dining room overlooks fine formal gardens and ancient yew hedges. Chef David Kinnes upholds the hotel's reputation for fine dining and interesting dishes that use fresh and local produce. Balbirnie has 2 AA Rosettes. "There is an air of quiet, friendly efficiency pervading the whole establishment – outstanding."

Open all year
- 🏨 Rooms: 30 with private facilities
- 🆂🅿 Special rates available
- ✘ Lunch ££
- ✘ Dinner £££
- Ⅴ Vegetarians welcome
- 🧍 Children welcome
- ♿ Facilities for disabled visitors
- 🐄 Member of the Scotch Beef Club

Tartlet of quails eggs with crisp pancetta, mushroom duxelle and sauce mousseline. Loin of Perthshire venison baked in a salt crust lattice, served with a sauce of Dijon mustard, honey and cabernet sauvignon. Granny Smith apple parfait with candied apples and caramel syrup.

STB Deluxe 👑 👑 👑 👑 👑
- 💳 Credit cards: Access/Mastercard/Eurocard, American Express, Visa, Diners Club
- 🅽 Proprietors: The Russell Family

RESCOBIE HOTEL
6 Valley Drive
Leslie
Fife KY6 3BQ
Tel: 01592 742143
Fax: 01592 620231

At west end of village of Leslie, by Glenrothes.

A small country house with a family atmosphere.

- Country house hotel.
- Country house cooking.
- "Rescobie has a comfortable, warm atmosphere, friendly staff and homely cooking."

Rescobie is an unpretentious and comfortable small Listed country house, built in the 1920s and retaining something of the feel of that era with antique furniture, comfortable armchairs and an open fire in the lounge. It stands in two acres of secluded gardens on the edge of the village of Leslie and is personally run by its friendly owner Tony Hughes-Lewis. The cuisine merits a Rosette from the AA. Chefs Stuart Aitken and David Lessles specialise in unusual and appropriate sauces on their menus (table d'hôte, à la carte and vegetarian); the flavours are positive and delicious. All meals are very reasonably priced. French and German spoken.

    Open all year except 24 to 27 Dec
🛏 Rooms: 10 with private facilities
SP Special rates available
✗ Lunch £
✗ Dinner ££
Ⓥ Vegetarians welcome
⊀ Children welcome
♿ Facilities for disabled visitors

Avocado tartlet. Venison with rowanberry jelly. Rhubarb mousse.

STB Commended 👑 👑 👑 👑
💳 Credit cards: Access/Mastercard/Eurocard, American Express, Visa, Diners Club
Ⓝ Owner: Tony Hughes-Lewis

DALMUNZIE HOUSE HOTEL
Spittal of Glenshee
Blairgowrie
Perthshire PH10 7QG
Tel: 01250 885 224
Fax: 01250 885 225

Approx 22 miles from Blairgowrie.

The hotel in the hills.

- Country house hotel.
- Traditional Scottish cooking.
- "A friendly, informal hotel with a friendly atmosphere."

Dalmunzie House Hotel is a substantial Victorian baronial mansion standing in its own 6,500 acre mountain estate. It has its own 9-hole golf course (every Sunday there is a 'Golf Marathon', where non-golfers are partnered with good golfers); fishing, stalking and grouse shooting are available, and the ski slopes of Glenshee are not far away. The Winton family who own the hotel have lived in the glen for decades and are genuine and experienced hosts. The house has a wonderfully friendly atmosphere, with log fires and comfy chairs and is hospitable and informal – the tone set by Simon and Alexandra Winton. The menu is table d'hôte (four-five choices) with a couple of à la carte supplements. The cooking is homestyle but imaginative; everything is fresh and cooked to order.

    Open 28 Dec to first wk Nov
🛏 Rooms: 17, 16 with private facilities
SP Special rates available
✗ Lunch £
✗ Dinner ££-£££
Ⓥ Vegetarians welcome
⊀ Children welcome
♿ Limited facilities for disabled visitors

Fresh Orkney mussels with a white wine sauce. Roast haunch of venison with a juniper and redcurrant sauce. Home-made brandy basket filled with Blairgowrie raspberries and cream.

STB Commended 👑 👑 👑
💳 Credit cards: Access/Mastercard/Eurocard, Visa
Ⓝ Owners: Simon & Alexandra Winton

Grantown-on-Spey 92

ARDCONNEL HOUSE
Woodlands Terrace
Grantown-on-Spey
Moray PH26 3JU
Tel: 01479 872104
Fax: 01479 872104

On A95, south-west entry to town.

A family run guest house in Grantown-on-Spey.

- Victorian villa guest house/hotel.
- Wholesome home cooking.
- "Relaxing, friendly and capable service – just enjoy yourself."

Built in 1890, Ardconnel House is a typical example of a Victorian villa, and this combines with the high standard of renovation and interior design that Jim and Barbara Casey have achieved to make for an attractive and comfortable place to stay. Their attention to detail is apparent throughout the house and this care extends also to the food, wines and whiskies on offer. Dinner is a nightly changing, small set menu, cooked in traditional style by Barbara and drawing on the local seasonal availability of produce. With the Spey practically on the doorstep, salmon and trout make regular appearances. Booking for dinner is advisable.

Open Easter to 31 Oct
- 🏠 Rooms: 6 with private facilities
- ✗ Residents only
- ♀ Restricted licence
- ✗ Dinner ££
- ✝ Children over 10 years welcome
- 🚭 No smoking throughout

Home-made wild mushroom soup. Roast of Scottish beef. Rhubarb and banana compote.

STB Deluxe 👑 👑 👑
- 💳 Credit cards: Access/Mastercard/Eurocard, Visa
- ⛊ Owners: Jim & Barbara Casey

THE ARDLARIG
Woodlands Terrace
Grantown-on-Spey
Moray PH26 3JU
Tel: 01479 873245

On A95 south west entry to town.

Comfortable and friendly guest house with good food.

- Carefully maintained Victorian house.
- Fresh home cooking.
- "Modern comforts with good hospitality."

The Ardlarig is a fine country house, set in a large garden, built at the turn of the century. It retains the grandeur and splendour of that time offering warm traditional Scottish hospitality, well-appointed rooms and fine food. Neil Cairns is an accomplished owner/chef – and excellent food, freshly prepared and presented, emerges from the kitchen making for a very pleasant Scottish experience. Typical of the area – a large selection of Speyside and island malts are offered. Neil will often join guests for a glass of wine or a 'wee dram'. Please note that Neil also shares his home with three Persian cats.

Open all year except Christmas Day, Boxing Day + New Year's Eve
- 🏠 Rooms: 7, 1 with private facilities
- ⛊ Special rates available
- ✗ Residents only
- ⛑ Picnic hampers/packed lunch only ££
- ✗ Dinner ££
- Ⓥ Vegetarians welcome
- ✝ Children welcome
- 🚭 Smoking allowed in lounge only

West Coast scallops and prawns in a garlic and lime sauce. Fillet steak with home-made pâté, served on oatcakes with a Glayva, cream and green peppercorn sauce. Summer sponge cheesecake.

STB Highly Commended 👑 👑
- 💳 No credit cards
- ⛊ Owner/Chef: Neil Cairns

CULDEARN HOUSE
Woodlands Terrace, Grantown-on-Spey
Moray PH26 3JU
Tel: 01479 872106
Fax: 01479 873641

Entering Grantown on A95 from south west, turn
left at 30mph sign. Culdearn faces you.

A country house on the outskirts of Grantown.

- Victorian country house.
- Traditional home cooking.
- "Highly accomplished home cooking. Be
  prepared to relax – the hospitable atmosphere
  is highly infectious."

This charming deluxe establishment has achieved
many accolades for the style in which it is run.
Alasdair and Isobel Little are enthusiastic hosts,
and quickly put their guests at ease. Their house
itself is elaborately and expensively furnished
throughout; service is professional and attention to
detail meticulous. Isobel is a talented chef and
prepares local produce in classic Scots ways. Fifty
malt whiskies now on offer and interesting new
wine list.

Open 1 Mar to 30 Oct
🏨 Rooms: 9 with private facilities
SP Special rates available
✗ Residents only
♀ Restricted licence
🍴 Picnic lunches to order
✗ Dinner – residents only
🚭 No smoking in dining room

**Smoked Scottish salmon served with freshly
scrambled eggs and dill sauce. Roast leg of
Moray lamb served with redcurrant, orange and
mint jelly with minted new potatoes and fresh
vegetables. Coffee and walnut sponge with
custard or ice cream.**

STB Deluxe 👑 👑 👑
💳 Credit cards: Access/Mastercard/Eurocard,
  American Express, Visa, Diners Club,
  Mastercharge, Switch, Delta, JCB
👤 Proprietors: Isobel & Alasdair Little

Gullane 93

GREYWALLS
Muirfield, Gullane, East Lothian EH31 2EG
Tel: 01620 842144
Fax: 01620 842241

At the eastern end of Gullane village (on the A198),
signposted left as a historic building.

**First-rate food and accommodation in a building
of national importance on the edge of Muirfield.**

- An Edwardian architectural masterpiece.
- Refined country house cuisine.
- "Enjoy good food and wine in historic
  surroundings."

This charming, grand but understated house was
designed at the turn of the century by Sir Edwin
Lutyens and his collaborator Gertrude Jekyll to be a
holiday home for the Hon Alfred Lyttelton. It was one
of the architect's favourite buildings and is
deservedly listed as being of national importance. It
became an hotel in 1948, and is still family-owned.
Greywalls has a wonderful situation overlooking
Muirfield Golf Course and the Firth of Forth. The
hotel's lovely walled garden complements the
serenity of the house itself, which still has the feel of
a family home: relaxed, refined, elegant... a perfect
backdrop for the discreetly attentive service one
meets with in this distinguished hotel. Chef Paul
Baron's menus are table d'hôte. His cooking is deft
and light, with classical influences: "a refreshing
combination of well-chosen ingredients, interestingly
blended." The wine list is exceptional. Greywalls has
2 AA Rosettes. Winner of Taste of Scotland Country
House Hotel of the Year Award 1992.

Open mid Apr to mid Oct
🏨 Rooms: 22 with private facilities
✗ Lunch ££
✗ Dinner ££££
Ⓥ Vegetarians welcome – prior notice required
🧒 Children welcome
♿ Facilities for disabled visitors
🚭 No smoking in dining room

**The best local produce skillfully prepared, menus
constantly changing.**

STB Highly Commended 👑 👑 👑 👑
💳 Credit cards: Access/Mastercard/Eurocard,
  American Express, Visa, Diners Club, Switch
👤 Manager: Sue Prime

`HADDINGTON`

MAITLANDFIELD HOUSE HOTEL

Sidegate, Haddington, East Lothian EH41 4BZ
Tel: 01620 826513
Fax: 01620 826713

Haddington on A1, take route to town centre. At east end of High Street take Sidegate (signposted Gifford and Lauder B6368) – about 300 yards – opposite St Mary's church.

This large modern hotel offers a high degree of comfort and two restaurants.

- A recently renovated and expanded large townhouse.
- Modern and classic Scottish cooking.
- "Unusual dishes using the freshest of produce."

Maitlandfield House Hotel is set in landscaped gardens within minutes of the centre of Haddington. The hotel has been completely refurbished in the last few years to provide high standards of accommodation and facilities. The 16 Kings Restaurant – named after the number of kings who have visited Haddington since 1124 – has a tent-like, canopied ceiling and offers candlelit dinner on polished wooden tables. The table d'hôte menus here use fresh local produce. Chef Mike Scotford trained at the Waldorf in London and offers a balanced menu with interesting influences. The Conservatory Bistro is more informal. The hotel also has a beer garden and children's play area.

Open all year
🏠 Rooms: 22 with private facilities
SP Special rates available
✗ Food served all day ££
✗ Lunch £
✗ Dinner £££
♿ Facilities for disabled visitors
Ⓥ Vegetarians welcome
☆ Children welcome

Tain of West Coast lobster and tomato with chervil jelly. Loin of Scottish lamb on a bed of crispy leeks and carrots. Sable of fresh Highland berries with a Drambuie sabayon.

STB Commended ♔ ♔ ♔ ♔
💳 Credit cards: Access/Mastercard/Eurocard, American Express, Visa, Mastercharge, Switch, Delta
👤 General Manager: Jacqui Scotford

`HAWICK`

MANSFIELD HOUSE HOTEL

Weensland Road, Hawick
Roxburghshire TD9 8LB
Tel: 01450 373988
Fax: 01450 372007

On the A698 Hawick to Kelso road. On the outskirts of the town.

An attractive newly extended mansion overlooking the outskirts of Hawick.

- Family-run small country house hotel.
- Traditional Scottish and contemporary cooking.
- "A warm welcome awaits within these hospitable walls."

A Victorian mansion overlooking the River Teviot and the town itself and standing in 10 acres of well-kept terraced lawns and mature shrubs and trees. Approached by a private drive, the hotel is secluded and quiet, yet it is within walking distance of the town centre. The building retains many of its original features – panelled doors, open fireplaces, ornate plasterwork – and a modern extension provides a large open bar and terrace. The hotel has been owned and run by the MacKinnon family for the past 11 years and under their supervision Chef David Tate presents well-priced à la carte and 'business lunch' menus in the formal dining room, and bar meals are also available. As well as the usual grills, the à la carte menu features some unusual combinations and meats (hare, kid, duck livers). *(See advert Page 22.)*

Open all year except 26, 27 Dec, 1 + 2 Jan
🏠 Rooms: 12 with private facilities
SP Special rates available
✗ Lunch £
✗ Dinner ££
Ⓥ Vegetarians welcome
☆ Children welcome
♿ Facilities for disabled visitors
🚭 No smoking area in restaurant

Kipper tartare. Roast quail with red cabbage and apple and a light grape sauce. Iced nougat soufflé.

STB Commended ♔ ♔ ♔
💳 Credit cards: Access/Mastercard/Eurocard, American Express, Visa, Diners Club
👤 Owners: Ian & Sheila MacKinnon

WHITCHESTER CHRISTIAN GUEST HOUSE

Borthaugh, Hawick
Roxburghshire TD9 7LN
Tel: 01450 377477
Fax: 01450 371080

¼ mile off A7, 2 miles south of Hawick on B711 to Roberton.

A former Dower House on the Buccleuch Estate.

- Peaceful small country house in its own grounds.
- Excellent home cooking.
- "Home cooking at its best."

The circumstances which guided David Maybury, an Episcopal priest, and his wife Doreen (now a priest), to establish a place where 'people could go and feel loved ... pampered' are extraordinary, but ten years ago they achieved their goal. Whitchester House was established as a Christian Centre with charitable status. Everything here – the growing of vegetables and fruit in the garden, the preparation of local game, the cooking and baking by Doreen, the waiting by David – is done 'For the Greater Glory of God'. And it shows: the friendliness and thoughtfulness, cheerfulness and warmth, is palpable. And the cooking is blessed!

Open Feb to Dec
🏠 Rooms: 8, 4 with private facilities
SP Special rates available
UL Unlicensed
🍴 Lunch – prior booking recommended £
🍴 Dinner – prior booking recommended ££
V Vegetarians welcome
⃠ Children welcome
⃝ Facilities for disabled visitors
⃠ No smoking throughout

Cream of artichoke soup. Roast Border grouse with rosemary and blackcurrant sauce. Spiced apple cake.

STB Commended 👑 👑 👑
💳 Credit cards: Access/Mastercard/Eurocard, Visa
🗿 Proprietors: David & Doreen Maybury

Helmsdale 96

NAVIDALE HOUSE HOTEL

Helmsdale
Sutherland KW8 6JS
Tel: 01431 821258
Fax: 01431 821531

¾ mile north of Helmsdale on main A9 road overlooking the sea.

A country house hotel in its own gardens overlooking the Moray Firth.

- Comfortable and friendly small hotel in dramatic Sutherland.
- Excellent home cooking with flair.
- "Marcus Blackwell buys his seafood direct from the fishing boats and collects his vegetables from the garden. The same care is taken with cooking and presentation."

Built as a shooting lodge for the Dukes of Sutherland in the 1830s, Navidale retains that atmosphere. Public rooms are elegant, spacious and well-appointed. Set in five acres of woodland and garden that lead down to the sea the hotel affords dramatic views over the Moray Firth and the Ord of Caithness, alongside modern comforts. Chef and manager Marcus Blackwell's menus make good use of the fine supply of local seafood, Highland lamb, beef and game. The hotel's own kitchen garden supplies fresh vegetables in season.

Open 30 Jan to 7 Nov
🏠 Rooms: 14 with private facilities
SP Special rates available
✕ Lunch ££
✕ Dinner £££
V Vegetarians welcome
⃠ Children welcome
⃝ Limited facilities for disabled visitors
⃠ No smoking in restaurant

Half Ogen melon filled with smoked salmon and local prawns. Local Helmsdale scallops in a cream sauce with chives and orange. Summer pudding.

STB Commended 👑 👑 👑
💳 Credit cards: Access/Mastercard/Eurocard, Visa
🗿 Managers: Marcus & Colleen Blackwell

THE OLD MANSE OF MARNOCH
Bridge of Marnoch, by Huntly
Aberdeenshire AB54 7RS
Tel: 01466 780873
Fax: 01466 780873

On B9117, less than 1 mile off A97 midway between Huntly and Banff.

A delightful country house hotel on the river Deveron in unspoilt Aberdeenshire.

- Secluded and peaceful, a small hotel of rare distinction.
- Outstanding creative cuisine.
- "Off the beaten track, but well worth a visit."

Remarkable for its solitude and peace, this fine Georgian house was built in the 1780s as the manse for the ministers of Marnoch Old Church. Its owners Patrick and Keren Carter have preserved the Georgian elegance in a tasteful and sympathetic conversion to an intimate country house hotel. Using fresh local produce and, in season, herbs and vegetables from their own four acre garden, Keren Carter deserves her growing reputation for imaginative, fine cooking. Her four course dinner changes every day. Her breakfasts are unrivalled. For a small establishment, the wine list is a triumph, both familiar and adventurous and always reasonably priced. Fluent German spoken. The hotel has 2 AA Rosettes.

Open all year except 2 wks Nov, Christmas + New Year
- 🛏 Rooms: 5 with private facilities
- ✕ Dinner 4 course menu £££
- ⋈ Reservations essential for non-residents
- Ⓥ Vegetarians welcome – prior notice required
- 🕏 Children over 12 years welcome
- ⼺ No smoking in dining room

Silver darlings: home-cured herring with salad leaves and thyme oatcakes. Pan-fried breast of wood pigeon with rhubarb and ginger. Bitter orange curd tart.

STB Deluxe ♛ ♛ ♛
- ⊞ Credit cards: Access/Mastercard/Eurocard, Visa, Delta
- 🕴 Proprietors: Patrick & Keren Carter

TRAQUAIR ARMS HOTEL
Traquair Road, Innerleithen
Peebles-shire EH44 6PD
Tel: 01896 830 229   Fax: 01896 830 260

On A72 midway between Peebles and Galashiels. Midway along Innerleithen High Street take B709 Yarrow. Hotel 150 yards on left.

An attractive Victorian village hotel in Innerleithen in the Scottish Borders.

- An attractive Victorian village inn.
- Good home cooking.
- "Good home cooking – speciality Aberdeen Angus beef flavoured with famous Traquair Ale."

A pleasant family-owned hotel close to the centre of this small Borders town. It is a sturdy stone building in a quiet street with a well-kept garden. The town, made famous by Sir Walter Scott, is popular with visitors, especially those looking for the cashmeres and tweeds for which these parts are renowned. Hugh and Marian Anderson run their hotel in a relaxed and friendly manner with genuine concern for the comfort of their guests. Extensive imaginative menus use fresh local produce, and everything is cooked to order. You can eat, depending on the weather, in the charming secluded garden or beside the blazing fire in the dining room. The bar prides itself in its real ales and there is a range of lighter meals available all day. *(See advert Page 28.)*

Open all year except Christmas Day, Boxing Day, 1 + 2 Jan
- 🛏 Rooms: 10 with private facilities
- ⓢⓟ Special rates available
- ✕ Food served all day £
- ✕ Lunch £
- ✕ Dinner £££
- Ⓥ Vegetarians welcome
- 🕏 Children welcome
- ♿ Facilities for disabled visitors – dining only
- ⼺ No smoking in dining room

Smoked Shetland salmon. Traquair steak pie. Scottish cheeseboard.

STB Commended ♛ ♛ ♛
- ⊞ Credit cards: Access/Mastercard/Eurocard, American Express, Visa, Diners Club, Switch, Delta
- 🕴 Owners: Hugh & Marian Anderson

INVERKEILOR

GORDON'S RESTAURANT
Main Street, Inverkeilor
by Arbroath, Angus DD11 5RN
Tel: 01241 830364

A92 Arbroath to Montrose, turn off at sign for
Inverkeilor

Cottage style restaurant with two rooms.

- Victorian terrace house.
- Classic/Scottish cooking.
- "A gem of a restaurant with consistent standards."

This small restaurant is run by Maria and Gordon
Watson and their son Garry. They took it over as a
bed and breakfast establishment and have now
built up a reputation for excellent food. Gordon
was a head waiter and manager in hotels before
opening here and Maria is a trained patisserie
chef. He has a flair and a sound sense of show-
manship, having trained classic flambé cooking at
diners' tables. Being so close to Arbroath and
Lunan Bay, Gordon's Restaurant has access to
fresh catches; soft fruits come from the berry
fields which surround them; herbs from their own
herb garden. Everything is cooked from scratch,
using the classic recipes which were familiar in
large hotels twenty years ago. The à la carte menu
changes regularly according to seasonal availability
and the range of dishes covers the spectrum of
good Scottish foods. Gordon's has 1 AA Rosette.

Open all year except last 2 wks Jan
🏨 Rooms: 2 with private facilities
✕ Closed Mon – residents only
✕ Lunch except Mon – residents only ££
✕ Dinner except Mon – residents only £££
Ⓥ Vegetarians welcome
⚘ Children welcome
♿ Facilities for disabled visitors
🚭 No smoking area in restaurant

**Chicken liver terrine layered with pheasant,
venison and Madagascar green peppercorns.
Seared fillet of salmon with prawns, chanterelles
and a nut brown butter sauce accompanied with a
timbale of rice pilaff. Chocolate parfait served
with poached pear and chocolate liqueur sauce.**

STB Commended 👑 👑
💳 Credit cards: Access/Mastercard/Eurocard, Visa
👤 Proprietors: Gordon & Maria Watson

INVERMORISTON

GLENMORISTON ARMS HOTEL
Invermoriston
Inverness-shire IV3 6YA
Tel: 01320 351206
Fax: 01320 351308

At junction of A82 and A887 in Invermoriston.

**A Highland sporting hotel with a village inn
atmosphere; ideal location for country sports and
holidays combined with spectacular scenery.**

- A traditional coaching inn in Glenmoriston for
over 200 years.
- Imaginative Scottish cooking featuring
speciality game dishes.
- "Friendly, busy hotel, ideal location for exploring
the Loch Ness area."

Glenmoriston Arms is a traditional Highland
sporting hotel which has stood in Glenmoriston for
over 200 years. It is situated in a beautiful part of
the Highlands only a few hundred yards from Loch
Ness with woodlands behind. There is an 'olde
worlde' atmosphere inside with the Moriston Bar
and Restaurant decorated with antique guns and
fishing rods evoking a sporting theme. The
restaurant menu is short and fresh with seasonally
changing dishes. Resident owners Neil and Carol
Scott ensure that guests enjoy their experience at
Glenmoriston. *(See advert Page 263.)*

Open all year except Christmas Day
🏨 Rooms: 8 with private facilities
SP Special rates available
✕ Lunch ££
✕ Dinner £££
Ⓥ Vegetarians welcome
⚘ Children welcome
♿ Facilities for disabled visitors – please
telephone prior to booking
🚭 No smoking in restaurant

**Wafer-thin slices of smoked venison served with
a pepperonata salad. King scallops sautéd with
julienne of leek and diced bacon topped with a
garlic and herb butter. Home-made Gaelic
coffee trifle.**

STB Commended 👑 👑 👑 👑
💳 Credit cards: Access/Mastercard/Eurocard,
Visa, Switch, Delta
👤 Resident Owners: Neil & Carol Scott

BUNCHREW HOUSE HOTEL

Inverness , Inverness-shire IV3 6TA
Tel: 01463 234917
Fax: 01463 710620

On A862 Inverness-Beauly, c. 10 minutes from centre of Inverness.

A country house hotel on the Beauly Firth.

- 17th century mansion.
- Country house cooking.
- "Consistently offers a high standard of comfort and food."

Bunchrew House is a short way out of Inverness nestling on the shores of the Beauly Firth, in 20 acres of woodland. The house dates back to 1621 when it was built by the 8th Lord Lovat, whose marriage the same year is commemorated by a stone fireplace lintel in the drawing room. Stewart and Lesley Dykes are continuing to renovate this lovely house and their painstaking attention to detail is apparent throughout the public and private rooms. The magnificent dining room overlooks the sea. Menus are innovative and interesting, and, like the rest of the house, the attention to detail is painstaking. Chef Walker's cooking embraces a variety of traditional and modern styles, with a penchant for deliciously complex sauces. Bunchrew has 1 AA Rosette.

Open all year
🏨 Rooms: 11 with private facilities
SP Special rates available
✗ Food served all day £££
✗ Lunch ££
✗ Dinner £££
Ⓥ Vegetarians welcome
⚹ Children welcome
♿ Facilities for disabled visitors
✄ No smoking in dining room
🐂 Member of the Scotch Beef Club

Marinade of Scottish salmon served with a beetroot vinaigrette. Pan-fried breast of Guinea fowl with pink grapefruit and prosciutto. Caramelised lemon tart with an Armagnac sauce.

STB Highly Commended 👑 👑 👑 👑
💳 Credit cards: Access/Mastercard/Eurocard, American Express, Visa
👤 Proprietors: Stewart & Lesley Dykes

DUNAIN PARK HOTEL

(On The A82) Inverness IV3 6JN
Tel: 01463 230512
Fax: 01463 224532

On A82, 1 mile from the Inverness town boundary.

A country house hotel in a beautiful setting, offering outstanding cuisine, cooked by a Master Chef.

- A handsome 19th century 'Georgian Italianate' hunting lodge.
- First rate Scottish cooking, with assured French influences.
- "Ann Nicoll's cooking is simply superb. The combinations of her food along with the charm of Dunain Park Hotel makes each meal a memorable experience."

Dunain Park is a fine Georgian country house, standing in six acres of gardens and woodlands, overlooking the Caledonian Canal. The large kitchen garden supplies herbs, vegetables and soft fruit. Ann and Edward Nicoll have won a high reputation for their establishment and several awards. Public and private rooms are immaculately furnished – and there is an indoor swimming pool and sauna. But it is for its food that Dunain is particularly renowned – the hotel has 1 AA Rosette. Ann Nicoll is self taught, with spells of training in France and encouragement from the famous John Tovey of Miller Howe. She goes to great length to source top quality local produce – the only beef she will use is from Highland cattle – and her style of cooking brings out the flavour of fresh produce, and enhances it with wonderfully assured sauces.

Open all year
🏨 Rooms: 14 with private facilities
SP Special rates available
✗ Dinner £££
Ⓥ Vegetarians welcome
⚹ Well-behaved children welcome
♿ Facilities for disabled visitors – residents only
✄ No smoking in dining room
🐂 Member of the Scotch Beef Club

Terrine of Guinea fowl and chicken enriched with port and wine, layered with venison, rabbit and pigeon. Salmon baked in a salt crust and served with a sorrel sauce. Chocolate roulade.

STB Deluxe 👑 👑 👑 👑
💳 Credit cards: Access/Mastercard/Eurocard, American Express, Visa, Diners Club, Switch, Delta
👤 Owners: Ann & Edward Nicoll

GLEN MHOR HOTEL & RESTAURANT
9-12 Ness Bank
Inverness IV2 4SG
Tel: 01463 234308
Fax: 01463 713170

On river bank below castle.

Family-run hotel in Inverness.

- Handsome buildings dating back to c. 1850.
- Both modern Taste of Scotland cooking and traditional Scottish and cosmopolitan.
- "Glen Mhor offers two contrasting restaurants, one formal one informal, but common to each is the good fresh food and excellent service."

The family run Glen Mhor Hotel is situated in the centre of Inverness just below the castle. It is a large 19th century townhouse which offers full private facilities in its 30 bedrooms, which are chintzy and mellow, one with four-poster. The public rooms are comfortable and furnished with a baronial Scottish theme. The Riverview Seafood Restaurant, overlooking the River Ness, offers an extensive à la carte menu stressing seafood, but with other meat and game choices. The Bistro, Nico's, which offers a less complex range of dishes, from char-grilled steaks to traditional Scottish and cosmopolitan dishes, vegetarian options available.

Open all year
Note: Riverview Restaurant closed Sun evenings Oct to Apr
- 🏨 Rooms: 29 with private facilities
- 🆂🅿 Special rates available
- ✗ Residents only
- ✗ Lunch (Nico's) £-££
  (Riverview – by arrangement)
- ✗ Dinner (Riverview Restaurant) £££
- Ⓥ Vegetarians welcome
- 🕈 Children welcome
- ♿ Facilities for disabled visitors
- ⌀ No smoking area in Nico's

Giant seafood platter. Neptune's pot pourri of local seafood. Almond basket with Glayva cream and fresh fruit.

STB Commended 👑 👑 👑 👑
- 💳 Credit cards: Access/Mastercard/Eurocard, American Express, Visa, Diners Club, Switch
- Ⓜ Proprietors: Nicol & Beverley Manson

GLENDRUIDH HOUSE HOTEL
by Castle Heather
Old Edinburgh Road South
Inverness IV1 2AA
Tel: 01463 226499
Fax: 01463 710745

2 miles from Inverness centre. ½ mile south off Sir Walter Scott Drive (formerly Inverness southern distributor road).

A quiet oasis two miles from Inverness, with extensive grounds, comfortably furnished bedrooms, and good quality cooking.

- A most unusual building, dating mainly from the 1850s.
- Traditional Scottish cooking.
- "The best of Highland produce, cooked traditionally and served in the immaculate surroundings of Glendruidh."

This is an unusual and attractive small country house set in three acres of woodland and lawns overlooking the Moray Firth: seclusion and privacy within minutes of Inverness, and with two golf courses close by, and a haven for non-smokers – smoking is prohibited even in the grounds. The Druid's Glen Bar provides an excellent range of whiskies and the relaxing sitting room has the unusual feature of being completely circular, its windows and doors shaped to the contour of the room. The elegant dining room (residents only) has an Italian marble fireplace and overlooks the tidy gardens. Christine Smith's simple table d'hôte menus change daily and offer classic dishes employing local game and fish.

Open all year except Christmas Day
- 🏨 Rooms: 7 with private facilities
- 🆂🅿 Special rates available
- ✗ Lunch – residents only ££
- ✗ Dinner – residents only ££-£££
- Ⓥ Vegetarians welcome
- 🕈 Children welcome
- ♿ Limited facilities for disabled visitors
- ⌀ No smoking throughout

Cullen skink. Highland game pie. Vanilla bavarois with cherry sauce.

STB Highly Commended 👑 👑 👑
- 💳 Credit cards: Access/Mastercard/Eurocard, American Express, Visa, Diners Club, Switch, JCB
- Ⓜ Proprietors: Michael & Christine Smith

MOYNESS HOUSE
6 Bruce Gardens
Inverness IV3 5EN
Tel: 01463 233836
Fax: 01463 233836

From A9 (north + south) and A862 Beauly, follow signs for A82 Fort William holiday route. Through Tomnahurich Street to Glenurquhart Road (A82), turn into Bruce Gardens diagonally opposite Highland Regional Council offices.

Lovely Victorian house in the centre of Inverness – close to Eden Court Theatre and Balnain House.

- A detached villa built in 1880, formerly the home of Neil Gunn, the celebrated Scottish author.
- First class home cooking.
- "Imaginative enjoyable food with some interesting variations on classic dishes."

Moyness House is situated in a quiet residential part of Inverness, within ten minutes walk of the town centre and Eden Court Theatre. It is tastefully decorated and appointed in a way which respects the Victorian nature of the house, and retains its elegance. The bedrooms are charmingly decorated and have en suite facilities; the principal rooms are smart and spacious. A large garden to the rear of the house is also available for guests to enjoy. Moyness is run by Jenny and Richard Jones – with Jenny being responsible for the cooking and her daily changing menus show flair and imagination. She goes to great lengths to source high quality Scottish produce, and treats her ingredients imaginatively, within a classic context – just as her many regular guests like it!

Open all year except Christmas wk
🏠 Rooms: 7 with private facilities
SP Special rates available
✘ Residents only
♀ Residents licence
✘ Dinner ££
Ⓥ Vegetarians welcome
★ Children welcome
✔ No smoking in restaurant

Stilton pears with poppyseed dressing. Grilled trout with lemon grass stuffing and julienne chips. Amaretto crème caramel.

STB Deluxe 👑 👑 👑
💳 Credit cards: Access/Mastercard/Eurocard, Visa, Switch, Delta
🔪 Proprietors: Richard & Jenny Jones

RESTAURANT NO 1
Greig Street
Inverness IV3 5PC
Tel: 01463 716363
Fax: 01463 234125

Centrally situated on the corner of Greig Street/ Huntly Street, on the west side of the River Ness.

A small congenial restaurant on the banks of the Ness.

- Restaurant specialising in fish.
- Modern Scottish cooking.
- "A well-appointed small restaurant with excellent fish dishes."

This comfortable and intimate L-shaped restaurant is on the corner of Greig Street/Huntly Street, on the west bank of the River Ness in the capital of the Highlands. It was formerly a shop and has fine views of the river, the old town and the castle. Now it has been refurbished in a style in keeping with the building and has a cosy atmosphere, somewhat Victorian. Fergus and Avril Ewart specialise in fresh West Coast seafood – lobsters and langoustines, crabs and scallops, halibut and turbot. Lamb and beef is also offered on the daily changing à la carte menu. The restaurant has 2 AA Rosettes.

Open all year except 24 to 26 Dec + 1 to 3 Jan
Closed Sun all year + Sun Mon Oct to Mar
✘ Lunch £
✘ Dinner £££
Ⓥ Vegetarians welcome
★ Children welcome
♿ Facilities for disabled visitors
✔ No smoking in restaurant

Cream of mushroom soup. Seafood casserole. Crème caramel.

💳 Credit cards: Access/Mastercard/Eurocard, Visa, Switch
🔪 Proprietors: Avril & Fergus Ewart

INVERURIE

PITTODRIE HOUSE HOTEL
Chapel of Garioch
by Inverurie, Aberdeenshire AB51 5HS
Tel: 01467 681444
Fax: 01467 681648

Off A96 just north of Inverurie 21 miles north of Aberdeen, 17 miles north of airport.

A country house hotel offering indoor and outdoor recreational facilities.

- Scottish baronial mansion, incorporating many architectural details of its long history.
- Well-cooked Scottish cuisine.
- "Welcoming historic family home set at the foot of Bennachie."

Standing in the shadow of Bennachie, in 2,000 acres of gardens and parkland, Pittodrie House originally belonged to a branch of the family of the Earls of Mar, the estate being granted to them by Robert the Bruce for their loyalty at the Battle of Bannockburn. The house was built in 1480, and added to in the baronial style in 1850. The latter influence is reflected in the opulent interiors of the public rooms, and the period atmosphere has been carefully maintained throughout the hotel. In the dining room the robust table d'hôte menus are well-balanced and offer just the kind of dishes one would expect in a grand country house, accompanied by herbs and vegetables from the hotel's own garden and a delicious selection of desserts.

Open all year
🏨 Rooms: 27 with private facilities
SP Special rates available
✕ Food served all day £££
✕ Lunch £-££
✕ Dinner £££
V Vegetarians welcome
🕇 Children welcome
🚭 No smoking in dining room

Grilled goats cheese with truffle oil dressing. Roast monkfish with stir-fry vegetables and oyster sauce. Almond and cinnamon cheesecake.

STB Commended 🏴 🏴 🏴 🏴
💳 Credit cards: Access/Mastercard/Eurocard, American Express, Visa, Diners Club, Mastercharge, Switch, Delta
👤 Managing Director: Martin McIlrath

ISLE OF ARRAN

APPLE LODGE
Lochranza
Isle of Arran KA27 8HJ
Tel: 01770 830229
Fax: 01770 830229

From Brodick, head north and follow the road to Lochranza (around 14 miles). As you enter the village pass the distillery and Apple Lodge is situated 300 yards on the left opposite golf course.

Attractive country house in charming island village.

- Edwardian house with adjoining cottage.
- High quality home cooking.
- "An impressive new addition to the 1997 Taste of Scotland Guide."

Originally the village manse, Apple Lodge is tranquilly located on the northern part of Arran in the delightful village of Lochranza, where the ferry from Kintyre docks. Set in its own appealing gardens, both the lodge – and the south-facing suite addition – Apple Cottage – are furnished beautifully to a very high standard. One can relax in the comfortable surroundings watching wild deer graze a few yards from the garden, whilst an eagle soars overhead. Meanwhile, Jeannie Boyd will be creating a deliciously mouth-watering dinner for all to enjoy.

Open all year except Christmas wk
🏨 Rooms: 4, 3 with private facilities (+ 1 suite)
SP Special rates available
✕ Residents only
Ⓤ Ⓨ Unlicensed – guests welcome to take own wine
🥪 Packed lunches £
✕ Dinner ££
V Vegetarians welcome
🕇 Children over 12 years welcome
🚭 No smoking in dining room + bedrooms

Slices of locally smoked salmon with lemon, watercress and fennel salad. Whole roast leg of Arran lamb with garlic, coriander, and rosemary, served with orange, redcurrant and port sauce. Arran hot strawberries and mangoes with cream.

STB Highly Commended 🏴 🏴 🏴
💳 No credit cards
👤 Proprietor/Chef: Jeannie Boyd

ARGENTINE HOUSE HOTEL
Shore Road, Whiting Bay
Isle of Arran KA27 8PZ
Tel: 01770 700662
Fax: 01770 700693

8 miles south of ferry terminal. First hotel on seafront at village entrance.

Family-run guest house with comfortable bedrooms.

- Victorian seaside villa.
- Scottish produce with a continental touch.
- "A delightful eating experience with good attention to detail."

Assya and Bruno bring an interesting blend of their Swiss hospitality combined with skilful use of Scottish produce to create meals with a lightly continental touch to delight the palate of their guests. Ideally located on the promenade there is the feeling of being invited into Assya and Bruno's home. From the moment you walk up the path, past a colourful array of flags on their three flag poles, European hints as to your hosts' nationality abound. Assya's impressive cooking mirrors this with appealing menus brimming over with local produce, including organically home-grown ingredients, and is influenced by her native Switzerland and neighbouring countries.

Open Dec to Oct
🏠 Rooms: 6 with private facilities
SP Special rates available
✗ Non-residents – by arrangement
ⓊⓁ ♀ Unlicensed – guests welcome to take own wine
✗ Dinner ££
Ⓥ Vegetarians welcome
⚹ Children welcome
⤧ No smoking in dining room

Barley risotto with Arran goats cheese and flowers. Salmon, scallops and scampi on a special red sauce. Trio of mousses au chocolat.

STB Commended 👑 👑 👑
⊞ Credit cards: Access/Mastercard/Eurocard, Visa
Ⓜ Owners: Assya & Bruno Baumgartner

AUCHRANNIE COUNTRY HOUSE HOTEL
Brodick
Isle of Arran KA27 8BZ
Tel: 01770 302234
Fax: 01770 302812

One mile north of Brodick Ferry Terminal and 400 yards from Brodick Golf Club.

Country house hotel and country club in Brodick.

- 19th century mansion, with substantial additions.
- Country house cooking.
- "Top quality dining in surroundings to match."

Auchrannie House is a pink sandstone Victorian country house, formerly the home of the Dowager Duchess of Hamilton. Today it has been fully refurbished in a reproduction period style with modern comforts. A number of self-catering 'lodges' have been built in the grounds, STB Deluxe 5 Crowns, (each accommodating up to six people), also a state-of-the-art leisure complex with 20m pool. Brambles Bistro is a popular venue for families for snacks and meals, and the Garden Restaurant (which extends the original dining room with a conservatory) offers more formal dining. The sizeable table d'hôte menu offers a good range of local Scottish meat and fish dishes complemented by fresh vegetables and a daily vegetarian speciality. Auchrannie has 1 AA Rosette.

Open all year
🏠 Rooms: 28 with private facilities
SP Special rates available
✗ Food served all day £
✗ Lunch £
✗ Dinner ££££
Ⓥ Vegetarians welcome
⚹ Children welcome
♿ Facilities for disabled visitors
⤧ No smoking in Garden Restaurant
⤧ Smoking area in Brambles Bistro

Marinaded red mullet, fried basil and sauce vierge. Tenderloin of pork centred by an apricot mousse with Aegean prunes and Armagnac sauce. Cloutie dumpling with Drambuie parfait.

STB Highly Commended 👑 👑 👑 👑 👑
⊞ Credit cards: Access/Mastercard/Eurocard, American Express, Visa, Switch
Ⓜ Managing Director: Iain Johnston

CREELERS SEAFOOD RESTAURANT
The Home Farm, Brodick
Isle of Arran KA27 8DD
Tel: 01770 302810
Fax: 01770 302797

From Brodick Pier, go north following coast road towards Brodick Castle and Corrie for 1½ miles. Restaurant on right.

Seafood bistro within Arran Visitors Centre.

- Sophisticated seafood bistro.
- Fish and modern Scottish cooking.
- "An outstanding restaurant for lovers of fine food."

Creelers Seafood Restaurant is based in the old bothy of the Brodick Castle Home Farm. Tim and Fran James have established it as an excellent seafood restaurant, where the decor is simple and colourful and the atmosphere has something continental about it. Tim once a trawlerman on the West Coast still provides much of the shellfish through his own boat. The rest of the produce is either purchased on the quayside of Kintyre or carefully sourced on the island or the mainland. There is also their own smokery adjacent, with the resulting produce appearing on the menu or for sale. Daily changing menus appear on black-boards, and are extremely good value. Service is friendly and efficient. Chef Robin Gray, who also grows the vegetables for the restaurant, organically, is professional and enthusiastic, and the style of his cooking is minimalistic, with flashes of colour and fascinating textures. Winner of Taste of Scotland Special Merit Award 1993.

Open mid Mar to 31 Oct
Closed Mon except Bank Holidays + during Jul/Aug
✕ Lunch except Mon £-££
✕ Dinner except Mon ££
Ⓥ Vegetarians welcome
⚲ Children welcome
♿ Facilities for disabled visitors

Rendezvous of local sea and shellfish with Pernod and dill sauce. Kintyre salmon with lemon and chive fumet. Cranachan cheesecake.

▤ Credit cards: Access/Mastercard/Eurocard, Visa
▮ Proprietors: Tim & Fran James

DUNVEGAN HOUSE HOTEL
Shore Road
Brodick
Isle of Arran KA27 8AJ
Tel: 01770 302811

Situated on the coast road, 500 yards from Ferry.

A well-run small hotel, right on the seafront at Brodick.

- Traditional red sandstone seafront hotel overlooking Brodick Bay on the Isle of Arran.
- Daily changing table d'hôte menu offering good traditional cooking.
- "Immaculately kept with a high standard of traditional cooking offering good value for money."

Dunvegan House Hotel is set back from the village's waterfront promenade by its own garden, and affords good views across the bay to Brodick Castle and Goatfell. David and Naomi Spencer arrived here from England seven years ago with no experience of the hotel business. They have learned fast, do all of the work with the help of a small dedicated team, and maintain a very high standard. Dunvegan is the past winner of the Booker Prize for Excellence – judged Best Hotel/Guest House in the UK. The dinner menus offer seasonally available local produce in a small choice of familiar dishes. The breakfasts are memorable, especially the locally smoked kippers.

Open Mar to Jan
🛏 Rooms: 9 with private facilities
✕ Residents only
⚲ Restricted licence
✕ Dinner ££
Ⓥ Vegetarians welcome
⚲ Children welcome
⚲ No smoking in bedrooms

Haggis with onion sauce. Arran lamb with rosemary gravy. Traditional puddings with home-made custard.

STB Highly Commended 👑 👑 👑
▤ No credit cards
▮ Proprietors: Mr David Spencer & Mrs N Spencer

GLEN CLOY FARMHOUSE

Glencloy Road, Brodick
Isle of Arran KA27 8DA
Tel: 01770 302351

On heading out of Brodick, towards Brodick Castle, turn left up the road with the post box on the wall. Follow signs for Glen Cloy – road becomes farm track.

A family-run farm guest house on Arran.

- Old farmhouse.
- Home cooking.
- "Fresh, traditional dishes in a Victorian farmhouse setting."

This is a charming old sandstone building in a little glen on the road to Brodick Castle. The bedrooms have a very homely air about them and two have private facilities. Mark and Vicki Padfield run the house and cook themselves. They bake their own bread, and the vegetables and herbs come from the garden. The food is traditional fare, locally sourced and carefully prepared and is served in the attractive, homely dining room overlooking the countryside. Coffee is served in the drawing room where one is surrounded by interesting local books, Vicki Padfield's embroideries, family photos, etc. – a most relaxing and enjoyable experience.

    Open 1 Mar to 7 Nov
🏨 Rooms: 5, 2 with private facilities
SP Special rates available
UL ♀ Unlicensed – guests welcome to take own wine
✗ Dinner ££
Ⓥ Vegetarians welcome
⚘ Children welcome
⚹ Facilities for disabled visitors
⚌ No smoking in dining room

Home-made mushroom and Arran mustard soup. Roast leg of Arran lamb with Glen Cloy redcurrant jelly. Ginger and marmalade sponge with custard sauce.

STB Commended 👑 👑
⊕ No credit cards
N Proprietors: Mark & Vicki Padfield

GLENISLE HOTEL

Shore Road, Lamlash
Isle of Arran KA27 8LS
Tel: 01770 600 559/258
Fax: 01770 600 966

On main street of Lamlash. 17 miles to Lochranza, alternate ferry for Kintyre.

Quiet, island hotel of considerable charm, where you will encounter friendly hospitality and efficient service.

- Traditional whitewashed hotel set in a neat garden overlooking Lamlash Bay.
- Home cooking.
- "Traditional fare in comfortable surroundings."

This hotel on the main street of Lamlash has a clean, scrubbed look with hanging flower baskets and awnings. The bedrooms are comfortably furnished, and those at the front have fine views of Lamlash Bay and Holy Isle (now a Buddhist retreat). There is a relaxed and friendly atmosphere about the place. In the cocktail lounge a feature has been made of wooden carvings from the famous old Clyde steamer, 'The Talisman'. The restaurant menu offers a decent range of dishes reflecting the Scottish and local Arran produce available.

    Open 1 Feb to 1 Nov + 1 Dec to 3 Jan
🏨 Rooms: 13 with private facilities
✗ Lunch £
✗ Dinner ££
Ⓥ Vegetarians welcome
⚘ Children welcome
⚹ Limited facilities for disabled visitors

Home-made soups and pâtés. Chicken suprême stuffed with haggis, with a cream and whisky sauce. Apple and mincemeat crumble.

STB Commended 👑 👑 👑 👑
⊕ Credit cards: Access/Mastercard/Eurocard, Visa, Switch
N Proprietor: Fred Wood

GRANGE HOUSE HOTEL
Whiting Bay
Isle of Arran KA27 8QH
Tel: 01770 700263
Fax: 01770 700263

8 miles south of ferry terminal at Brodick, ¼ mile past the centre of Whiting Bay village.

A delightful hotel with memorable gardens and fine views over Whiting Bay.

- Seaside house hotel.
- Traditional and innovative cooking.
- "The beautifully restored house plus Janet Hughes' excellent cooking add up to a memorable stay."

Grange House Hotel was built in dressed stone in 1896 and retains many of its original features. It has been sensitively decorated and furnished, and has fine views over Whiting Bay. Within the acre of garden is a putting green, and the hotel has a sauna. Clive and Janet Hughes have many years experience in the catering trade in England and their experience is manifested by the efficient service and the well-prepared and presented dinners they offer.

Open 15 Mar to 15 Nov + Christmas/New Year
🏠 Rooms : 9, 7 with private facilities
SP Special rates available
✕ Non-residents – by arrangement
✕ Dinner ££
V Vegetarians welcome
† Children welcome
♿ Facilities for disabled visitors
🚭 No smoking throughout

Venison sausage braised in red wine served with spiced cabbage. Lamlash Bay scallops with wild rice timbale. Quince parfait with tropical fruits.

STB Highly Commended 👑 👑 👑
💳 Credit cards: Access/Mastercard/Eurocard
👤 Proprietors: Clive & Janet Hughes

KILMICHAEL COUNTRY HOUSE HOTEL
Glen Cloy, by Brodick
Isle of Arran KA27 8BY
Tel: 01770 302219
Fax: 01770 302068

From Brodick Pier take road north 1½ miles, then turn inland at golf course following signs about ¾ mile.

Charming country house hotel set in a beautiful glen.

- Historic house with great period character.
- Superb modern cooking.
- "The practice of elegant hotel-keeping, brought to a fine art."

Kilmichael is believed to be the oldest house on Arran – the present building is late 17th century, but there was an early christian cell on the site. Described as a 'mansion' in the records, in fact it is an elegant and compact lodge, exquisitely furnished by its present owners (oriental antiques are a feature), who engagingly describe its attractions in order of importance as "... comfort, tranquillity, books and home-made ice cream." It is the only hotel on Arran graded 'Deluxe' by the STB and has two Red entries in Michelin and 2 AA Rosettes. The menus presented in the dining room are very interesting and demonstrate French and Italian influences. A five course table d'hôte menu and à la carte menu are available at dinner. Every dish has something unique and authentic about it, with piquant flavours and delicately spiced sauces.

Open all year except Christmas wk
🏠 Rooms: 6 with private facilities
SP Special rates available
✕ Dinner £££
✕ Dinner for non-residents – booking essential
V Vegetarians welcome
♿ Facilities for disabled visitors
🚭 No smoking in dining room + bedrooms

Mille feuille of Arran king scallops seared in Pernod with a wasabi beurre blanc. Valentines of lamb with Grenadine pomegranate sauce and Glen Cloy chanterelles. Soured crème brûlée with strawberries and rhubarb in gin.

STB Deluxe 👑 👑 👑 👑
💳 Credit cards: Access/Mastercard/Eurocard, Visa
👤 Partners: Geoffrey Botterill & Antony Butterworth

ISLE OF BENBECULA

DARK ISLAND HOTEL
Liniclate, Isle of Benbecula
Western Isles PA88 5PJ
Tel: 01870 603030/602414
Fax: 01870 602347

Benbecula lies between North and South Uist (Western Isles). A865 to Liniclate. Hotel is c. 6 miles from the airport.

A modern, purpose built hotel in the Outer Hebrides.

- A motel with vivid antique red roof.
- Traditional Scottish cooking.
- "Plain good traditional style cooking – generous portions."

The Dark Island Hotel – the name comes from a well-known Hebridean song – is a surprising discovery in the Outer Hebrides. The Lace Restaurant – offering table d'hôte and à la carte menus; a wonderful range of fresh local shellfish, cheeses and smoked produce including salmon, venison, chicken and eel which is equally matched by a lengthy list of steaks and grills with salad, chips or baked potato on offer. Flavours are fresh and positive. As an alternative for lunch, 'Carriages' carvery offers a selection of cold seafoods and hot roasts.

Open all year
🏨 Rooms: 42 with private facilities
🆂🅿 Special rates available
✗ Lunch £
✗ Dinner ££
Ⓥ Vegetarians welcome
🇰 Children welcome
♿ Facilities for disabled visitors

Cold poached salmon. Roast haunch of venison. Lemon mousse.

STB Commended 🛏 🛏 🛏 🛏
💳 Credit cards: Access/Mastercard/Eurocard, Visa
𝕞 General Manager: Mr Stephen Peteranna

ISLE OF BUTE

NEW FARM RESTAURANT WITH ROOMS
New Farm, Mount Stuart
Isle of Bute PA20 9NA
Tel: 01700 831646

Just 6 miles from the ferry and 1 mile from Mount Stuart House and Gardens.

Whitewashed converted cottage farmhouse on working dairy and sheep farm.

- Whitewashed farmhouse.
- Enthusiastic, adventurous and talented cooking.
- "A welcoming comfortable farmhouse on a beautiful island."

New Farm is set on a 1,000 acre farm on the beautiful Island of Bute. Formerly four cottages it is now home to Carole and Michael Howard and their three children. The views from the farmhouse are magnificent and the warm welcome and homely atmosphere ensure that guests quickly settle in. On arrival you are offered home-baked afternoon tea – Carole is an accomplished baker. Her cooking is tackled with enormous enthusiasm and interest and produces imaginative and tasty meals making full use of locally sourced supplies. As Carole says "if we are unable to grow it, make it or rear it we will certainly source it locally from our Island, the Isle of Bute." Guests can choose to eat on their own but most people prefer to join the other guests and have an interesting and convivial evening after being welcomed in Gaelic to the table. A most welcome addition to Taste of Scotland.

Open all year
🏨 Rooms: 3
🅤🅛 ♀ Unlicensed – guests welcome to take own wine
✗ Lunch – reservation essential ££
✗ Dinner – reservation essential £££
Ⓥ Vegetarians welcome
🇰 Children welcome
♿ Facilities for disabled visitors

Home-made soups and broths served with home-baked bread. Honey glazed New Farm lamb casseroled on a bed of apricots, fresh tarragon and scallions. Bournville baked bananas served in a puddle of cream.

💳 No credit cards
𝕞 Proprietor: Carole Howard

ISLE OF GIGHA

GIGHA HOTEL
Isle of Gigha, Argyll PA41 7AA
Tel: 01583 505 254
Fax: 01583 505 244

A83 Lochgilphead-Campbeltown, c. 18 miles south of Tarbert turn into Tayinloan. Follow Gigha Ferry sign.

A traditional, family-run hotel and island with glorious views.

- A classic stone-built and white-painted 18th century hostelry.
- Traditional Scottish home cooking.
- "A relaxing place to stay on a most beautiful and friendly island."

Overlooking the Sound of Gigha towards the hills of Kintyre, Gigha Hotel is the island's original inn and traces its origins back two centuries. The island was described by our inspector "one of the wonders of our western seaboard", and although it is only 20 minutes ferry trip from Kintyre, you immediately step back a couple of decades. Life is gentle and slow-moving. The hotel combines old-world charm with modern comfort. The accommodation is cottage style; and the friendly hotel bar is popular with locals and visiting yachts-men. The hotel also has several cottages on the island if you wish to be more independent. The restaurant specialises in Scottish country cooking, and makes good use of the seafood landed by local fishing and lobster boats. Table d'hôte menus change daily. William and Sandra Howden, the resident owners of the hotel, are attentive and happy to accept any special requests.

Open Mar to Oct
🛏 Rooms: 13, 11 with private facilities
🆂🅿 Special rates available
✕ Lunch £
✕ Dinner 4 course menu £-££
🆅 Vegetarians welcome – prior notice required
🧒 Children welcome

Haggis with gooseberry sauce. Grilled Gigha salmon coated with lime and hazelnut butter. Mandarin zig-zag.

STB Commended 👑 👑 👑
💳 Credit cards: Access/Mastercard/Eurocard, Visa
👤 Proprietors: William & Sandra Howden

ISLE OF HARRIS

ALLAN COTTAGE GUEST HOUSE
Tarbert
Isle of Harris HS3 3DJ
Tel: 01859 502146

Upper road overlooking ferry road, c. 600 yards from ferry.

An attractive family-run guest house in Harris' main village.

- A converted telephone exchange on Tarbert's main street.
- Traditional Scottish cooking.
- "Good traditional cooking – perfect after a day's hill-walking in Harris."

This attractive old building has been interestingly converted maintaining many of the original features. It has been extended to form a house of unusual charm; quiet and homely. Rooms are all well furnished in cottage style and the bedrooms have private facilities. Bill and Evelyn Reed are wonderfully enthusiastic and look after guests with true island hospitality. The dinner menu is discussed with guests in the morning, so that individual preferences can be taken into account. The cooking is interesting and imaginative and of a very high standard; Bill makes use of fresh local produce whenever it can be obtained. A charming unpretentious establishment.

Open 1 Apr to 30 Sep
🛏 Rooms: 3 with private facilities
🆂🅿 Special rates available
✕ Residents only
🆄🅻 Unlicensed
✕ Dinner 4 course menu ££
🆅 Vegetarians welcome – by prior arrangement
🧒 Children welcome
🚭 No smoking in dining room + bedrooms

Grilled avocado with prawns in a cheese sauce. Wild Harris salmon served with whisky cream sauce. Almond tart with apricot coulis.

STB Highly Commended 👑 👑 👑
💳 No credit cards
👤 Joint Proprietors: Bill & Evelyn Reed

ARDVOURLIE CASTLE
Isle of Harris
HS3 3AB
Tel: 01859 50 2307
Fax: 01859 50 2348

¼ mile off A859. 24 miles from Stornoway, 8 miles from Tarbert.

A lovingly restored house run by Derek and Pamela Martin, with four elegant and comfortable bedrooms.

- Recently restored 19th century hunting lodge on the island of Harris.
- Traditional Scottish cooking.
- "This is a very special place, stunning setting – wonderful food, beautiful house. I wish I could keep it a secret."

Ardvourlie stands on the shores of Loch Seaforth under the imposing crags of Clisham. It was built in 1863 by the Earl of Dunmore but fell into a semi-ruinous state in recent years – which makes the achievement of Derek and Pamela Martin all the more remarkable. They have restored the place magnificently, with sensitivity and outstandingly good taste. The castle is furnished in keeping with its period. The dining room offers views over the wilderness beyond and it uses designs and furniture from the Victorian and Art Nouveau periods. Here you will encounter the Martins' fine cooking. Much of the raw materials that are unavailable locally are very carefully sourced on the mainland which comprises dishes to suit all tastes using as much local produce as is available on this remote island, and where necessary fresh foods are brought in by sea from the mainland.

Open 1 Apr to 31 Oct
- Rooms: 4
- ✕ Residents only
- ♀ Restricted licence
- ✕ Dinner 4 course menu £££
- Ⓥ Vegetarians welcome – advance notice essential
- ☆ Children welcome
- ♿ Facilities for disabled visitors
- ⚬ No smoking in dining room

Melon with orange, yoghurt and mint. Grilled monkfish kebabs marinated with onion, fennel and lime. Burnt cream with raspberries.

- ⊞ No credit cards
- 🅺 Owner: D G Martin

LEACHIN HOUSE
Tarbert
Isle of Harris
HS3 3AH
Tel: 01859 502157

1 mile from Tarbert on A859 to Stornoway, sign-posted on lochside.

Charming Victorian house of local interest.

- Substantial lochside Victorian house.
- Modern Scottish cooking.
- "I wish I could have stayed for longer, the food was delicious and the house fascinating."

Linda and Diarmuid Evelyn Wood have turned Leachin House (which means house among the rocks) into a most attractive and welcoming guest house, without losing any of the charms and gracious proportions of this lovely Victorian building. Dining at Leachin is a most enjoyable experience. The views across the loch are breath-taking, the dining room itself is fascinating with its 100 year old French hand-painted wallpaper, and the skill and care with which Linda cooks and presents the food is worth a journey to Harris just to eat there! The wonderful produce of the islands, particularly lamb and seafood, feature regularly on the fixed menu and each course illustrates a well-judged mix of both simple and complex food preparation. French spoken.

Open all year except Christmas + New Year
- Rooms: 3, 1 en suite, 1 with private facilities
- SP Special rates available
- ✕ Residents only
- Ⓤ Unlicensed
- ✕ Dinner ££
- ☆ Children over 10 years welcome
- ⚬ No smoking in dining room

Scallops in vermouth. Fillet of lamb with port wine and redcurrant sauce. Treacle tart with Mascarpone and nutmeg ice cream.

- ⊞ Credit cards: Access/Mastercard/Eurocard, Visa, Delta
- 🅺 Owners: Linda & Diarmuid Evelyn Wood

SCARISTA HOUSE
Isle of Harris PA85 3HX
Tel: 01859 550 238
Fax: 01859 550 277

On A859, 15 miles south-west of Tarbert
(Western Isles).

**Distinctive country house hotel in a peaceful
island location.**

- Converted Georgian mansion house with
  magnificent views.
- Modern Scottish country house cooking.
- "Top quality food carefully sourced, well-
  prepared and cooked."

Scarista House overlooks a three mile long shell
sand beach on the dramatic Atlantic coast of
Harris. The eight bedrooms all have views out to
sea. This makes for an ever-changing panorama of
scenery and atmosphere. The bedrooms are
comfortably and traditionally furnished with
bathrooms en suite. The public rooms which also
include an extensive library are cheery and
welcoming and the absence of radio and television
is an asset not a liability. The hotel's dining room
has featured in many guides worldwide and is
known particularly for its superb fish and shellfish.
There is a very decent wine list chosen to
complement the dishes on offer.

Open May to Sep
🏠 Rooms: 8 with private facilities
♀ Residents licence
✗ Dinner £££
Ⓥ Vegetarians welcome
🖈 Children over eight years welcome
♿ Facilities for disabled visitors
🚭 No smoking throughout

**Scallops in oatmeal. Fillet of lamb with a Madeira
sauce and saffron potatoes. Poached pears in
red wine.**

💳 No credit cards
🋥 Proprietors: Ian & Jane Callaghan

Isle of Islay   108

THE CROFT KITCHEN
Port Charlotte
Isle of Islay
Argyll PA49 7UN
Tel: 01496 850230

On the main road into Port Charlotte opposite the
Museum of Islay Life.

A charming family restaurant.

- Informal village bistro style restaurant.
- Home cooking.
- "Simple or sophisticated – whatever you
  choose is well-cooked and exceptional value."

Joy and Douglas Law took over the Croft Kitchen in
1995, having run a hotel on the island for ten years.
The Croft Kitchen itself was established 18 years
ago in a fine situation close to a sandy beach, with
views of the Paps of Jura and Loch Indaal. As well
as home baking, home-made soups, family snacks
and sandwiches, the Kitchen now also offers a
good range of daily 'specials', chosen from a
blackboard, which features local scallops, oysters,
mussels, lamb and so on – at incredibly reasonable
prices. A friendly, informal place where the whole
family is made welcome.

Open mid Mar to mid Oct
Note: Closed second Thu in Aug (Islay
Show Day)
Ⓤ Unlicensed
✗ Food served all day £
✗ Lunch £
✗ Dinner £
Ⓥ Vegetarians welcome
🖈 Children welcome

Local produce as in season.

💳 No credit cards
🋥 Joint Proprietors: Joy & Douglas Law

GLENMACHRIE FARMHOUSE
Port Ellen, Isle of Islay
Argyll PA42 7AW
Tel: 01496 30 2560

Midway on A846 between Port Ellen and
Bowmore.

Farm guest house near Port Ellen.

- Traditional island farmhouse.
- Highland speciality table.
- "Attractive and cleverly presented dishes using ingredients sourced from the farm."

Glenmachrie is a mixed farm of 450 acres, with cattle, sheep, ponies, horses and a small fold of Highland cattle. Rachel and Alasdair Whyte welcome guests into their home with great warmth and a genuine Hebridean hospitality. Generous helpings of home cooking are cheerfully served in the candlelit dining room. Rachel offers a choice of dishes which include meat and game from the farm and salmon and wild brown trout from their own loch and river which overlooks the famous Machrie golf links. With access to private fishing guests are also offered the opportunity to make their own catches.

Open all year
🛏 Rooms: 5 with private facilities
✗ Residents only
🍷 Unlicensed – guests welcome to take own wine
✗ Dinner ££
🧒 Children over five years welcome
♿ Facilities for disabled visitors (ground floor bedroom)
🚭 No smoking throughout

Courgette and Brie soup with warmed oatcakes and warmed continental bread. Rendezvous of local sea and shellfish in a cream sauce, lightly scented with fresh fennel. Fresh garden rhubarb fool served with home-made shortbread and jug of cream.

STB Highly Commended 👑 👑 👑
💳 No credit cards
🅗 Proprietor: Rachel Whyte

KILCHOMAN HOUSE
by Bruichladdich, Isle of Islay
Argyll PA49 7UY
Tel: 01496 850382
Fax: 01496 850277

Take B8018 road signposted Kilchoman, off A847.
6 miles from Bruichladdich.

A Georgian manse in rural Islay.

- Informal restaurant with rooms.
- Imaginative home cooking.
- "Combined good standards with informal atmosphere."

Kilchoman is a charming Georgian, small 'C Listed' former manse tucked away in a little hollow, well off the beaten track on the Atlantic side of the Rhinns of Islay. It is the home of Stuart and Lesley Taylor, who have two rooms in the house itself and five self-catering cottages nearby (minimum 3 nights stay, early booking advised). Lesley's cooking is popular locally (reservations must be made in advance); she uses local produce to present a straightforward table d'hôte menu offering a good choice of starters and main courses.

Open all year
🛏 Rooms: 2, 1 with private facilities
🍷 Table licence
✗ Dinner except Sun ££
Ⓥ Vegetarians welcome – prior notice required
🧒 Children welcome
🚭 No smoking in restaurant

Islay scallops with terrine of leeks and Lanark Blue dressing. Pan-fried saddle of Rhinns venison with home-made rowan jelly. Chocolate and orange bombe and Kilchoman mist.

💳 No credit cards
🅗 Proprietors: Stuart & Lesley Taylor

ISLE OF ISLAY

KILMENY FARMHOUSE

Ballygrant, Isle of Islay
Argyll PA45 7QW
Tel: 01496 840 668
Fax: 01496 840 668

½ mile south of Ballygrant village – look for sign at road end, ¾ mile up private road.

A charming house with spectacular views.

- 19th century farmhouse.
- Home cooking.
- "A perfect setting and home in which to indulge in the pleasures of genuine care and hospitality."

Kilmeny is a working farm of 300 acres, within easy reach of Port Askaig. Margaret and Blair Rozga have been running their guest house for over 20 years and enjoy a loyal following of guests from all over the world. The bedrooms and public rooms are very elegantly decorated, with many fine antiques and luxurious furnishings. Margaret is an accomplished cook and uses only the finest produce all of which is locally sourced. Her menus are well-planned and imaginative requiring a great deal of skill and careful organisation – all of which she accomplishes single-handedly to great effect.

Open all year except Christmas + New Year
- Rooms: 3 with private facilities
- Special rates available
- Residents only
- Unlicensed – guests welcome to take own wine
- Dinner except Sun ££
- Vegetarians welcome
- Children welcome
- No smoking throughout

Terrine of salmon, prawns and avocado. Pot-roasted Jura pheasant with Hunter sauce. Little summer puddings with chantilly cream.

STB Deluxe 👑 👑 👑
- No credit cards
- Proprietor: Margaret Rozga

ISLE OF LEWIS

CLEASCRO GUEST HOUSE

Achmore, Lochs
Isle of Lewis HS2 9DU
Tel: 01851 860 302
Fax: 01851 860 302

A859 from Stornoway for 7 miles. Right turn onto A858. Cleascro is on right 2 miles on.

Attractive modern family-run guest house in rural Lewis.

- Modern villa.
- Skilled traditional cooking.
- "One of the best lamb dishes I have ever tasted."

Cleascro is a most comfortable and welcoming small guest house, ideally situated for exploring the Isle of Lewis. Gaelic speaking Donna Murray is a gifted and imaginative cook making use of her formal training to devise menus based around the top quality local ingredients of fish, venison and lamb. All vegetables and herbs are from the garden, bread is made daily.

Open all year except Christmas Day
- Rooms: 3 with private facilities
- Special rates available
- Residents only
- Unlicensed – guests welcome to take own wine
- Dinner ££
- Vegetarians welcome
- Children welcome
- No smoking in dining room

Asparagus and seafood salad in lemon and oil dressing. Rack of lamb with herby crust with kidney and celery stuffing. Spiced apple and raisin bake with a crunchy rolled oat topping.

STB Highly Commended 👑 👑 👑
- No credit cards
- Owners: Donna & Geoff Murray

ESHCOL GUEST HOUSE

Breasclete, Callanish
Isle of Lewis HS2 9ED
Tel: 01851 621 357

On A858, 17 miles from Stornoway, 40 miles from Tarbert.

A guest house on the Isle of Lewis.

- A small croft in the weaving village of Breasclete.
- Home cooking.
- "A most attractive small guest house with excellent home cooking and friendly hosts."

Isobel and Neil Macarthur run this croft on the West Coast of Lewis, within walking distance of the mysterious Stones of Callanish. There are wonderful views across Loch Roag to the island of Great Bernera and beyond, with the hills of South Uig and Harris in the distance. The three bedrooms all have their own bathrooms and have a nice simple rustic feel to them. This is a small establishment and Neil will regale you for hours (in Gaelic if you desire) with tales and folklore of the area and its past. The food here is home cooking at its best with no pretensions. Eshcol really does offer 'real island hospitality.'

Open 1 Mar to 31 Oct
🏠 Rooms: 3 with private facilities
✗ Residents only
Ⓤ ♀ Unlicensed – guests welcome to take own wine
✗ Dinner 4 course menu ££
Ⓥ Vegetarians welcome
🕏 Children over 10 years welcome
🚭 No smoking in dining room

Carrot and coriander soup. New season roast gigot of lamb with fresh vegetables from the garden. Lemon mousse.

STB Highly Commended 👑 👑 👑
💳 No credit cards
🏶 Owners: Neil & Isobel Macarthur

HANDA

18 Keose Glebe (Ceos), Lochs
Isle of Lewis HS2 9JX
Tel: 01851 830 334

1½ miles off A859, 12 miles south of Stornoway, 25 miles north of Tarbert, Harris: last house in village of Ceos.

A hilltop house on the Hebridean island of Lewis; a small family-run guest house which provides comfortable accommodation and good food.

- This is a lovely home, furnished in pine with all modern facilities.
- Traditional Scottish home cooking.
- "This wonderful little guest house illustrates just what is meant by a Taste of Scotland."

This is the last house in the Hebridean haven of Keose village. It is idyllically appointed on top of a hill overlooking a private loch and ideally positioned for exploring the island and nearby Harris. Stepping from the house itself you can follow a range of pursuits from bird-watching to hill-walking and (if you are fortunate) otter sighting. The loch provides brown trout fishing and a boat and equipment can be hired from the house. The owner, Christine Morrison, runs the guest house with genuine island hospitality. Alongside traditional recipes, she does all of her own baking and uses the best of local seafood and fresh produce from her garden. Winner of The Macallan Personality of the Year Award 1995.

Open 2 May to 5 Oct
🏠 Rooms: 3, 1 with private facilities
SP Special rates available
Ⓤ ♀ Unlicensed – guests welcome to take own wine
✗ Dinner ££
🚭 No smoking throughout
Ⓥ Vegetarians welcome

Celery and apple soup. Chicken in tarragon with fruity aubergine boats. Coffee meringue gâteau.

STB Highly Commended 👑 👑
💳 No credit cards
🏶 Owners: Murdo & Christine Morrison

THE PARK GUEST HOUSE & RESTAURANT
30 James Street, Stornoway
Isle of Lewis Western Isles HS1 2QN
Tel: 01851 70 2485

500 yards from ferry terminal. At junction of Matheson Road, James Street and A866 to airport and Eye peninsula.

A traditional family-run guest house in the centre of town.

- A stone-built Victorian guest house.
- Traditional Scottish cooking.
- "Excellent fresh fish and shellfish, will suit the most robust of appetites."

A substantial stone-built B Listed building dating from the 1880s, standing in the centre of Stornoway, this house has a homely atmosphere and Roddy and Catherine Afrin are friendly hosts. Catherine was trained in interior design at the Glasgow School of Art, and the house has benefited from her skill and good taste. Note the original Glasgow-style fireplace in the dining room. Roddy was formerly head chef on an oil rig in the North Sea. His robust à la carte menus use fresh fish from Stornoway and the West Coast fishing boats, and local lamb and venison. Each dish is cooked to order. The restaurant is popular with local people.

Open all year except 24 Dec to 5 Jan
Note: Restaurant closed Sun Mon
🏠 Rooms: 8, 3 with private facilities
🎒 Packed lunches available £
✗ Dinner – residents only ££
✗ Dinner (Restaurant) Tue to Sat £££
Ⓥ Vegetarians welcome
🧍 Children welcome
♿ Facilities for non-residential disabled visitors

Scaliscro oysters – naturelle or au gratin. Grilled collops of Lewis lamb with minted cabbage and rosemary jus. Deep-fried ice cream and home-made butterscotch sauce.

STB Commended 👑 👑
💳 No credit cards
👤 Proprietor: Catherine Afrin
👤 Chef/Proprietor: Roddy Afrin

Isle of Mull 110

ARDFENAIG HOUSE
by Bunessan, Isle of Mull, Argyll PA67 6DX
Tel: 01681 700210
Fax: 01681 700210

2 miles west of Bunessan on A849, turn right on private road to Ardfenaig House, ½ mile.

A lovely old country house hotel surrounded by woodland, sea and moorland on the Isle of Mull.

- Originally an estate factor's house then shooting lodge in a glorious position on the shores of Loch Caol on the Ross of Mull.
- Assured country house cooking.
- "A delightful way to spend an evening is to dine at Ardfenaig."

Ardfenaig House stands in the southwest corner of Mull midway between Bunessan and Fionnphort. The house is home to Malcolm and Jane Davidson, hospitable and welcoming hosts who look after you charmingly. It has five en suite bedrooms and the newly refurbished Coach House by a small burn 50 yards away provides additional self-catering accommodation for four to six people. In front of the house is a small jetty and Malcolm will be happy to take you for a sail in the bay or an early morning fishing trip. The drawing room has magnificent views over Loch Caol and a new conservatory dining room is being added for 1997. The excellent food is freshly prepared in the kitchen from fresh local produce and is beautifully presented. Menus are short but imaginative, and since the Davidsons have a share in a French vineyard, the wine list is rather special.

Open 26 Mar to 25 Oct
🏠 Rooms: 5 with private facilities
♧ Restricted licence
✗ Dinner 4 course menu £££
Ⓥ Vegetarians welcome
🚭 No smoking in dining room + bedrooms

Asparagus and pine nut tartlets. Medallions of halibut with scallops and prawns in white wine cream sauce. Iced Grand Marnier nougat with an apricot coulis.

STB Highly Commended 👑 👑 👑
💳 Credit cards: Access/Mastercard/Eurocard, Visa
👤 Owners: Malcolm & Jane Davidson

ARDRIOCH FARM GUEST HOUSE
Dervaig, Isle of Mull
Argyll PA75 6QR
Tel: 01688 400264
Fax: 01688 400264

1 mile from Dervaig on Calgary road (B8073).

A delightful farm guest house with four bedrooms and pine-panelled annexe in an informal garden setting, with wonderful views.

- A modern bungalow/farmhouse on a working 70 acre farm.
- Scottish home cooking.
- "A delightful home to stay in and explore Mull."

This cedar-built bungalow on the west coast of Mull can accommodate eight guests. It is the pleasant, comfortable home of Jenny and Jeremy Matthew – tastefully furnished with antiques, good pictures and lots of books. It is redolent of cedar wood and you will find yourself living very much amongst the busy clutter of a warm family home. Jenny's meals are delicious and homely; all dishes use fresh local produce. The day's menu is fixed, according to what is available, but she is more than happy to accommodate any preferences or requests from her guests where possible, if you ask her in advance. The house is two miles from Croig harbour, where Ardrioch's inter-island day cruises depart for wildlife and sightseeing trips.

Open 1 Apr to 30 Oct
🏨 Rooms: 5, 2 with private facilities
✕ Dinner ££
✕ Residents only
🍷 ♀ Unlicensed – guests welcome to take own wine
Ⓥ Vegetarians welcome
ᚲ Children welcome
🚭 No smoking throughout

Salad of smoked Tobermory trout and Mull prawns with home-made savoury scones. Local venison casserole with mushrooms, rowan jelly and sherry. Gooseberry and ginger ice cream.

STB Commended 👑 👑
💳 No credit cards
👤 Owners: Jenny & Jeremy Matthew

ASSAPOL HOUSE HOTEL
Bunessan
Isle of Mull
Argyll PA67 6DW
Tel: 01681 700 258
Fax: 01681 700 445

From Craignure-A849 towards Fionnphort. When approaching Bunessan, pass village school on the right, take first road on left signed Assapol House.

A delightful, spacious old house in a sheltered corner of Mull.

- Small country house hotel.
- Stylish country cooking.
- "A very comfortable, friendly house."

The feature that immediately impresses the visitor to Assapol is the care and attention to detail that your hosts, the Robertson family, manifest in every department: fresh flowers in the bedrooms, beds turned down, sewing kits supplied, etc. Assapol House, itself a former manse, is 200 years old and overlooks the loch of the same name, with the Burg Peninsula, the Treshnish Isles and Staffa beyond. Wildlife, secluded beaches and historical sites abound in this delightful corner of Mull. The dinner menu offers a choice of starters and puddings and a set main course. The food is locally sourced and features local delicacies; it is sensitively cooked and imaginatively presented; and it is extremely good value. Assapol has 1 AA Rosette.

Open Apr to Oct
🏨 Rooms: 6 with private facilities
🆂🅿 Special rates available
✕ Residents only
♀ Restricted hotel licence
✕ Dinner ££
Ⓥ Vegetarians welcome – by prior arrangement
ᚲ Children over 10 years welcome
🚭 No smoking in dining room

Salad of smoked mackerel, hot smoked trout and mussels. Roast fillet of venison served with a port jus. Apricot, ginger and orange crumble.

STB Highly Commended 👑 👑 👑
💳 Credit cards: Access/Mastercard/Eurocard, Visa, Switch, Delta
👤 Partners: Onny, Thomas & Alex Robertson

BREMENVOIR HOUSE

Ardtun, Bunessan
Isle of Mull, Argyll
PA67 6DH
Tel: 01681 700527

Follow main Craignure to Iona road for approx 32 miles. Turn right immediately past sign 'Lee' down small road. Go through 2 gates across the road – house is next on right.

Comfortable modern home in lovely setting.

- Modern farmhouse.
- Skilled home cooking.
- "A comfortable and considerate home with excellent cooking."

This is definitely 'off the beaten track' and well worth a visit for those wishing to get away from it all. Mr and Mrs Acey are friendly, welcoming young hosts. He is a sea fisherman and brings home some of the day's catch to the table. Mrs Acey is considerably skilled in the kitchen and serves excellent dishes to the table. Much of the charm here is the comfort and attractiveness of the interior. Mrs Acey is a skilled needlewoman and this is evident throughout with thoughtful touches in her home.

Open all year except Christmas
🏠 Rooms: 3, 1 with private facilities
🍶 Unlicensed – guests welcome to take own wine
🍴 Packed lunch £
✖ Dinner except Sun £££
🚭 No smoking in upstairs/bedrooms

Home-made seafood soup. Lobster salad. Home-made sponge pudding.

STB Commended 👑 👑
💳 No credit cards
👤 Owner: Mrs Melanie Acey

CALGARY FARMHOUSE HOTEL

Calgary, nr Dervaig
Isle of Mull, Argyll
PA75 6QW
Tel: 01688 400256
Fax: 01688 400256

About 9 miles from Dervaig on B8073, just up hill from Calgary beach.

A farm guest house with tea-room and gallery.

- Converted farm steadings.
- Home cooking.
- "Delicious home baking and freshly prepared food."

Calgary Farmhouse is just up the hill from the beautiful white sands of Calgary Beach. The farm buildings and courtyard have recently been sensitively converted by Julia and Matthew Reade into nine bedrooms with private facilities, and two public rooms. Exposed stonework, wooden furniture and wood-burning stoves all contribute to a warm and cosy environment. The Dovecote Restaurant offers an à la carte menu which changes four times a week according to the seasonal produce available. The accent is on simple, home cooking in an informal atmosphere while the family's fishing connections ensure a wonderful supply of Mull's bountiful catches. There is also a tea-room, The Carthouse Gallery, charmingly converted and open throughout the day for light lunches and home baking. A changing exhibition of pictures by local artists is displayed here, many of them for sale.

Open Apr to Oct inclusive
🏠 Rooms: 9 with private facilities
✖ Lunch £
✖ Dinner ££
Ⓥ Vegetarians welcome
👶 Children welcome
🚭 Smoking discouraged whilst others are eating

Escalopes of seared salmon with a piquant marinated cucumber salad. Locally dived scallops meunière, pan-fried with parsley butter and finished with cream. Mulberry and apple crumble.

STB Commended 👑 👑 👑
💳 Credit cards: Access/Mastercard/Eurocard, Visa, Switch
👤 Proprietors: Matthew & Julia Reade

DRUIMARD COUNTRY HOUSE

Dervaig, Isle of Mull
Argyllshire PA75 6QW
Tel: 01688 400345/400291
Fax: 01688 400345

Situated adjacent to Mull Little Theatre, well signposted from Dervaig village.

A small country house hotel run by husband and wife.

- A restored Victorian manse.
- Modern Scottish cooking.
- "Cooked to perfection – what more can one say!"

Druimard is just on the outskirts of the pretty village of Dervaig, eight miles from Tobermory. The old house has been beautifully restored by Haydn and Wendy Hubbard, who run their hotel with the standards of comfort one would expect from a country house: service is professional, the en suite bedrooms are very comfortable, the restaurant has a strong reputation, and has been recognised by the award of an AA Rosette. The table d'hôte menus have moved with the current eating trends towards a large choice of fish which is locally caught and meat which is traditionally reared. The cooking is assured, fresh and imaginative with unusual sauces and everything is prepared to order.

Open 1 Apr to end Oct
🏠 Rooms: 6 with private facilities
SP Special rates available
♀ Restaurant licence only
✗ Lunch – residents only £
✗ Dinner – non-residents except Sun £££
Ⓥ Vegetarians welcome
🧒 Children welcome
🚭 No smoking in restaurant

Filo pastry baskets filled with a medley of seafood. Noisettes of Scotch lamb with hotpot potatoes, braised lentils, caramelised shallots and rosemary and thyme-scented juices. Sinful chocolate truffle terrine with fresh Mull raspberry sauce.

STB Highly Commended 👑 👑 👑 👑
💳 Credit cards: Access/Mastercard/Eurocard
👤 Partners: Mr & Mrs H R Hubbard

KILLIECHRONAN HOUSE

Isle of Mull
Argyll PA72 6JU
Tel: 01680 300403
Fax: 01680 300463

Leaving ferry turn right to Tobermory A849. At Salen turn left to B8035. After 2 miles turn right to Ulva ferry B8073. Killiechronan House on right after 300 metres.

A comfortable and secluded corner in one of the prettiest parts of Mull.

- Small Victorian country house hotel.
- Best of Scottish and European.
- "A discovery you won't want to leave behind when the time comes."

Killiechronan is the lodge house of its own 5,000 acre estate. Six charming en suite bedrooms offer comfort and style in a peaceful setting, while the dining room and two distinctively furnished lounges are a quiet haven to relax and enjoy. The house has a happy and relaxed atmosphere, reflected also by the staff under the professional eye of Patrick and Margaret Freytag, who moved here from The Manor House, Oban. The food here is excellent, deserving of the AA Rosette, and customers every needs are well-catered for with menus made available early afternoon so that any dietary requirements can be met. Ideal for a relaxed holiday in a wonderful setting.

Open 4 Apr to 31 Oct
🏠 Rooms: 6 with private facilities
SP Special rates available
♀ Residents licence
✗ Lunch Sun only ££
✗ Dinner £££
Ⓥ Vegetarians welcome
🚭 No smoking in dining room

Loch na Keal oysters with fennel and honey. Isle of Mull venison with juniper berry sauce and black cherries. Parfait Flora Macdonald with Drambuie sauce.

STB Highly Commended 👑 👑 👑 👑
💳 Credit cards: Access/Mastercard/Eurocard, American Express, Visa, Switch, Delta
👤 Managers: Patrick & Margaret Freytag

THE OLD BYRE HERITAGE CENTRE
Dervaig
Isle of Mull PA75 6QR
Tel: 01688 400229

1½ miles from Dervaig. Take Calgary road for ¾ mile, turn left along Torloisk road for ¼ mile, then left down private road following signs.

A small gift shop, tea-room and small heritage centre on the Isle of Mull.

- Converted barn with self-service restaurant.
- Home cooking and baking.
- "Great for a warming plate of soup – or a full tuck-in."

A remotely situated, picturesque old cattle byre in Glen Bellart (near Dervaig) has been restored and converted into a heritage centre which explores the traditions and natural history of the Isle of Mull, from the first settlers to the present day. There are audio-visual displays and exhibits as well as a gift shop with souvenirs and crafts for sale. The licensed tea room offers a range of light meals and home baking and daily specials, using fresh Mull produce. By prior arrangement meals can be arranged for groups and vegetarians are well catered for.

Open 31 Mar to 25 Oct
✗ Light meals served throughout day £
♀ Licensed
Ⓥ Vegetarians welcome
☆ Children welcome

Crofter's soup served with warm rolls. Ploughman's lunch with Mull cheese. Cloutie dumpling a speciality.

Ⓔ No credit cards
Ⓚ Joint Owners: Ursula & Michael Bradley

THE WESTERN ISLES HOTEL
Tobermory
Isle of Mull PA75 6PR
Tel: 01688 302012
Fax: 01688 302297

High above the little town the hotel is reached in a few minutes by a steep side road out of the main seafront shopping area.

Fine old Victorian hotel in superb position above the harbour.

- Town hotel of Scottish baronial architecture.
- Substantial Scottish cooking.
- "Continuous refurbishment and innovation has kept this fine old hostelry well to the forefront of the island's town hotels."

The hotel occupies one of the finest positions in the Western Isles set above the village of Tobermory with glorious views over the Sound of Mull. You can enjoy the ever-changing, dramatic scenery from all of the hotel's public rooms and many of the bedrooms. There is a choice of three places in which to eat here – the dining room; Spices Restaurant; and the conservatory which is a particularly delightful spot and is popular with guests and visitors to the island who drop in for lunch or even coffee. The bar lunch menu is extensive with a very wide choice, from soup of the day and filled sandwiches to a full three or four course meal of hot and cold dishes and salads. The dinner menu offers four courses on a table d'hôte menu of good, traditional Scottish cooking accompanied by a reasonably priced wine list. *(See advert Page 263.)*

Open 1 Feb to 18 Dec
🛏 Rooms: 23 with private facilities
ⓈⓅ Special rates available
✗ Lunch £
✗ Dinner £££
Ⓥ Vegetarians welcome
☆ Children welcome
⚊ No smoking in dining room

Chicken bouchée in a puff pastry case glazed with cream. Sauté of venison and woodpigeon and wild mushrooms with a hawthorn sauce. Home-made desserts.

STB Highly Commended 👑 👑 👑 👑
Ⓔ Credit cards: Access/Mastercard/Eurocard, American Express, Visa, Switch
Ⓚ Proprietors: Sue & Michael Fink

ALBERT HOTEL
Mounthoolie Lane
Kirkwall
Orkney KW15 1JZ
Tel: 01856 876000
Fax: 01856 875397

50 yards from Harbour. Just off Junction Road (A963).

Old town hotel in Kirkwall.

- Hotel at the hub of things in Old Kirkwall.
- Wholesome traditional cooking.
- "Good Orcadian fare, a popular place with locals and visitors."

The Albert Hotel has played an important role in the life of Kirkwall for over a 100 years. It stands within the conservation area in the centre of the town, between the harbour and St Magnus Cathedral, and has recently been refurbished in a style which retains its character and atmosphere. Attached to the hotel is the intimate Stable's Restaurant, which offers table d'hôte and à la carte menus, featuring local seafood, beef and lamb, all prepared to order. Its personable owner, Anjo Casey, also runs a busy local 'both bar' (with a fine open fire) and a nightclub which is one of the most popular venues in Kirkwall, so you are never at a loss for entertainment at the Albert.

Open all year except Christmas Day + New Year
🏠 Rooms: 19 with private facilities
🆂🅿 Special rates available
✖ Lunch £
✖ Dinner ££
Ⓥ Vegetarians welcome
⚐ Children welcome
✖ Children's menu available.
♿ Facilities for the disabled in dining room + bar

Smoked salmon and prawn coronets. Noisettes of lamb. Stable's cheesecake.

STB Commended 👑 👑 👑
💳 Credit cards: Access/Mastercard/Eurocard, American Express, Visa, Mastercharge, Switch
👤 Proprietors: Anjo & Paddy Casey

CLEATON HOUSE HOTEL
Cleaton
Westray
Orkney KW17 2DB
Tel: 01857 677508
Fax: 01857 677442

Signposted 5 miles from Rapness (Westray) Ferry terminal on road to Pierowall Village.

A friendly, family-run hotel on the Island of Westray.

- Victorian manse of distinctive 'ink bottle' design.
- Orcadian produce – modern cooking.
- "The best of island hospitality."

A regular roll-on, roll-off ferry service connects Westray to Kirkwall, and Cleaton's owner, Malcolm Stout, is happy to meet you at the pier. Such personal concern for guests is manifested in every aspect of this delightful small hotel. Chef Lorna Reid combines her many years working in 'top class' kitchens, with outstanding local ingredients, to produce quality cuisine. The hotel has been sympathetically restored and refurbished and has splendid views. An excellent base from which to explore Westray's beaches, cliffs and Heritage Centre – and the second largest sea-bird colony in Britain.

Open all year except New Year's Day
🏠 Rooms: 5 with private facilities
🆂🅿 Special rates available
✖ Lunch £
✖ Dinner ££
Ⓥ Vegetarians welcome
⚐ Children welcome
♿ Facilities for disabled visitors
🚭 No smoking in dining room

Spoots in butter (razor clams) served with bere bannocks. Westray scallops draped with red pepper and Noilly Prat sauce. Cloutie dumpling with whisky liqueur parfait.

STB Highly Commended 👑 👑 👑
💳 Credit cards: Access/Mastercard/Eurocard, Visa, Delta
👤 Proprietor: Malcolm Stout

CREEL RESTAURANT & ROOMS

Front Road, St Margaret's Hope, Orkney KW17 2SL
Tel: 01856 831 311

Take A961 south across the Churchill Barriers into St Margaret's Hope. 14 miles from Kirkwall.

Alan Craigie consistently achieves a very high standard and is rightfully acknowledged for his culinary achievements.

- Historic seafront house, stark, whitewashed and gabled, overlooking St Margaret's Hope.
- Innovative modern cooking with strong influences of traditional Orcadian recipes.
- "Carefully selected Orkney produce, perfectly cooked."

The clean white walls of the Creel shine out on the quayside; a small, family-run restaurant with an international reputation. Chef/owner Alan Craigie presents a short menu which changes daily according to the availability of local produce and features Orcadian specialities. He cooks with great skill, respecting textures and flavours, creating original and unusual sauces, and spectacular desserts. The atmosphere of the place is informal and friendly; the restaurant has three spacious and comfortable bedrooms, with bathrooms en suite. Since Alan's television appearances (in Keith Floyd's Britain and Ireland, Scotland's Larder and Rhodes Around Britain) the Creel has become a place of pilgrimage for gourmets, but its cheerful understated ambience has not changed – nor have its incredibly reasonable prices. The Creel has 1 AA Rosette. One of 12 establishments shortlisted for The Macallan Taste of Scotland Awards 1996.

Open weekends Oct to Mar except Jan: daily Apr to Sep – advisable to book, especially in low season
Closed Christmas Day + Boxing Day + Jan
🏠 Rooms: 3 with private facilities
✕ Dinner £££
Ⓥ Vegetarians welcome
⚐ Children 5 years and over welcome
🚭 No smoking in restaurant

Prime rump steak marinated in a sweet beer, pickle smoked over oak chips. Orcadian Fish Stew: halibut, scallops, salmon and haddock. Home-baked shortbread filled with local strawberries and double cream.

💳 Credit cards: Access/Mastercard/Eurocard, Visa
👤 Owners: Joyce & Alan Craigie

FOVERAN HOTEL & RESTAURANT

Foveran, St Ola
Kirkwall, Orkney
KW15 1SF
Tel: 01856 872389
Fax: 01856 876430

On A964 Orphir road, 2½ miles from Kirkwall.

Rural modern hotel in the Isles of Orkney.

- Scandinavian style, purpose-built hotel.
- Traditional Scottish cooking.
- "The best of Orcadian produce full of flavour in a lovely location."

This is a modern Scandinavian bungalow, purpose built as an hotel, with views over Scapa Flow. The interior is warm and inviting, and the Corsies are happy and charming hosts. Their menus rely heavily on the outstanding fresh seafood and meat of the islands, and familiar dishes are given a local twist (rich sauce laced with Highland Park whisky, Orkney Raven Ale sauce, etc.). There is a separate vegetarian menu with a delicious looking range of dishes: this in itself is indicative of the attention you will encounter here. The Pine Restaurant and chef Clare Cooper (at Foveran four years now) are achieving an excellent reputation for the quality of cooking here. Restaurant requires to be booked in advance.

Open all year except Christmas Day + Jan
Closed Sun – residents only
🏠 Rooms: 8 with private facilities
✕ Dinner except Sun £££
Ⓥ Vegetarians welcome
⚐ Children welcome
♿ Facilities for disabled visitors
🚭 No smoking in restaurant

Arbroath smokies served hot with butter. King of scallops served with a cheese and garlic sauce. Orkney bouillabaisse.

STB Commended 👑 👑 👑 👑
💳 Credit cards: Access/Mastercard/Eurocard, Visa, Switch, Delta
👤 Owners: Bobby & Ivy Corsie

ISLES OF SHETLAND

BUSTA HOUSE HOTEL
Busta, Brae
Shetland ZE2 9QN
Tel: 01806 522 506
Fax: 01806 522 588

On the Muckle Roe road, 1 mile off A970
Hillswick road.

Historic Shetland house with wonderful views.

- 16th century laird's house.
- Scottish produce with modern influences.
- "Good food in historic surroundings."

The history of Busta House is full of superstition, ghosts and family feuds. Fear not, as the hospitality and enthusiasm of Peter and Judith Jones make you welcome to their tastefully restored home. One of the few Listed buildings in Shetland, it has many interesting features, amongst which are its walled gardens and private pier. Enjoy an aperitif in the Long Room before dinner, gently absorbing the atmosphere of the historic Busta House. Cooking is Scottish and international using local produce where possible, all freshly cooked.

Open all year except 22 Dec to 2 Jan
- ⊞ Rooms: 20 with private facilities
- ⊠ Special rates available
- ✗ Lunch £
- ✗ Dinner £-£££
- Ⓥ Vegetarians welcome
- ☆ Children welcome
- ✗ No smoking in dining room

Layered fish terrine (turbot, salmon and prawns) with fresh herbs and fresh dill cream. Pan-fried pheasant breast on a bed of leeks with a whisky and bacon sauce. Grand Marnier parfait with a Maraschino cherry and Earl Grey syrup.

STB Commended ♕ ♕ ♕ ♕
- ⊞ Credit cards: Access/Mastercard/Eurocard, American Express, Visa, Diners Club, Switch, Delta
- ⋈ Owners: Peter & Judith Jones
- ⋈ Manageress: Jeanette Watt

ISLE OF SKYE

ARDVASAR HOTEL
Ardvasar, Sleat
Isle of Skye IV45 8RS
Tel: 01471 844223

15 miles south of Broadford, ½ mile south of Armadale/Mallaig ferry.

A small roadside hotel in the 'Wild Garden of Skye'.

- Traditional whitewashed coaching inn.
- Innovative home cooking.
- "The Fowlers serve a wide range of customers, with considerable experience."

Ardvasar Hotel is situated at the south end of the Sleat Peninsula, near Armadale (the ferry point for Mallaig) and enjoys lovely views over the Sound of Sleat to the mountains of Knoydart. The hotel is run by Bill and Greta Fowler who show personal concern over their guests' comfort and well-being, and encourage many to become regular visitors. Bill cooks imaginatively and with great attention to detail, with local fresh produce complemented by unusual sauces and accompaniments. An appetising à la carte menu is presented in the restaurant and bar food is also available. Ardvasar has 1 AA Rosette.

Open 1 Mar to 28 Oct
- ⊞ Rooms: 10 with private facilities
- ✗ Lunch ££
- ⋈ Dinner – reservations please £££
- Ⓥ Vegetarians welcome
- ☆ Children welcome
- ✗ Smoking discouraged

Warm fresh local mussels with leeks and wine. Roast marinated venison fillet with juniper and plums. Chocolate meringue.

STB Commended ♕ ♕ ♕
- ⊞ Credit cards: Access/Mastercard/Eurocard, Visa, Delta
- ⋈ Partners: Bill & Greta Fowler

ATHOLL HOUSE HOTEL
& CHIMES RESTAURANT
Dunvegan
Isle of Skye IV55 8WA
Tel: 01470 521 219
Fax: 01470 521 481

In the centre of the village of Dunvegan. From the bridge – follow A850 to Sligachan, turn left to Dunvegan – 22 miles.

A small hotel in 'heart of the village'.

• Late 19th century manse now a comfortable small hotel.
• Modern Scottish cooking with care.
• "A small hotel that makes a big effort to please."

Situated at the head of Loch Dunvegan, the Atholl looks out on to the twin flat-topped mountains – the Macleod's Tables. Built in 1910 the Atholl is a former manse which retains many of the original features. The atmosphere is friendly and the cooking accomplished using much of the excellent local Skye produce.

Open all year except Jan
🏨 Rooms: 10, 8 with private facilities
SP Special rates available
✕ Food served all day £££
✕ Lunch £
✕ Dinner £££
Ⓥ Vegetarians welcome
☆ Children welcome
♿ Facilities for disabled visitors
🚭 No smoking in restaurant

Home-made soup. Marriage of wild Raasay salmon, monkfish and Skye scallops with tomatoes, shallots and fresh basil enveloped in a filo pastry purse and set on a Silver Birch sauce. Selection of Highland and local cheeses.

STB Commended 👑 👑 👑
💳 Credit cards: Access/Mastercard/Eurocard, American Express, Visa, Switch
🗎 Owner: Joan M Macleod

BOSVILLE HOTEL
Bosville Terrace
Portree
Isle of Skye IV51 9DG
Tel: 01478 612846
Fax: 01478 613434

Town centre above Portree Harbour and Cuillin Mountains.

A bustling hotel in the centre of Portree village.

• Town centre hotel.
• Traditional Scottish cooking.
• "Bosville has an excellent local reputation which grows every year."

Centrally situated on a busy corner in Portree, the Bosville has old fashioned award-winning Highland hospitality. The popular restaurant fronts the street; diners come and go and locals drop in for a chat, or to deliver goods and fresh produce. The hotel stands on a brae and commands fine views across the harbour, with the Cuillin Mountains beyond. Table d'hôte lunch and dinner menus are presented, using local produce wherever possible and featuring a number of Scottish specialities.

Open all year
🏨 Rooms: 15 with private facilities
SP Special rates available
✕ Food served all day £
✕ Lunch £
✕ Dinner ££
Ⓥ Vegetarians welcome
☆ Children welcome
♿ Facilities for disabled visitors
🚭 No smoking throughout

Highland terrine of veal sweetbreads and Scottish lobster studded with pistachio, placed on a lime and Pernod vinaigrette. Layers of spinach, sole, salmon, king scallops lightly steamed and glazed with a tomato and basil butter. Poached pear with honey cream, vintage port and lime syrup.

STB Commended 👑 👑 👑 👑
💳 Credit cards: Access/Mastercard/Eurocard, American Express, Visa, Mastercharge, Switch, Delta
🗎 Hotel Manager: Donald W MacLeod, MHCIMA

DUNORIN HOUSE HOTEL

Herebost
Dunvegan
Isle of Skye IV55 8GZ
Tel: 01470 521488
Fax: 01470 521488

From Kyleakin A850 to Sligachan, then A863 to Dunvegan. 2 miles south of Dunvegan turn left at Roag/Orbost junction, 200m on right.

A small and modern, family-run hotel in a beautiful
corner of Skye.

- Purpose-built with modern comforts in mind.
- Scottish cooking with island recipes/hotel cooking.
- "Local people offering truly Highland comfort and hospitality."

Dunorin House is the brainchild of Gaelic-speaking native islanders Joan and Alasdair MacLean. Built in 1989, it offers comfortable accommodation in ten en suite rooms. The hotel enjoys panoramic views across Loch Roag to the Cuillin Hills. All bedrooms and public rooms are on ground level with wide corridors and so are specially suitable for the disabled. In the evenings, Joan and Alasdair's son Darren, a Gaelic Festival winner, entertains guests with traditional Scottish music. With many local recipes, the hotel's à la carte menu seeks to make the most of fresh local produce such as scallops, venison and salmon. It also offers more routine hotel fare. The wine list is reasonably priced and varied.

Open 1 Apr to 15 Nov except 2 wks Oct
🏠 Rooms: 10 with private facilities
SP Special rates available
🍴 Non-residents – bookings only
🍷 Restricted hotel licence
✖ Dinner £££
Ⓥ Vegetarians welcome
🧒 Children welcome
♿ Facilities for disabled visitors
🚭 No smoking in dining room

Scallops in garlic butter. Medallions of venison with a port and redcurrant sauce. Cloutie dumpling.

STB Highly Commended 👑 👑 👑
💳 Credit cards: Access/Mastercard/Eurocard, Visa
👥 Partners: Alasdair & Joan MacLean

FLODIGARRY COUNTRY HOUSE HOTEL & THE WATER HORSE RESTAURANT

Staffin, Isle of Skye
Inverness-shire IV51 9HZ
Tel: 01470 552203
Fax: 01470 552301

A855 north from Portree to Staffin, 4 miles from Staffin to Flodigarry.

Country hotel at the north end of Skye.

- Unsurpassed views.
- Fine Scottish cuisine.
- "A relaxed-home-in-the-country atmosphere."

This historic country house hotel nestles between the towering pinnacles of the Quiraing and has panoramic sea views over Flodigarry Island, and across Staffin Bay to the mainland. Its 19th century castellate additions lend it the air of folklore, especially being so close to the mysterious 'Fairy Glen', and adjacent is Flora Macdonald's cottage (now converted to provide seven luxury en suite rooms, five with sea view). In the Water Horse Restaurant, residents and non-residents can enjoy a daily changing table d'hôte menu, featuring traditional dishes, or choose from an à la carte menu. Bar meals are served in the conservatory and on the terrace. Winner of The Macallan Taste of Scotland Country House Hotel of the Year Award 1995. *(See advert Page 7.)*

Open all year
🏠 Rooms: 19 with private facilities
SP Special rates available
✖ Lunch (Restaurant) ££
✖ Dinner 4 course menu £££
Ⓥ Vegetarians welcome
🧒 Children welcome
♿ Facilities for disabled visitors
🚭 No smoking in restaurant or conservatory

Roulade of local cured wild salmon and cottage cheese served with a fresh raspberry vinaigrette. Medallions of Highland venison served with a blaeberry wine sauce. Iced Drambuie soufflé served with home-made shortbread.

STB Highly Commended 👑 👑 👑 👑
💳 Credit cards: Access/Mastercard/Eurocard, Visa, Switch, Delta
👥 Proprietors: Andrew & Pamela Butler

GLENVIEW INN & RESTAURANT
Culnacnoc, Staffin
Isle of Skye
Inverness-shire IV51 9JH
Tel: 01470 562 248
Fax: 01470 562 211

12 miles from Portree on the Staffin road –
signposted off the A855.

A comfortable West Highland inn near Staffin.

* Restaurant with rooms.
* Good quality cooking of fresh local seafood.
* "Small and cosy with good food and attentive service."

Tucked into a sheltered corner up in the north end of the island, this little hostelry is big in all the home comforts. The fresh sea catch of the day is quickly brought to the table, while in the afternoon, home baking is a temptation to longer over. Whatever the time of day – the Glenview will rise to the occasion. Paul's cooking uses local produce and eclectic techniques to produce well-priced and varied meals selected from an à la carte menu and blackboard featuring daily specials – from fresh local seafood and game to vegetarian and ethnic dishes.

Open mid Mar to early Nov
🏠 Rooms: 4 with private facilities
SP Special rates available
✕ Lunch ££
✕ Dinner £££
Ⅴ Vegetarians welcome
🕺 Children welcome
🚭 Smoking restricted to certain areas

Warm salad of Skye scallops, cockles and squat lobster tails with dulse. Fricassée of pheasant with oyster mushrooms, leeks, apple, cream and vermouth with pilau rice and warm pitta bread. Slice of home-made hot chocolate fudge pie.

STB Commended 👑 👑 👑
💳 Credit cards: Access/Mastercard/Eurocard, Switch
🅽 Owners: Paul & Cathie Booth

HARLOSH HOUSE
by Dunvegan
Isle of Skye IV55 8ZG
Tel: 01470 521 367
Fax: 01470 521 367

Off A863, 4 miles south of Dunvegan.

A small hotel in a remote setting on the shores of Loch Bracadale.

* Charming 18th century tacksman's house with six bedrooms.
* Modern restaurant cooking.
* "Scenically one of the most dramatic corners of Skye – and one of the best to eat in."

This converted farmhouse is not far south of Dunvegan in the north-west of the island, and has splendid views of the Cuillins and the islands which speckle the sea loch it sits beside. It has a relaxed atmosphere inspired by its owners, Peter and Lindsey Elford who also prepare and serve the dinners. Peter cooks, making use of the fresh seafood, which is predominant in the restaurant. His attention to detail is meticulous (he also makes his own breads, desserts and chocolates) and the dishes on his menus are complex with subtle flavours. Harlosh has 2 AA Rosettes Food Award.

Open Easter to end Oct
🏠 Rooms: 6 with private facilities
✕ Dinner ££££
🕺 Children welcome
🚭 No smoking in restaurant

Fresh asparagus risotto with local langoustine tails. Tranche of cod with a brioche crust on a plum tomato salsa. A trio of home-made sorbets.

STB Highly Commended 👑 👑 👑
💳 Credit cards: Access/Mastercard/Eurocard, Visa, Switch
🅽 Owners: Peter & Lindsey Elford

HOTEL EILEAN IARMAIN
Sleat, Isle Ornsay
Inverness-shire IV43 8QR
Tel: 01471 833 332
Fax: 01471 833 275

Situated between Broadford and Armadale, follow A851 for 15 minutes then on right-hand side follow sign A852 Eilean Iarmain. 20 minutes from Skye Bridge.

Gaelic charm at 'The Inn on the Sea'.

- Small whitewashed island hotel.
- Modern Scottish cooking.
- "A taste of the natural hospitality of Skye."

Hotel Eilean Iarmain (Isle Ornsay Hotel) stands on the small rocky bay of Isle Ornsay in the south of Skye, with expansive views over the Sound of Sleat to the hills of Knoydart. The hotel was built in 1888 and retains the charm and old-world character of a gentler age, with log fires in the public rooms and a panelled dining room. It is owned by Sir Iain Noble – who has done so much for Gaelic culture and language: staff and locals are all Gaelic speakers. The award-winning restaurant serves a four course table d'hôte menu (in Gaelic, but translated) which features local shellfish (landed only yards from the hotel), game and vegetables. The restaurant has an AA Rosette. *(See advert Page 22.)*

Open all year
- **⌂** Rooms: 12 with private facilities
- **SP** Special rates available
- **✕** Lunch – booking essential ££
- **🍴** Dinner – advance reservation advisable £££
- **Ⅴ** Vegetarians welcome
- **✝** Children welcome
- **½** No smoking in restaurant

Locally dived scallops sautéd with Stornoway black pudding and apple. Monkfish baked in its own juices with garlic and fennel. Crème brûlée served with berries and fresh dairy cream.

STB Commended 👑 👑 👑
- **£** Credit cards: Access/Mastercard/Eurocard, American Express, Visa, Mastercharge,
- **ⱡ** Proprietors: Sir Iain & Lady Noble

KINLOCH LODGE
Sleat
Isle of Skye IV43 8QY
Tel: 01471 833214
Fax: 01471 833277

8 miles south of Broadford on A851. 10 miles north of Armadale on A851. 1 mile off A851.

The home of the High Chief of Clan Donald and Lady Macdonald.

- Country house hotel in Sleat.
- Outstanding traditional cooking with innovative influences.
- "The atmosphere is relaxed and friendly and the food delicious."

Kinloch was built in 1680, as a farmhouse, and was expanded into a sporting lodge in the 19th century. As the home of Lord Macdonald of Macdonald, it is full of portraits of ancestors, old furniture and family treasures. It is very much a family home, with two comfortable drawing rooms, log fires and a variety of bedrooms. Lady Claire Macdonald is one of the best known cooks in Scotland: an award-winning journalist and the author of 12 cookbooks. Assisted by a small team she presents a five course table d'hôte menu each night which uses only fresh seasonal produce. The breakfasts are a very special treat.

Open Mar to Nov incl
- **⌂** Rooms: 10 with private facilities
- **SP** Special rates available
- **✕** Dinner 5 course menu ££££
- **Ⅴ** Vegetarians welcome – prior notice required
- **✝** Children welcome by arrangement
- **½** No smoking in dining room
- **🐄** Member of the Scotch Beef Club

Leek and goats cheese tart with cheese pastry. Roast leg of lamb with apricot sauce and red wine and rosemary gravy. White chocolate mousse with raspberry sauce.

STB Highly Commended 👑 👑 👑 👑
- **£** Credit cards: Access/Mastercard/Eurocard, Visa
- **ⱡ** Proprietors: Lord & Lady Macdonald

LOCHBAY SEAFOOD RESTAURANT
Stein, Waternish
Isle of Skye IV55 8GA
Tel: 01470 592235

Take B886, 4 miles down single track road to village of Stein. Last house in the village.

A small fish restaurant in Waternish, with two en suite bedrooms.

- Two restored 18th century cottages with gorgeous views over to the Outer Isles.
- Seafood handled with care and skill.
- "Prime seafood, and a charming corner to find it in."

Situated in the old fishing village of Stein and located just 30 yards from the pier with some lovely unspoilt views, these fisherman's cottages have been restored rather than converted. The old black range is still there, (and working), the copper kettle on the hob; whitewashed walls and original pine panelling. The place has great charm, and this is enhanced by the hospitality of its owners, Peter and Margaret Greenhalgh. The fish and shellfish is brought up from the pier and cooked simply and deliciously by Margaret – it simply could not be fresher. Bookings essential in the evenings.

Open Easter to end Oct incl Easter Sat
Closed Sat
🏨 Rooms: 2
✕ Food served all day except Sat ££
✕ Lunch except Sat £
✕ Dinner except Sat ££
Ⓥ Vegetarians welcome
🛉 Children welcome
🚭 No smoking throughout

Squat lobster. Seafood platter: halibut. Chocolate bread and butter pudding.

💳 Credit cards: Access/Mastercard/Eurocard, Visa
👥 Proprietors: Margaret & Peter Greenhalgh

THE LOWER DECK SEAFOOD RESTAURANT
The Harbour, Portree
Isle of Skye IV51 9DD
Tel: 01478 613611
Fax: 01478 613611

Lower deck is on the ground floor of the old buildings that line the harbour frontage. It is clearly signposted with parking nearby or in town square.

A small seafood bistro popular with yachtsmen, visitors and locals.

- Old harbourside building.
- Confident and quick with respect for fresh fish.
- "A new watering hole that will quickly make its presence known."

The Lower Deck opened in Spring 1996, and is a small seafood bistro. Its owner is a fishmonger and thus ensures that a particular respect is shown to fish in its cooking. The bistro has fine views across the bay and, if in luck, diners will be able to enjoy watching local fishermen landing their daily catch in the harbour. The decor is reminiscent of a traditional ship's passenger saloon – thus the name! Cooking here is excellent and according to our Inspector is the right time and place, and the perfect setting.

Open all year except New Year's Day
Note: Opening hours may vary in winter
✕ Lunch ££
✕ Dinner £££
Ⓥ Vegetarians welcome
🛉 Children welcome
♿ Facilities for disabled visitors

Fresh Skye mussels steamed with shallots and white wine. Salmon fillet with ginger, coriander and walnuts. Cranachan: whipped cream, raspberries, whisky and toasted oats.

💳 Credit cards: Access/Mastercard/Eurocard, Visa, Mastercharge, Switch
👥 Manageress: Carolyn Johnston

ROSEDALE HOTEL

Beaumont Crescent, Portree
Isle of Skye IV51 9DB
Tel: 01478 613131
Fax: 01478 612531

Harbourside location, 100 yards from village square.

A small hotel in Skye's principal village with views directly over the harbour.

- Harbourside fishermen's cottages comfortably converted to accommodate this friendly hotel.
- Modern Scottish.
- "The harbourside is like a little village on the waterfront of the town of Portree."

The Rosedale was originally a row of William IV cottages adjacent to the harbour in the heart of old Portree. The hotel has now spread its wings in all directions so that it now occupies practically all of one side of the Portree waterfront. Growth was in response to demand and demand was created by satisfied guests returning yet again for another stay. There are many unique and interesting features – not least of which is finding your way to the first floor restaurant! – from which there are splendid views out over the bay. Chef Tony Parkyn presents a daily changing table d'hôte dinner menu which offers a good choice of imaginative dishes (there is always a speciality vegetarian main course), based upon fresh local produce whenever it is available. The hotel has 1 AA Rosette.

    Open 11 May to 1 Oct
🏨 Rooms: 23 with private facilities
✕ Lunch – residents only
✕ Dinner ££££
Ⓥ Vegetarians welcome
⅄ No smoking in restaurant

Banana, raisin and carrot salad with a coconut dressing scattered with zest of orange. Breast of Letterfinlay duck with a purée of gingered beans and smoked aubergine. Local strawberries, gently sautéd in Calvados and served lightly sprinkled with black pepper.

STB Highly Commended 👑 👑 👑 👑
💳 Credit cards: Access/Mastercard/Eurocard, Visa, Mastercharge, Switch, Delta
🅝 Manager: Keith White

SKEABOST HOUSE HOTEL

Skeabost Bridge, Isle of Skye IV51 9NP
Tel: 01470 532 202
Fax: 01470 532 454

4 miles north of Portree on Dunvegan road.

An imposing family-run hotel on the shores of Loch Snizort.

- A 19th century hunting lodge set in lovely grounds.
- Skilled contemporary cooking.
- "A very delightful place to come to eat well with the aura of a fine old country house."

Built in 1870 this former hunting lodge has been a family-run establishment by the Stuart and McNab families for over 26 years (granny, aged 84, still prepares the traditional afternoon teas) It is an oasis of cultivated serenity within the wild and rugged terrain of Skye. Positioned in 12 acres of lovely grounds which stretch down to the water-side, its well-kept gardens also incorporate a nine hole golf course. During 1994 a period conservatory overlooking the loch was added to the main building and extended the hotel's dining facilities. A buffet menu is available during the day and in the more formal surroundings of the elegant, wood-panelled dining room Angus McNab presents daily changing table d'hôte menus which demonstrate considerable flair and skill, particularly with fish and game.

    Open Mar to Nov
🏨 Rooms: 26 with private facilities
🆂🅿 Special rates available
✕ Lunch £
✕ Dinner £££
Ⓥ Vegetarians welcome
🜨 Children welcome
♿ Facilities for disabled visitors
⅄ No smoking in dining room
🐄 Member of the Scotch Beef Club

A fine parfait of chicken livers and port served with home-made toasted brioche and a cranberry and onion chutney. Best end of prime Scottish lamb with a herb crust and served with a carrot dauphinoise and a rosemary-scented gravy. Home-made cloutie dumpling ice cream with a crisp coconut biscuit.

STB Commended 👑 👑 👑 👑 👑
💳 Credit cards: Access/Mastercard/Eurocard, Visa, Switch
🅝 Proprietors: Stuart & McNab

THREE CHIMNEYS RESTAURANT
Colbost, by Dunvegan
Isle of Skye IV55 8ZT
Tel: 01470 511258

4 miles west of Dunvegan on B884 road to
Glendale. Look out for Glendale Visitor Route signs.

Island restaurant in a gem of a setting.

- Delightful restaurant in converted crofter's
  cottage.
- Natural scottish cooking.
- "A delight to the eye as well as the palate."

This restaurant is off the beaten track, right on the
shore of Loch Dunvegan at Colbost, on the scenic
Glendale Visitor Route which takes you to the most
westerly point of Skye. It is open almost all day.
Morning coffee, lunch and afternoon tea are
served until 4.30 pm. Dinner, from 7 pm, is a really
full blown occasion with a wide choice à la carte
menu accompanied by a well-chosen wine list
offering a good choice of New World and
European wines. As you would expect, given its
location, seafood is a speciality of the menu but fish,
lamb, beef, venison and an intriguing vegetarian
choice are also among the selection on offer. This
is Scottish cooking at its best — simple,
imaginative, delicious. Shirley is a brilliant and
artistic cook — not to be missed! Disabled visitors
are asked to contact the restaurant prior to visit.
Three Chimneys has 2 AA Rosettes. Winner of
Taste of Scotland Special Merit Award 1992.
Talisker Quality Award for finest food '93, '94, '95.

Open end Mar to end Oct
Closed Sun except Easter + Whitsun
✗ Food served all day except Sun £-££££
✗ Lunch except Sun ££
✗ Dinner except Sun 3 course menu £££-££££
Ⓥ Vegetarians welcome
⚘ Children welcome
⚞ No smoking throughout

**Seared West Coast scallops with roast red pepper
cream. Three Chimneys hot lobster and
langoustines in brandy and cream sherry sauce.
Fresh lemon almond roulade with home-made
lemon curd sauce.**

💳 Credit cards: Access/Mastercard/Eurocard,
Visa, Switch
🅜 Owners: Eddie & Shirley Spear

UIG HOTEL
Uig, Portree
Isle of Skye IV51 9YE
Tel: 01470 542 205
Fax: 01470 542 308

Entering Uig from Portree on A856, hotel is halfway
down hill on right.

Former coaching inn in charming island location.

- Popular family-run hotel.
- Traditional Scottish cooking.
- "A comfortable base, with good food and caring
  atmosphere."

The hotel is blessed with an extremely attractive
location on a hillside overlooking Uig Bay and Loch
Snizort. It is a well-known and popular stopping off
point to or from the Hebridean ferries and is also
an ideal base from which to explore Skye. Grace
Graham has owned the hotel since 1946 and her
personal touch is everywhere. Bedrooms and public
rooms are comfortable and tastefully furnished
and some are also self-catering apartments,
particularly attractive for those looking for a family
break. The hotel also has its own pony-trekking
centre. Food and standards of hospitality are good
with simple Scottish fare on a reasonably priced
table d'hôte menu. *(See advert Page 263.)*

Open 1 Apr to 30 Oct
🛏 Rooms: 17 with private facilities
🆂🅿 Special rates available
✗ Lunch £
✗ Dinner 4 course menu ££££
Ⓥ Vegetarians welcome
⚘ Children welcome
⚭ Facilities for disabled visitors
⚞ No smoking in restaurant

**Home-made fish cakes. Sauté of chicken with
oranges, lemons, tomatoes and cinnamon.
Home-made sweets.**

STB Commended ♛ ♛ ♛ ♛
💳 Credit cards: Access/Mastercard/Eurocard,
American Express, Visa, Diners Club, Switch
🅜 Proprietors: Grace Graham & David Taylor

ISLE OF TIREE

THE GLASSARY RESTAURANT AND GUEST HOUSE

Sandaig, Isle of Tiree
Argyll PA77 6XQ
Tel: 01879 220 684
Fax: 01879 220 684

On west coast of island. On leaving pier turn left through Scarinish to Heylipol, Middleton and Sandaig at west end of the island.

A restaurant and guest house on the beautiful Isle of Tiree.

- The restaurant is a pine-lined converted byre.
- Traditional Scottish with modern influences.
- "Wonderful views to be enjoyed."

The Glassary is situated on the picturesque west coast of the island, close to long stretches of unspoiled white sandy beaches. The name is taken from the nearby ruined kelp (seaweed) factory which operated during the last century. The house offers limited, accommodation. Proprietor Mabel Macarthur and her son, chef Iain, create a warm atmosphere. Almost all the beef, lamb and seafood are local and you can order lobster in advance. Home-made soups are excellent and a speciality is carageen pudding, made from kelp (on request). The menu prices are very reasonable and the cooking is imaginative with some original and inventive touches, making eating here a most enjoyable experience.

Open Easter to Oct
🏠 Rooms: 3
✗ Lunch £-££
✗ Dinner ££-£££
Ⓥ Vegetarians welcome
⊀ Children welcome
& Facilities for disabled visitors

Melon, prawn and smoked trout. Strips of lamb pan-fried and flamed in brandy, pink peppercorns and cream. Bread and butter pudding, traditionally made and laced with Drambuie.

💳 No credit cards
🅝 Proprietors: Mabel & Iain Macarthur

JEDBURGH

SIMPLY SCOTTISH

High Street
Jedburgh
Roxburghshire TD8 6AG
Tel: 01835 864696
Fax: 01835 822989

Centre of Jedburgh just off A68.

Modern bistro/restaurant specialising in local quality produce.

- Modern bistro-style town restaurant.
- Fresh modern Scottish cooking.
- "A friendly and attractive modern informal restaurant serving good honest food."

The Simply Scottish restaurant, coffee shop and craft cook-shop has been recently converted from the old Co-op department store to very high standards, and with great effect. The interior of the bistro/restaurant has a light, modern country feel with heavy pine furniture and stripped pine flooring. As the name suggests the emphasis on the food is using good freshly sourced local produce and served simply but with some interesting combinations of flavours and presented with style.

Open all year
✗ Food served all day £-££
✗ Lunch £
✗ Dinner except some week nights in winter (please phone) ££
Ⓥ Vegetarians welcome
⊀ Children welcome
& Facilities for disabled visitors
⌖ No smoking area

Smoked trout mousse. Grilled Border lamb with Arran mustard sauce. Summer fruit pudding with fresh fruit coulis and heather honey ice cream.

💳 Credit cards: Access/Mastercard/Eurocard, Visa
🅝 Proprietors: Linda Fergusson & Charles Masraff

Kelso 116

EDNAM HOUSE HOTEL
Bridge Street, Kelso, Roxburghshire TD5 7HT
Tel: 01573 224168
Fax: 01573 226319

Situated on Bridge Street, halfway between town square and abbey.

Very traditional, independent, grand sporting hotel.

- Georgian mansion – banks of Tweed.
- Traditional and modern Scottish cooking.
- "Relaxed but grand country house hotel – very traditional and well-run."

Standing on the banks of the Tweed in Kelso and enjoying wonderful views, this is considered to be the finest Georgian mansion in Roxburghshire. It was built in 1761 and its elegant facade is complemented by an interior with ornate ceilings, fireplaces and carved woodwork. In spite of this grandeur, Ednam is not a daunting house, and you are very warmly received. It has a homely, attractively 'old fashioned' feel, and a genuine country house atmosphere, encouraged by the numbers of salmon fishermen who stay here. The proprietor/chef Ralph Brookes describes his cooking as 'straightforward, but along classical lines' and creates original dishes using unusual ingredients such as oxtail and wood pigeon, preferring to fashion his menus from the fresh ingredients he can obtain locally and seasonally.

Open all year except Christmas + New Year
🏠 Rooms: 32 with private facilities
SP Special rates available
✕ Food served all day £-££
✕ Lunch £
✕ Dinner ££
Ⓥ Vegetarians welcome – prior notice required
⚘ Children welcome
🐄 Member of the Scotch Beef Club

Home-cured gravadlax. Medallions of Aberdeen Angus beef fillet with a red wine and shallot sauce. Cider syllabub served with home-made shortbread biscuits.

STB Commended 👑 👑 👑 👑
💳 Credit cards: Access/Mastercard/Eurocard, Visa, Switch
Ⓜ Proprietors: R A & R W Brooks

SUNLAWS HOUSE HOTEL AND GOLF COURSE
Heiton, Kelso
Roxburghshire TD5 8JZ
Tel: 01573 450331
Fax: 01573 450611

Situated at the village of Heiton, on the A698 Kelso-Hawick road. Signposted at western end of village.

One of Scotland's leading country house hotels in a lovely secluded setting.

- Country house hotel.
- Traditional Scottish, with grand hotel touches.
- "Picturesque countryside providing gracious accommodation and excellent food."

The Duke and Duchess of Roxburghe, who own Sunlaws, turned it into a gracious hotel in the 1970s. The building itself is in the Scottish baronial style and stands on the banks of the River Teviot in many hundreds of acres of park and woodland. The hotel offers a variety of country pursuits and in April 1997 its own golf course will open. Although it is an imposing mansion, Sunlaws retains the common touch. The welcome is genuinely hospitable; there are many thoughtful, cosy touches; the overall manner and atmosphere is unpretentious. Well-constructed table d'hôte menus are offered for lunch and dinner (an à la carte menu is also available in the evening) – offering both light and complex dishes and a good range of meat, fish and poultry. Chef David Bates gives careful thought to combinations of flavour and presentation. Sunlaws has 2 AA Rosettes.

Open all year
🏠 Rooms: 22 with private facilities
SP Special rates available
✕ Lunch ££
✕ Dinner £££-££££
Ⓥ Vegetarians welcome
⚘ Children welcome
⌇ No smoking in dining room
🐄 Member of the Scotch Beef Club

Venison broth with beetroot and root vegetables. Steamed brill with salmon soufflé and chervil butter sauce. Brandy-snap basket filled with praline ice cream.

STB Highly Commended 👑 👑 👑 👑 👑
💳 Credit cards: Access/Mastercard/Eurocard, American Express, Visa, Diners Club, Switch
Ⓜ General Manager: David A Webster

ARDSHEAL HOUSE
Country House Hotel of the Year 1996

Kentallen, Argyll PA38 4BX
Tel: 01631 740227 Fax: 01631 740342

On A828 Oban road, 4 miles south of Ballachulish Bridge.

A luxurious country house hotel.

- An outstanding country house hotel.
- Modern Scottish cooking.
- "Excellent food can be enjoyed in an atmosphere of old world charm."

Everywhere you turn, as you travel up the mile-long drive, there are ancient trees, and between them glimpses of sea and mountains. The original house was built by the Stewarts of Appin in the 1500s. It is beautifully appointed, with a magnificent oak-panelled hall, a traditional billiards room and a dining room conservatory in the garden area. Throughout it is furnished with fine antiques, and log fires burn in the sitting rooms on chilly days. The cooking is elegant and assured. Vegetables, fruits and herbs come from the two acre kitchen garden; meat, fish and shellfish is sourced locally; all preserves are made in the kitchen. The atmosphere of the place is very much that of an elegant private house, and to stay at Ardsheal is like joining a very select house party. A very special place. Ardsheal has 2 AA Rosettes. *(See advert Page 13.)*

Open all year except 10 Jan to 10 Feb
- 🛏 Rooms: 13 with private facilities
- 🆂🅿 Special rates available
- ✕ Lunch £-££
- ✕ Dinner £££
- Ⓥ Vegetarians welcome
- 🧍 Children welcome
- 🚭 No smoking in restaurant

Pan-fried crab cakes with a Champagne and chive butter sauce. Rosette of beef fillet with a coarse grain mustard sabayon, red wine and shallot sauce. Rhubarb and ginger pudding with home-made vanilla ice cream.

STB Highly Commended 👑 👑 👑 👑
- 🆔 Credit cards: Access/Mastercard/Eurocard, American Express, Visa, Switch
- Ⓜ Managers: Mr & Mrs George Kelso

ARDANAISEIG HOTEL

Kilchrenan
by Taynuilt
Argyll PA35 1HE
Tel: 01866 833333
Fax: 01866 833222

1 mile east of Taynuilt, turn sharp left. Follow B845 to Kilchrenan. At Kilchrenan Inn turn left – 3 miles on single track road to Ardanaiseig.

Small luxury hotel.

- Skilfully restored early 19th century mansion.
- A very high standard of food superbly cooked and presented.
- "First class!"

Ardanaiseig is an elegantly appointed hotel offering excellent standards of care and comfort. Under its new owner, Benny Gray, the house has been skilfully restored and furnished with beautiful antiques, paintings and eye-catching objet d'art. In the dining room true Scottish hospitality is delivered by new chef Dale Thornber who selects the very best fresh, local ingredients and presents them with flair and sophistication. Everything about Ardanaiseig is exquisite from the gardens and nature reserve to the tiniest details. A very welcome addition to Taste of Scotland. *(See advert Page 13.)*

Open all year except 2 Jan to 14 Feb
- 🛏 Rooms: 14 with private facilities
- ✕ Food served all day £££
- ✕ Lunch ££
- ✕ Dinner £££

Home-made red cabbage and apple soup. French-roasted poussin. Lemon yoghurt mousse.

STB Highly Commended 👑 👑 👑 👑
- 🆔 Credit cards: Access/Mastercard/Eurocard, American Express, Visa, Diners Club
- Ⓜ Manager: Nigel Liston

TAYCHREGGAN HOTEL

Kilchrenan, Taynuilt
Argyll PA35 1HQ
Tel: 01866 833 211/833 366
Fax: 01866 833 244

Leave A85 at Taynuilt on to B845 through village of Kilchrenan to the loch side.

A beautiful small country hotel set in the grandeur of Argyll.

- A highly regarded, award-winning hotel of great distinction.
- Elegant British cuisine.
- "What an elegant and charming place this is."

There has been an hotel here, nestling on the shores of Loch Awe, for 300 years. Taychreggan was a drovers' inn. With its cobbled courtyard and great charm, it retains that sense of peace and history. But under proprietor Annie Paul no effort has been spared to restore and enhance the hotel's unique ambience. Her emphasis and that of her dedicated staff is to make visitors feel like house guests, even well-behaved canine ones. Award-winning chef Neil Mellis presents imaginative fine cuisine in the hotel's dining room. Simpler bar lunches are no less carefully prepared. Euan Paul's wine list is a revelation. The hotel has 2 AA Rosettes.

Open all year
⌂ Rooms: 20 with private facilities
SP Special rates available
✕ Lunch ££
✕ Dinner 5 course menu £££
Ⓥ Vegetarians welcome
♿ Facilities for disabled visitors
⅟ No smoking in dining room
🐄 Member of the Scotch Beef Club

Seared Loch Etive scallops with a speck and citrus vinaigrette. Fillet of Highland beef with fondant potatoes, roasted shallots and garlic on a red wine jus. Vanilla and fresh raspberry mille feuille.

STB Highly Commended 👑 👑 👑 👑
💳 Credit cards: Access/Mastercard/Eurocard, American Express, Visa, Switch
👤 Proprietor: Annie Paul

KILDRUMMY CASTLE HOTEL

Kildrummy, Alford
Aberdeenshire AB33 8RA
Tel: 019755 71288
Fax: 019755 71345

On A97 Ballater-Huntly, 35 miles west of Aberdeen.

A grand country house hotel on Donside amidst acres of gardens.

- A very grand Victorian house converted into a luxurious hotel.
- Good hotel cooking.
- "A very comfortable hotel with pleasant surroundings and good food."

Kildrummy is a magnificent house near Alford, deep in rural Aberdeenshire and standing in 12 acres of gardens – one of several splendid castles and country houses in the area, many of them open to the public. Having been lavishly appointed when it was built and well-maintained ever since, it has a wonderful period charm. Its sumptuous colour schemes and ornately panelled ceilings, walls and fire surrounds create an atmosphere of opulence, and the attention to detail in furnishing the public rooms complements this well. Upstairs, the 16 en suite bedrooms are equally tastefully furnished. The menu is heartily luxurious – fine country house cooking, substantial and locally sourced fish, game and meat – and professionally served. The hotel has 1 AA Rosette.

Open all year except Jan
⌂ Rooms: 16 with private facilities
SP Special rates available
✕ Lunch ££
✕ Dinner 4 course menu £££
Ⓥ Vegetarians welcome
⛄ Children welcome
⅟ No smoking in dining room

North Sea crab claws and king prawns with garlic butter. Fillet of Aberdeen Angus beef with a haggis and Drambuie sauce. Selection of home-made sweets from the trolley.

STB Deluxe 👑 👑 👑 👑
💳 Credit cards: Access/Mastercard/Eurocard, American Express, Visa, Mastercharge, Switch, Delta
👤 Proprietors: Thomas & Mary Hanna

KILMARNOCK

THE COFFEE CLUB
30 Bank Street, Kilmarnock
Ayrshire KA1 1HA
Tel: 01563 522048

City centre.

Town centre coffee shop/bistro.

- Popular and busy town restaurant.
- Home-cooking.
- "Now an institution in Kilmarnock – the only place to visit."

Situated in one of the oldest streets in Kilmarnock opposite the Laigh Kirk, this cheerful restaurant offers something for everyone. There is a large varied menu with lots of choice including grills and vegetarian dishes and a range of quick snack meals. Service is fast, friendly and efficient. All food is produced on the spot using fresh produce wherever possible and the home baking is a speciality. There is a welcoming atmosphere at The Coffee Club.

Open all year except Christmas Day,
Boxing Day, 1 + 2 Jan
🍽 ♀ Unlicensed – guests welcome to take own wine
✗ Food served all day £
✗ Lunch except Sun £
✗ Dinner except Sun ££
Ⓥ Vegetarians welcome
⚘ Children welcome
♿ Facilities for disabled visitors
🚭 No smoking area in air-conditioned restaurant

Sandwiches, salads, omelettes etc. Children's menu. Vegetarian dishes. Grilled salmon steak with hollandaise sauce. Sole with almonds in a rich cream sauce. Steaks with a variety of sauces.

⊞ Credit cards: Access/Mastercard/Eurocard, American Express, Visa, Switch
🗓 Proprietor: Svend Kamming

KILMUN BY DUNOON

BISTRO AT FERN GROVE
Kilmun, by Dunoon
Argyll PA23 8SB
Tel: 01369 840 334
Fax: 01369 840 334

6 miles from Dunoon on A880 on the side of the Holy Loch.

Restaurant with rooms.

- Bistro in village.
- Home cooking.
- "Good cooking and a bright personality in host Ian Murray."

This 19th century house was at one time the home of the Campbells of Kilmun overlooking Holy Loch. The hospitable hosts Ian and Estralita Murray have built up a strong reputation for their little bistro over the years. Simple cooking is their forte. A daily changing blackboard menu of chef's specials is supplemented by an à la carte menu of snacks. Accommodation is limited to three rooms, and plays a secondary role to the restaurant.

Open all year except Nov, weekends only Dec to 1 Apr
🛏 Rooms: 3 with private facilities
🆂🅿 Special rates available
✗ Food served all day £
✗ Lunch ££
✗ Dinner ££
Ⓥ Vegetarians welcome
⚘ Children welcome
♿ Facilities for disabled visitors
🚭 No smoking in restaurant + bedrooms

Carrot roulade filled with creamy smoked haddock. Breast of pheasant with mustard sauce. Warm pear and almond tart with home-made honey ice cream.

⊞ Credit cards: Access/Mastercard/Eurocard, Visa
🗓 Proprietors: Ian & Estralita Murray

KINCRAIG

MARCH HOUSE

Lagganlia, Feshiebridge, Inverness-shire PH21 1NG
Tel: 01540 651 388 Fax: 01540 651 388

Follow B970 to Feshiebridge. Cross the bridge and climb until red telephone box on right. Turn right and follow no through road for ½ mile. Turn left down drive.

A family-run guest house, beautifully situated in Glenfeshie.

- Secluded Alpine style house.
- Traditional Scottish cooking with European overtones.
- "Daily selected produce freshly cooked."

Standing in a glade of mature pines at the mouth of lovely Glenfeshie, March House enjoys wonderful views of the Cairngorm Mountains and is an ideal base for the many outdoor pursuits that Speyside offers, such as skiing, gliding, birdwatching, etc. The house is modern and Alpine in style – with timber cladding, a large wood-burning stove and old stripped pine furniture. It has six bedrooms, all en suite and the spacious conservatory overlooking the mountains provides an idyllic setting for dinner (non-residents are welcome, but should telephone). It is owned and enthusiastically run by Caroline and Ernie Hayes, whose cooking and baking matches the clean, fresh atmosphere of March House itself. They use fresh local produce and present a very well-priced table d'hôte menu.

Open all year except 26 Nov to 26 Dec
🛏 Rooms: 6 with private facilities
SP Special rates available
UL ♀ Unlicensed – guests welcome to take own wine
✗ Lunch – pre-arranged parties ££
✗ Dinner ££
🛏 Reservations essential for non-residents
V Vegetarians welcome
🧒 Children welcome
✗ Smoking permitted after dinner

Seasonal soups served with wholemeal and walnut soda bread rolls. Chicken breasts baked with wild mushrooms, white wine and home-grown thyme. Hot pancakes with caramelised oranges.

STB Highly Commended 🌟 🌟 🌟
💳 Credit cards: Visa
🛏 Proprietors: Ernie & Caroline Hayes

KINGUSSIE

THE CROSS

Tweed Mill Brae, Ardbroilach Road
Kingussie, Inverness-shire PH21 1TC
Tel: 01540 661166 Fax: 01540 661080

From traffic lights in centre of village, travel uphill along Ardbroilach Road for c. 200 yards, then turn left down private drive (Tweed Mill Brae).

Outstanding award-winning restaurant.

- Restaurant with rooms.
- Innovative Scottish cooking.
- "Nothing is too much trouble for the Hadleys – they deserve all the accolades they receive."

The Cross was built as a tweed mill in the late 19th century and is situated in a wonderful waterside setting. Here they have retained some interesting features including the exposed original beams in the dining room and the upstairs lounge with its coombed ceilings. Ruth Hadley is a member of the Master Chefs of Great Britain. She treats her ingredients deftly and there is an experimental energy behind some dishes. Where she can, she uses less common produce such as wild mushrooms, mountain hare, pike or fresh turbot, and she grows her own herbs in the restaurant's four acre garden. Tony Hadley's waiting style is renowned; he also makes a nightly selection of wines, from one of the best cellars in Scotland, which will complement the menu. The Cross has 3 AA Rosettes.

Open 1 Mar to 1 Dec + 27 Dec to 5 Jan
Closed Tue
🛏 Rooms: 9 with private facilities
✗ Lunch – private party bookings by arrangement
✗ Dinner except Tue ££££
V Vegetarians welcome – prior notice required
♿ Facilities for non-residential disabled visitors
✗ No smoking in dining room + bedrooms

Seafood Sausage: a sausage of halibut, prawns and scallop served with fresh asparagus. Venison 'Francatelli': fillet of local wild red deer, lightly cooked with port wine and redcurrants. Iced Hazelnut Parfait: a frozen-textured parfait, accompanied by Blairgowrie raspberries and cream.

💳 Credit cards: Access/Mastercard/Eurocard/Visa, Switch, Delta
🛏 Partners/Proprietors: Tony & Ruth Hadley

THE OSPREY HOTEL

Ruthven Road
Kingussie
Inverness-shire PH21 1EN
Tel: 01540 661510
Fax: 01540 661510

South end of Kingussie main street.

An attractive small hotel in a quiet Highland town.

- A stone-built town house.
- Traditional Scottish cooking with French influences.
- "Comfortable accommodation and imaginative, delicious cooking."

Conveniently situated in the centre of Kingussie, overlooking the memorial gardens, The Osprey Hotel is an excellent base from which to explore this part of the Highlands. Robert and Aileen Burrow are friendly, caring and attentive hosts, and these qualities, alongside Aileen's considerable culinary skills have earned them both 2 AA Rosettes and a large number of returning guests each year. One regular from London returns every year and has done so for a long time; she is now 101 years old! Aileen is a talented cook; her menus, which are table d'hôte, are appetising and offer only freshly prepared dishes, carefully and imaginatively cooked. The home baking is a very special treat; the bread is fresh each day – and be sure to leave some space for a pudding!

Open all year
🏠 Rooms: 8 with private facilities
SP Special rates available
✗ Dinner £££
Ⓥ Vegetarians welcome
🕇 Children over 10 years welcome
🕭 Facilities for disabled visitors

Choux pastry cups filled with onion and red pepper casserole. Braised lamb cutlets with garlic, apple and rosemary. Whisky and hazelnut parfait served with seasonal fruits.

STB Commended 👑 👑 👑
💳 Credit cards: Access/Mastercard/Eurocard, American Express, Visa, Diners Club
🏠 Proprietors: Robert & Aileen Burrow

SCOT HOUSE HOTEL

Newtonmore Road
Kingussie
Inverness-shire PH21 1HE
Tel: 01540 661351
Fax: 01540 661111

South end of main road through village of Kingussie (B9152 off A9 trunk road).

An attractive, well-appointed hotel set amid the unique natural splendour of the Highlands.

- A converted manse.
- Outstanding home cooking.
- "Friendly, comfortable and relaxing – a Highland welcome awaits you."

George MacKenzie was a local man who made his fortune in Canada by founding the Singer Sewing Machine Company. In 1884 he provided the funds to build the village's Free Presbyterian Church manse. Converted in the 1960s, it is now the Scot House Hotel. Its present owners have recently restored and refurbished the entire building. With both table d'hôte and à la carte menus, the dining room makes the most of the area's excellent beef, fish and game yet also offers a vegetarian menu. Unpretentious and good, the hotel's cooking is matched by a varied and affordable wine list. Bar lunches and suppers are distinguished by wholesome ingredients, freshly prepared. Scot House Hotel has 1 AA Rosette.

Open 8 Feb to 31 Dec except Christmas Day + Boxing Day
🏠 Rooms: 9 with private facilities
✗ Lunch £
✗ Dinner ££-£££
🕇 Children welcome
🕭 Facilities for disabled visitors
🚭 No smoking in dining room
🕭 Entry ramp and toilets for disabled visitors

Home-made fine chicken liver pâté with a hot, fresh, redcurrant and orange sauce. Breast of chicken stuffed with leeks and shrimps with a lemon and cucumber sauce. Fresh local strawberry pavlova.

STB Highly Commended 👑 👑 👑
💳 Credit cards: Access/Mastercard/Eurocard, Visa, Switch, Delta
🏠 Chef/Proprietor: W E Gilbert

KINLOCHOURN

SKIARY
Loch Hourn, Invergarry, Inverness-shire PH35 4HD
Tel: 01809 511214

From Invergarry (on A82 Fort William–Inverness road) take A87 Invergarry–Kyle road. After 5 miles turn left to Kinlochourn. Proceed for 22 miles to end of single track road. You will then be met by boat by arrangement.

Remote, small guest house accessible only by boat or on foot.

- A unique guest house on the very shore of a dramatic West Highland sea-loch.
- Home cooking.
- "The spectacular journey to this century old fisherman's cottage ends happily with a genuinely warm welcome to their home from John and Christina."

This must be the most remote guest house in Scotland but the journey is worth it. Christina's cooking is miraculous, she uses excellent fresh local game, meat and fish. Vegetables, herbs and soft fruit come from the garden; and bread, scones and pastry are baked daily. The bedrooms are small but charming. Views from the house are truly spectacular with an abundance of wild life to be seen. A fantastic experience, not for the faint-hearted.

```
     Open 1 May to 30 Sep
🏠  Rooms: 3
SP  Special rates available
✗  Residents only
🍷 Unlicensed – guests welcome to take own wine
✗  Food served all day
✗  Lunch
✗  Dinner
Ⓥ  Vegetarians welcome
🜨  Children welcome
♿  Downstairs bedroom suitable for mildly
     disabled visitors
🅿  No parking at establishment but parking at
     end of the road
```

Salmon and sour cream pie. Casserole of local venison with red wine and orange. Rhubarb and orange meringue pie.

💳 No credit cards
👤 Owners: John & Christina Everett

KINLOCH RANNOCH

BUNRANNOCH HOUSE
Kinloch Rannoch
Perthshire PH16 5QB
Tel: 01882 632407

Turn right after 500 yards on Schiehallion road, just outside Kinloch Rannoch off B846.

A family-run country guest house in Highland Perthshire.

- An old hunting lodge in lovely surroundings.
- Traditional cooking.
- "Warm hospitality in a family Highland home."

Set amidst mature trees, Bunrannoch is a Listed building and stands on the site of a medieval settlement, in the shadow of the 'sleeping giant' mountain, close to Loch Rannoch. There is an easy informality within this comfortable family home, making guests feel completely at ease and totally relaxed. The cosy lounge, log fires and uninterrupted Highland views complement the delicious aromas from the kitchen. Jennifer Skeaping is the chef/proprietor and her good cooking and friendly manner assure you of an enjoyable stay. The menus (a choice of two main courses) change daily, fresh food is sourced locally and tastefully prepared.

```
     Open all year except Christmas + New Year
🏠  Rooms: 7, 5 with private facilities
SP  Special rates available
✗  Dinner ££
Ⓥ  Vegetarians welcome – prior notice required
🚭  No smoking throughout
```

Spicy avocado soup. Fillet of Scottish lamb pan-fried and served with a Madeira sauce. Chocolate truffle cake with Cointreau strawberries.

STB Commended 👑 👑
💳 Credit cards: Access/Mastercard/Eurocard, Visa
👤 Proprietor: Jennifer Skeaping

CUILMORE COTTAGE

Kinloch Rannoch
Perthshire
PH16 5QB
Tel: 01882 632 218
Fax: 01882 632 218

From Kinloch Rannoch take unclassified road signed Rannoch School on south side of Loch. Pass War Memorial. Cuilmore Cottage 100 yards along first road on left.

A tiny restaurant with rooms and an unrivalled reputation.

- An 18th century converted croft house.
- Fresh home cooking with flair.
- "Cuilmore is unique – a standard and style in a class of its own!"

Anita Steffen has made a tremendous success of this cosy little croft house overlooking Loch Rannoch and the standard and style of her food has been lauded and publicised to a degree that is remarkable for so small an establishment. Much of her produce is grown in the cottage garden and the rest is locally sourced to ensure freshness and quality. Thereafter Anita displays her own culinary skill and flair to the great satisfaction of her diners. Dinners are served at the candlelit table in the intimate dining room of the cottage. Cuilmore is delightfully secluded and guests have the complimentary use of mountain bikes, a dinghy and canoe to explore the beautiful countryside. Gleneagles Best B&B 1995.

Open 1 Feb to 30 Oct
🏠 Rooms: 2 with private facilities
SP Special rates available
UL ♀ Unlicensed – guests welcome to take own wine
✕ Dinner £££
V Vegetarians welcome
✗ No smoking throughout

Tay salmon mousse flavoured with lime and dill. Half baby Guinea fowl filled with celery and chestnut forcemeat. Layered Valrohna chocolate delice.

STB Deluxe 👑 👑 👑
💳 Credit cards: Access/Mastercard/Eurocard, Visa
👤 Proprietors: Jens & Anita Steffen

Kinnesswood 126

THE LOMOND COUNTRY INN

Kinnesswood, by Loch Leven
Perthshire KY13 7HN
Tel: 01592 840253
Fax: 01592 840693

4 miles from Kinross. From south, M90 junction 5, B9097 via Scotlandwell. From north, M90 Junction 7, A911 via Milnathort.

Family-run hotel/inn overlooking Loch Leven and popular meeting place for locals.

- Hotel in an historic village.
- Scottish/home cooking.
- "Good food and Scottish hospitality."

This is an honest and unpretentious country hotel in the village of Kinnesswood. People come here for the food and the fine views as the inn is conveniently situated just minutes off the motorway. The food is freshly prepared and the dishes have a traditional Scottish character. A good wine list and some interesting real ales complement the menus and food available throughout the day. The hotel has 1 AA Rosette.

Open all year
🏠 Rooms: 12 with private facilities
SP Special rates available
✕ Food served all day £
✕ Lunch £
✕ Dinner ££
V Vegetarians welcome
☆ Children welcome
♿ Facilities for disabled visitors
✗ No smoking in restaurant

Highland game terrine with orange and whisky marmalade. Puff pastry parcel of wild salmon with vermouth sauce. Raspberry cranachan.

STB Commended 👑 👑 👑
💳 Credit cards: Access/Mastercard/Eurocard, American Express, Visa, Diners Club, Switch, Delta
👤 Proprietor: David Adams

Kinross 127

CARLIN MAGGIES RESTAURANT

191 High Street
Kinross
Fife KY13 7DB
Tel: 01577 86 3652
Fax: 01577 86 3652

Junction 6, M90 approach to Kinross.

Restaurant with inventive Scottish cuisine with Scottish flavour.

- Small town restaurant.
- Good Scottish cooking by an accomplished chef.
- "Good use of local and regional produce in this very pleasant little restaurant."

Tom McConnell, international Master Chef and culinary olympic medallist, and his Australian wife Dala, run this restaurant focusing on skilfully prepared Scottish produce. The surroundings are comfortable and Dala's friendly and welcoming manner ensures an enjoyable dining experience.

Open all year except Mar
Closed Sun Mon
✗ Lunch (Sun Mon Tue Wed – by appointment) £
✗ Dinner except Sun Mon £££
Ⓥ Vegetarians welcome – prior notice required
✝ Children welcome
♿ Facilities for disabled visitors
✄ Smoking area in restaurant

Marinated Orkney scallops and prawns on horseradish, potato, sesame bread ring, parsley juices, mustard oil and red pepper juices. Pork fillet parcel with avocado, mushroom, Edam and cottage cheese, crumbled and pan-fried with lemon and tarragon sauce. Atholl Brose parfait.

💳 Credit cards: Access/Mastercard/Eurocard, Visa
🔪 Chef/Owner: Tom McConnell

THE GROUSE AND CLARET

Heatheryford Country Centre
by Kinross
Tayside KY13 7NQ
Tel: 01577 864212
Fax: 01577 864920

20 metres from M90 at junction 6, opposite service station. 500 metres up private road.

Restaurant with rooms.

- Converted farm.
- Home/traditional cooking.
- "Excellent cuisine, relaxed atmosphere in country setting."

Situated in 25 acres of wild meadow surrounded by ten acres of water stocked with wild rainbow and brown trout, The Grouse and Claret (named after a fishing fly) offers good home cooking, with many traditional dishes appearing on the menus. Seasonal game and fresh shellfish are a speciality and vegetarians are well catered for. Meriel Cairns and her sister Vicki Futong take great pride in their successful establishment, assuring you of a warm welcome in lovely surroundings. The detached accommodation has comfortable ground floor rooms overlooking the fishing lochans. The Heatheryford Gallery has regular exhibitions of contemporary art.

Open 2 Jan to 15 Jan + 7 Feb to 31 Dec
Closed Boxing Day + New Year's Day
Note: Closed Mon Jan to Mar
🛏 Rooms: 3 with private facilities
♀ Table licence
✗ Lunch except Mon Jan to Mar ££
✗ Dinner except Sun Mon Jan to Mar ££-£££
Ⓥ Vegetarians welcome
✝ Children welcome
♿ Facilities for disabled visitors
✄ No smoking in restaurant

A soufflé with three Scottish cheeses and fresh herbs. Noisettes of Scottish lamb on a bed of Provençale vegetables with a tarragon and port jus. Heatheryford cranachan.

STB Commended 👑 👑 👑
💳 Credit cards: Access/Mastercard, Visa
🔪 Proprietor: Meriel Cairns
🔪 Manager: Vicki Futong

THE MUIRS INN KINROSS
49 Muirs, Kinross
Kinross-shire KY13 7AU
Tel: 01577 862270
Fax: 01577 862270

M90 exit junction 6 and follow A922 Milnathort for a short distance. At 'T' junction, Inn is diagonally opposite to right.

A popular village inn offering Scottish hospitality.

- Good, fresh, honest food at sensible prices.
- The best of straightforward home cooking – and more.
- "Good food at affordable prices, good home baking and cooking. A true village inn."

Built in the early 19th century as a farmhouse, the Muirs Inn is near the shores of Loch Leven. Mary, Queen of Scots, was imprisoned on an island there in 1567. The inn merits its excellent and growing reputation for attention to detail and care for guests' comfort in its five bedrooms, all with private facilities. The same care is evident in the inn's food and ethos. The Maltings restaurant has a warm, homely feel and offers a vast menu from traditional pub food to Caribbean and Chinese. All are freshly prepared and well-presented. This is an establishment run by and for people who care.

Open all year
- Rooms: 5 with private facilities
- Special rates available
- Lunch £
- Dinner ££/Supper £
- Vegetarians welcome
- Children welcome
- Facilities for disabled visitors

Freshly baked tomato filled with a smoked salmon mousse and garnished with leek in a tartan effect. A succulent piece of gammon topped with smoked haddock. Traditionally made cloutie dumpling made to 'granny's' recipe.

STB Commended 👑 👑 👑
- Credit cards: Access/Mastercard/Eurocard, Visa, Switch, Delta
- Innkeepers: G M Westwood & G Philip

Kirkcudbright 128

AULD ALLIANCE RESTAURANT
Castle Street
Kirkcudbright DG6 4JA
Tel: 01557 330569

Kirkcudbright town, opposite the castle.

Small restaurant in Kirkcudbright.

- A Listed stone terraced cottage.
- French/Scottish cooking.
- "Good cooking making the best use of fresh local ingredients."

This is a converted tradesman's cottage built from stones quarried from Kirkcudbright Castle on the other side of the street. The restaurant is unfussy, plain and simple inside which is just as well for the dishes cooked by Alistair Crawford will focus your attention. They are a wonderful mixture of fresh local foods cooked in opulent, classical French style – the style in which Alistair was trained. The spirit of the establishment echoes the ancient union between Scotland and France – and what better way to express the bond than through the confluence of technique and supply.

Open Easter to 31 Oct
- Sun lunch only £
- Dinner £££
- Vegetarians welcome
- Children welcome
- Facilities for disabled visitors

Smoked Scotch salmon wrapped around lightly sautéd Kirkcudbright queen scallops and salmon mousse with apple and mint jelly and a hint of Pernod. Fresh local lobster in a creamy mushroom and mustard sauce topped with melted Dunlop cheese. 'Witches foam' flavoured with Drambuie served in a brandy snap (jumble) basket.

- No credit cards
- Proprietors: Alistair & Anne Crawford

Kyle of Lochalsh **129**

THE SEAFOOD RESTAURANT

Railway Station, Kyle of Lochalsh
Ross-shire IV40 8XX
Tel: 01599 5344813

At Kyle of Lochalsh railway station on platform 1.
Parking on slipway to station.

An informal bistro and cafe in scenic location.

- Converted station waiting room.
- Modern Scottish home cooking.
- "The appeal is the same as when I first inspected it a few years ago – all railway stations should have a place like this."

A railway platform is not the obvious choice of location for a restaurant but it is worth taking the trouble to track down The Seafood Restaurant for you will not be disappointed. The station is right next to the harbour in Kyle of Lochalsh close to the ferry terminal which, until the recently opened bridge, was the main crossing point to Skye. From your table in the converted waiting room you can look out over the Cuillins. The philosophy here is to present high quality local produce, predominantly fish and shellfish cooked simply. Although the abundant seafood is prominent on the menu there is also an interesting selection of meat and vegetarian dishes. In the peak season there is a breakfast and lunch menu with a selection of simple, home-cooked fare which changes to give a more sophisticated à la carte choice in the evening. You are advised to check opening hours as they vary depending on the time of year.

Open Easter to Oct
♀ Table licence
✗ Lunch except Sun Sat £
✗ Dinner ££
Ⓥ Vegetarians welcome
☆ Children welcome
♿ Limited facilities for disabled visitors
🚭 No smoking in restaurant

Langoustines in garlic butter. Flambéd Drambuie and mushroom steaks. Raspberry cranachan.

💳 Credit cards: Access/Mastercard/Eurocard, Visa
Ⓜ Owners: Jann Macrae & Andrea Matheson

SEAGREEN RESTAURANT & BOOKSHOP

Plockton Road
Kyle of Lochalsh IV40 8DA
Tel: 01599 534388

North of Kyle of Lochalsh, on road to Plockton.

A relaxed, informal bistro combined with bookshop and gallery.

- Charming stone-built schoolhouse conversion.
- Modern Scottish cooking.
- "At any time of day or in the evening, a friendly place."

Situated on the outskirts of Kyle of Lochalsh this is a very attractive complex of an open plan kitchen and large, spacious dining area with a bookshop at one end which sells literature and traditional music CDs and cassettes. The dining room exhibits shows of local painters and photographers. Outside there is a sheltered sunny garden and terrace, popular with guests. An all day counter service offers delicious salads, soups, home baking, etc., all made on the premises from fresh local ingredients. The restaurant offers very good wholefood but the emphasis is increasingly on fish and shellfish. In the evening a full à la carte dinner menu is served in a separate dining room. The style of the food is different from that served during the day with a more sophisticated continental/European influenced menu.

Open all year except 25, 26 Dec,
1 Jan, 6 Jan + end Feb
✗ Lunch £
✗ Dinner ££-£££
Ⓜ Reservations preferred for dinner
Ⓥ Vegetarians welcome
☆ Children welcome
♿ Facilities for disabled visitors
🚭 No smoking in restaurant

Green pea and leek soup. Monkfish and mussel kebabs served on a bed of couscous with watercress sauce. Home-made ice creams.

💳 Credit cards: Access/Mastercard/Eurocard, Visa, Switch
Ⓜ Chef/Proprietor: Fiona Begg

KYLESKU

LINNE MHUIRICH
Unapool Croft Road, Kylesku
by Lairg, Sutherland IV27 4HW
Tel: 01971 502227

½ mile south of the new Kylesku Bridge on A894, last house in a cul-de-sac road.

Lochside bed and breakfast in Assynt.

- Modern shoreside crofthouse.
- Home cooking.
- "Excellent, substantial home cooking using only the freshest ingredients."

Fiona and Diarmid MacAulay welcome guests to their home close to the Kylesku Bridge which links Assynt to Scourie and the far north-west. A modern house of traditional design, it is peacefully positioned overlooking Loch Glencoul. The Handa Island Nature/Bird Reserve and lovely, lonely sandy beaches are nearby. Directions and maps for many local walks are provided. The dinner menus change daily and they are discussed with you after breakfast. Local fish and seafood including smoked haddock; Kylesku prawn vol-au-vents; and Loch Beag mussels and Ullapool prawns; appear on the menu alongside tempting desserts. All quiches and pâtés are home-made. Vegetarians are extremely well catered for and all the dishes are prepared in a homely style, using fresh local ingredients and taking account of guests' preferences. The food is unpretentious and wholesome. The house proudly proclaims itself to be a 'non-smokers' sanctuary'; guests are invited to bring their own wine. French and German spoken.

Open Easter to 30 Oct
- 🏠 Rooms: 2, 1 with private facilities
- ✗ Residents only
- ✗ Dinner except Sun Sat Wed ££
- Ⓥ Vegetarians welcome
- ⚘ Children welcome
- ⚸ No smoking throughout

Celtic salmon medallions with lime and almonds. Pork, pepper and apple casserole. Scottish honey and cheeses.

STB Commended 👑 👑
- 💳 No credit cards
- ⋈ Proprietors: Fiona & Diarmid MacAulay

LAIDE

THE OLD SMIDDY
Laide, nr Gairloch, Wester Ross IV22 2NB
Tel: 01445 731425
Fax: 01445 731425

A835 Inverness-Ullapool. At Braemore junction (44 miles north-west of Inverness) take A832 via Dundonnell to Laide (29 miles).

Unique cottage guest house with small restaurant in the tiny village of Laide.

- Small guest house.
- Imaginative, creative, Scottish home cooking.
- "The food is beautifully presented, and tastes every bit as good as it looks."

Seven miles north of the famous Inverewe Gardens and opposite the church sits The Old Smiddy, an attractive and well-converted white cottage (formerly the village blacksmith shop). Kate is a self-taught enthusiastic cook assisted by her husband Steve who ensures that menus are created around guests desires. The trend now being towards seafood of which there is an abundance in Wester Ross but also encompassing all the finest Highland produce which can be sourced locally. The dishes are then compiled with interesting finishing sauces, imaginative presentation using home-grown herbs. Genuine warm hospitality in superior Highland cottage providing a culinary oasis for those who enjoy above average fayre.

Open 3 Mar to 14 Nov
Note: Tea-room closed Sun Sat
- 🏠 Rooms: 2 with private facilities
- 🅂🄿 Special rates available
- 🅄🄻 ♀ Unlicensed – guests welcome to take own wine
- ✗ Lunch except Sun Sat £
- ✗ Dinner – early booking advisable for non-residents ££
- Ⓥ Vegetarians welcome
- ♿ Facilities for non-resident disabled visitors
- ⚸ No smoking throughout

Roasted red pepper soup with oatmeal bread. Monkfish fillets finished with a saffron, ginger and dill sauce. Rum and Mascarpone trifle.

STB Highly Commended 👑 👑 👑
- 💳 Credit cards: Access/Mastercard/Eurocard, Visa
- ⋈ Proprietors: Kate & Steve Macdonald

LANGBANK

GLEDDOCH HOUSE HOTEL & COUNTRY ESTATE
Langbank, Renfrewshire PA14 6YE
Tel: 01475 540711
Fax: 01475 540201

M8 towards Greenock. Take B789 Langbank/
Houston exit. Follow signs to left and then right
after ½ mile – hotel is on left.

**Country house hotel in its own sporting estate
overlooking the Clyde.**

- First class country house hotel in lovely grounds.
- Modern Scottish cooking.
- "A truly relaxing location with Scotland's
  finest cuisine."

Gleddoch House Hotel was once the home of the
shipping baron, Sir James Lithgow. It stands in a 360
acre estate with dramatic views across the River
Clyde to Ben Lomond and the hills beyond. The
estate allows the hotel to offer a variety of outdoor
pursuits including an 18-hole golf course, horse
riding, clay pigeon shooting and off-road
driving. Public and private rooms are all decorated
and furnished to a very high standard. The
restaurant is spacious and gracious; the four
course, table d'hôte menu is succinct but superbly
cooked and presented by a highly professional chef.
The hotel also has conference and private dining
facilities and has been awarded 2 AA Rosettes.

Open all year
- 🛏 Rooms: 39 with private facilities
- 🆂🄿 Special rates available
- ✗ Food served all day £-££££
- ✗ Lunch ££
- ✗ Dinner ££££
- Ⓥ Vegetarians welcome
- 🗲 Children welcome
- 🐂 Member of the Scotch Beef Club

**Grilled king scallops on an Oban mussel, chive, shallot
and Pernod cream. Rosettes of spring Lanarkshire
lamb with a hazelnut and woodland mushroom
duxelle, with a duo of Madeira and Arran mustard
sauces. White chocolate and raspberry delice with a
gratin of fresh raspberries and blueberries.**

STB Highly Commended 👑 👑 👑 👑 👑
- 💳 Credit cards: Access/Mastercard/Eurocard,
  American Express, Visa, Diners Club, Switch
- 🗡 General Manager: Leslie W Conn

LARGS

FINS SEAFOOD RESTAURANT
Fairlie, Largs, Ayrshire KA29 0EG
Tel: 01475 568989
Fax: 01475 568921

On A78, 1 mile south of Fairlie near Largs.

**Fish farm, smokehouse, farm shop and
bistro/seafood seafood restaurant.**

- Renovated farm bistro.
- Imaginative, modern fish cookery.
- "Informal-style country restaurant serving
  brilliantly fresh seafood."

Fins is part of Fencebay Fisheries in Fairlie and fish
of all kinds are cured and smoked by traditional
methods; an agreement with the oyster farm across
the way also provides them with scallops, prawns
and other seafood (since they also have a fishing
boat). So the fish at Fins is landed daily. The enterprise, owned by Jill and Bernard Thain, won the
Scottish Seafood Product of the Year Award 1995
at the Scottish Food Proms. Chef Gillian Dick's
lunch and dinner menus are à la carte, supplemented
by a blackboard 'catch of the day' (there is also a
steak dish for non-'fishies'). The cooking is modern
and accomplished. The restaurant itself is situated
in an old barn, very tastefully decorated (with a
fishy theme), bright, friendly and cheerful. Service
is excellent. A thoroughly good fish restaurant.

Open all year except Christmas Day,
Boxing Day + New Year's Day
Closed Mon
- ✗ Lunch except Mon ££
- ✗ Dinner except Mon £££
- Ⓥ Vegetarians welcome
- 🗲 Children welcome – lunch only
- ♿ Facilities for disabled visitors
- 🚭 Diners are requested to refrain from smoking
  until after 2.30pm (lunch) + 9pm (dinner)

**Cullen skink. Pan-fried peppered salmon fillet
with The Macallan whisky sauce. Christine's
prune and apple cake with prune and Armagnac
ice cream.**

- 💳 Credit cards: Access/Mastercard/Eurocard,
  American Express, Visa, Diners Club,
  Mastercharge, Switch, Delta
- 🗡 Owner: Jill Thain
- 🗡 Head Chef: Gillian Dick

ACHRAY HOUSE HOTEL
St Fillans
Perthshire PH6 2NF
Tel: 01764 685 231
Fax: 01764 685 320

On A85, 12 miles from Crieff.

Family-run rural hotel beside Loch Earn.

- Traditional white-painted hotel.
- Traditional cooking based on quality produce.
- "Friendly, smiling, welcoming hotel in a delightful location."

Now owned and run by John and Lesley Murray, this popular and well-established hotel has a stunning lochside position with its own foreshore and jetty, in this area of outstanding natural beauty. They set impressively high standards and the food is offered across a range of menus in both bar and restaurant and provides and excellent choice. The dining room is tastefully appointed. *(See advert Page 27.)*

Open 5 Feb to 5 Jan
- 🏠 Rooms: 9, 8 with private facilities
- SP Special rates available
- ✕ Lunch £
- ✕ Dinner ££
- V Vegetarians welcome
- ⚘ Children welcome
- ♿ Facilities for disabled visitors
- ⚞ No smoking in restaurant

Wide choice of Scottish produce – salmon, lamb, beef, venison, seafood. Good choice of freshly made vegetarian dishes always available. Home-made puddings a speciality.

STB Commended 👑 👑 👑
- 💳 Access/Mastercard/Eurocard, American Express, Visa, Switch
- ⚐ Proprietors: John & Lesley Murray

FOUR SEASONS HOTEL
St Fillans
Perthshire PH6 2NF
Tel: 01764 685 333
Fax: 01764 685 333

On A85, 12 miles west of Crieff, at west end of St Fillans overlooking Loch Earn.

Rural hotel in charming village of St Fillans.

- Edwardian building with tasteful extensions.
- Traditional/modern Scottish cooking.
- "An attractive family-run hotel overlooking the loch."

Loch Earn is one of the most beautiful Perthshire lochs, surrounded by woods and hills. The Four Seasons has a wonderful unspoiled view from where the seasons can truly be seen to change over the year. The hotel has well-maintained bedrooms and rather quaint public rooms and bar. The Scott family run the hotel very efficiently and Chef Andrew Scott produces menus which have a strong emphasis on seafood and game in the best traditions of the Taste of Scotland. On warmer days dine 'al freso' on the south facing terrace. The Four Seasons has 2 AA Rosettes.

Open Mar to 24 Dec
Note: Open weekend only from mid Nov
- 🏠 Rooms: 18 with private facilities
- SP Special rates available
- ✕ Lunch ££
- ✕ Dinner £££
- V Vegetarians welcome
- ⚘ Children welcome
- ♿ Facilities for disabled visitors
- ⚞ No smoking in dining room

Steamed lemon sole with West Coast scallop mousse, Skye mussels, tomato and vermouth. Fillet of venison and woodpigeon, juniper, apples and local chanterelles. Honeyed pastry basket of local berries, praline ice cream.

STB Commended 👑 👑 👑 👑
- 💳 Credit cards: Access/Mastercard/Eurocard, American Express, Visa, Diners Club, Switch
- ⚐ Owners: The Scott Family

LOCH LOMOND

CAMERON HOUSE COUNTRY HOTEL
Loch Lomond, Alexandria
Dunbartonshire G83 8QZ
Tel: 01389 755565
Fax: 01389 759522

On A82 near Balloch, on the banks of Loch Lomond. At Balloch roundabout follow signs for Luss. Approx 1 mile, first right.

Luxury hotel and leisure complex on the shores of Loch Lomond.

- Converted baronial mansion with time-shared lodges and a state-of-the-art leisure complex.
- Award-winning grand hotel cuisine.
- "Fine old Scots baronial house, adapted well to modern luxury."

A luxury hotel resort on the southern shore of Loch Lomond, standing in 108 acres of parkland. Executive Chef Jeff Bland presents a highly sophisticated and imaginative menu in the hotel's main restaurant, the elegant Georgian Room. The bright and airy Brasserie has a more informal atmosphere and offers grill/brasserie style of dishes from an à la carte menu; bar snacks are available in the Marina Clubhouse. Cameron House has 3 AA Rosettes.

Open all year
🛏 Rooms: 68 with private facilities
✕ Food served all day £-££££
✕ Lunch except sun Sat ££
✕ Dinner ££££
Ⓥ Vegetarians welcome
⚘ Children welcome
♿ Facilities for disabled visitors
🚭 No smoking in Georgian Room
🐄 Member of the Scotch Beef Club

Oban langoustine soup garnished with lentils and beans served with a nettle dumpling. Casserole of Scottish lobster in a vegetable sauce accompanied by saffron potatoes. Hot banana soufflé and a vanilla ice cream.

STB Deluxe 👑 👑 👑 👑 👑
💳 Credit cards: Access/Mastercard/Eurocard, American Express, Visa, Diners Club, Mastercharge
👤 Executive Chef: Jeff Bland
👤 Restaurant Manager: Dale Dewsbury

LOCHCARRON

CARRON RESTAURANT
Cam-Allt, Strathcarron
Ross-shire IV54 8YX
Tel: 01520 722488

Lochcarron to Kyle of Lochalsh road, 4 miles from Lochcarron village.

Restaurant overlooking Loch Carron.

- Charming purpose-built restaurant.
- Home cooking.
- "Freshly cooked food from early breakfasts to evening meals."

This restaurant lies at the side of Loch Carron and is most attractively positioned. Its appeal is enhanced by the clean-cut exterior adorned with hanging flower baskets and tubs of flowers. It is adjacent to the Carron Pottery which makes the charming hand-thrown crockery used in the restaurant. The restaurant itself is furnished in pine, and paintings for sale by local Highland artists line the walls. Apart from the daily specials which depend on local catches and seasonal produce, there is a range of dishes from substantial grills to smaller dishes like home-made salmon quiche. For travellers, the restaurant is also now open for an early hearty breakfast.

Open 1 Apr to end Oct
Closed Sun
✕ Food served all day £
✕ Lunch £
✕ Dinner ££
Ⓥ Vegetarians welcome
⚘ Children welcome
♿ Facilities for disabled visitors
🚭 No smoking throughout

Queen scallops pan-fried in herbs and garlic butter. Whole Lochcarron prawns in shells. Fresh strawberry pavlova.

💳 Credit cards: Access/Mastercard/Eurocard, American Express, Visa
👤 Proprietors : Seamus & Sarah Doyle

ROCKVILLA HOTEL & RESTAURANT
Main Street, Lochcarron
Ross-shire IV54 8YB
Tel: 01520 722379
Fax: 01520 722379

Situated in centre of village, c. 20 miles north of
Kyle of Lochalsh.

Little hotel in centre of village.

- Small family-run hotel.
- Traditional Scottish cooking.
- "A simple but delightful base from which to
  explore the area."

This is an attractive little restaurant with bar and
four comfortable rooms above. The restaurant has
an open outlook to the loch and hills, and Lorna
and Kenneth Wheelan are attentive hosts. An à la
carte dinner menu offers excellent value and gives
a good choice of starters, main courses and
puddings. Local specialities and traditional
favourites mean that there is something for everyone. After a hearty breakfast guests are well set
up for a day's walking, fishing or exploring the
West Highlands with its dramatic scenery.

Open all year except Christmas Day + 1 Jan
🏠 Rooms: 4 with private facilities
SP Special rates available
✕ Lunch £
✕ Dinner ££
Ⓥ Vegetarians welcome
☆ Children welcome
⤬ No smoking in restaurant

**Smoked Highland venison. Home-baked Scottish
steak pie. Home-made desserts.**

STB Commended 👑 👑 👑
💳 Credit cards: Access/Mastercard/Eurocard,
Visa, Switch, Delta
🏠 Proprietors: Lorna & Kenneth Wheelan

THE ALBANNACH
Lochinver, Sutherland IV27 4LP
Tel: 01571 844407
Fax: 01571 844407

From Lochinver follow signs for Baddidarroch.
After ½ mile, pass turning for Highland Stoneware,
turn left for The Albannach.

**An excellent small restaurant overlooking
Lochinver.**

- Restaurant with rooms.
- Contemporary Scottish cooking.
- "Flamboyant service and creative Scottish
  cooking at its best."

The Albannach is a 19th century house of
considerable architectural character standing in a
small glen overlooking Lochinver and the wild
country beyond. It has been tastefully decorated
by Colin Craig and has a Victorian feel and a cosy
atmosphere. Meals are available in the conservatory,
which has a paved patio and stone balustrade
beyond it. Dinner is served in the wood-panelled,
candlelit dining room. Lesley Crosfield presents a
set, four course dinner menu which relies entirely
on the availability of fresh, free-range produce, her
cooking is creative and assured. Colin Craig serves
at table, resplendent in kilt and Jacobean shirt and
some nights a piper plays outside before dinner.

Open last 2 wks Mar to 27 Dec
🏠 Rooms: 5 with private facilities
SP Special rates available
✕ Non-residents welcome – by prior
arrangement
♀ Table licence
✕ Dinner 4 course menu £££
Ⓥ Vegetarians welcome – by prior arrangement
☆ Children over 10 years welcome
♿ Facilities for disabled visitors
⤬ No smoking throughout

**Warm tartlet of Badnaban crab with a leek and
nutmeg purée. Roast tronçon of Lochinver turbot
with two sauces. Lemon and lime cheese gâteau
with strawberry and Cassis sauce.**

STB Highly Commended 👑 👑 👑
💳 Credit cards: Access/Mastercard/Eurocard,
Visa
🏠 Co-Proprietors: Colin Craig & Lesley Crosfield

INVER LODGE HOTEL

Iolaire Road, Lochinver
Sutherland IV27 4LU
Tel: 01571 844496
Fax: 01571 844395

A837 to Lochinver, first turn on left after village
hall. ½ mile up private road to hotel.

**A new West Highland hotel in the 'grand hotel'
tradition.**

- A modern luxury hotel with outstanding views.
- Modern Scottish cooking, with classic/grand
  hotel influences.
- "Views, views, views!"

Inver Lodge was opened in 1988. It stands on the
hill above Lochinver village and bay, and enjoys
panoramic views across the Minch and the wild
country of Assynt. The building itself is long, low
and plain – even spartan. Inside, however, it is
comfortably and tastefully appointed, with a 'highland shooting lodge' theme (it has good private
fishing for salmon and trout); public rooms and
bedrooms are spacious and airy, and all share the
terrific view . It has a snooker room, solarium and
sauna. Members of staff are uniformed in tartan,
well-trained and courteous. À la carte and table
d'hôte menus feature Lochinver-landed fish and
shellfish and Assynt venison. The cooking is highly
professional, and the presentation and service is in
the 'grand hotel' style. Great care and effort goes
into every aspect of Inver Lodge's hospitality. *(See
advert Page 23.)*

Open 28 Mar to 1 Apr + 26 Apr to 19 Oct
🛏 Rooms: 20 with private facilities
SP Special rates available
✗ Lunch £
✗ Dinner £££
Ⓥ Vegetarians welcome
🏃 Children welcome
✍ No smoking in dining room

**Achiltibuie smoked salmon wrapped around fresh
Ardvar salmon mousse served with an avocado
and garlic sauce. Assynt venison collops, pan-
fried and served with a wild rowan jelly and
blackcurrant sauce. Orange and Drambuie cream.**

STB Deluxe 👑 👑 👑 👑
💳 Credit cards: Access/Mastercard/Eurocard,
  American Express, Visa, Diners Club, Switch,
  Delta, JCB
👤 General Manager: Nicholas Gorton

LOCHINVER LARDER'S RIVERSIDE BISTRO

Main Street, Lochinver
Sutherland IV27 4JY
Tel: 01571 844356

A837 to Lochinver, second property on right as
enter village.

A fresh restaurant on the banks of the River Inver.

- Bistro and restaurant.
- Home cooking.
- "Quite possibly the best cup of coffee to be had
  in Scotland."

Ian and Debra Stewart run this delicatessen shop
with a restaurant in Lochinver. The dining room is
situated behind the shop, next to the river, and
looks out to where the River Inver flows into the
bay. The emphasis here is on the delicious
selection of sturdy home-made pies with a large
variety of fillings. A selection of freshly cooked
steaks and seafood is also offered every night
given the easy access of excellent seasonal
produce. During the day there is a self-service
 policy although at night the atmosphere is less
informal. Another of the booming areas of business
here is the take away food to heat at home, which
is similar to that offered on the menu. It is no
wonder their regulars return year after year.
Lochinver Larder has 1 AA Rosette.

Open 1 Apr to 31 Oct
✗ Food served all day ££-£££
✗ Lunch £
✗ Dinner ££-£££
Ⓥ Vegetarians welcome
🏃 Children welcome
♿ Facilities for disabled visitors
✍ No smoking throughout

**Garlic prawns. Halibut steak in lime and ginger
butter. Home-made cheesecake.**

💳 Credit cards: Access/Mastercard/Eurocard,
  Visa, Mastercharge, Switch, Delta
👤 Proprietors: Ian & Debra Stewart

LOCKERBIE

SOMERTON HOUSE HOTEL
Carlisle Road
Lockerbie DG11 2DR
Tel: 01576 202583
Fax: 01576 204218

Follow High Street eastwards towards M74, 1 mile from town centre.

A well-run, beautifully kept hotel on the outskirts of the town.

- Sandstone mansion.
- Classic contemporary.
- "Familiar dishes served with flair."

Situated on the outskirts of town, with views to open countryside yet within easy striking distance of the M74, the hotel stands in its own spacious grounds facing the road with well-kept pretty gardens to one side and ample private parking. Inside this attractive merchant's villa/mansion has retained many of its superb original features in excellent order and combined these expertly with all the best of modern comforts making the hotel a relaxing and charming place to stay. A bar menu is served in the extensive cosy lounge and adjoining patio lounge bar while a full à la carte is served in the delightful dining room. The food is hearty and the dishes familiar but served with some style in these pleasant surroundings. Popular with locals and visitors alike, a warm welcome awaits guests at the Somerton.

Open all year
- ⌂ Rooms: 7 with private facilities
- ✕ Lunch £
- ✕ Dinner ££-£££
- Ⓥ Vegetarians welcome
- ✶ Children welcome
- ⌇ No smoking in dining room

Lowland Ham and Haddie: a local speciality of smoked haddock and ham in a cream sauce topped with croutons, tomato and cheese. Barbary duckling on a nest of crispy noodles surrounded by a raspberry pond. Strawberry tiramisu.

STB Commended 👑 👑 👑 👑
- 💳 Credit cards: Access/Mastercard/Eurocard, American Express, Visa, Diners Club
- ⚑ Proprietors: Alex & Jean Arthur

LUNDIN LINKS

OLD MANOR HOTEL
Leven Road, Lundin Links
Fife KY8 6AJ
Tel: 01333 320368
Fax: 01333 320911

On A915 Kirkcaldy–St Andrews, 1 mile east of Leven, on right overlooking Largo Bay.

An excellent small country hotel in a golfer's paradise.

- An award-winning informal restaurant and pub.
- Good Scottish cuisine in the restaurant; pub grub in the bar.
- "Family-run hotel offering ideal accommodation for business, holiday or golfing break."

Owned and run by the Clark family, their commitment to what they do here is obvious. The Clarks are a mine of information and advice on the game of golf. Their Aithernie Restaurant serves both à la carte and table d'hôte dishes, based on fresh local meat and fish, imaginatively prepared and presented. The wine list is sound and reasonably priced. The restaurant's success has been reflected by a number of awards for chef Alan Brunt. The hotel's Coachman's Grill caters for a different market, serving upmarket, inexpensive food simply and unpretentiously. The Old Manor has 2 AA Rosettes.

Open all year except Boxing Day + New Year's Day
- ⌂ Rooms: 25 with private facilities
- ⓈⓅ Special rates available
- ✕ Food served all day ££
- ✕ Lunch ££
- ✕ Dinner £££
- Ⓥ Vegetarians welcome
- ✶ Children welcome
- ♿ Facilities for disabled visitors
- ⌇ No smoking in restaurant

Gâteau of lime marinated salmon. Roast loin of Scotch lamb crowned with a chicken and tarragon mousse. Warm rose grapefruit and pistachio nut tart with cinnamon ice cream.

STB Highly Commended 👑 👑 👑 👑
- 💳 Credit cards: Access/Mastercard/Eurocard, American Express, Visa, Mastercharge, Switch, Delta, JCB
- ⚑ Owners: Clark Family

LYBSTER

THE PORTLAND ARMS HOTEL
Lybster
Caithness KW3 6BS
Tel: 01593 721208
Fax: 01593 721446

On A9, 12 miles south of Wick.

A small, family-run hotel in a beautiful Caithness village.

- A historic roadside hotel.
- Unpretentious and wholesome cooking.
- "Plenty of straightforward good food."

This hotel was built as a staging post for the turnpike roads in the 19th century. Today, it makes for an excellent base from which to explore the charms of the surrounding countryside. The emphasis now is on attentive, cheerful service. All bedrooms are comfortable and well-equipped. Some even have jacuzzi baths en suite. Local weddings and small conferences enjoy the hotel's new function room. The menus are straightforward, using local produce when available, and represent good value for money.

    Open all year except 1 + 2 Jan
🛏 Rooms: 19 with private facilities
SP Special rates available
✗ Food served all day £
✗ Lunch ££
✗ Dinner £££
Ⓥ Vegetarians welcome
🕏 Children welcome
♿ Facilities for disabled visitors
🚭 No smoking in dining room

Oak-smoked salmon with dill sauce. Fillet of beef Wellington with Madeira sauce. Baked fillet of lemon sole with cream and prawns.

STB Commended 👑 👑 👑 👑
💳 Credit cards: Access/Mastercard/Eurocard, American Express, Visa, Diners Club, Mastercharge, Switch
🗝 Owners: Helen & Gerald Henderson

MALLAIG

MARINE HOTEL
Mallaig
Inverness-shire PH41 4PY
Tel: 01687 462217
Fax: 01687 462821

Adjacent to railway station. First hotel on right off A82, and a 5 minute walk from ferry terminal.

A family-run hotel in the fishing port of Mallaig.

- Long established local small town hotel.
- Traditional wholesome cooking.
- "The smoked fish soup and home-made bread was almost a meal in itself."

Mallaig is at the end of the famous West Highland Railway Line and also marks the termination of The Road to the Isles. Once the busiest herring port in Britain, the town has still a busy fishing harbour and is the main ferry terminal to the Hebrides. The hotel has well-appointed bedrooms all of which are en suite, bar one which has a private but separate bathroom. The menus take full advantage of freshly landed fish and shellfish and is offered in both lounge bar and restaurant. Cooking is simple and wholesome. Good selection of malt whiskies available.

    Open all year except Christmas Day + New Year's Day
    Note: Restricted served Nov to Mar
🛏 Rooms: 19, 18 with private facilities, 1 with private separate facilities
SP Special rates available
✗ Lunch ££
✗ Dinner ££
Ⓥ Vegetarians welcome
🕏 Children welcome
♿ Limited facilities for disabled visitors
🚭 No smoking in restaurant

Cullen skink. Local scallops in cream and wine sauce. Home-made liqueur ice creams, meringues and cloutie dumpling.

STB Commended 👑 👑 👑
💳 Credit cards: Access/Mastercard/Eurocard, Visa
🗝 Proprietor: Dalla Ironside

BY MAYBOLE

LADYBURN
by Maybole, Ayrshire KA19 7SG
Tel: 01655 740 585
Fax: 01655 740 580

A77 (Glasgow-Stranraer) to Maybole then B7023 to Crosshill. Turn right at War Memorial (Dailly-Girvan). After exactly 2 miles, turn left and follow signs. 5 miles south of Maybole.

Country house hotel.

* 17th century country house.
* Home cooking.
* "Ladyburn is a wonderful place to stay and Jane extends a very warm welcome."

Ladyburn is an historic house set deep in 'the most beautiful valley in Ayrshire' and is the family home of Jane and David Hepburn. You are surrounded by family heirlooms and portraits, and comfortable antique furniture. There is a homely authenticity about the food served in the dining room, reflecting Jane Hepburn's commitment to produce genuine dishes cooked with original touches of flavours and textures; neither overbearing nor trendily understated. Substantial well-tried recipes cooked with care are the order of the day. Dining room open at all times for residents. Italian, French, German and Russian spoken.

Open all year except 2 wks Nov + 4 wks during Jan to Mar
🏠 Rooms: 8 with private facilities
SP Special rates available
♀ Restricted licence
🍴 Reservations essential for non-residents
✕ Lunch except Mon ££
✕ Dinner except Sun Mon £££
Ⓥ Vegetarians welcome
🕇 Children over 16 years welcome
👌 Facilities for disabled visitors
🚭 No smoking in dining room + drawing room + bedrooms

'Grive Smetana' (Russian mushroom starter). Oxtail and grape casserole. Peach Amaretto.

STB Deluxe 👑 👑 👑
💳 Credit cards: 1, 2, 3
🛏 Proprietors: Jane & David Hepburn

MELROSE

BURTS HOTEL
Market Square, Melrose, Roxburghshire TD6 9PN
Tel: 01896 822285 Fax: 01896 822870

A6091, 2 miles from A68, 38 miles south of Edinburgh.

A family-run 18th century hostelry.

* Delightful 18th century inn.
* Modern Scottish cooking.
* "An establishment of much character, a haven for both the serious and amateur angler."

Burts Hotel, is a delightful 18th century Scottish inn. It stands in the centre of the square of this Borders market town, and is always bustling with activity. It is run by Graham, Anne and Nicholas Henderson, professional and friendly hosts, who make their guests feel very welcome. Their restaurant has a good local reputation. The à la carte menu is extensive and displays a thorough familiarity with contemporary eating fashions. Both it and the regularly changing table d'hôte menu are ambitious and display imaginative combinations, creative confidence and a sound appreciation of appropriate flavours. The cooking and presentation is akin to that you would expect to find in a refined country house. Burts has 2 AA Rosettes. *(See advert Page 27.)*

Open all year except Boxing Day
🏠 Rooms: 20 with private facilities
SP Special rates available
✕ Lunch except Christmas Day + Boxing Day ££
✕ Dinner except Christmas Day + Boxing Day £££
Ⓥ Vegetarians welcome
🕇 Children welcome
🚭 No smoking in restaurant
🐄 Member of the Scotch Beef Club

Deep-fried wedges of Teviotdale cheese enveloped with smoked salmon served with a citrus marmalade. Loin of Border lamb rolled with wild mushrooms and spinach centred with kidney accompanied with a minted apple chutney. Warm Selkirk bannock pudding scented with lemon accompanied with a shortbread ice cream.

STB Highly Commended 👑 👑 👑 👑
💳 Credit cards: Access/Mastercard/Eurocard, American Express, Visa, Diners Club, Switch, Delta, JCB
🛏 Manager: Nicholas Henderson

MELROSE STATION RESTAURANT
Palma Place, Melrose
Roxburghshire TD6 9PR
Tel: 01896 822546

100 yards from Market Square. Take Dingleton
Road signposted B6359 to Lilliesleaf – first right
just before bridge.

**An important building converted into a stylish,
modern restaurant.**

* Converted 19th century station-master's house.
* Modern Scottish, with international influences.
* "Imaginative menu using the very best of fresh
  local produce."

Close to the Market Square at the centre of the
town, Melrose station is one of the very few
notable pre-1850 Scottish railway stations to have
survived. It was closed in 1969, lay derelict until
1985 and has now been completely renovated as a
Grade A Listed building. The restaurant is situated
in what used to be the station-master's house and
overlooks the leafy town and famous abbey. The
style is modern and tasteful, simple and elegant,
friendly and informal – the approach is bistro-style.
Ian and Claire Paris gained hotel experience in
Australia and their excellent small restaurant is
much patronised by locals. Claire is responsible for
the cooking and her scones and other specialities
are not be missed, whilst Ian attends to the front of
house. A blackboard menu is presented at
lunchtime and a very well-priced table d'hôte
menu for dinner, as well as a newly introduced à la
carte menu.

Open all year except 25 Dec to 31 Dec +
first 3 wks Feb
Closed Mon
✗ Lunch except Mon ££
✗ Dinner except Sun Mon Tue £££
Ⓥ Vegetarians welcome
ㅊ Children welcome
ㅅ Facilities for disabled visitors

**Lime and ginger marinated salmon fillet served on
a julienne of vegetables. Rolled leg of Border
lamb stuffed with apricots, mint and mushrooms.
Brown bread ice cream with rich fudge sauce.**

⊞ Credit cards: Access/Mastercard/Eurocard,
Visa, Delta
Ⓜ Proprietors: Ian & Claire Paris

Melvich

MELVICH

THE SHEILING GUEST HOUSE
Melvich
Sutherland KW14 7YJ
Tel: 01641 531 256
Fax: 01641 531 356

North Coast, main road overlooking Melvich Bay,
18 miles west of Thurso.

Comfortable family home in beautiful countryside.

* Small guest house known for its hospitality.
* Scottish home cooking at its best.
* "Joan Campbell shops for the best produce in
  the North of Scotland to entertain her guests."

The Sheiling is a family-run guest house in an
outstanding location, blessed with wonderful
views over the Halladale River and Melvich Bay.
The Campbells open their home to visitors
between April and October and guests return year
after year to enjoy their unfailing hospitality. Two
bedrooms are en suite, the third bedroom has
private facilities. Food is home-cooked and based
on local produce, the set menu changing daily,
using a variety of fresh vegetables. Breakfast is a
special treat, with traditional porridge and home-
made jams and marmalade. Not to be missed!

Open 1 Apr to mid Oct
⌂ Rooms: 3 with private facilities
✗ Residents only
Ⓤ♀ Unlicensed – guests welcome to take own
wine
✗ Dinner ££
ㅊ No smoking in dining room + bedrooms
Ⓥ Vegetarians welcome

**Scotch broth with fresh herbs. Peppered scallops
of wild Atlantic salmon with creamy seafood
sauce served with a variety of fresh vegetables.
Pavlova with Scotch raspberries and cream.**

STB Highly Commended 👑 👑 👑
⊞ No credit cards
Ⓜ Proprietor: Joan Campbell

MOFFAT

WELL VIEW HOTEL
Ballplay Road, Moffat
Dumfriesshire DG10 9JU
Tel: 01683 220184
Fax: 01683 220088

Leaving Moffat take A708. At crossroads, left into Ballplay Road – hotel on right.

A small town hotel offering first class cuisine.

- Victorian town house with gardens.
- Modern Scottish cooking.
- "This undiscovered treasure is a real credit to The Taste of Scotland."

Janet and John Schuckardt run this traditional hotel, which has a peaceful garden and stands on the outskirts of Moffat. It is within easy walking distance of the centre of this charming town which sits in a fertile plain below the dramatic Devil's Beef Tub. John has a good knowledge of wine and has over 100 bins available. The six course menu demonstrates an inventive approach to more familiar dishes, accompanied by light fruity sauces and dressings. The meat is served pink and the vegetables al dente, which is a good sign of use of fresh produce. The owners go out of their way to look after their guests every need. German and a little French spoken. Well View has 2 AA Rosettes.

Open all year
🏠 Rooms: 6 with private facilities
SP Special rates available
✗ Lunch except Sat ££
✗ Dinner 6 course menu £££
🍴 Prior reservation essential for both lunch + dinner
Ⓥ Vegetarians welcome
🧒 Children welcome
🚭 No smoking throughout

Cream of celery, apple and Stilton soup. Honey-roast ham with Cumberland sauce. Steamed orange and sultana castle pudding.

STB Deluxe 👑 👑 👑
💳 Credit cards: Access/Mastercard/Eurocard, American Express, Visa
👤 Owners: Janet & John Schuckardt

MONTROSE

THE LINKS HOTEL
Mid Links, Montrose
Angus DD10 8RL
Tel: 01674 671000
Fax: 01674 672698

From town centre follow signs to the Links and the beach. Links Hotel is situated in a pleasant residential area.

A town hotel in a pleasant setting, a short walk from the beach.

- Town hotel.
- Scottish cooking with French influence.
- "A friendly young team of staff determined to make your visit a pleasure."

The Links is a comfortable hotel overlooking a tree-lined park, where the emphasis is on the informal. Its location makes it ideal for golfers, anglers, bird-watchers and general touring. The cooking is good Scottish with French influences, and Head Chef Franc Rivault ensures that only the freshest produce is used. Menus are interesting with French influences and offer good value for money.

Open all year except 27 Dec to 2 Jan
🏠 Rooms: 21 with private facilities
SP Special rates available
✗ Food served all day
✗ Lunch ££
✗ Dinner £££
Ⓥ Vegetarians welcome
🧒 Children welcome
♿ Facilities for disabled visitors

Howgate Brie on toast triangles. Trio of salmon, sole and plaice poached in dill. Orange mousse with local strawberries.

STB Approved 👑 👑 👑 👑
💳 Credit cards: Access/Mastercard/Eurocard, American Express, Visa, Mastercharge, Switch, Delta
👤 General Manager: Andrew Dacey

MUIR OF ORD BY INVERNESS

ORD HOUSE HOTEL
Muir of Ord
Ross-shire IV6 7UH
Tel: 01463 870 492
Fax: 01463 870 492

On A832 Ullapool-Marybank, ½ mile west of Muir of Ord.

A relaxed and friendly small country house hotel in beautiful surroundings.

- Comfortable and homely living.
- Good country cooking.
- "Simple well-planned menus using fresh ingredients."

John and Eliza Allen offer their guests the unhurried peace of a bygone age in this 17th century laird's house. Open fires and an elegant drawing room match the calm beauty of the hotel's 50 acres of grounds. Bedrooms are tastefully and well-appointed. The dining room offers unpretentious and reasonably-priced honest country cooking that uses fresh meat, game and fish and vegetables, in season, from the hotel's own garden. Service is attentive without being fussy. The wine list is sound and inexpensive. Fluent French is spoken.

Open 1 May to 20 Oct
🏠 Rooms: 11 with private facilities
✖ Lunch £
✖ Dinner 4 course menu ££
Ⓥ Vegetarians welcome
☆ Children welcome
🚭 No smoking in dining room

Cassoulet of wild mushrooms. West Coast scallops served in the shell in a leek and mushroom sauce. Raspberry mille feuille with a whisky and honey cream.

STB Commended 👑 👑 👑
💳 Credit cards: Access/Mastercard/Eurocard, American Express, Visa
🅺 Proprietors: John & Eliza Allen

NAIRN

CAWDOR TAVERN
The Lane, Cawdor
Nairn-shire IV12 5XP
Tel: 01667 404 777
Fax: 01667 404 777

Turn off A96 to Cawdor. Tavern is clearly signposted.

Traditional village inn with friendly atmosphere.

- An historic inn.
- Modern, freshly prepared cooking.
- "Wholesome food and hospitality to suit all tastes."

Cawdor Tavern is a country pub located in the quiet conservation village by Cawdor Castle. The building itself was originally the castle workshop and the old oak panelling that decorates the walls was gifted by the old laird. The Sinclair family who run the tavern also run the Moorings Hotel in Fort William and are well-known for their skill in the hospitality business. The food here is wholesome making good use of fresh products, with a blackboard menu featuring daily speciality dishes offering good value for money. A popular place for the traveller and locals.

Open all year except 25, 26 Dec, 1 + 2 Jan
✖ Lunch £
✖ Dinner ££
Ⓥ Vegetarians welcome
☆ Children welcome
♿ Facilities for disabled visitors
🚭 No smoking area in restaurant

Seafood platter featuring smoked salmon, prawns, herring and mackerel with dill mayonnaise. Breast of Culloden chicken filled with haggis and served with a Drambuie and mushroom sauce. Warm date pudding with sticky toffee sauce.

💳 Credit cards: Access/Mastercard/Eurocard, American Express, Visa
🅺 Proprietor: Norman Sinclair

THE GOLF VIEW HOTEL
& LEISURE CLUB
Seabank Road
Nairn IV12 4HD
Tel: 01667 452301
Fax: 01667 455267

At west end of Nairn. Seaward side of A96. Turn off at large Parish Church.

A large sporting hotel with a leisure club.

- 19th century seafront mansion converted into a modern hotel, leisure club and terrace restaurant.
- Modern Scottish cooking.
- "The Terrace Restaurant must have one of the most stunning views in Scotland. The cooking is equally good."

Adjacent to the Nairn Golf Club, the appropriately named 'Golf View' is also within an hour's drive of 25 further courses. The hotel has a fully equipped leisure club has a magnificent swimming pool and multi-gym. The restaurant offers a nightly changing, invitingly descriptive, table d'hôte menu. Fish and shellfish are featured strongly, and locally sourced meat and game. Creative and well-made sauces complement the dishes and demonstrate the chef's expertise. Vegetarian dishes show skill and imagination, and delicious fresh bread is baked every day. The Conservatory is open all day, every day, serving food.

Open all year
🏠 Rooms: 47 with private facilities
SP Special rates available
✕ Food served all day ££
✕ Lunch £
✕ Dinner 4 course menu £££
Ⓥ Vegetarians welcome
ⵆ Children welcome
& Facilities for disabled visitors
🚭 No smoking in restaurant + conservatory

Home-made langoustine and lobster ravioli on a spaghetti of courgettes and carrots with a lemon and basil butter sauce. Loin of lamb pan-fried with garlic and rosemary with a leek and mustard crumble and a Burgundy and red wine tarragon essence. Terrine of two chocolates with a coffee bean sauce.

STB Highly Commended 👑 👑 👑 👑 👑
💳 Credit cards: Access/Mastercard/Eurocard, American Express, Visa, Diners Club, Switch
🍴 General Manager: Greta Anderson

Newburgh 149

UDNY ARMS HOTEL
Main Street, Newburgh, Aberdeenshire AB41 6BL
Tel: 01358 789444
Fax: 01358 789012

On A975, 2½ miles off A92 Aberdeen-Peterhead, 15 minutes from Aberdeen.

A hotel situated in the centre of Newburgh village, overlooking the golf course, it has a function suite and cafe bar.

- A traditional Victorian stone-built house with the style and character of an old village inn.
- Creative Scottish cooking.
- "A genial atmosphere with creative use of Scottish produce."

The Udny Arms Hotel overlooks the Ythan Estuary and has attracted sportsmen, nature lovers and tourists to the Aberdeenshire village of Newburgh for over 100 years. It is an unpretentious and intimate hotel, run by the Craig family, and the service is cheerful and efficient. Some recent changes to the building have made room for a cosy residents lounge. Dining is in the bistro, a split-level restaurant overlooking the lovely Sands of Forvie. The extensive à la carte menu changes every six weeks, and includes a handful of 'specials' which change daily. Meat and game come from the famous Bain of Tarves – and fish a speciality. The hotel also has a brasserie-style restaurant, in the Parlour, with table d'hôte menu. Udny Arms has an AA Rosette and is a member of the Certified Aberdeen Angus Scheme.

Open all year except Christmas Night + Boxing Night
🏠 Rooms: 26 with private facilities
SP Special rates available
✕ Lunch £-£££
✕ Dinner £-££
Ⓥ Vegetarians welcome
ⵆ Children welcome
& Facilities for disabled visitors

Home-cured gravadlax. Udny creel. 'The original' sticky toffee pudding.

STB Commended 👑 👑 👑 👑
💳 Credit cards: Access/Mastercard/Eurocard, American Express, Visa, Diners Club, Mastercharge, Switch, Delta
🍴 Proprietors: Denis & Jennifer Craig

CREEBRIDGE HOUSE HOTEL
Minnigaff, Newton Stewart
Wigtownshire DG8 6NP
Tel: 01671 402121
Fax: 01671 403258

From roundabout signposted Newton Stewart on A75, through the town, cross bridge over river to Minnigaff. 250 yards – hotel on left.

Friendly hotel on the banks of the River Cree.

- An old Galloway family house with character and charm.
- Imaginative country house cooking.
- "Expertly run by an accomplished chef and his wife."

Creebridge House Hotel was formerly owned by the Earls of Galloway and its present resident owners, Chris and Sue Walker, have made sure that it retains an atmosphere of unhurried elegance, peace and tranquillity. The drawing room has an ornate ceiling and period fireplace, not to mention a baby grand piano. There is a choice of eating during the day, either in the bar or in the main restaurant. Chef/proprietor Chris Walker and his Head Chef Paul Sommerville present imaginative table d'hôte menus for the Garden Restaurant and outstanding à la carte bar menus. They have a deserved reputation. Winner of The Taste of Scotland Scotch Lamb Challenge Classic Category 1996. *(See advert Page 19.)*

Open all year except 24 to 26 Dec
🏠 Rooms: 20 with private facilities
SP Special rates available
✕ Lunch £
✕ Dinner ££
Ⓥ Vegetarians welcome
🧒 Children welcome
♿ Facilities for disabled visitors
🚭 No smoking in restaurant

Smoked salmon and lobster tagliatelle. Chefs own baked fillet of Galloway beef with shallots, red wine and horseradish sauce. Ecclefechan butter tart.

STB Commended 👑 👑 👑 👑
💳 Credit cards: Access/Mastercard/Eurocard, American Express, Visa, Switch, Delta
🗓 Proprietors: Chris & Sue Walker

GLEN ROY RESTAURANT
Monreith, nr Newton Stewart
Wigtownshire, DG8 9LJ
Tel: 01988 700466

Approximately 17 miles from A75 at Newton Stewart. Take A714 to Port William then A747 coast road to Monreith. Restaurant at southern end of main street.

Small specialist restaurant overlooking the sea.

- Old fisherman's cottage.
- Best modern British.
- "Superb seafood, a wonderful view and accomplished cooking skills."

Monreith is a tiny village set up on the cliffs overlooking Luce Bay and the Mull of Galloway. The restaurant is at one end of a row of tiny whitewashed cottages on the main road looking out to the sea. The interior is simply furnished with open fireplace, candles and has a welcoming feel to it. The food is described by our Inspector as "contemporary cooking at its best" and who predicts that Glen Roy will become one of Taste of Scotland's sought after gems. All produce is freshly sourced with an emphasis on seafood whilst not forgetting good Galloway beef. Three rooms with private facilities are planned to open for the 1997 season.

Open all year except 2 wks end Nov
Note: closed Tue Nov to Easter
Closed Mon
✕ Lunch except Mon £
✕ Dinner except Mon ££
Ⓥ Vegetarians welcome
🧒 Children welcome
♿ Facilities for disabled visitors
🚭 No smoking in one of two dining rooms

Soufflé of haggis and black pudding with an apple and whisky sauce. Symphony of hot seafood with two sauces. Chocolate Marquise with Grand Marnier and chocolate sauce.

💳 Credit cards: Access/Mastercard/Eurocard, Visa, Delta
🗓 Joint Owners: Patrick & Jenny Crawley

KIRROUGHTREE HOUSE
Newton Stewart
Wigtownshire DG8 6AN
Tel: 01671 402141
Fax: 01671 402425

From A75 take A712 New Galloway road, hotel 300 yards on left.

Delightful, grand Scottish country hotel in the very best tradition.

- 18th century mansion converted into a stylish, family-run country house hotel.
- Gourmet Scottish cooking.
- "Superb surroundings and service only surpassed by exquisite cuisine."

Kirroughtree has all the grandeur and opulence of an historical mansion, it is sumptuously furnished and elegantly decorated, yet it has an atmosphere which is welcoming and considerate rather than over-formal. There are two dining rooms, reached from the panelled lounge. Head Chef, Ian Bennett, was trained by the celebrated Michel Roux, and his cooking is highly accomplished. The menus are short (three main courses at dinner, two at lunch), creative and well-balanced. Special golfing packages at sister hotel, Cally Palace and local Newton Stewart course. Kirroughtree has 2 AA Rosettes. Winner of The Taste of Scotland Special Merit Award 1993.

Open 14 Feb to 3 Jan
- 🏠 Rooms: 17 with private facilities
- 🆂🅿 Special rates available
- ✕ Lunch – booking essential ££
- ✕ Dinner 4 course menu £££
- Ⓥ Vegetarians welcome – prior notice required
- 🕏 Children over 10 years welcome
- 🚭 No smoking in dining rooms
- 🐂 Member of the Scotch Beef Club

Terrine of corn-fed chicken and Ayrshire bacon, layered with herbs and accompanied by tomato chutney and toasted brioche. Tournedos of prime Scottish beef set on fondant potato, topped by parsley mousse and surrounded by sauce bordelaise. Caramelised lemon and banana tart served with caramel ice cream.

STB Deluxe 👑 👑 👑 👑
- 💳 Credit cards: Access/Mastercard/Eurocard, Visa, Switch
- 🅽 Manager: James Stirling

Oban   151

ARDS HOUSE
Connel, by Oban
Argyll PA37 1PT
Tel: 01631 710255

On main A85 Oban–Tyndrum, 4½ miles north of Oban.

Family-run guest house overlooking Loch Etive.

- Victorian villa.
- Home cooking.
- "A blend of talented cooking and charming ease."

This is a comfortable guest house standing on the shores of a loch, with views over the Firth of Lorn and the Morvern Hills. All the bedrooms have private facilities and there is a happy air of the family home here, encouraged by the owners John and Jean Bowman, who take great trouble over their guests. The daily changing set menu is displayed in the afternoon and any special requirements are easily catered for. The dishes rely on local produce where possible, combining a taste for detail and fresh home cooking.

Open Feb to mid Nov
- 🏠 Rooms: 6 with private facilities
- 🆂🅿 Special rates available
- ✕ Non-residents – by arrangement
- ♀ Restricted licence
- ✕ Dinner 4 course menu ££
- Ⓥ Vegetarians – by arrangement
- 🕏 Children over 12 years welcome
- 🚭 No smoking throughout

Four cheese tartlet with a tomato coulis. Scottish lamb cutlets with onion confit and sultanas. Crème de Menthe parfait with strawberries and camomile syrup.

STB Commended 👑 👑 👑
- 💳 Credit cards: Access/Mastercard/Eurocard, Visa, Switch, Delta
- 🅽 Proprietors: John & Jean Bowman

DUNGALLAN HOUSE HOTEL
Gallanach Road
Oban
Argyllshire PA34 4PD
Tel: 01631 563799
Fax: 01631 566711

In Oban, at Argyll Square, follow signs for
Gallanach. ½ mile from Square.

**A fine old Victorian house offering a tranquil,
country atmosphere.**

- A small and friendly country house hotel.
- Traditional fresh Scottish/home cooking.
- "A welcoming house hotel on the edge
  of the town."

Set in its own five acres of mature woodland yet
close to Oban's bustling centre, Dungallan House
was built in 1870 by the Campbell family. It was
used as a hospital in the First World War and as
HQ for the Flying Boat Squadrons in the Second.
Now owned and refurbished by George and Janice
Stewart, Dungallan House enjoys magnificent
panoramic views over Oban Bay to the Island of
Mull, Lismore and the Hills of Morvern. As is
appropriate for this prime West Coast port, menus
take full advantage of the range of fresh fish and
shellfish available locally. Janice Stewart does the
cooking in person. The well-balanced table d'hôte
menu offers four-five choices for each course. The
wine list offers something to match each dish on
Dungallan's rounded menu. Dungallan has 1 AA
Rosette. *(See advert Page 19.)*

....

  Open all year
🏠 Rooms: 13, 9 with private facilities
SP Special rates available
✖ Lunch £
✖ Dinner £££
Ⓥ Vegetarians welcome
大 Children welcome
ᕫ Limited facilities for disabled visitors
⌿ No smoking in dining room
🐄 Member of the Scotch Beef Club

**Squat lobsters in a hot vinaigrette dressing.
Scotch beef olives stuffed with whisky flavoured
haggis. Fresh fruit meringue roulade.**

STB Commended 3 Crowns 👑 👑 👑
💳 Credit cards: Access/Mastercard/Eurocard,
  Visa
👤 Owners: Janice & George Stewart

THE GATHERING SCOTTISH RESTAURANT
AND O'DONNELL'S IRISH BAR
Breadalbane Street, Oban
Argyll PA34 5NZ
Tel: 01631 565421/564849/566159
Fax: 01631 565421

Entering Oban from A85 (Glasgow) new one-way
system. Turn left at Deanery Brae into
Breadalbane Street (signs for swimming pool etc.)
then right at bottom of Deanery Brae.

**An informal, distinctively Scottish, town
restaurant.**

- An unpretentious restaurant and bar with a
  Celtic theme.
- Good, plain cooking.
- "Its history is on the walls – its food is up to
  date."

First opened in 1882 as a supper room for the
famous annual Gathering Ball, The Gathering has a
distinguished pedigree and is rightly popular with
Oban's many tourists. With antlers and targes on
the walls, the restaurant's ambience is decidedly
and memorably Scottish. The menu offers first-
class, straightforward dishes made from local
meat and seafood, as well as a range of imaginative
starters and popular 'lighter bites'. The wine list is
predictable but dependable. Portions are generous,
prices modest and service cheerful. During July to
September live music is available every night in
O'Donnell's Irish Bar e.g. ceilidhs, folk music and
local musicians. Live music at weekends
off season.

....

  Open Easter to New Year except Christmas
  Day, New Year's Day + some Suns
  Closed Sun off season – please telephone
  Note: closed to public last Thu in Aug
✖ Lunch £-££: off season – by reservation
✖ Dinner ££-£££
Ⓥ Vegetarians welcome
大 Children welcome
ᕫ Facilities for disabled visitors
⌿ No smoking in restaurant

**Oban Bay seafood platter. Venison haunch
roasted with Madeira sauce. Cranachan.**

💳 Credit cards: Access/Mastercard/Eurocard,
  Visa, Switch, Delta, JCB
👤 Owner/Chef: Elaine Cameron

ISLE OF ERISKA
Ledaig, by Oban
Argyll PA37 1SD
Tel: 01631 720 371
Fax: 01631 720 531

A85 north of Oban, at Connel Bridge take A828 for 4 miles. North of Benderloch village follow signs to Isle of Eriska.

Exceptional hotel by any standards.

- An impressive, grey granite Scottish baronial house built in 1884, romantically situated on an island reached by a short road bridge.
- Gourmet country house cuisine.
- "The very best of country living – an occasion to remember."

Robin and Sheena Buchanan-Smith have run their home on the island of Eriska as a hotel for over 20 years and manage to combine the intimate atmosphere of a family-run country house with the highest standard of professional service. In the dining room, internationally acclaimed standards of cuisine are meticulously maintained. Isle of Eriska is one of the best hotels on the West Coast and its 300 acre grounds offer golf, tennis, putting, croquet, clay-pigeon shooting and magnificent gardens. The hotel also has a new leisure complex with swimming pool, etc. Isle of Eriska has 2 AA Rosettes. Winner of The Macallan Taste of Scotland Hotel of the Year Award 1994.

Open all year except Jan + Feb
- ⌂ Rooms: 17 with private facilities
- ✕ Open to non-residents for dinner only
- ✕ Lunch – residents only
- ✕ Dinner 7 course menu ££££
- Ⓥ Vegetarians welcome
- ⚘ Children welcome (dinner – over 10 years old)
- ♿ Facilities for disabled visitors
- ✄ No smoking in dining room
- 🐂 Member of the Scotch Beef Club

Ravioli of local goats cheese with rocket sauce. Roasted loin of venison with baby spinach and blackberry vinegar sauce. Chocolate and Drambuie Marquise.

STB Deluxe 👑 👑 👑 👑 👑
- 💳 Credit cards: Access/Mastercard/Eurocard, American Express, Visa, Mastercharge, Switch
- 👤 Partner: B Buchanan-Smith

THE MANOR HOUSE
Gallanach Road, Oban
Argyll PA34 4LS
Tel: 01631 562087
Fax: 01631 563053

From Argyll Square, Oban, follow signs for Gallanach and the car ferry. Continue for approx ½ mile.

An historic house overlooking Oban Bay.

- Small country house hotel.
- Scottish cooking with French influences.
- "A little Manor House with a big reputation and a restful setting close to the water."

Situated on the southern tip of Oban Bay, the Manor House was built in 1780 by the Duke of Argyll, and was first a factor's residence and then a Dower House. In 1826 Oban's first bank, 'The National', opened here and in 1845 Admiral Otter used it as his base which conducted hydrographic surveys on the West Coast. Latterly it was the home of the MacLeans of Drimnin. The house retains much of the charm and atmosphere of the past. The five course table d'hôte dinner menu (three-four starters, three-four main courses) changes every day, according to what is available and seasonal. The cooking is fresh and creative. The Manor House has 1 AA Rosette.

Open 1 Feb to 3 Jan
- ⌂ Rooms: 11 with private facilities
- ⑤ Special rates available
- ✕ Lunch £
- ✕ Dinner 5 course menu £££
- Ⓥ Vegetarians welcome
- ✄ No smoking in dining room

Timbale of smoked salmon with a farcie of crabmeat and squat lobsters, with a lemon and thyme dressing. Haunch of venison with caramelised parsnips, and a compote of wild berries with a rosemary and juniper jus. Hazelnut parfait infused with Drambuie caramel sauce, served with home-baked shortbread.

STB Highly Commended 👑 👑 👑 👑
- 💳 Credit cards: Access/Mastercard/Eurocard, American Express, Visa, Switch
- 👤 Manageress: Gabriel Wijker

THE SCOTTISH SALMON CENTRE
Kilninver, Oban
Argyll PA34 4QS
Tel: 01852 316202
Fax: 01852 316262

7 miles south of Oban on A816 on the shores of Loch Feochan.

Attractive building overlooking Loch Feochan with shop, restaurant, and Visitors Centre.

- Well-planned centre well worth a visit for all ages.
- Good Scottish cooking.
- "An interesting place to eat and look around."

The Scottish Salmon Centre has successfully combined a shop, educational exhibition and restaurant, making it one of the very interesting places to visit near Oban. The centre itself has been carefully decorated and finished with pleasing individual touches and the shop – which you pass through to the restaurant – is crammed with interesting gifts of food and non-perishables – all that is best from Argyll and the islands. The food, as you would expect, specialises in seafood but not exclusively so and everything is well-cooked. There is something to suit all pockets here and children are especially welcome and thoughtfully catered for. Traditional Scottish afternoon teas are a speciality. Now open for dinner the setting is ideal to watch the glorious West Coast sunsets shimmering on the loch. The centre has 1 AA Rosette.

Open Mar to end Oct
- ✕ Food served all day £
- ✕ Lunch £
- ✕ Dinner ££
- Ⓥ Vegetarians welcome
- ⚘ Children welcome
- ♿ Facilities for disabled visitors

Speciality seafood soup – Scottish salmon and prawn chowder. Escalope of salmon topped with local langoustine in a white wine and saffron sauce. Iced honey and whisky creams served with a small home-made Highlander shortbread biscuit.

- 💳 Credit cards: Access/Mastercard/Eurocard, Visa
- Ⓜ Managing Director: Robert Provan

THE WATERFRONT RESTAURANT
No 1 The Waterfront
The Pier, Oban
Argyll PA34
Tel: 01631 563110

The waterfront, Oban.

Right on the pier – the fish couldn't be fresher.

- Seafood restaurant.
- Straightforward cooking.
- "Good fresh fish in a cheerful, happy atmosphere."

'From the pier to the pan as fast as we can' reads the Waterfront's slogan. The restaurant is on the first floor, with Creel's Coffee Shop below (specialises in home baking and sandwiches with seafood fillings). The à la carte menus are supported by daily blackboard specials, although predominantly fish and shellfish, meat dishes are also offered. Weather permitting it is also planned to serve meals 'al fresco' outside. The cooking is straightforward and the treatments uncomplicated in the main, as befits the quality of the seafood. Service is friendly and obliging. The overall atmosphere is cheerful and unpretentious – including the price.

Open all year
- ✕ Creel's coffee shop £
- ✕ Lunch £
- ✕ Dinner ££

Balvicar Bay oysters. Tobermory scallops and prawns in a cream sauce. Fresh seafood platter of the day.

- 💳 Credit cards: Access/Mastercard/Eurocard, Visa
- Ⓜ Proprietor: Stuart Walker

WILLOWBURN HOTEL
Clachan Seil, Isle of Seil
by Oban PA34 4TJ
Tel: 01852 300276

11 miles south of Oban, via A816 and B844, sign-posted Easdale, over Atlantic Bridge.

A small privately owned hotel on the Isle of Seil standing in two acres of ground with fine views over the Sound of Seil.

- A waterside hotel with dining room, bistro bar and comfortable well-equipped bedrooms.
- Excellent home cooking.
- "Once found a place to return to – often."

The lovely little island of Seil is noted for its wildlife, and for being connected to the mainland by 'the bridge over the Atlantic' (built in 1792). Willowburn is a small family-owned hotel; guests are made very welcome. The dining room has stunning views across the Sound of Seil, and the à la carte and table d'hôte menus are especially strong on local seafood. The cooking is skilled and assured. The six bedrooms are all very comfortable and have their own bathrooms. The hotel has 1 AA Food Rosette.

Open Easter to late Oct
🏨 Rooms: 6 with private facilities
🆂🅿 Special rates available
✘ Lunch £
✘ Dinner ££
Ⓥ Vegetarians welcome
⚹ Children welcome
⚹ Facilities for disabled visitors
✄ No smoking in dining room

Warm Atlantic prawn pot with herb bread. Pan-roasted salmon fillet with orange and Drambuie. Warm blackcurrant and applemint soufflé cake.

STB Highly Commended 👑 👑 👑
💳 Credit cards: Access/Mastercard/Eurocard, Visa
👤 Proprietors: Archie & Maureen Todd

YACHT CORRYVRECKAN
Dal an Eas
Kilmore, nr Oban
Argyll PA34 4XU
Tel: 01631 770246
Fax: 01631 770246

Stylish yacht exclusively designed for West Coast cruising and gourmet eating.

- Charter yacht.
- Skilful cooking.
- "It's not every Master Chef that needs a Master Mariner. Douglas and Mary make a great team!"

Douglas and Mary Lindsay have been offering chartered cruises on the West Coast for many years and brought all their experience to bear when they designed Corryvreckan (strictly speaking Corryvreckan II, since their earlier vessel had the same name). She is 65 feet overall, 16 feet in the beam and has a wonderfully spacious feel – standing room is available throughout. There are five double guest cabins, and the dining table seats 12 comfortably. Mary's cooking is wonderful: everything (even baking and canapés) is cooked fresh; the galley is full of potted herbs; every night is a dinner party. Guests are members of the crew and help with washing up as well as actually sailing the ship. This is a memorable experience! One of 12 establishments shortlisted for The Macallan Taste of Scotland Awards 1996.

Open Apr to Oct
⚓ Cabins: 5
🆂🅿 Special rates available for whole boat charter
🆄🅻 ♀ Unlicensed – wine provided with dinner
✄ No smoking below deck
🚗 Parking available

Arbroath smokies baked in cream with basil and tomato. Ragoût of venison with toasted walnuts. Bramble whisky syllabub.

💳 No credit cards
👤 Proprietors: Douglas & Mary Lindsay

Oldmeldrum 152

MELDRUM HOUSE
Oldmeldrum
Aberdeenshire AB51 0AE
Tel: 01651 872294
Fax: 01651 872464

A947 Aberdeen to Oldmeldrum (15 miles). 13 miles north of Aberdeen airport.

An historic house in rural Aberdeenshire.

* Scottish baronial mansion, now a country house hotel.
* Creative Scottish cooking.
* "Very good food, interesting surroundings."

Local tradition maintains that King Charles I spent part of his childhood here, when a ward of the Seton family of nearby Fyvie Castle. The historic atmosphere of the house is enhanced by antiques, portraits and faded furniture. The house stands in 15 acres of lawns and woodland, with its own small loch. The resident proprietors are Douglas and Eileen Pearson, attentive and courteous hosts who make you very welcome to their home. Eileen presents an imaginative and well-constructed four course table d'hôte menu which changes every month.

Open all year
🏠 Rooms: 9 with private facilities
SP Special rates available
♀ Restricted licence
✗ Food served all day £££
✗ Lunch ££
✗ Dinner £££
V Vegetarians welcome
☇ Children welcome
♿ Facilities for disabled visitors
✗ No smoking in restaurant

Rabbit tarragon and potato cake on a light game jus. Roast quail stuffed with an almond and apricot sausagemeat on straw potatoes and a Madeira jus. White and dark chocolate cheesecake served with an Amaretto nest and diamond of praline.

STB Commended 👒 👒 👒 👒
🔲 Credit cards: Access/Mastercard/Eurocard, Visa, Mastercharge, Switch
🔲 Proprietors : Douglas & Eileen Pearson

Onich by Fort William 153

ALLT-NAN-ROS HOTEL
Onich, by Fort William
Inverness-shire PH33 6RY
Tel: 0185 582 1210
Fax: 0185 582 1462
On A82, 10 miles south of Fort William.

Highland country hotel.

* Victorian house on the shores of Loch Linnhe.
* Country house cooking.
* "A very welcoming family-run hotel overlooking Loch Linnhe and the beautiful hills beyond."

Situated halfway between Ben Nevis and Glencoe, Allt-nan-Ros is an attractive 19th century shooting lodge standing in an elevated position above the loch and commanding spectacular views: a most picturesque situation. The Gaelic name means Burn of the Roses, and derives from the cascading stream which passes through the gardens of the hotel. The decoration is modern, rooms are comfortably furnished, service is personal and dinner is served in a new conservatory. The menus offer a range of familiar Scottish dishes, prepared from locally sourced ingredients, and the style of the cooking has French influences. An accordionist serenades guests in the dining room from time to time! Allt-nan-Ros has 2 AA Rosettes.

Open 1 Jan to 10 Nov
🏠 Rooms: 21 with private facilities
SP Special rates available
✗ Lunch ££-£££
✗ Dinner 5 course menu £££-££££
V Vegetarians welcome
✗ No smoking in dining room

Ravioli of monkfish flavoured with chives and a cream sauce infused with coriander. Fillet of salmon grilled with garlic butter on a bed of spinach. Baked apple strudel with crème anglaise.

STB Highly Commended 👒 👒 👒 👒
🔲 Credit cards: Access/Mastercard/Eurocard, American Express, Visa, Diners Club, Mastercharge, Switch
🔲 Proprietor: James Macleod

CUILCHEANNA HOUSE
Onich
by Fort William
Inverness-shire PH33 6SD
Tel: 01855 821226

250 yards off A82 in village of Onich – 9 miles south of Fort William.

An attractive and welcoming West Highland hotel.

- A small country house hotel with a warm welcome and peaceful setting.
- Quality home cooking.
- "A peaceful hotel in a picturesque location."

This is an old farmhouse (17th century foundation) now a traditional family hotel run by Russell and Linda Scott, who are most welcoming hosts. It stands in its own grounds overlooking Loch Linnhe, peacefully situated with views towards Glencoe and the Isle of Mull, and is pleasantly furnished – with piles of books of local interest and a cosy log fire in the lounge. The set four course dinner menu changes daily, and is complemented by a well thought out wine list, as well as a fine selection of quality malt whiskies. The emphasis is on genuine home-cooking and Linda makes good use of prime local produce and fresh Scottish-grown herbs. The comprehensive breakfast choice includes local favourites such as venison sausage, haggis, herring in oatmeal and Mallaig kippers.

Open 26 Mar to 26 Oct
🏠 Rooms: 7 with private facilities
SP Special rates available
✗ Residents only
✗ Dinner 4 course menu £££
V Vegetarians welcome
✗ No smoking throughout

Spiced lentil and apricot soup. Suprême of chicken with a raspberry and red onion sauce. Lemon and bramble meringue gâteau.

STB Commended 3 Crowns 👑 👑 👑
💳 Credit cards: Access/Mastercard/Eurocard, Visa, Delta
👤 Proprietors: Linda & Russell Scott

FOUR SEASONS BISTRO & BAR
Inchree, Onich
by Fort William
Inverness-shire PH33 6SD
Tel: 01855 821393
Fax: 01855 821287

8 miles south of Fort William. Take Inchree turn-off, ¼ mile south of Corran Ferry, then 250 yards.

Friendly bistro bar in lovely setting.

- Log cabin style building.
- Traditional Scottish cooking.
- "A casual and happy place with a holiday atmosphere."

Four Seasons Bistro and Bar is a warm and welcoming haven in lovely leafy surroundings with views of Loch Linnhe and Ardgour. It is a family business and the staff are all pleasant, exuding a happy atmosphere. The interior is unusual but suits the timber of the building and furniture and decor is pleasing, complementing the style of the establishment. The menus are interesting, food well-cooked with much evidence of fresh, locally caught seafood prepared and presented with care and attention to detail.

Open Christmas + New Year period
winter limited opening until Easter
Closed Tue except Jul + Aug
✗ Dinner except Tue ££
V Vegetarians welcome
🧒 Children welcome
♿ Facilities for disabled visitors
✗ No smoking in eating areas

Selection of local smoked meats with an apple and tarragon jelly. Whole lemon sole with parsley butter. Steamed sponge pudding.

💳 Credit cards: Access/Mastercard/Eurocard, American Express, Visa
👤 Manageress: Susan Heron

THE LODGE ON THE LOCH HOTEL
Onich, by Fort William
Inverness-shire PH33 6RY
Tel: 0185 582 1237
Fax: 0185 582 1238

On A82, 1 mile north of the Ballachulish Bridge.

A comfortable hotel with good views.

- Victorian country hotel, with modern additions.
- Traditional Scottish cooking.
- "The panoramic views enhance the warm, friendly atmosphere."

The Lodge on The Loch hotel is a granite Victorian villa with new additions and an attractive conservatory. It stands within yards of Loch Linnhe and enjoys good views towards the hills of Morvern. Guests of the Lodge on The Loch have automatic membership of a sister hotel's swimming pool, sauna, steam room, turbo pool, solarium and multi-gym. The bedrooms are comfortable and the dining room has delightful loch views. The table d'hôte menus feature several Scottish dishes.

Open Christmas/New Year + 2 Feb to 4 Jan
🏠 Rooms: 20, 18 with private facilities
SP Special rates available
✗ Food served all day ££
✗ Lunch ££
✗ Dinner 4 course menu £££
V Vegetarians welcome
⅄ Children welcome
♿ Facilities for disabled visitors
⅄ No smoking in dining room

Sautéd wild mushrooms with fine herbs served on a puff pastry case, set on a Moniack Castle wine and cream sauce. Baked suprême of Loch Linnhe salmon on a cucumber and ginger butter. Blackcurrant and whisky charlotte presented with a lime crème anglaise.

STB Highly Commended 👑 👑 👑 👑
💳 Credit cards: Access/Mastercard/Eurocard, Visa, Mastercharge, Switch, Delta
👤 General Manager: Mr Iain Coulter

Peat Inn 154

THE PEAT INN
Peat Inn, by Cupar, Fife KY15 5LH
Tel: 01334 840206 Fax: 01334 840530

At junction of B940/B941, 6 miles south west of St Andrews.

A superb country restaurant now firmly established in a class of its own.

- Restaurant with rooms in a converted village inn.
- Innovative Scottish cooking which has won many awards for chef David Wilson.
- "A gastronomic experience prepared by one of Scotland's finest chiefs."

Food and style writers have waxed lyrical about The Peat Inn almost since the day it opened its doors. Chef and owner David Wilson has literally re-written the rule book on Scottish cooking and has created a world class restaurant whose name is synonymous with good food. His bold imaginative cooking style has gained him all the top food and wine awards including his most recent – the Scottish Chef Achievement Award. All ingredients are of the utmost freshness and quality and, with tremendous flair, they are transformed into truly memorable dishes. His wine list is formidable but provides great choice even in the lowest price range. Menus are table d'hôte, à la carte and a tasting menu of six or seven courses which must be ordered for a complete table. The Peat Inn has 3 AA Rosettes.

Open all year except Christmas Day + New Year's Day
Closed Sun Mon
🏠 Rooms: 8 all with sitting room + private facilities
✗ Lunch except Sun Mon 4 course menu ££
✗ Dinner except Sun Mon 4 course menu £££
V Vegetarians welcome
⅄ Children welcome
♿ Facilities for disabled visitors
⅄ No smoking in dining rooms
🐄 Member of the Scotch Beef Club

Sauté of scallops, monkfish and spiced pork with apple. Roast saddle of venison with wild mushroom and truffle crust. Trio of caramel desserts.

💳 Credit cards: Access/Mastercard/Eurocard, American Express, Visa, Diners Club, Switch, JCB
👤 Partners: David & Patricia Wilson

CRINGLETIE HOUSE HOTEL
nr Peebles EH45 8PL
Tel: 01721 730 233
Fax: 01721 730 244

Off A703 Edinburgh-Peebles, 2½ miles north of Peebles.

Award-winning family-run hotel in the Borders.

- 19th century baronial mansion.
- Home cooking.
- "A joy to visit – wonderful hospitality in delightful surroundings."

A charming Victorian baronial house designed for the Wolfe Murray family by the famous Scottish architect David Bryce. It stands in beautifully kept gardens, amidst the gentle Tweedsmuir countryside, with rolling hills and glens all about. The exterior of the house has an understated dignity which is echoed in the tasteful decor of public and private rooms. There is a two acre walled garden and some beehives which supply the kitchen; as far as possible fresh local meat and fish is used, and the table d'hôte menu changes every day. The dishes created by chef/owner Aileen Maguire use positively flavoured sauces and dressings and draw inspiration from continental and Eastern traditions.

Open 8 Mar to 1 Jan
- 🏠 Rooms: 13 with private facilities
- ✗ Lunch £-££
- ✗ Dinner 4 course menu £££
- Ⓥ Vegetarians welcome
- ⚡ Children welcome
- ⚡ No smoking in restaurant

Game terrine with rhubarb and date chutney. Baked salmon in saffron cous-cous crust with tomato and olive salsa. Iced triple chocolate parfait with vanilla sauce.

STB Highly Commended 👑 👑 👑 👑
- 💳 Credit cards: Access/Mastercard/Eurocard, American Express, Visa
- 🛎 Proprietors: Stanley & Aileen Maguire
- 🛎 Head Chef: Sheila McKellar

PARK HOTEL
Innerleithen Road, Peebles
Tweeddale EH45 8BA
Tel: 01721 720451
Fax: 01721 723510

At eastern end of High Street (A72).

A peaceful country house hotel with good accommodation and food.

- Attractive baronial style country house set in parkland with views over the River Tweed.
- Traditional hotel cuisine.
- "Friendly, peaceful country house hotel."

An attractive mansion standing in its own grounds on the outskirts of Peebles, on the banks of the River Tweed. It has a peaceful and relaxing atmosphere and caters primarily for the older visitor. The hotel is surrounded by well-tended gardens and lawns. The comfortable public rooms are on the ground floor, as are a number of en suite bedrooms. The leisure and sporting facilities of the Peebles Hydro are available to the Park's guests, who are then able to retreat from the family bustle of the larger hotel! The oak-panelled restaurant has splendid views of the Tweed and the rolling Border hills beyond, you will find a wide choice of familiar and more unusual dishes, plainly cooked and nicely presented.

Open all year
- 🏠 Rooms: 24 with private facilities
- SP Special rates
- ✗ Lunch £
- ✗ Dinner 4 course ££
- Ⓥ Vegetarians welcome
- ⚡ Children welcome
- ♿ Facilities for non-residential disabled visitors

Lightly poached salmon with warm potato salad. Roast Border turkey with grilled bacon and tomato, stuffed with skirlie. Chocolate mousse with fruit coulis.

STB Commended 👑 👑 👑 👑
- 💳 Credit cards: Access/Mastercard/Eurocard, American Express, Visa, Diners Club, Mastercharge, Switch
- 🛎 Manager: Lawson Keay

BALLATHIE HOUSE HOTEL
Kinclaven, by Stanley, Perthshire PH1 4QN
Tel: 01250 883268 Fax: 01250 883396

Off A9, 2 miles north of Perth – turn off at Stanley
and turn right at sign to Kinclaven.

A fine country house hotel.

- A Victorian baronial house on the River Tay.
- Award-winning modern and classic Scottish cooking.
- "Wonderful food in a beautiful setting."

An elegant turreted mansion, well-seated in superb shooting country on one of the best salmon beats on the mighty River Tay. The hotel itself is furnished and decorated in keeping with its age and station as a top-flight country house hotel: the public rooms are graciously proportioned and comfortably chintzy, the bedrooms well-appointed. Chris Longden, Ballathie's Manager, is very experienced, and his Chef, Kevin McGillivray, presents lunches and dinners which one inspector described as 'exceptional' His menus change daily, use local produce and offer subtle variations on classic Scottish dishes. Ballathie has 2 AA Rosettes. Winner of The Macallan Taste of Scotland Country House Hotel of the Year Award 1994. *(See advert Page 13.)*

....

Open all year
🏠 Rooms: 28 with private facilities
SP Special rates available
✗ Food served all day ££
✗ Lunch £££
✗ Dinner £££
Ⓥ Vegetarians welcome
🌲 Children welcome
⛴ Facilities for disabled visitors
🚭 No smoking in dining rooms
🐃 Member of the Scotch Beef Club

Salad of Skye squat lobster, avocado and fried leek with basil pesto. Loin of lamb roasted in a herb crust served with local chanterelle mushrooms and jus. Steamed marmalade and whisky pudding, apricot ice cream and a vanilla sauce.

STB Deluxe 👑 👑 👑 👑
💳 Credit cards: Access/Mastercard/Eurocard, American Express, Visa, Diners Club, Mastercharge, Switch, Delta, JCB
🗝 Manager: Christopher J Longden

HUNTINGTOWER HOTEL
Crieff Road
Perth PH1 3JT
Tel: 01738 583771
Fax: 01738 583777

Signposted off A85, 1 mile west of Perth, towards Crieff.

An elegant mansion in its own garden a mile outside Perth.

- Country house hotel.
- Country house cooking with French influences.
- "A well-run country house hotel, minutes from Perth."

Huntingtower is a half-timbered Edwardian mansion standing in a four acre garden, with a pretty little stream meandering through it. Both the spacious conservatory and the dining room overlook the garden. The former offers unusual bar meals – including Mexican Fajitas, pasta, omelettes and filled croissants, as well as substantial meat and fish dishes. The latter is an elegant room, panelled from ceiling to floor, with crystal chandeliers, ornate cornices and a very handsome ingle-nook fireplace. Both à la carte and table d'hôte menus are offered, with table d'hôte is reasonably priced and offering some unusual dishes and classic sauces. The hotel is a popular venue for weddings and business meetings. Huntingtower has 1 AA Rosette.

....

Open all year
🏠 Rooms: 27 with private facilities
SP Special rates available
✗ Lunch £
✗ Dinner ££
Ⓥ Vegetarians welcome
🌲 Children welcome
⛴ Facilities for disabled visitors

Char-grilled smoked salmon steak set on a tossed salad of herbs with a tomato and pesto dressing. Braised brace of quail stuffed with truffle and mushroom duxelle on a port jus. Steamed chocolate sponge pudding with white chocolate ice cream and Cointreau anglaise.

STB Commended 👑 👑 👑 👑
💳 Credit cards: Access/Mastercard/Eurocard, American Express, Visa, Diners Club, Switch
🗝 General Manager: Stephen Owen

THE LANG BAR & RESTAURANT, PERTH THEATRE
185 High Street, Perth PH1 5UW
Tel: 01738 472709
Fax: 01738 624576

Perth city centre in pedestrian zone at middle section of High Street.

Restaurant and bar which is part of Perth Theatre.

- Theatre restaurant.
- Innovative/traditional Scottish cooking.
- "Excellent Scottish fare in thespian surroundings."

Perth Theatre was built in 1900, and has recently been beautifully restored. The bar, restaurant and coffee bar benefits both from its situation and the refurbishment. The menus are changed to suit the current production (a novel touch!). However being theatrical, when the stage is 'dark' so is the restaurant. The food is of a high standard and covers the range of Scottish meat, fish and game in really rather interesting dishes with continental touches. There is a creative touch in the more traditional dishes which demonstrates chef Colin Potter's culinary energy. During the summer the restaurant is open Thursday to Saturday evening with live music adding to the atmosphere. Winner of Martini/TMA British Regional Theatre Award for Most Welcoming Theatre in Britain 1995.

Open all year except Christmas Day +
Public Holidays
Closed Sun
Note: Please telephone to ensure Restaurant is open
✗ Food served all day ££
✗ Lunch except Sun £
♨ Dinner except Sun – booking advised ££
Ⓥ Vegetarians welcome
⅄ Children welcome
♿ Facilities for disabled visitors
⅄ Smoking areas in restaurant + coffee bar

Gruyère and red pesto tartlets served warm with a salad garnish. Spinach and hazelnut cannelloni steamed with a mirepoix of vegetables and gratinated with a white sauce and Camembert cheese, served with garlic potatoes and salad. Pink grapefruit and lemon meringue pie served with a lemon sauce.

💷 Credit cards: Access/Mastercard/Eurocard, American Express, Visa, Diners Club, Mastercharge, Switch, Delta
▨ Catering Manager: Peter Hood
▨ Restaurant Manager: Debbie Riddle

LET'S EAT
77/29 Kinnoull Street
Perth PH1 5EZ
Tel: 01738 643377
Fax: 01738 621464

Stands on corner of Kinnoull Street and Atholl Street, close to North Inch. 3 minutes walk from High Street.

A popular city bistro restaurant.

- Attractive town centre restaurant.
- Modern Scottish cooking with a continental influence.
- "One of the best and not to be missed. Booking essential."

Let's Eat opened in December '95 under the skilled hands of Tony Heath and Shona Drysdale. Tony gained an excellent reputation and won awards for his cooking at The Courtyard in Aberdeen, and is continuing this excellence. Shona's expertise is front of house and between them they have a very successful blend of hospitality, comfortable welcoming surroundings and excellent food. The style of food is bistro in style with classic influences, the atmosphere relaxed. Winner of The Scottish Chefs Association 'New Restaurant of the Year'. Let's Eat has 2 AA Rosettes.

Open all year except 2 wks mid Jul
Closed Sun Mon
✗ Lunch except Sun Mon ££
✗ Dinner except Sun Mon ££
Ⓥ Vegetarians welcome
⅄ Children welcome
♿ Facilities for disabled visitors
⅄ No smoking in restaurant area
🐄 Member of the Scotch Beef Club

Salad of smoked Rannoch venison and Galia melon with a balsamic dressing. Brioche and herb crusted fillet of Isle of Skye cod on a bed of creamy mash with queen scallops and squat lobster and a langoustine essence. Warm chocolate brownie with chocolate fudge sauce and vanilla ice cream.

💷 Credit cards: Access/Mastercard/Eurocard, American Express, Visa, Mastercharge, Switch, Delta
▨ Partners: Tony Heath & Shona Drysdale

MURRAYSHALL COUNTRY HOUSE HOTEL
Scone
nr Perth PH2 7PH
Tel: 01738 551171
Fax: 01738 552595

4 miles out of Perth, 1 mile off A94.

A country house hotel with its own golf course.

• Baronial country house set in parkland converted to a golf course.
• Elegant Scottish cuisine.
• "A paradise for golf-loving gourmets."

Golfers will feel particularly at home in this small, grey-stoned mansion house, surrounded by its own 300 acres and private, 18-hole golf course, covered bay driving range, indoor golf school, tennis etc. Bowls and clay pigeon shooting are also available in the hotel's grounds. The Old Masters Restaurant is an elegant, spacious and well-furnished room, its menus based on the best of seasonally-available produce. Many of the herbs and vegetables are grown in the hotel's own kitchen garden. Service is polished and friendly. The wine list is extensive, and in accord with the menus. Special dietary needs catered for. French spoken. Some refurbishment is taking place to be completed for March 1997, including the addition of a conservatory dining room and a new Clubhouse and leisure facilities.

Open all year
🏢 Rooms: 26 with private facilities
SP Special rates available
✕ Lunch (Clubhouse) £
✕ Dinner (Old Masters) ££
Ⓥ Vegetarians welcome
🧒 Children welcome

Fillet of Scotch beef topped with a tarragon and mushroom duxelle accompanied with a whisky and pickled walnut sauce. Fillet of North Sea turbot and scallops topped with a creamed leek sauce. Caramelised pear and apple pastry with a rocher of vanilla ice cream.

STB Highly Commended 👑 👑 👑 👑
💳 Credit cards: Access/Mastercard/Eurocard, American Express, Visa, Diners Club, Switch
🙍 Sales Development Manager: Lin Mitchell

NEWMILN
Newmiln Estate
by Scone Palace, Perth PH2 6AE
Tel: 01738 552364
Fax: 01738 553505

4 miles north of Perth on A93 Blairgowrie road. Follow signs for Scone Palace. 3 miles after Scone Palace, Newmiln driveway on left.

A country house and sporting estate just outside Perth.

• Country house hotel.
• Scottish/modern cooking.
• "The excellent standards here are being rewarded with a fast growing reputation."

Standing within its own 700 acre estate – pheasant, duck and trap shooting are available to guests – the house itself is Edwardian in character, although it dates from the 18th century. Its owner, Elaine McFarlane, succeeds in making Newmiln a 'home from home' for guests; although imposing and beautifully appointed, the house is cosy and the welcome warm. Their young and talented chef, J Paul Burns (ex Auchterarder House, and The Cellar Restaurant, Anstruther) presents a sophisticated menu in the handsome dining room. Altogether a delightful experience. Newmiln has 3 AA Rosettes. One of 12 establishments shortlisted for The Macallan Taste of Scotland Awards 1996. *(See advert Page 22.)*

Open all year except Christmas Day + Boxing Day
🏢 Rooms: 7 with private facilities
SP Special rates available
✕ Lunch Sun – otherwise by prior arrangement ££
🍴 Dinner: Thu to Sat non-residents – reservations essential £££
Ⓥ Vegetarians welcome
🧒 Children over 12 years welcome
♿ Facilities for disabled visitors
🚭 No smoking in dining room

Seared escalope of Tay salmon with dill marinated cucumber spaghetti and plum tomato dice. Honey-roasted Gressingham duck served with Crème de Cacao, green peppercorn and orange sauce. Iced banana parfait centred with pear water-ice served with fruit coulis and crème anglaise.

STB Highly Commended 👑 👑 👑
💳 Credit cards: Access/Mastercard/Eurocard, American Express, Visa
🙍 Owners: James & Elaine McFarlane

NUMBER THIRTY THREE SEAFOOD RESTAURANT

33 George Street
Perth PH1 5LA
Tel: 01738 633771

Perth city centre.

A stylish city centre restaurant.

- Well-established and popular seafood restaurant in Perth.
- Formal Scottish cooking with a choice of eating styles.
- "Traditional Scottish seafood presented with modern style."

Number Thirty Three is now an established presence on George Street, easily identified by its distinctive seahorse sign. The theme is Art Deco in muted tones of pink and grey with a clever use of sea imagery creates a stylish atmosphere, the perfect setting for an extremely good meal. The menu is based principally on fish and seafood balanced by interesting and original starters and puddings. Mary Billinghurst does all the cooking and her own home-made gravadlax with dill mayonnaise is something of a house speciality. There is a choice of menu with light meals available in the Oyster Bar and more formal dining in the restaurant. Whichever option you choose, the food and wine list are impressive, confirming the restaurant's well-earned reputation for quality. Number Thirty Three has 1 AA Rosette.

Open all year except 25, 26 Dec, 1, 2 Jan, also last 2 wks Jan + first wk Feb
Closed Sun Mon
✗ Lunch except Sun Mon ££-££££
✗ Dinner except Sun Mon ££-££££
Ⓥ Vegetarians welcome
☆ Children over 5 years welcome
⤤ Guests are asked not to smoke cigars

Creamy crab and prawn terrine. Marinaded brochette of pollack and coley served with savoury rice. Mary's sticky toffee pudding with butterscotch sauce.

Ⓔ Credit cards: Access/Mastercard/Eurocard, American Express, Visa
Ⓧ Proprietors: Gavin & Mary Billinghurst

PARKLANDS HOTEL

St Leonards Bank
Perth PH2 8EB
Tel: 01738 622451
Fax: 01738 622046

Junction of St Leonards Bank and Marshall Place in centre of Perth adjoining South Inch Park.

Classical town house, city centre hotel.

- Well-restored town house with parkland views.
- Modern Scottish quality cooking.
- "Good Scottish food at a restful haven near the city centre."

Formerly the home of the Lord Provost of Perth, Parklands Hotel has been luxuriously refurbished maintaining original features whilst offering the comforts expected of a city centre hotel. Every effort is made by the chefs to ensure the finest produce is cooked and presented with care and attention. Lunch is particularly suited to the business user with an inviting table d'hôte menu or as an alternative the bar snacks in the Conservatory are worth a visit. At dinner both à la carte and table d'hôte menus are offered – bistro style bar meals are also provided in the evening. With its own small car park and central location Parklands is deservedly popular with business and leisure visitors alike.

Open 6 Jan to 24 Dec
🏠 Rooms: 14 with private facilities
ⓢⓟ Special rates available
✗ Food served all day ££
✗ Lunch £
✗ Dinner £££
Ⓥ Vegetarians welcome
☆ Children welcome
♿ Facilities for disabled visitors
⤤ No smoking in restaurant

Local pheasant, pistachio and green peppercorn terrine laced with sherry and garnished with salad leaves. Fresh Scottish salmon lightly poached, set upon a bed of fresh mussels and king prawns with a white wine and dill cream. Brandy snap basket filled with a trio of chef's home-made parfaits, set on a Cointreau anglaise.

STB Highly Commended 👑 👑 👑 👑
Ⓔ Credit cards: Access/Mastercard/Eurocard, American Express, Visa, Diners Club, Mastercharge, Switch, Delta
Ⓧ Manager: Catriona Baron

PETERHEAD

ALBERT HOTEL
75 Queen Street
Peterhead
Aberdeenshire AB42 1TU
Tel: 01779 472391
Fax: 01779 479696

32 miles north of Aberdeen.

A family-run hotel of long standing.

- Town house.
- Good wholesome cooking.
- "A rustic establishment, unpretentious and good value for money."

The Albert Hotel has been family-run for over 34 years. Chef Albert Reid, son of the owners, has a commitment to fresh Scottish produce of the highest standards and menus are interesting, varied and offer excellent value for money. The hotel's location makes it an ideal place to tour the history and drama of the Grampians from one of Europe's premier fishing ports.

Open all year
🏠 Rooms: 9, 6 with private facilities
✘ Lunch £-££
✘ Dinner ££
Ⓥ Vegetarians welcome
🕏 Children welcome
🚭 No smoking in dining room

Fresh Ugie smoked salmon pâté parcel. Noisettes of lamb with a Drambuie sauce. Fresh poached peaches with a malt whisky syrup and fresh cream.

STB Commended 👑 👑 👑
💳 Credit cards: Access/Mastercard/Eurocard, Visa
🅺 Proprietor: Albert Reid

PITLOCHRY

ACARSAID HOTEL
8 Atholl Road
Pitlochry
Perthshire PH16 5BX
Tel: 01796 472389
Fax: 01796 473952

On main road at the Perth end of Pitlochry occupying a prominent position.

An attractively furnished town hotel ideal for theatre goers.

- Victorian villa with later additions.
- Good British/Scottish cooking.
- "Courteous and attentive staff see to every detail – one wants for nothing."

Acarsaid is a haven where comfort of guests and attention to detail are priorities. Attractively furnished throughout the hotel is comfortable with care given to small details, and residents receive complimentary afternoon tea upon arrival. Of the public rooms one is 'smoking' and one 'non-smoking'. The cooking is very good offering sound, well-prepared and thought out dishes. A healthy choice menu is also available. Mary and Howard Williams, owners, are attentive hosts who care for their guests comfort and experience of this is evident throughout.

Open 15 Mar to 5 Dec
🏠 Rooms: 18 with private facilities
✘ Lunch £
✘ Dinner ££
Ⓥ Vegetarians welcome
🕏 Children 10 years and over welcome
🚭 No smoking in dining room

Softly poached free-range eggs on a little potato cake served with a creamy shallot, bacon and fresh garden herb sauce. Oven-baked Scottish lamb shank with a rich red wine jus and dauphinois potatoes. Tayberry meringue roulade: a soft meringue roll filled with thick dairy cream and tayberries with a fresh raspberry coulis.

STB Highly Commended 👑 👑 👑
💳 Credit cards: Access/Mastercard/Eurocard, Visa, Switch, Delta
🅺 Owners: Howard & Mary Williams

AUCHNAHYLE

Pitlochry
Perthshire PH16 5JA
Tel: 01796 472318
Fax: 01796 473657

Off East Moulin Road, at end of Tomcroy Terrace.
Keep going to end of farm road.

An unusual private house, in the heart of rural Perthshire.

- An 18th century farmhouse and steading with a self-catering cottage.
- Scottish home cooking.
- "Wonderful hospitality – and a most delicious dinner."

This delightful little 18th century farmhouse has a lovely garden which is home to the family's peacocks. The land was once owned by the monks of Dunfermline Abbey, one of the richest monasteries in Scotland. Auchnahyle is home to Penny and Alastair Howman who are attentive hosts. Penny is a skilled and accomplished cook and prepares the best of fresh farm and local produce and herbs from the herb garden to provide imaginative dishes for their guests. Dinner is served by candlelight around the family dining table and guests are offered genuine hospitality, every comfort and memorable meals. If you are a theatre-goer – pre-theatre supper is available. One of Taste of Scotland's gems.

Open all year except Christmas + New Year
Note: Winter months – please book well beforehand
🏠 Rooms: 3 with private facilities
✘ Residents only
⚱♀ Unlicensed – guests welcome to take own wine
🍴 Picnic lunches £
✘ Dinner 4 course menu ££
Ⓥ Vegetarians welcome – prior notice required
✝ Children over 12 years welcome
♿ Facilities for disabled visitors
✐ No smoking in dining room

Baked avocado with bacon, smoked cheese and walnuts. Honey-glazed duck breast with a ginger and grapefruit sauce accompanied by fresh garden vegetables. Home-made ice creams and meringues.

💳 Credit cards: Access/Mastercard/Eurocard, Visa, Mastercharge
👤 Proprietors: Penny & Alastair Howman

BIRCHWOOD HOTEL

East Moulin Road
Pitlochry, Perthshire
PH16 5DW
Tel: 01796 472477
Fax: 01796 473951

200 yards off Atholl Road on Perth side of Pitlochry.

A comfortable hotel with attractive accommodation.

- An old stone Victorian mansion set on a wooded knoll with four acres of grounds and gardens.
- Traditional Scottish cooking.
- "Good food freshly prepared – a soundly run establishment in lovely grounds."

Birchwood is a grand country villa built in the 1870s on the south side of Pitlochry surrounded by four acres of woodland gardens. Unpretentious and welcoming. It is managed by partners, Brian and Ovidia Harmon, who are committed to making their guests welcome and providing every comfort. Hospitality is allied to good food and spacious bedrooms, all with private facilities. The pleasant restaurant overlooks the garden and the chef uses fresh produce to create table d'hôte and à la carte menus with a strong Scottish flavour, giving good value for money. The chef is also happy to cater for personal dietary preferences. There is a modern bungalow adjacent to the hotel which has five bedrooms with full facilities.

Open Mar to Nov
🏠 Rooms: 17 with private facilities
SP Special rates available
✘ Lunch £-££
✘ Dinner ££-£££
Ⓥ Vegetarians welcome
✝ Children welcome
✐ No smoking in restaurant

Tomato stuffed with Drambuie haggis. Chicken breast with skirlie stuffing on a leek sauce. Ben Vrackie meringue with local berries.

STB Highly Commended 👑 👑 👑
💳 Credit cards: Access/Mastercard/Eurocard, American Express, Visa
👤 Partners: Ovidia & Brian Harmon

DUNFALLANDY HOUSE

Logierait Road, Pitlochry
Perthshire PH16 5NA
Tel: 01796 472648
Fax: 01796 472017

On south side of Pitlochry, signposted off road leading to Festival Theatre.

A country house hotel just outside Pitlochry.

- Attractive Georgian house in lovely gardens and woodland.
- Country house cooking.
- "Stylish meals particularly handy for pre-theatre dining."

Dunfallandy House is approached up a hill through magnificent mature trees and rhododendrons. The view is spectacular. The three-storey stone mansion was built in 1790 for General Archibald Fergusson, Chief of Clan McFergus of Atholl. There has been a settlement on this site for centuries and the famous Dunfallandy Stone, a 9th century Pictish monolith stands close by. The house has been sensitively restored and retains its period character in the clean lines of the exterior and the extremely tasteful interior decorations and antique furniture. Public rooms and bedrooms are comfortable and very well-appointed. The Georgian Dining Room retains its original black slate fireplace, the furniture is Louis XV and it sparkles with crystal, silver and cut flowers. Jane and Michael Bardsley are the resident owners, and present a short but creative table d'hôte menu (two main courses), with dishes made from absolutely fresh local ingredients. There are two sittings for dinner – one for theatre goers and one for later dining.

Open Feb to Oct
🏠 Rooms: 9 with private facilities
🆂🅿 Special rates available
✗ Dinner ££
Ⓥ Vegetarians welcome
⚹ No children
🚭 No smoking in dining room + bedrooms

Beetroot soup (borscht). Fillet of salmon with lemon and garden herb sauce. Chocolate and Cointreau truffle tart.

STB Highly Commended 👑 👑 👑
💳 Credit cards: Access/Mastercard/Eurocard, American Express, Visa
👤 Proprietors: Jane & Michael Bardsley

EAST HAUGH COUNTRY HOUSE HOTEL & RESTAURANT

Special Merit Award for Best Informal Lunch 1996

THE TASTE OF MACALLAN AWARDS SCOTLAND

Pitlochry, Perthshire PH16 5JS
Tel: 01796 473121 Fax: 01796 472473

1½ miles south of Pitlochry on old A9 road.

Charming country house hotel.

- 17th century turreted stone house.
- Elegant Scottish cooking.
- "An exceptionally delightful eating experience in a beautiful setting."

Built originally as part of the Atholl Estate around 300 years ago, East Haugh is a turreted stone house, standing in its own gardens. It is run by Neil and Lesley McGown who bought the property in 1989 and have converted it sympathetically. They are helped by their two daughters and all aim to offer a very personal service. Both Neil and Lesley are keen fishermen and Neil also shoots and stalks – these are encouraging pastimes for Neil who is the chef, since the bag or catch often appear on the menu. There is a great deal of food on offer at East Haugh, with children's menus, lunchtime bistro style menus and those offered in The Gamekeeper's Restaurant for dinner. The lunch dishes are very wide ranging and are prepared to order; dinner is a more formal affair, with a well-composed menu which changes every two days and features local produce.

Open all year except Christmas Day, Boxing Day + first 2 wks Feb
🏠 Rooms: 8 with private facilities
🆂🅿 Special rates available
✗ Lunch ££
✗ Dinner ££-£££
Ⓥ Vegetarians welcome
⚹ Children welcome
🚭 No smoking in restaurant

Selection of home-smoked fish – mussels, sea trout, salmon and scallops served with fresh mayonnaise and horseradish. Rack of Perthshire lamb cooked pink, with a fresh herb crust on a sauce of fresh mint and cream. Warm treacle tart with orange pastry, served with ginger ice cream.

STB Commended 👑 👑 👑
💳 Credit cards: Access/Mastercard/Eurocard, Visa
👤 Proprietors: Neil & Lesley McGown

THE KILLIECRANKIE HOTEL
by Pitlochry
Perthshire PH16 5LG
Tel: 01796 473220
Fax: 01796 472451

B8079 on old A9, 3 miles north of Pitlochry.

An attractive country house overlooking the River Garry.

- Small country house hotel.
- Modern Scottish cooking with classic influences.
- "Very commendable food in a lovely Perthshire setting."

This is a former manse built in 1840 and stands in four acres of well-kept gardens and woodland above the River Garry and the historic Pass of Killiecrankie, where a notable battle was fought in 1689. The surrounding country abounds with wildlife and the hotel has the atmosphere of a sporting lodge. Its resident owners, Colin and Carole Anderson, have decorated and furnished the house very tastefully; and have provided a high standard of comfort. Head Chef John Ramsay was commended by the Scottish Chef's Association as 'Newcomer of the Year'. His cooking is highly professional and imaginative, and his table d'hôte menus (four starters, four main courses) are well balanced and appetising. A most attractive and well-run establishment. Killiecrankie has 2 AA Rosettes.

Open 7 Mar to 3 Jan except 1 wk mid Dec
- Rooms: 10 with private facilities
- Special rates available
- Lunch ££
- Dinner 5 course menu £££
- Vegetarians welcome
- Children welcome
- No smoking in dining room

Ragoût of smoked chicken and herbs with fresh tagliatelle. Roast loin of Scottish lamb stuffed with wild mushrooms and Camargue rice, served with cooking juices enriched with port. Hazelnut and chocolate mousse galette.

STB Highly Commended 👑 👑 👑 👑
- Credit cards: Access/Mastercard/Eurocard, Visa, Switch, Delta
- Owner/Proprietors: Colin & Carole Anderson

KNOCKENDARROCH HOUSE
Higher Oakfield, Pitlochry
Perthshire PH16 5HT
Tel: 01796 473473
Fax: 01796 474068

High on a hill overlooking village – just off main road in the centre of town, up Bonnethill Road and take first right turn.

An imposing Victorian villa with a period atmosphere.

- Victorian mansion in Pitlochry.
- Excellent classic cooking
- "Delicious food in a very happy atmosphere."

Knockendarroch is a sturdy villa, built in 1870 on a steep hillock in Pitlochry, and accordingly enjoying wonderful views up the Tummel Valley to the south, and of Ben Vrackie to the north. The house is well-proportioned; the public rooms well-appointed and comfortable; the 12 bedrooms individually furnished. It was opened as an hotel in 1985 by its current owners, the McMenemie family, who are courteous and enthusiastic hosts. The cooking is of a high standard, and has earned Knockendarroch a Red Rosette from the AA. Booking is essential for non-residents.

Open all year
- Rooms: 12 with private facilities
- Special rates available
- Dinner ££
- Vegetarians welcome
- Children welcome
- No smoking throughout

Salad of smoked chicken served on a crisp lettuce panache with a red onion marmalade. Roast haunch of venison with a lemon and rosemary seasoning served with a Burgundy sauce. Berry fruits cheesecake served with a Drambuie scented cream.

STB Highly Commended 👑 👑 👑
- Credit cards: Access/Mastercard/Eurocard, American Express, Visa
- Proprietors: The McMenemie Family

PITLOCHRY FESTIVAL THEATRE RESTAURANT
Port-na-Craig, Pitlochry
Perthshire PH16 5DR
Tel: 01796 473054
Fax: 01796 473054

On south bank of the River Tummel, approx ¼ mile from centre of town. Clearly signposted.

An informal restaurant for theatre goers with a relaxed atmosphere.

- Restaurant and coffee bar.
- Modern Scottish cooking enlivened with imaginative touches.
- "The atmosphere and views from this restaurant set the scene for diners before a performance."

The Pitlochry Festival Theatre is beautifully situated on the banks of the River Tummel at the gateway to the Highlands. The theatre's restaurant and coffee bar are a boon to theatre patrons as well as Pitlochry locals who drop in regularly to enjoy the home baking which is such a feature of the coffee bar in the foyer. At lunchtime the restaurant is buffet style with a choice of hot and cold dishes including local fish from the 'Summer Festival Buffet'. Portions are generous with lots of healthy eating options. In the evening table d'hôte dinner is served at 6.30 pm to accommodate theatre goers. Booking is essential.

Open 2 May to 11 Oct
Note: open early Apr for Coffee + Lunch only
✕ Lunch £
🍴 Dinner – booking essential £-££
🍴 Note: If theatre performance Sun, buffet served – booking essential
Ⓥ Vegetarians welcome
☆ Children welcome
♿ Facilities for disabled visitors
✗ No smoking in restaurant during dinner
✗ Smoking area in Coffee Bar

Scampi, scallops, salmon and prawns in a cream and dill sauce. Poached fillet of Scottish salmon with spinach and leek sauces. Mincemeat roulade filled with a Glayva flavoured cream.

💳 Credit cards: Access/Mastercard/Eurocard, American Express, Visa, Diners Club, Mastercharge
👤 Catering Manager: Alistair Barr

QUEENS VIEW HOTEL
Strathtummel, by Pitlochry
Perthshire PH16 5NA
Tel: 01796 473 291
Fax: 01796 473 515

Take old A9 (B8079) north from Pitlochry, turn left onto B8019 'Queens View' 4 miles. Hotel is ½ mile before 'Queens View' between road and Loch Tummel.

A country house hotel in a beautiful setting.

- Stone built baronial house overlooking Loch Tummel.
- Innovative, yet traditional cooking.
- "Warm hospitality, good food and all the comforts of home."

The Queens View Hotel is on a fabulous position 100 feet or more above Loch Tummel. The building itself was built in several phases and dates back to the early 1800s the interior of which has a very traditional Scottish feel to it. Norma and Richard Tomlinson run the hotel using the wide experience gained in the catering business over the years and their care and professionalism shows throughout. Nine of the bedrooms are en suite and five have king-size beds. Norma's cooking is the best of Scottish with some imaginative touches and the experience to be found here was described by our Inspector as like staying as a guest in someone's home.

Open 1 Mar to mid Jan
Closed Christmas Eve, Christmas Day + Boxing Day
🍴 Note: Telephone bookings required for Jan
🛏 Rooms: 10, 9 with private facilities
SP Special rates available
✕ Food served all day £
✕ Lunch £-££
✕ Dinner £££
Ⓥ Vegetarians welcome
☆ Children welcome
✗ No smoking in dining room

Puff pastry horns filled with a mélange of ceps, morel mushrooms, chestnuts and Madeira. Venison steak on a bed of clapshot with a red wine and port sauce. Chocolate meringue roulade with a raspberry coulis and shortbread garnish.

STB Commended 👑 👑 👑 👑
💳 Credit cards: Access/Mastercard/Eurocard, Visa, Switch, Delta
👤 Proprietors: Richard & Norma Tomlinson

WESTLANDS OF PITLOCHRY

160 Atholl Road, Pitlochry
Perthshire PH16 5AR
Tel: 01796 472266
Fax: 01796 473994

A924 into Pitlochry, Westlands at north end of
town on right hand side.

Attractive stone-built hotel.

- Country town hotel.
- Traditional cooking.
- "A centrally based hotel with welcoming
  atmosphere."

An attractive stone building with an extension,
built in keeping with the rest. The lawn, which is
bordered by mature trees, slopes down to the main
road, and Westlands has attractive views. The
hotel is personally run by its resident proprietors,
Andrew and Sue Mathieson, supported by their
manager and chef. There is a straightforward table
d'hôte menu and an à la carte menu which offers a
wide range of Scottish dishes. Both are reasonably
priced. Meals are served in the Garden Room
Restaurant, which has pleasant views of the Vale
of Atholl.

Open all year except 25, 26 Dec
🏠 Rooms: 15 with private facilities
SP Special rates available
✕ Lunch £
✕ Dinner ££
Ⓥ Vegetarians welcome
† Children welcome
✕ No smoking in restaurant

**Fresh local salmon fishcakes in home-made
crispy coating set on a pool of tomato and basil
sauce. Roast gigot of Highland lamb roasted with
heather honey and grain mustard, served with a
grain mustard and white wine sauce. Carse of
Gowrie and caraway meringue set on a pool of
raspberry coulis with fresh cream.**

STB Commended 👑 👑 👑 👑
💳 Credit cards: Access/Mastercard/Eurocard,
Visa
🏠 Partners: Andrew & Sue Mathieson

Plockton 159

THE HAVEN HOTEL

Innes Street, Plockton, Ross-shire IV52 8TW
Tel: 01599 544223
Fax: 01599 544467

In the village of Plockton.

A small West Highland hotel.

- Converted 19th century merchant's house.
- Modern Scottish cooking.
- "A haven indeed – excellent food in a most
  charming old village setting."

Plockton is known as the 'jewel of the Highlands.'
With its palm trees along the waterfront and shining
views out over the sea, it is really one of the
country's loveliest villages. The Haven was built
for a Victorian merchant and has a pleasing
simplicity in its architecture, sandstone-fronted
and harled sides and rear. Although detached, it
stands in the terrace of traditional houses at
Plockton, only yards from the beach. The hotel
continues to offer the same high standard of
cuisine for which it has long had such a good
reputation. Accommodation is currently being
refurbished to include 2 suites, one with a four-
poster bed. Dinner menus are table d'hôte (six
choices of main course) and combine fresh local
produce with interesting sauces, changing daily.
The Haven has 1 AA Rosette, and is a member of
the Certified Aberdeen Angus Scheme.

Open 1 Feb to 20 Dec incl
🏠 Rooms: 15, 12 with private facilities
SP Special rates available
♀ Restricted licence
✕ Lunch – 24 hours notice required ££
✕ Dinner 5 course menu £££
Ⓥ Vegetarians welcome
† Children over 7 years welcome
♿ Facilities for disabled visitors
✕ No smoking in restaurant

**A Dunsyre Blue flavoured soufflé set on a port wine
sauce. West Coast king scallops set on a shellfish,
paprika and tarragon sauce accompanied by a
timbale of wild rice. Ecclefechan butter tart.**

STB Highly Commended 👑 👑 👑 👑
💳 Credit cards: Access/Mastercard/Eurocard,
Visa, Switch, Delta
🏠 Owners: Annan & Jill Dryburgh

THE LAKE HOTEL
Port of Menteith, Perthshire FK8 3RA
Tel: 01877 385258
Fax: 01877 385671

On A81 – at Port of Menteith – 200 yards on road
south to Arnprior.

An Art Deco country hotel overlooking the lake.

• A well-established, comfortable and recently
  refurbished country hotel.
• Excellent cooking. Imaginative use of the best of
  Scottish produce.
• "Wonderful panoramic views of the Lake of
  Menteith."

Standing on the southern shore of Scotland's only
'lake', the hotel enjoys splendid views towards the
Trossachs. The heart of the building was a 19th
century manse, but it became an hotel over 50
years ago, with many well-integrated additions,
and from the outside it is a classic example of a
traditional Scottish country hotel. The interior
provides a surprise: the theme is Art Deco, well
executed, with many original pieces of furniture.
The Conservatory Restaurant is on the lakeside,
entered from the spacious lounge. Like all the
other rooms, it is pleasantly appointed. The table
d'hôte menus (lunch and dinner) are very well-
priced and offer some unusual traditional dishes
which have all but disappeared from more
'precious' restaurants. The excellence of the
cooking has been recognised with 2 AA Rosettes.

Open all year
🏠 Rooms: 16 with private facilities
🍴 Lunch – booking essential ££
✗ Dinner 4 course menu £££
Ⓥ Vegetarians welcome
🚭 No smoking in restaurant

**Pressed mixed fish terrine with Provençale
dressing. Game sausage with braised lentils,
apple chutney and raspberry vinegar sauce.
Banana beignets with fudge ice cream and
butterscotch sauce.**

STB Highly Commended 👑 👑 👑 👑
💳 Credit cards: Access/Mastercard/Eurocard,
   American Express, Visa, Switch
👤 Manager: Douglas Little

CORSEMALZIE HOUSE HOTEL
Port William
Newton Stewart
Wigtownshire DG8 9RL
Tel: 01988 860254
Fax: 01988 860213

Halfway along B7005 Glenluce-Wigtown, off A714
Newton Stewart-Port William or A747 Glenluce-
Port William.

Sporting country house hotel.

• Victorian country mansion.
• Traditional hotel cooking.
• "A comfortable sporting country house hotel in
  delightful surroundings."

This 19th century house with its own 40 acre
estate is a popular venue for those who enjoy the
pursuit of country sports. The sprawling gardens
and woodlands around the house are most
attractive and peacocks strut proudly across the
lawns, with the occasional courageous pheasant
which has avoided the pot, ducking between them.
The menus feature much locally shot game and
locally caught wild salmon trout and local shellfish.
(See advert Page 18.)

Open 1 Mar to 20 Jan except Christmas Day +
Boxing Day
🏠 Rooms: 15 with private facilities
SP Special rates available
✗ Lunch £££
✗ Dinner £££
Ⓥ Vegetarians welcome
🧒 Children welcome
♿ Facilities for disabled visitors
🚭 No smoking in dining room

**Filo parcels filled with spinach and Scottish
cream cheese. Local lamb cutlets en croûte.
Meringue roulade with a Drambuie cream.**

STB Commended 👑 👑 👑 👑
💳 Credit cards: Access/Mastercard/Eurocard,
   American Express, Visa, Mastercharge,
   Switch, Delta
👤 Proprietor: Peter McDougall

Portpatrick 162

FERNHILL HOTEL
Heugh Road, Portpatrick
nr Stranraer DG9 8TD
Tel: 01776 810220
Fax: 01776 810596

On entering Portpatrick take right fork – Heugh Road – and hotel is c. 300 yards on left.

A comfortable hotel overlooking the pretty seaside village and sea.

- Victorian house with modern conservatory extension.
- Modern Scottish cooking.
- "Interesting menus, with local seafood particularly well-used."

Set above the harbour of the beautiful, unspoiled fishing village of Portpatrick, The Fernhill Hotel has been family run by Anne and Hugh Harvie for over 30 years. It began as a single Victorian villa-boardinghouse, and has gradually expanded in all directions, so that it now has 20 bedrooms and a sizeable conservatory restaurant with splendid views over the village to the sea. The chef, John Henry, uses locally landed fish and shellfish and Galloway beef and lamb. His cooking is fresh and healthy and his menus sensible and well-priced.

Open all year except Christmas Day + Boxing Day
- ⌂ Rooms: 20 with private facilities
- SP Special rates available
- ✕ Food served all day £-££
- ✕ Lunch £-££
- ✕ Dinner ££
- Ⓥ Vegetarians welcome
- ☆ Children welcome
- ♿ Facilities for disabled visitors
- 🚭 No smoking in conservatory

Smoked salmon and spinach mousse with roast red pepper sauce. Pan-fried collops of venison saddle with sautéd wild mushrooms and red wine sauce. Tangy lemon cheesecake topped with toffee meringue.

STB Highly Commended 👑 👑 👑 👑
- 💳 Credit cards: Access/Mastercard/Eurocard, American Express, Visa, Diners Club, Switch, Delta, JCB
- 👤 Proprietor: Mrs Anne Harvie

KNOCKINAAM LODGE
Portpatrick, Dumfries & Galloway DG9 9AD
Tel: 01776 810471 Fax: 01776 810435

Take A77 towards Portpatrick. 2 miles west of Lochans, Knockinaam sign on right. Take first left turning, past smokehouse. Follow signs for 3 miles to lodge.

Outstanding cuisine in a beautiful and untouched corner of rural Galloway.

- A 19th century hunting lodge converted into a first class country house hotel.
- Best modern British cooking.
- "An idyllic country house hotel with a true artist in charge of the kitchens."

Knockinaam was built in 1869 and was described 'as delightful a maritime residence as is anywhere to be seen'. It is remotely situated on the Galloway coast, close to the shore and facing toward the sunset (with Ireland on the horizon), surrounded on three sides by cliffs: tranquil and timeless. The public rooms are small and cosy, with open log fires in winter; the bedrooms, varying in size, are superbly appointed. The lodge's resident owners, Michael Bricker and Pauline Ashworth, are attentive and hospitable hosts, and their Head Chef Tony Pierce prepares dishes which are both contemporary, unusual and outstandingly successful. A memorable place. Knockinaam has 3 AA Rosettes.

Open all year
- ⌂ Rooms: 10 with private facilities
- SP Special rates available
- ✕ Food served all day ££
- ✕ Lunch £££
- ✕ Dinner ££££
- Ⓥ Vegetarians welcome
- ☆ Children welcome
- ♿ Facilities for disabled visitors – restaurant only
- 🚭 No smoking in dining room

Roast Mallaig sea scallops with a carrot and vanilla emulsion. Noisettes of Galloway lamb with a turnip fondant and a juniper scented jus. Layered jellied terrine of native berries with Drambuie ice cream.

STB Deluxe 👑 👑 👑 👑
- 💳 Credit cards: Access/Mastercard/Eurocard, American Express, Visa, Diners Club, Switch, Delta
- 👤 Proprietors: Michael Bricker & Pauline Ashworth

POWMILL

WHINSMUIR COUNTRY INN
Powmill, by Dollar, Clackmannanshire FK14 7NW
Tel: 01577 840595 Fax: 01577 840779

On A977 Kincardine Bridge-Kinross.

Country inn with excellent views of surrounding countryside.

- Restaurant with accommodation.
- Modern Scottish bistro style cooking.
- "Country inn offering good food in a bistro style atmosphere."

Formerly the Gartwhinzean Hotel, it has now been taken over by the Brown family, run by Paul and Diane Brown, who are real experts in running hotels demonstrated by the success they have achieved at Auchterarder House, and Roman Camp. Many changes have been introduced including a recently completed new dining room with a large open fireplace and beautiful views. The bedroom accommodation is in the process of complete modernisation. Menus offer something for everyone and cater for all tastes and budgets with a good choice of lunch and snack dishes as well as a more sophisticated à la carte dinner menu giving five-six choices per course. Accompanying wine lists are well-chosen and relatively competitively priced. Whinsmuir has 1 AA Rosette. *(See advert Page 263.)*

Open all year
- 🛏 Rooms: 13 with private facilities
- SP Special rates available
- ✕ Food served all day ££
- ✕ Lunch £
- ✕ Dinner £££
- Ⅴ Vegetarians welcome
- ⚥ Children welcome
- ⚭ Facilities for disabled visitors
- ⚥ No smoking area in restaurant

A warm Stilton and apple flan accompanied by a beetroot and walnut chutney. Grilled fillet of halibut topped with Welsh rarebit and served with a vermouth and chive cream sauce. Frosted Turkish delight soufflé with Italiène meringue.

STB Commended 👑 👑 👑 👑
- 💳 Credit cards: Access/Mastercard/Eurocard, American Express, Visa, Switch
- 🅝 Proprietor: Paul M Brown

ROGART

SCIBERSCROSS LODGE
Strath Brora, Rogart
Sutherland IV28 3YQ
Tel: 01408 641246
Fax: 01408 641465

A9 over Dornoch Firth Bridge for c. 10 miles, then A839 for 4 miles. In Rogart turn right onto single-track road (Balnacoil) for 7 miles, lodge on left.

An attractive sporting lodge in secluded surroundings.

- Country house hotel.
- Country house cooking.
- "An idyllic retreat with good food, lovely accommodation and caring hosts."

Sciberscross is the home of Peter and Kate Hammond, and this classic Victorian sporting lodge built for the Duke of Sutherland in 1876 is full of homely touches – masses of fresh cut flowers, framed photographs and family portraits, antique furniture. Peter usually dines with his guests, and the lodge offers fishing for salmon, sea trout, brown trout and char. It stands in spectacular scenery just across the Dornoch Firth. Kate uses whatever can be sourced locally. Her five course dinners have set menus (choices for starter and dessert), and her cooking is delicious. Their motto is "Arrive as strangers, leave as friends."

Open 1 Feb to 31 Oct
- 🛏 Rooms: 5 with private facilities
- SP Special rates available
- ✕ Lunch – by special arrangement ££££
- ✕ Dinner 5 course fully inclusive menu – non-residents by prior booking only ££££
- Ⅴ Vegetarians welcome
- ⚥ Children welcome at owners' discretion

Salmon quartet. Rack of Rogart lamb with orange and rosemary jus. Pear ice cream/sorbet in a brandy basket with chocolate and Crème de Cacao sauce.

- 💳 Credit cards: Access/Mastercard/Eurocard, Visa
- 🅝 Joint Resident Owner: Peter Hammond
- 🅝 Chef/Patron: Kate Hammond

ROTHES

ROTHES GLEN
Rothes, Morayshire
AB38 7AQ
Tel: 01340 831 254
Fax: 01340 831 566

Beside the A941, 6 miles south of Elgin and 3 miles north of Rothes.

Excellent country house hotel within a castle style building.

- Turreted baronial mansion.
- Traditional Scottish with modern influences.
- "Freshly prepared quality food in beautiful surroundings."

New resident proprietors, Michael MacKenzie and Frederic Symonds have wasted no time in making their impression on Rothes Glen. They have a commitment to training and use of fresh Scottish produce that is immediately apparent. The building itself is very impressive and stands in ten acres of well-kept mature grounds with Highland cattle in fields fronting the hotel. Inside the furnishings are grand with sweeping staircase and grand piano greeting you on arrival. The new proprietors have a programme to constantly improve the already high standards achieved here. Cooking is accomplished by a chef who is highly skilled and taking courage from the new owners to broaden the menus and experiment with more modern combinations whilst still making the most of the excellent local produce to hand in Moray. Rothes Glen has 1 AA Rosette.

Open all year
🏠 Rooms: 16 with private facilities
✗ Lunch ££
✗ Dinner £££
Ⓥ Vegetarians welcome
⚲ Children welcome
✍ No smoking in dining room

Local crab cakes with a grain mustard sauce. Fillet of halibut with a chive butter sauce. Raspberry crème brûlée.

💳 Credit cards: Access/Mastercard/Eurocard, American Express, Visa
🄽 Resident Proprietors: Michael MacKenzie & Frederic Symonds

ST ANDREWS

THE GRANGE INN
Grange Road, St Andrews
Fife KY16 8LJ
Tel: 01334 472670
Fax: 01334 472604

From centre of town follow A917 Crail road past hospital to double mini roundabout. Take middle road signposted Grange – ¾ mile to Inn.

A charming country Inn overlooking St Andrews Bay.

- 17/18th century buildings.
- Modern and traditional Scottish cooking.
- "Delightful Inn created from centuries old Scottish cottages, with fine food and log fires."

Charming restaurant dating back to the 17th/18th century situated on a hillside overlooking St Andrews Bay. A short distance from the historic old town of St Andrews, The Grange offers fresh Scottish produce imaginatively prepared and cooked to order. Under the capable management of Proprietor Peter Aretz, The Grange has prospered and grown busy yet still managed to retain much of its old fashioned charm and atmosphere. There are three separate dining areas where you'll find high standards of hospitality with uncomplicated, tasty, home-cooked food. A range of draught and bottled beers, spirits and liqueurs are available in the cosy, stone-flagged Caddies Bar, with a personally selected wine list.

Open all year but closed Mon Tue Nov to Apr incl
✗ Lunch £-££
✗ Dinner £££
Ⓥ Vegetarians welcome
⚲ Children welcome
✍ No smoking in Patio Room + Bay Room

Smoked goose breast with apple and kumquat chutney. Pan-fried loin of venison served on a bed of red cabbage and beetroot, finished with damson and sloe gin sauce. Upside down apple tart glazed and flavoured with orange zest, served cold or warm with heather honey cream.

💳 Credit cards: Access/Mastercard/Eurocard, American Express, Visa, Diners Club, Switch, Delta
🄽 Proprietor: Peter Aretz

THE OLD COURSE HOTEL
St Andrews, Fife KY16 9SP
Tel: 01334 474371
Fax: 01334 477668

A91 to St Andrews on outskirts of town.

A large modern hotel standing on the edge of the most famous golf course in the world.

- Grand resort hotel .
- Modern Scottish/grills.
- "Fine Scottish cuisine to enjoy whilst overlooking the world famous golf course."

The hotel is set in a spectacular location overlooking the infamous 17th Road Hole and the historic Royal and Ancient clubhouse. All 125 bedrooms, including 17 suites, have unrivalled views, some looking over the Old Course to the sea, others towards the hotel's own Duke's Course and the surrounding countryside. The hotel offers its guests (residents and non-residents) a unique choice of dining experiences – the Road Hole Grill with its open kitchen, the Conservatory – serving light meals throughout the day in summer, and the Jigger Inn, originally a 19th century cottage, now a popular golfing pub serving real ale and good wholesome food. Chef Bruce Price was winner of The Taste of Scotland Scotch Lamb Challenge Gourmet Category 1996, and The Taste of Scotland Scotch Lamb Challenge Overall Winner 1996.

Open all year
- 🏠 Rooms: 125 with private facilities
- 🆂🅿 Special rates available
- ✗ Food served £-££
- ✗ Lunch ££
- ✗ Dinner ££££
- Ⓥ Vegetarians welcome
- ✝ Children welcome
- ♿ Facilities for disabled visitors
- 🚭 Pipe and cigar smoking not permitted in dining room + restaurants

Smoked haddock gâteau: lightly tea-smoked with tomato, avocado and a beetroot and ginger dressing. Pan-fried fillet of Aberdeen Angus beef with sun-dried tomato, mashed potato, and a ragoût of beans and spring onion. Tasting of Old Course desserts.

STB Deluxe 👑 👑 👑 👑 👑
- 💳 Credit cards: Access/Mastercard/Eurocard, American Express, Visa, Diners Club, Mastercharge, Delta, JCB
- 🅺 Food & Beverage Manager: Andrew Phelan

RUFFLETS COUNTRY HOUSE & GARDEN RESTAURANT
Strathkinness Low Road, St Andrews
Fife KY16 9TX
Tel: 01334 472594
Fax: 01334 478703

On B939, 1½ miles west of St Andrews.

A most attractive country house near St Andrews.

- Country house hotel.
- Fine country house cooking.
- "A delightful experience for dining and Scottish hospitality."

Rufflets is one of the oldest established country house hotels in Scotland, and has the distinction of being privately owned and managed by the same family since 1952. The house itself was built in 1924 and stands in formal gardens; furnishings are extremely tasteful (a mix of antique and contemporary country house); bedrooms are all individually designed and furnished. The attractive Garden Restaurant has an AA Rosette, among other awards. The daily changing menus are table d'hôte (six main courses) and the cooking combines the fresh seafood available from the East Neuk and good local meats and vegetables with imaginative sauces and stuffings. A four course, Scottish 'tasting' menu is also available. Service is smart and professional under the guidance of Manager, John Angus.

Open all year
- 🏠 Rooms: 25 with private facilities
- 🆂🅿 Special rates available
- ✗ Lunch (Restaurant Sun Sat) ££
- ✗ Dinner £££
- Ⓥ Vegetarians welcome
- ✝ Children welcome
- ♿ Facilities for non-residential disabled visitors

Crinan king scallops seared in the pan and glazed with a tomato hollandaise. Medallions of pork fillet grilled with fresh lemon thyme and honey. Amaretto burnt cream.

STB Highly Commended 👑 👑 👑 👑
- 💳 Credit cards: Access/Mastercard/Eurocard, American Express, Visa, Diners Club, Mastercharge, Switch
- 🅺 Proprietor: Ann Russell

ST ANDREWS GOLF HOTEL
40 The Scores, St Andrews
Fife KY16 9AS
Tel: 01334 472611
Fax: 01334 472188

A91 to St Andrews, turn left at Golf Place then
follow round to right to The Scores.

**A golfing hotel close to the links with splendid
views.**

- Town hotel.
- Traditional Scottish cooking.
- "Enjoy good, traditional Scottish cooking in this
  well-appointed family-run hotel."

The Golf is a family-run hotel with fine views over
St Andrews Bay to the distant Highlands, a mere
200 yards from the famous Royal and Ancient Gold
Club and the championship courses. It is a
Victorian terraced house, tastefully modernised
and decorated with quality prints. The restaurant is
oak-panelled and candlelit; à la carte and table
d'hôte menus feature locally sourced Scottish fish,
game and meat. In the basement is the convivial
'Ma Bells' pub, where bar food is served all day.
Italian and some French spoken. The hotel has
1 AA Rosette.

Open all year
🛏 Rooms: 23 with private facilities
SP Special rates available
✗ Food served all day £££
✗ Lunch ££
✗ Dinner ££££
Ⓥ Vegetarians welcome
✶ Children welcome
⚹ Facilities for disabled visitors
⚞ No smoking in restaurant

**Pheasant, bacon and dried apricot terrine with
apricot and basil chutney. Noisette of Perthshire
lamb topped with woodland mushrooms and
rosemary duxelles and sweet shallot jus.
Crabbies chocolate cake with vanilla cream
cheese.**

STB Highly Commended 🏆 🏆 🏆 🏆
⊞ Credit cards: Access/Mastercard/Eurocard,
  American Express, Visa, Diners Club,
  Mastercharge, Switch, Delta
🅺 Proprietors: Maureen & Brian Hughes

St Boswells 167

BUCCLEUCH ARMS HOTEL
The Green
St Boswells
Roxburghshire
TD6 0EW
Tel: 01835 822243
Fax: 01835 823965

Situated on the main A68, 60 miles north of
Newcastle. 40 miles south of Edinburgh.

An historic coaching inn, once a hunting lodge.

- Sportsman's hotel/inn.
- Contemporary hotel cooking.
- "Friendly hotel popular with local sportsmen
  and visitors alike."

The Buccleuch Arms dates from the 16th century,
when it was a hunting lodge for the Dukes of
Buccleuch. Situated on one of the main roads into
Scotland (now the A68), beside the pretty village
cricket pitch and green in the old village of St
Boswells (established in the 11th century by a
French monk, Boisil). Now a coaching inn, it is a
popular base from which to tour the Tweed Valley,
fish, shoot or golf (there are 14 golf courses within
a 20 mile radius). Lunch and suppers/dinners are
served in the bar and in the restaurant. The
cooking is adventurous, uses as much local
produce as possible and favours aromatic sauces
and combinations.

Open all year except Christmas Day
🛏 Rooms: 18, 17 with private facilities
SP Special rates available
✗ Food served all day £
✗ Lunch ££
✗ Dinner ££
Ⓥ Vegetarians welcome
✶ Children welcome
⚞ No smoking in dining room

**Smoked Scottish oysters served on a toasted
croûte, coated with a dressing of sour cream and
chives. Tournedos of Scottish beef set on a bed of
leaf spinach with a glazed wine and peppercorn
sauce. Home-made strawberry shortcake.**

STB Commended 🏆 🏆 🏆 🏆
⊞ Credit cards: Access/Mastercard/Eurocard,
  Visa
🅺 Director: Sue Dodds

DRYBURGH ABBEY HOTEL

Dryburgh, Melrose
Roxburghshire TD6 0RQ
Tel: 01835 822261
Fax: 01835 823945

Off A68 at St Boswells onto B6404. 2 miles turn left onto B6356. Continue for 1½ miles, hotel signposted.

A splendid luxury hotel in the Scottish Borders with leisure facilities and comfortable accommodation. Popular with anglers and country sportsmen.

- Scottish baronial red sandstone mansion on the banks of the River Tweed.
- International and modern Scottish cuisine.
- "The menu concentrates on thoughtful flavour combinations and makes good use of superb local produce."

In a tranquil setting on the banks of the River Tweed, not far from the ruins of the historic Abbey, this mansion has been restored and converted into a first class hotel. The public rooms, bedrooms and suites are grand, comfortably appointed and maintained to high standards and there is also an indoor heated swimming pool. The Tweed Restaurant is situated on the first floor, with views over the lawns and gardens to the river: a spacious, elegant room with decorative cornicing and ornate chandeliers. The Head Chef, Patrick Ruse, offers a table d'hôte menu (lunch and dinner) which changes daily, and uses only fresh local produce. During the day a range of light meals is also available, served in the lounge or bar.

Open all year
🍴 Rooms: 26 with private facilities
SP Special rates available
✕ Food served all day ££
✕ Lunch £
✕ Dinner £££
Ⓥ Vegetarians welcome
⚘ Children welcome
⚲ Facilities for disabled visitors
🚭 No smoking in restaurant

Quenelles of avocado and walnut mousse with coriander dressing. Halibut with watercress sauce. Scottish cheeseboard.

STB Highly Commended 🏅🏅🏅🏅🏅
💳 Credit cards: Access/Mastercard/Eurocard, American Express, Visa, Mastercharge, Switch, Delta, JCB
👤 General Manager: John Sloggie
👤 Deputy Manager: Fiona Fleming

Selkirk 168

PHILIPBURN HOUSE HOTEL

Selkirk TD7 5LS
Tel: 01750 20747
Fax: 01750 21690

Situated on A707 Moffat-Peebles, 1 mile from A7 on outskirts of Selkirk.

Country house hotel offering a great deal of individual character.

- 18th century country mansion.
- Modern British cooking.
- "Comfortable and welcoming family-run hotel of high standards."

The Hill family has enhanced this already delightful Georgian house, built in the mid 18th century, with their own distinctive style. The hotel has earned increasingly high ratings for all of the last decade as it has increased the range and scope of its facilities. Jim Hill is an energetic progressively minded hotelier and is constantly seeking to improve standards. Guests have the choice of dining in the Garden and Poolside Restaurants, or perhaps in the informal atmosphere of Soutars Bar. The kitchen team led by Pelham Hill produces imaginative menus with distinctive touches and presents food to a very high standard. Re-opening early 1997.

Open all year
🍴 Rooms: 17 with private facilities
SP Special rates available
✕ Lunch £-££
✕ Dinner ££-£££
Ⓥ Vegetarians welcome
⚘ Children welcome
⚲ Facilities for disabled visitors
🚭 Smoking restricted in dining room

Grilled black pudding served on a sweet potato mash with a parsley and garlic essence. Fillet of sea bass with red and yellow pepper sauces. Philipburn passion fruit soufflé.

STB Highly Commended 🏅🏅🏅🏅
💳 Credit cards: Access/Mastercard/Eurocard, American Express, Visa, Diners ClubMastercharge, Switch, Delta
👤 Contacts: Pelham Hill & Jodie Hannan

Spean Bridge 169

BY SPEAN BRIDGE

CORRIEGOUR LODGE HOTEL
Loch Lochy, nr Spean Bridge
Inverness-shire PH34 4EB
Tel: 01397 712685
Fax: 01397 712696

Follow A82, 17 miles north of Fort William; 47 miles south of Inverness – between Spean Bridge and Invergarry.

A charming former hunting lodge set in breathtaking scenery.

- A small, personally owned and managed country house hotel.
- Excellent modern Scottish cuisine.
- "Well-run and beautifully appointed."

Corriegour was built in the late 19th century, now extensively and tastefully refurbished in an antique style, the hotel commands outstanding views over Loch Lochy. Its six acres of mature woodland and garden include a small lochside beach with jetty and waterfall. Corriegour Lodge's resident proprietors, Rod and Lorna Bunney, place their emphasis on guests' relaxation and comfort. Set with crisp white linen cloths and napkins, their Loch View Conservatory restaurant with its panoramic views, offers a range of high quality cuisine, all home-made, using the very best of Scottish produce including fresh seafood. The hotel's wine list is extensive and reasonably priced. Corriegour prides itself on its ethos, its position, its cooking and the friendliness of its staff.

Open all Mar to Nov
- 🏨 Rooms: 8 with private facilities
- 🆂🅿 Special rates available
- 🍴 Dinner – reservations strongly recommended ££
- Ⓥ Vegetarians welcome
- 🧒 Children welcome
- 🚭 No smoking in restaurant

Home-made soup and pâté. Fillet of Angus beef en croûte. Cloutie dumpling with Drambuie ice cream.

STB Highly Commended 🏵 🏵 🏵
- 💳 Credit cards: Access/Mastercard/Eurocard, American Express, Visa, Switch
- 👥 Proprietors: Rod & Lorna Bunney

OLD PINES RESTAURANT WITH ROOMS
Spean Bridge
Inverness-shire PH34 4EG
Tel: 01397 712324
Fax: 01397 712433

From Spean Bridge take A82 to Inverness. One mile north take B8004 next to Commando Memorial 300 yards on right.

A family home with a restaurant and guest rooms.

- Scandinavian-style log and stone chalet overlooking Glen Spean and the Nevis Range.
- Modern Scottish cooking.
- "Outstanding and sophisticated Scottish cuisine."

Old Pines is a little jewel set amongst mature pine trees in the Great Glen, an ideal base from which to explore Aonoch Mor and the countryside around Ben Nevis. It is the family home of Bill and Sukie Barber who describe it as a 'restaurant with rooms', and dinner by crystal and candlelight in the conservatory will certainly be the highlight of your stay. To dine here is to experience the very best of Scottish food, cooked superbly by Sukie who brings unlimited enthusiasm and skill to her craft. All ingredients are sourced locally, and they have their own smokehouse.

Open all year except 2 wks Nov: Closed Sun to non-residents
- 🏨 Rooms: 8 with private facilities
- 🆂🅿 Special rates available
- 🔒Ⓟ Unlicensed – guests welcome to take own wine
- ✕ Food served all day £
- 🍴 Lunch except Sun – restaurant lunch if booked £££
- ✕ Dinner 5 course menu except Sun (supper to residents) £££
- 🚭 No smoking throughout
- Ⓥ Vegetarians welcome – prior notice appreciated
- 🧒 Children welcome
- ♿ Facilities for disabled visitors

Monkfish, mussels and squat lobsters in a sauce of the sea. Roast leg of Scotch lamb stuffed with kidney and fresh herbs with rowan jelly. Caramelised rhubarb flan with ginger ice cream and orange sabayon sauce.

STB Highly Commended 🏵 🏵 🏵
- 💳 Credit cards: Access/Mastercard/Eurocard, American Express, Visa, Mastercharge, Switch, Delta
- 👥 Owners: Bill & Sukie Barber

`STEWARTON`

CHAPELTOUN HOUSE HOTEL
Irvine Road, nr Stewarton, Ayrshire KA3 3ED
Tel: 01560 482696
Fax: 01560 485100

From Fenwick exit on A77 (Glasgow to Ayr road),
take B778 to Stewarton then join B769 to Irvine.
Chapeltoun is 2 miles along on right hand side.

A country house hotel in Ayrshire.

- Country house hotel and restaurant.
- Country house cooking.
- "Unashamed luxury where standards remain
  year after year."

This attractive house was built in 1900 by a Glasgow
shipping merchant. It has all the elegant and refined
details of its period – rich oak panelling, grand fireplaces and ornate plasterwork (including a splendid
rose and thistle frieze). The house stands in 20
acres of gardens. The bedrooms are very comfortable and individually furnished, often with period
furniture, as are the public rooms. The dining room
is especially fine, with rich colours and
tapestry-covered chairs. The table d'hôte menu is
extensive (12 main courses) and changes every four
weeks. There is also a 'Chef's dish of the day'.
Dishes are cooked to order. The cooking draws
upon Eastern, French and Italian traditions; creamy
sauces are popular, and a lot of care is taken over
presentation. Chapeltoun has 1 AA Rosette.

    Open all year
🏠 Rooms: 8 with private facilities
✗ Lunch ££
✗ Dinner £££
Ⅴ Vegetarians welcome
ϯ Children welcome
✍ No smoking in restaurant

**Gâteau of Arbroath smokies encased in smoked
salmon, served with a dill and vermouth cream
sauce. Roast rack of lamb with a grain mustard
and rosemary herb crust served with a natural jus
and a selection of fresh vegetables and potatoes.
Individual Normandy apple tart.**

STB Highly Commended 🏅 🏅 🏅 🏅
💳 Credit cards: Access/Mastercard/Eurocard,
    American Express, Visa, Switch, Delta
🅺 Managing Directors: Colin McKenzie
    & Graeme McKenzie

`STIRLING (OUTSKIRTS)`

CROMLIX HOUSE
Kinbuck, by Dunblane
Perthshire FK15 9JT
Tel: 01786 822125
Fax: 01786 825450

Off A9, B8033 to Kinbuck, through village, cross
narrow bridge, drive is second on left. From Crieff
A822 to Braco, then B8033 Kinbuck.

**A baronial mansion recalling the splendours of a
bygone age.**

- A highly praised hotel with the atmosphere of a
  much loved home.
- Outstanding modern/traditional Scottish cuisine.
- "Cromlix is in a class of its own."

Proprietors David and Ailsa Assenti succeed in
exemplifying the true traditions of country house
hospitality, treating each of their guests as a
cherished individual. Under Head Chef Stephen
Robertson, Cromlix takes only the best of fresh
produce, either from the estate or procured locally,
and produces imaginative meals for the
discriminating palate. Menus change daily. The
wine list is discerning and extensive. Cromlix is
indeed a 'totally relaxing, seemingly effortless,
well-run ship'. Cromlix has 2 AA Rosettes.

    Open all year except 2 to 30 Jan
🏠 Rooms: 14 with private facilities
Ⓢ Special rates available
✗ Lunch ££
✗ Dinner 5 course menu ££££
Ⅴ Vegetarians welcome – extensive menu
ϯ Children welcome
✍ No smoking in dining rooms
🐄 Member of the Scotch Beef Club

**Warm avocado, smoked bacon and goats cheese
salad with a mild vinaigrette. Medallion of beef
glazed with bérnaise sauce and edged with Arran
mustard reduction. Warm pear tart with milk
chocolate sauce.**

STB Deluxe 🏅 🏅 🏅 🏅
💳 Credit cards: Access/Mastercard/Eurocard,
    American Express, Visa, Diners Club, Switch
🅺 Proprietors: David & Ailsa Assenti

ROYAL HOTEL

Henderson Street, Bridge of Allan
Stirlingshire FK9 4HG
Tel: 01786 832284
Fax: 01786 834377

Bridge of Allan town centre.

A traditional town centre hotel of distinction.

- A medium sized, privately owned hotel.
- Good traditional/modern Scottish cuisine.
- "A traditional Victorian hotel, typical of Scottish towns."

Built in 1842, this impressive Victorian hotel stands in the middle of Bridge of Allan, home to Stirling University. Carefully restored and refurbished, its atmosphere is of gracious comfort. The hotel's restaurant offers seasonal table d'hôte menus that make the most of fresh, local produce, and Henderson's Brasserie serves freshly prepared light meals and snacks at reasonable prices. The wine list of 55 bins is wide-ranging and fairly priced. Service is cheerful and considerate. The hotel has 1 AA Rosette.

Open all year
- 🛏 Rooms: 32 with private facilities
- SP Special rates available
- ✕ Food served all day £££
- ✕ Lunch ££
- ✕ Dinner £££
- Ⅴ Vegetarians welcome
- 术 Children welcome

Steamed West Coast mussels in a bacon and mushroom jus. Peppered fillet of Tay salmon on a julienne of leeks with red pepper and chive sauce. Iced Drambuie praline parfait with fruits of the forest compote.

STB Commended 👑 👑 👑 👑
- 💳 Credit cards: Access/Mastercard/Eurocard, American Express, Visa, Diners Club
- 🍴 Brasserie Manager: Brian Provan

THE TOPPS

Fintry Road, Denny
Stirlingshire FK6 5JF
Tel: 01324 822471
Fax: 01324 823099

On B818 Denny – Fintry road, off M80. 4 miles from Denny.

A family-run farm guest house in Stirlingshire.

- A farmhouse on a working sheep and cashmere goat farm.
- Excellent home cooking.
- "Comfortable, relaxed guest house in a perfect setting where good Scottish food can be appreciated."

This is a most informal farm guest house where you cannot help but share in the day to day activities of the country. The house itself is a modern bungalow with splendid views over the Fintry and Ochil Hills, pleasantly furnished with plenty of family bric-a-brac. The atmosphere is cosy and familiar. A popular restaurant complements the guest house facilities. It has a small bar and a comfortable dining room. Scottish owners Jennifer and Alistair Steel both cook. The menus are straightforward, usually offering a choice of four main courses and as much produce as possible comes from the farm itself.

Open all year
- 🛏 Rooms: 8 with private facilities
- ✕ Lunch ££
- ✕ Dinner ££
- Ⅴ Vegetarians welcome – prior notice required
- 术 Children welcome
- ♿ Facilities for disabled visitors
- 🚭 No smoking throughout

Jock's smoked trout with side salad and skinny toast. Spring gigot of lamb served with minted pears. Glenmorangie Gâteau: feather-light sponge, chocolate, yoghurt and just a hint of 'the water of life'.

STB Commended 👑 👑 👑
- 💳 Credit cards: Access/Mastercard/Eurocard, Visa
- 🍴 Owners/Chefs: Jennifer & Alistair Steel

`STRANRAER`

NORTH WEST CASTLE HOTEL
Portrodie, Stranraer
Wigtownshire DG9 8EH
Tel: 01776 704413
Fax: 01776 702646

Seafront – opposite ferry port.

Large resort hotel offering extensive facilities.

- 1820s town mansion.
- Traditional hotel cooking.
- "A well-known and popular hotel with so many enjoyable extras."

This castellated townhouse was built by Sir John Ross, the Arctic explorer, in 1820. It has been owned and run as a hotel by the McMillan family for many years and has been well-maintained with comfortable accommodation and function rooms. It has the distinction of being the first hotel in the world with its own indoor curling rink and also has bowling, swimming pool (with spa bath), sauna, sunbeds and multi-gym. The games room offers snooker, pool and table tennis. Overlooking Loch Ryan the large 'Regency' dining room has a grand hotel atmosphere with pianist playing each evening and both the à la carte and table d'hôte menus offer traditional Scottish dishes, treated in a creative way. The kitchen goes to great lengths to find fresh local produce.

Open all year
🛏 Rooms: 71 with private facilities
SP Special rates available
✕ Lunch ££
✕ Dinner ££££
Ⓥ Vegetarians welcome
⚘ Children welcome

Timbale of local oak-smoked salmon filled with a smoked trout mousse, accompanied by a cucumber and yoghurt sauce. Steamed fillet of Scottish salmon wrapped in spinach leaves and served with a hollandaise sauce. Warm Ecclefechan tart accompanied by a light caramel sauce.

STB Highly Commended 👑 👑 👑 👑 👑
⊡ Credit cards: Access/Mastercard/Eurocard, Visa, Switch, Delta
🕴 Proprietor: H C McMillan

`STRATHLACHLAN`

INVER COTTAGE RESTAURANT
Strathlachlan, by Cairndow
Argyll PA27 8BU
Tel: 01369 860396/275

B8000, 7 miles south of Strachur – signposted.

A friendly country restaurant overlooking Castle Lachlan.

- Small rural restaurant.
- Traditional Scottish cooking.
- "Personal, friendly service and good home cooking by the owners."

Inver Cottage has a grand view across a small bay to Castle Lachlan, ancient seat of the MacLachlans of MacLachlan. With an open fire and low ceilings, polished wood everywhere, and candles, both the restaurant and the adjacent lounge bar have a cosy welcoming atmosphere. Owners Tony and Gina Wignell and their team provide informal but efficient service. The cooking is unfussy and fresh; well contrived sauces accompanying excellent local meat, seafood and vegetables. The whole place has a great atmosphere.

Open Mar to 31 Oct (7 days)
Note: during Nov + Dec open Fri Sat Sun only
✕ Lunch £-££
✕ Dinner ££

Home-made chicken liver pâté. Ham n' Haddie. Home-made chocolate biscuit cake.

⊡ Credit cards: Access/Mastercard/Eurocard, Visa
🕴 Proprietors: Tony & Gina Wignell

Strathpeffer 174

COUL HOUSE HOTEL
Contin, by Strathpeffer
Ross-shire IV14 9EY
Tel: 01997 421487
Fax: 01997 421945

North of Inverness, continue on A9 over Moray Firth bridge. After 5 miles take second left at roundabout on to A835. Hotel is ½ mile up private drive to the right.

A country house near Strathpeffer.

* 19th century mansion.
* Country house cooking.
* "The cheeses were superb – they were made and smoked on the premises."

This elegant country house hotel commands fine views over unspoiled Highland scenery, little changed since its original inhabitants, the Mackenzies of Coul lived here. The spacious public rooms have open log fires and the recently refurbished en suite bedrooms are comfortable and tastefully decorated. Home to Martyn and Ann Hill, whose warm Highland welcome is only matched by their loveable Labradors. The bar lunches are notable – and the 'Kitchen Bar' itself is very popular with locals. Mackenzie's Taste of Scotland Restaurant offers table d'hôte and à la carte lunch and dinner menus which focus on Scottish specialities. Coul House has 1 AA Rosette. *(See advert Page 18.)*

Open all year
🏠 Rooms: 20 with private facilities
SP Special rates available
🍴 Lunch £-££ (Restaurant – prior booking only)
✕ Dinner 5 course menu ££££
Ⓥ Vegetarians welcome
🧒 Children welcome
♿ Facilities for disabled visitors
🚭 No smoking in restaurant

Smoked venison with melon. Summer Isles scallops. A selection of Scottish and chef's own home-smoked speciality cheese – apple and mint, whisky and thyme.

STB Highly Commended 👑 👑 👑 👑
💳 Credit cards: Access/Mastercard/Eurocard, American Express, Visa, Diners Club, Switch, JCB
🔖 Proprietors: Martyn & Ann Hill

Strathyre 175

CREAGAN HOUSE
RESTAURANT WITH ACCOMMODATION
Strathyre
Perthshire FK18 8ND
Tel: 01877 384638
Fax: 01877 384319

On A84, ¼ mile north of Strathyre.

Family-run restaurant with accommodation.

* 17th century farmhouse.
* Innovative Scottish cooking.
* "Full of old world charm and ambience."

Creagan House dates from the 17th century, and has been sympathetically restored to provide a 'baronial' dining room and five letting bedrooms. The house is eclectically furnished with all sorts of interesting pieces, and one of the bedrooms has a unique four-poster bed. Gordon and Cherry Gunn have been awarded an AA Rosette for their cooking. Guests choose from the 'menu of the day' or the 'chef's favourites menu'. The emphasis of cooking is to allow the fresh local ingredients to emerge, with herbs from the garden, meats sourced from within Perthshire and interesting Scottish cheeses. The care and attention to detail in preparation, cooking and presentation is obvious and the overall effect is excellent.

Open all year except 3 to 28 Feb + 1 wk Oct (Scottish half term)
🏠 Rooms: 5 with private facilities
SP Special rates available
🍴 Booking essential for all meals
✕ Lunch Sun ££ (Mon to Sat – lunch parties can be arranged)
✕ Dinner ££-£££
Ⓥ Vegetarians welcome – with prior notice
🧒 Children welcome
🚭 No smoking in dining hall + bedrooms

Fillet of rabbit, wild mushroom and seed mustard with tagliatelle. Duck in a thyme and ginger jus with sweetcorn crumble. Three berry terrine with framboise coulis.

STB Deluxe 👑 👑 👑
💳 Credit cards: Access/Mastercard/Eurocard, American Express, Visa
🔖 Chef/Proprietor: Gordon Gunn
🔖 Manageress: Cherry Gunn

STRONTIAN

KILCAMB LODGE HOTEL
Strontian
Argyll PH36 4HY
Tel: 01967 402257
Fax: 01967 402041

On A861, 13 miles from Corran Ferry (A82, 15 miles south of Fort William).

An attractive house on the shore of Loch Sunart.

- Small country house hotel.
- Traditional Scottish cooking.
- "Beautifully appointed, offering a high standard of comfort."

Kilcamb Lodge is a charming, substantial West Highland dowager house, with extensions at each end. Its situation is superb – standing in 28 acres of lawns and woodland, with half a mile of shoreline along Loch Sunart. The hotel is family-owned and run by Anne and Peter Blakeway. The excellence of the food has been recognised by the award of 2 AA Rosettes. Peter Blakeway cooks, presenting a short and highly professional table d'hôte menu which changes daily and uses the best of the produce available that day.

Open mid Mar to early Nov
⊞ Rooms: 11 with private facilities
✕ Light Lunch £
✕ Dinner 4 course menu £££
Ⓥ Vegetarians welcome – prior notice required
⊀ Children welcome
♿ Facilities for non-residential disabled visitors
🚭 No smoking in restaurant

Open ravioli of squat lobster and wild mushrooms. Roast saddle of venison with spiced red cabbage and a port and juniper sauce. Chocolate crème brûlée.

STB Deluxe 👑 👑 👑
💳 Credit cards: Access/Mastercard/Eurocard, Visa, Switch, Delta
👤 Directors: Peter & Anne Blakeway

SWINTON

THE WHEATSHEAF HOTEL
Main Street, Swinton
Berwickshire TD11 3JJ
Tel: 01890 860 257
Fax: 01890 860 257

On B6461 Kelso-Berwick-upon-Tweed, 12 miles west of Berwick or a few miles east of A697.

Quaint, attractive hotel in small Border village.

- A small country inn on the village green.
- Modern Scottish cooking.
- "Excellent menus using a range of fresh local produce."

That a great deal of care has been taken to preserve the character of a genuine country inn is evident. The result is a welcoming, comfortable and intimate atmosphere, the sort that takes years to acquire. Bedrooms are prettily furnished, light and airy with en suite bathrooms and there is a secluded, private residents' lounge upstairs. The menu is surprisingly extensive, very reasonably priced and changes quarterly with the seasons. Excellent local produce is given added flavour by the chef's individuality and flair. The Wheatsheaf has 1 AA Rosette.

Open all year except last wk Oct + last 2 wks Feb
Closed Mon
⊞ Rooms: 4, 3 with private facilities
ⓢ Special rates available
✕ Lunch except Mon £££
✕ Dinner except Mon £££
Ⓥ Vegetarians welcome
⊀ Children welcome
♿ Facilities for disabled visitors
🚭 No smoking in restaurant

Salmon, potato and spinach terrine with saffron vinaigrette. Fillet of venison in a sloe gin and juniper berry sauce with poached pear. Sticky ginger pudding with hot fudge sauce.

STB Highly Commended 👑 👑 👑
💳 Credit cards: Access/Mastercard/Eurocard, Visa
👤 Proprietors: Alan & Julie Reid

TAIN

MANSFIELD HOUSE HOTEL
Scotsburn Road, Tain
Ross-shire IV19 1PR
Tel: 01862 892052
Fax: 01862 892260

Approaching Tain from south, ignore first entrance and continue north on A9 to second turning, signposted to police station and Royal Academy. Hotel is opposite Royal Academy.

Modernised family-run hotel.

- 19th century baronial house.
- Good Scottish cooking.
- "Friendly and hospitable with good food."

Visitors to the Royal Burgh of Tain, chartered in 1066, are able to enjoy many architectural features of interest. Mansfield House was built in 19th century baronial style by Donald Fowler, the former Provost of Tain between 1898 and 1912. The house has been lovingly maintained and offers every comfort for travellers. The kitchen prides itself in preparing well-chosen Scottish produce for a selection of familiar and popular dishes. There is a friendly and relaxed atmosphere and the Lauritsen family, highly skilled and experienced, are excellent hosts – assisted by their two golden retrievers! *(See advert Page 19.)*

Open all year
🏨 Rooms: 18 with private facilities
SP Special rates available
✗ Food served all day £-£££
✗ Lunch £
✗ Dinner £-£££
Ⅴ Vegetarians welcome
⚡ Children welcome
♿ Facilities for disabled visitors
🚭 No smoking in restaurants

Home-made ravioli of Scottish smoked salmon and prawns. Breast of chicken stuffed with haggis and a Moniack mead sauce. Home-made shortbread layered with wild fruits.

STB Highly Commended 👑 👑 👑 👑
💳 Credit cards: Access/Mastercard/Eurocard, American Express, Visa, Switch
👤 Proprietors: Norman, Norma & David Lauritsen

TARBERT

THE COLUMBA HOTEL
East Pier Road, Tarbert
Argyll PA29 6UF
Tel: 01880 820808
Fax: 01880 820808

On East Pier Road, ½ mile to the left around the harbour. Hotel on roadside.

A well-appointed family-run hotel close to harbour at Tarbert.

- A Victorian waterfront hotel refurbished by the present owners as a comfortable and pleasant establishment.
- Scottish modern cooking.
- "Good cooking in a warm and friendly place with outstanding views of the loch and harbour."

This small hotel overlooks Loch Fyne at the entrance to Tarbert Harbour. It has been a labour of love to Gina and Bob Chicken, who have worked hard at sympathetically refurbishing this Victorian hotel and continue to do so. The decor is in keeping with the building; there is a cosy bar with an open fire, which is popular for its wholesomely different bar food (and its 30 malt whiskies). The restaurant has been elegantly restored; it offers a relaxed atmosphere and a menu which makes imaginative use of the excellent local produce – fish and shellfish from the harbour; game from Inveraray Castle. *(See advert Page 27.)*

Open all year except 25, 26 Dec
🏨 Rooms: 10 with private facilities
SP Special rates available
✗ Lunch £
✗ Dinner ££
Ⅴ Vegetarians welcome
⚡ Children welcome
🚭 No smoking in restaurant

Salad of seared Loch Tarbert scallops with gazpacho and turmeric oil. Pan-fried breast of pheasant on a bed of leeks with a Tain Hramsa cheese and mustard sauce. Peaches poached in white wine with a bramble coulis.

STB Commended 3 Crowns 👑 👑 👑
💳 Credit cards: Access/Mastercard/Eurocard, Visa
👤 Partners: Bob & Gina Chicken

TAYINLOAN

TAYINLOAN INN
by Tarbert
Argyll
PA29 6XG
Tel: 01583 441233

A83, 19 miles south of Tarbert.

A traditional West Highland pub in an old coaching inn.

- Family-run village inn.
- Home cooking.
- "Everything that a wayside inn should be – warm, friendly and deservedly popular."

Formerly a 17th century coaching inn, Tayinloan is on the main (A83) Campbeltown-Tarbert road, close to the Gigha ferry point, and retains many olde world features. You can eat either in the cosy bar or the adjacent sun-lounge, and there is a separate dining room available for larger parties. The food is wholesome, straightforward and extremely good value. You choose from a well-balanced menu, supplemented by blackboard specials. Fish from Tarbert features largely; there is always a vegetarian dish available, and a children's menu. Everything is cooked to order. A sound, friendly local inn.

Open all year
Note: Closed Mon Oct to Apr
🛏 Rooms: 3
SP Special rates available
✗ Lunch £
✗ Dinner ££
Ⓥ Vegetarians welcome
☆ Children welcome
✄ No smoking areas in dining room + bedrooms

Fruits of the sea soup. Liver and bacon served with port and rosemary gravy. Fresh raspberry pavlova.

💳 Credit cards: Access/Mastercard/Eurocard, Visa, Mastercharge
𝕄 Proprietors: Mya & Gerard Holloran

TAYVALLICH

TAYVALLICH INN
Tayvallich
Argyll PA31 8PL
Tel: 01546 870282
Fax: 01546 870333

On B8025 (via B841 [Crinan] off B816 at Cairnbaan).

An informal bistro style restaurant with an enviable reputation.

- Both a popular local hostelry and a destination for the discerning.
- Simple treatment of freshest ingredients.
- "A place to return to again and again."

Under the same dedicated ownership of John and Pat Grafton for 18 years, Tayvallich Inn has earned the reputation of being a firm favourite. Beautifully situated with a spectacular outlook onto Tayvallich Bay, its many regular customers are drawn to its friendly atmosphere and excellent cooking. The reasonably-priced menus concentrate on the abundance of local seafood – scallops, prawns, mussels, crab and oysters – but does equally well for carnivores and vegetarians. The cooking is simple, straightforward and unpretentious. Service is cheerful and relaxed.

Open all year
Note: Closed Mon Nov to Mar
✗ Lunch £
✗ Dinner ££
Ⓥ Vegetarians welcome
☆ Children welcome
✄ No smoking area in bar (meal times)

Roast beef-tomato with Parmesan shaving and asparagus. Pan-fried Sound of Jura scallops. Chocolate nut slab.

💳 Credit cards: Access/Mastercard/Eurocard, Visa, Mastercharge, Switch
𝕄 Proprietors: John & Pat Grafton

`TEMPLE NR GOREBRIDGE`

THE MILL HOUSE
Temple, Midlothian EH23 4SH
Tel: 01875 830 253
Fax: 01875 830 253

Temple is 3 miles off A7 on B6372. Turn right after village sign. Mill House is beside church on right hand side.

Set in a charming riverside garden within conservation area of Knights Templar enclave.

- House of fine architectural detail refurbished in 1710.
- Skilled Scottish cooking.
- "Cordon Bleu cooking in a relaxed atmosphere with interesting surroundings."

Mill House is set in a riverside garden within the conservation area of the Knights Templar and the garden has botanical interest throughout the year. Spring flowers and camomile lawn garden is open to the public on set days in the summer season. The house itself is interesting with fine architectural detail dating from its refurbishment in 1710. The interior is decorated to a high standard, very comfortable and offering many thoughtful additions for the guests. Caroline Yannaghas is a most welcoming hostess and treats her guests exceptionally well. Her cooking is highly accomplished, she is Cordon Bleu trained and uses only the best quality ingredients. A most relaxing place to stay.

Open Apr to Sep
- 🏠 Rooms: 3, 1 with private facilities
- 🆂🅿 Special rates available
  Note: Available for dinner parties/Directors' Lunches
- ✖ Non-residents by arrangement
- 🆄🅻 ♀ Unlicensed – wine supplied, if required
- ✖ Lunch – on request £££-££££
- ✖ Dinner £££-££££
- Ⓥ Vegetarians welcome
- ⚘ Children over 14 years welcome
- ⚡ No smoking throughout

Warm duck salad and walnut dressing. Plaited salmon and sole with tarragon cream sauce. Vanilla ice cream with apple fritters and apricot sauce.

- 🆎 No credit cards
- 🅺 Proprietor: Mrs Caroline Yannaghas

`THORNHILL DUMFRIES`

TRIGONY HOUSE HOTEL
Thornhill
Dumfries
DG3 5EZ
Tel: 01848 331211

Situated off A76, 13 miles north of Dumfries. 1 mile south of Thornhill on the Dumfries-Ayr trunk road.

An Edwardian country house standing in its own gardens.

- An attractive converted shooting lodge standing in its own gardens.
- Simple, elegant Scottish cooking.
- "A peaceful atmosphere of understated sophistication pervades."

Trigony is a small country house hotel built of pink sandstone, standing amidst its own four acres of mature trees and lawns. It was once the home of the oldest woman in Scotland, Miss Frances Shakerley, who lived to be 107, and became an hotel 17 years ago. Its owners, Robin and Thelma Pollock take justifiable pride in their hotel and provide homely comfort and good food made from local produce. Public and private rooms are bright and airy, prettily decorated and with charming views over the surrounding country. *(See advert Page 23.)*

Open all year
- 🏠 Rooms : 8 with private facilities
- 🆂🅿 Special rates available
- ✖ Lunch £
- ✖ Dinner ££
- Ⓥ Vegetarians welcome
- ⚘ Children over 8 years welcome
- ⚡ No smoking in dining room

Home-cured salmon with brandy and dill served with mustard and dill dressing. Venison medallions with black cherry sauce. Choux puff filled with crème custard and fresh fruit, served on a passion fruit coulis.

STB Highly Commended 👑 👑 👑
- 🆎 Credit cards: Access/Mastercard/Eurocard, Visa
- 🅺 Proprietors: Robin & Thelma Pollock

`THORNHILL BY STIRLING`

LION & UNICORN
Main Street, Thornhill
by Stirling FK8 3PJ
Tel: 01786 850204
Fax: 01786 850306

On A873, 9 miles west of Stirling, between Blair Drummond Safari Park and Aberfoyle.

A popular old coaching inn dating back to the 1600s.

- Informal restaurant and bar.
- Modern and traditional Scottish cooking.
- "This inn is worth a visit to soak up the atmosphere of hundreds of years of a travellers rest."

The Lion and Unicorn was built in 1635 as a coaching inn – with low ceilings, stone walls and open log fires. It is family-run and friendly: a popular local pub. A good range of reasonably priced dishes featuring fresh produce is offered on a blackboard. Vegetarian and children's options are also available. The lay out of the pub allows for there to be both smoking and non-smoking areas in the restaurant. Chef/owner Walter MacAulay is experienced and forthright, and his wife Ariane is Dutch and also speaks German. Walter speaks reasonable French!

Open all year
🛏 Rooms: 4
✖ Lunch ££
✖ Dinner ££
Ⓥ Vegetarians welcome
🉑 Children welcome
♿ Facilities for disabled visitors
🚭 No smoking in restaurant

Lentil and applemint soup. Perthshire venison in claret and cranberry sauce. Apple and toffee crumble.

💳 Credit cards: Access/Mastercard/Eurocard, American Express, Visa, Diners Club, Mastercharge
🕴 Proprietors: Walter & Ariane MacAulay

`TILLICOULTRY`

HARVIESTOUN COUNTRY INN
Dollar Road, Tillicoultry
Clackmannanshire FK13 6PQ
Tel: 01259 752522
Fax: 01259 752523

Just off A91 on eastern edge of Tillicoultry.

A cheerful hotel with brasserie and restaurant and a small number of comfortable rooms.

- A Listed farmhouse which has been tastefully converted.
- Menus which cater for all tastes.
- "The menus offer a wide range of dishes at moderate prices."

Transformations and restorations do not always succeed but this one comes off well. The original farm buildings form three sides of a courtyard, and additions have been fronted with similar sandstone. Behind the inviting frontage lies a pleasant inn offering an excellent standard of en suite accommodation and a choice of dining styles. On the ground floor is the bar-brasserie which has a lively and informal atmosphere, and for formal dining there is an elegant à la carte restaurant. The food is of a high standard and well-presented, with an unusually varied menu.

Open all year except Christmas Day, 1 + 2 Jan
🛏 Rooms: 10 with private facilities
SP Special rates available
✖ Food served all day ££
✖ Lunch ££
✖ Dinner £££
Ⓥ Vegetarians welcome
🉑 Children welcome
♿ Facilities for disabled visitors
🚭 No smoking in restaurant

Squid ink risotto with Mallaig scallops and langoustines. Pot-roasted Guinea fowl served on a bed of green lentils with a cèpe glaze, and braised chicory. Bitter chocolate mousse with coffee parfait and oranges.

STB Commended 👑 👑 👑
💳 Credit cards: Access/Mastercard/Eurocard, American Express, Visa, Switch
🕴 Proprietor: David Lapsley

TONGUE

BEN LOYAL HOTEL
Main Street, Tongue
Sutherland IV27 4XE
Tel: 01847 611216
Fax: 01847 611212

At junction of A838 and A836, midway between
John o' Groats and Cape Wrath – in village centre.

Comfortable Highland hotel.

- Well-appointed with panoramic views.
- Modern Scottish cooking.
- "Relaxing village hotel looking over the Kyle of Tongue to Castle Varrich."

Standing in a splendid location overlooking the Kyle of Tongue, the peaks of 'The Queen of Scottish Mountains' and ruined Castle Varrich, this hotel seems to have been designed with the sole intention of enabling guests to enjoy these quite stunning panoramas from the comfortably furnished lounge to the beautifully appointed bedrooms, nine of which are en suite, with their pine furniture, pretty fabrics and four-poster bed. But perhaps the best views of all can be had from the dining room, where you will find your loyalties torn between relishing the view and savouring the food. Only fresh local produce – much of it home-grown – is used in the preparation of traditional dishes presented in a modern way. Ben Loyal has 1 AA Rosette. *(See advert Page 18.)*

Open 1 Mar to 31 Oct
🏠 Rooms: 12, 9 with private facilities
SP Special rates available
✖ Lunch (Restaurant lunch by prior arrangement only) £
✖ Dinner ££
Ⓥ Vegetarians welcome
⃗ Children welcome
♿ Limited facilities for disabled visitors
🚭 No smoking in dining room

Chicken liver and Drambuie parfait with grape chutney. Breast of honey-roasted duckling with an orange and port wine gravy. Warm individual rhubarb tarts with a vanilla custard.

STB Highly Commended 👑 👑 👑
💳 Credit cards: Access/Mastercard/Eurocard, Visa, Switch, Delta
Ⓜ Proprietors: Mel & Pauline Cook

TROON

MARINE HIGHLAND HOTEL
Troon
Ayrshire KA10 6HE
Tel: 01292 314444
Fax: 01292 313727

South end of Troon overlooking golf course
and sea.

Traditional style grand hotel overlooking Royal Troon golf course.

- Four star resort hotel.
- Modern Scottish cooking.
- "Traditional and comfortable with high standards of service."

The Marine Highland overlooks the 18th fairway of the Royal Troon Golf Course with beautiful views over the Firth of Clyde towards the Isle of Arran. With 20 courses situated nearby, golf is the major attraction of the area but there is plenty for non-golfers to do and you don't even have to leave the hotel to enjoy the superb leisure facilities of the Marine Leisure and Sports Club. The hotel is luxurious and public rooms are tasteful and relaxing. The food is highly commended with a good choice of interesting and imaginative dishes available in the main restaurant, The Fairways. There is also an Italian restaurant, Rizzios. The hotel has 1 AA Rosette.

Open all year
🏠 Rooms: 72 with private facilities
SP Special rates available
✖ Food served all day in Arran Lounge
✖ Lunch £
✖ Dinner ££-£££
Ⓥ Vegetarians welcome
⃗ Children welcome
♿ Facilities for disabled visitors

Vegetable tartlet with crème fraîche and Pecorino cheese. Baked cod with herb crust served on a robust tomato sauce. Brandy snap basket filled with fresh strawberries macerated in Cointreau.

STB Highly Commended 👑 👑 👑 👑 👑
💳 Credit cards: Access/Mastercard/Eurocard, American Express, Visa, Diners Club, Switch
Ⓜ General Manager: Chris Hansen

PIERSLAND HOUSE HOTEL
15 Craigend Road, Troon
Ayrshire KA10 6HD
Tel: 01292 314747
Fax: 01292 315613

South corner of Troon, opposite Royal Troon
Golf Club.

A fine country house hotel in the town of Troon.

- A beautifully restored Tudor style mansion in the heart of Ayrshire golfing country.
- International cuisine.
- "A busy hotel attracting local as well as residential guests."

Piersland was built for Sir Alexander Walker, grandson of the Johnnie Walker who founded the whisky firm of the same name. Tudor outside, and very impressive, the house has some fine Jacobean-style features. It stands in four acres of immaculate grounds that include a Japanese water garden. The hotel also has seven cottage suites for guests wanting that little bit extra. All have their own lounge and twin-bedroom and are fully equipped. With ten championship courses within a 30 minute drive, this is a golfers' paradise. In the dining room, both table d'hôte and à la carte dishes justify the hotel's reputation for fine and varied cuisine. The Garden Room caters for private functions. The hotel has 1 AA Rosette.

Open all year
- 🍴 Rooms: 26 with private facilities
- SP Special rates available
- ✕ Lunch £
- ✕ Dinner £-££
- V Vegetarians welcome
- ★ Children welcome
- ⚹ Facilities for disabled visitors

Ragoût of wild mushrooms with spring leaves laced with a Drambuie sauce. Medallions of Highland venison layered with black pudding, masked by a mild black peppercorn sauce. Hot raspberry soufflé presented with shortbread fingers.

STB Highly Commended 👑 👑 👑 👑
- 💳 Credit cards: Access/Mastercard/Eurocard, American Express, Visa, Diners Club, Mastercharge, Switch, Delta
- ⚐ General Manager: Michael W Lee

Turnberry 188

MALIN COURT HOTEL
Turnberry
Ayrshire KA26 9PB
Tel: 01655 331457
Fax: 01655 331072

On A719 Ayr-Girvan, south of Maidens.

A country hotel with spectacular views.

- Popular, purpose built country hotel.
- Modern Scottish cooking.
- "A unique experience of hospitality."

Overlooking the famous Turnberry Open Championship Golf Course and close to Culzean Castle, Malin Court enjoys an attractive situation on the Ayrshire coast with a marvellous outlook over to the Isle of Arran. Accommodation is comfortable and well-furnished with every facility you could wish for. In the Carrick Restaurant, Andrea Beach has developed a successful blend of modern cooking combined with traditional Scottish dishes. Menus are imaginative and complemented by a short, well-priced wine list. The pleasure of dining is enhanced by spectacular sunset views of Arran. The hotel has 1 AA Rosette. *(See advert Page 264.)*

Open all year
- 🍴 Rooms: 17 with private facilities
- SP Special rates available
- ✕ Food served all day ££
- ✕ Lunch ££
- ✕ Dinner £££
- V Vegetarians welcome
- ★ Children welcome
- ⚹ Facilities for disabled visitors

Marinated salmon gâteau flavoured with dill, lime and juniper. Guinea fowl breast served with sweet thyme and mango essence. Deep-fried chocolate parcels with ice cream and vanilla sauce.

STB Highly Commended 👑 👑 👑 👑
- 💳 Credit cards: Access/Mastercard/Eurocard, American Express, Visa, Diners Club, Switch, Delta
- ⚐ General Manager: W R Kerr

TURNBERRY HOTEL
The Macallan Personality of the Year 1996 – Stewart Cameron

Turnberry, Ayrshire KA26 9LT
Tel: 01655 331000
Fax: 01655 331706

A77 – 17 miles south of Ayr. 2 miles after Kirkoswald.

One of Scotland's most exclusive hotels.

- Resort hotel of international standing.
- Grand hotel cooking; also spa and grill-room styles.
- "Truly one of the world's leading hotels."

Turnberry was purpose built as a golfing resort hotel at the turn of the century, and retains many opulent Edwardian features. It enjoys an elevated situation overlooking the championship golf courses, with gorgeous views across the Firth of Clyde to Ailsa Craig and Arran. Service is gracious and supremely professional, yet friendly. The hotel's main restaurant offers the best classical cooking – Chef Stewart Cameron is a member of the Academie Culinaire de France – and uses fresh, local ingredients. During the week, lunch is served in the Bay at Turnberry Restaurant, where a blissful menu for the health-conscious is presented. The Turnberry Clubhouse serves roasts, grills, fries and sandwiches. Turnberry has 2 AA Rosettes.

Open all year
🏠 Rooms: 132 with private facilities
SP Special rates available
✗ Food served all day ££
✗ Lunch £££
✗ Dinner ££££
Ⓥ Vegetarians welcome
⚹ Children welcome
&. Facilities for disabled visitors
⤫ No smoking in restaurants
🐄 Member of the Scotch Beef Club

Turnberry Bay prawns and crab, bound in a rich tomato and dill cream dressing. Medallions of Galloway beef charred with a confit of mushrooms and red onions, with a Dijon mustard and basil puree. Raspberry and honey quaich, with toasted oats, malt whisky and thickened cream.

STB Deluxe 🦢 🦢 🦢 🦢 🦢
⊞ Credit cards: Access/Mastercard/Eurocard, American Express, Visa, Diners Club, Mastercharge, Switch
Ⓜ Resident Manager: A R W Furlong

Turriff 189

FIFE ARMS HOTEL
The Square, Turriff
Aberdeenshire AB53 7AE
Tel: 01888 563124

Situated in Turriff town square on A947. 10 miles from Banff, 17 miles from Oldmeldrum.

A pleasant and relaxing restaurant offering traditional and modern dishes.

- Old market square building.
- Freshly cooked local produce.
- "A friendly restaurant offering simple, fresh and delicious food."

There is a tradition of a hostelry on this site since the early 1900s. Situated at the top of the square the Fife Arms with its Poachers Restaurant offers a cosy and informal venue for travellers and locals alike. The restaurant menu is written on a blackboard and changes daily, according to availability of local produce, particularly the seafood which comes form Macduff. The lounge bar is a relaxing place with oak beams, stained glass windows and open fire, and friendly service. Bedrooms are being renovated and opening is planned for March 1997.

Open all year
🏠 Rooms: 5 with private facilities
✗ Food served all day – bookings only £-££
✗ Lunch £
✗ Dinner £-££
Ⓥ Vegetarians welcome
⚹ Children welcome
⤫ No smoking in restaurant

Smoked salmon roses served on horseradish croûtons garnished with capers in olive oil and black pepper. Hough of ham cooked with ginger, nutmeg, cinnamon, cloves, demerara sugar and black treacle, served whole with a sauce made from reduction of cooking juices. Plum dumplings: whole fresh plums in sweet dumplings topped with brown sugar and flashed under the grill, served with egg custard.

⊞ Credit cards: Access/Mastercard/Eurocard, Visa, Delta
Ⓜ Chef/Manager: John Ferrier

THE TOWIE TAVERN
Auchterless
nr Turriff
Aberdeenshire AB53 8EP
Tel: 01888 511201

On main A947, 4 miles from Fyvie Castle, 4 miles from Turriff.

An old coaching inn with restaurants.

- Village inn.
- Traditional country style cooking.
- "A popular roadside inn with good atmosphere and excellent fare."

The Towie Tavern is a charming old coaching inn, built about 1800, standing close to the beautifully restored early 16th century Towie Barclay Castle. It has two restaurants – the Barclay (for dinners) and the Castle (for suppers). Lunches are served in both; there is a smaller chamber – the Post Room – off the Barclay for private parties, family gatherings, etc., and there is also a diner's bar and a lounge bar. The cooking makes use of the best of Grampian produce; à la carte menus are offered, and there are daily 'Towie Treats' of both supper and dinner dishes.

Open all year except 1 + 2 Jan
✖ Lunch £
✖ Dinner ££
Ⓥ Vegetarians welcome
✿ Children welcome
♿ Facilities for disabled visitors
☹ No smoking in restaurants

A pair of Scottish cheese parcels in filo with cranberry sauce. Selection of fresh fish: monkfish, langoustine, squid, mussels and scallops in a spicy pepper, herb and tomato sauce, served with rice, Home-made desserts.

▣ Credit cards: Access/Mastercard/Eurocard, Visa, Mastercharge
▥ Proprietors: Douglas & Eileen Pearson

Tyndrum 190

THE CLIFTON COFFEE HOUSE
Tyndrum
Central Scotland FK20 8RY
Tel: 01838 400271
Fax: 01838 400330

On A85 to Oban and Fort William. 5 miles north of Crianlarich.

Popular self-service restaurant.

- Craft and souvenir shopping eaterie.
- Home cooking.
- "A splendid location for the hungry traveller."

What began as a simple self-service restaurant has become a tourist attraction in its own right. The shopping complex which has grown up around it sells books, crafts, woollens, gifts and food, but the restaurant is still the focal point. The owners constantly review their standards, service is friendly and reliable, offering good home baking and cooking and a wide variety of traditional Scottish meals and snacks. Very popular with visitors to Glencoe.

Open 8 Feb to 4 Jan except Christmas Day + Boxing Day
✖ Food served all day £
✖ Lunch £
Ⓥ Vegetarians welcome
✿ Children welcome
♿ Facilities for disabled visitors
☹ No smoking area in restaurant

Home-made soups. Game pie. Clifton sticky toffee pudding with toffee sauce and cream.

▣ Credit cards: Access/Mastercard/Eurocard, American Express, Visa, Diners Club, Mastercharge, Switch, Delta
▥ Partners: DD, LV & IL Wilkie/L P Gosden/ F D Robertson

ULLAPOOL

MOREFIELD MOTEL AND MARINERS RESTAURANT

North Road, Ullapool, Ross-shire IV26 2TQ
Tel: 01854 612161
Fax: 01854 612171

After c. 1 mile leaving village heading north (A835) turn left immediately over the river bridge. Follow hotel signs.

An unpretentious hotel and restaurant on the outskirts of Ullapool with a well-earned reputation for fish and shell-fish.

- An inexpensive motel, good pub and restaurant.
- Specialists in seafood, but offer a variety of cooking.
- "To try fresh Scottish seafood at its best – look out for the daily 'specials'."

The Morefield is an excellent base from which to enjoy this beautiful part of Scotland. The Mariners Restaurant deserves its popularity, serving the best of freshly-caught seafood, cooked with flair and imagination, and outstanding Scottish meat. The Lounge Bar and newly added air-conditioned conservatory, offer pub grub that proves just how good this kind of cooking can be. Bookings advisable for dinner during high season. Accommodation closed Nov to mid March.

....

Open all year except Christmas Day, Boxing Day, 1 + 2 Jan
🏨 Rooms: 10 with private facilities
SP Special rates available
✗ Food served all day £-££
✗ Lunch £
✗ Dinner (Mariners Restaurant) ££
Ⓥ Vegetarians welcome
⚘ Children welcome
♿ Facilities for disabled visitors
🚭 No smoking in restaurant

Seafood Extravaganza: a large platter of seafood – lobster filled with prawns; fresh crab, langoustine, smoked salmon, salmon flakes, mussels, queenie scallops and pickled herring. Mixed brochette of cubed sirloin steak, scallops and prawns.

STB Commended 👑 👑 👑
💳 Credit cards: Access/Mastercard/Eurocard, American Express, Visa, Mastercharge, Switch
👤 Proprietor: David Smyrl

WALKERBURN

TWEED VALLEY HOTEL

Walkerburn, Peeblesshire EH43 6AA
Tel: 01896 870636
Fax: 01896 870639

A72 at Walkerburn – 8 miles east of Peebles and 10 miles west of Galashiels. 32 miles south of Edinburgh.

Hotel set halfway up the valley overlooking the River Tweed.

- An Edwardian country house hotel.
- Scottish country grill.
- "Home-smoked produce a treat!"

This pretty country house stands in its own grounds and has glorious views up the Tweed Valley. It was originally built in 1906 by the Borders wool mill owner John King Ballantyne, and retains its original panelling and ornate ceilings, although there are now significant modern additions such as a solarium, sauna and mini-gym. The hotel has a walled kitchen garden which provides vegetables, fruit and all the fresh herbs for the kitchen, and its owners, Charles and Keith Miller, also smoke their own fish and meat (these are available for sale). À la carte and table d'hôte menus are presented, and an extensive bar menu. Grills and traditional Scottish dishes abound. The restaurant has 1 AA Rosette.

....

Open all year except Christmas Day + Boxing Day
🏨 Rooms: 16 with private facilities
SP Special rates available
✗ Food served all day £
✗ Lunch ££
✗ Dinner ££
Ⓥ Vegetarians welcome
⚘ Children welcome
🚭 No smoking in restaurant

Smoked lamb on basil tomatoes masked with raspberry vinaigrette. Slivers of smoked salmon with monkfish and scallops on a julienne of vegetables topped with ginger and lime hollandaise. Warm Border tart with brandy cream.

STB Commended 👑 👑 👑 👑
💳 Credit cards: Access/Mastercard/Eurocard, American Express, Visa, Mastercharge, Switch
👤 Partner: Keith Miller

See entry Page 47

Reputation for Excellence

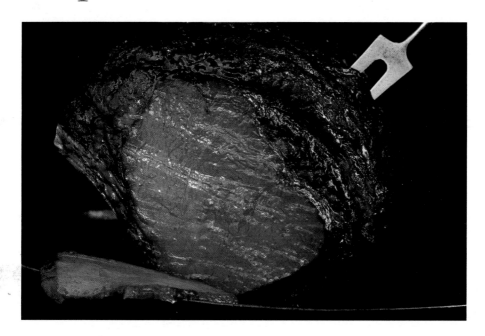

Like other products with a reputation for excellence it takes time and skill to produce specially selected Scotch Beef.

Taste of Scotland members have a commitment to quality and you will find this reflected in their presentation of Scotch Beef. Alternatively, for your own cooking, look throughout the UK for butchers who are Associate members of the Guild of Scotch Quality Meat Suppliers, and who are identified by the Guild's logo. And whilst in Scotland, look out too for butchers displaying the SFMTA's own 'Shop With Confidence' logo.

For a list of all your local stockists of
Scotch Beef and Scotch Lamb phone or fax us:
Scotch Quality Beef and Lamb Association
Tel: 0131 333 5335 Fax: 0131 333 2935

Scotch Lamb Challenge 1996

Scotch Lamb – Naturally, One of the Traditional Tastes of Scotland

Scotland, as every gourmet knows, boasts a natural larder which groans with a vast selection of quality foods – amongst them the Scotch Beef and Lamb which have been acclaimed for centuries.

Historically, Scottish cuisine was based on a 'one-pot' system which provided robust, nourishing dishes well suited to the times. Tradition will always have its honoured place on any nation's tables, but today appetites are more sophisticated, tastes are more international, and chefs more innovative than ever before. Appreciative of the natural fine qualities, flavour and versatility of Scotch Lamb, chefs now produce an annually widening selection of Scotch Lamb dishes to please the modern palate and to delight the eye.

For many of the world's top chefs Scotland is an instinctive first choice when sourcing beef and lamb for their restaurants – they know that the traditional stock rearing skills are linked to high standards of quality assurance throughout the Scottish meat industry. For some years, SQBLA and Taste of Scotland has, through the annual Scotch Lamb Challenge, provided an opportunity for all members chefs to develop new Scotch Lamb dishes. The success of this competition is clearly shown by an entry so large that the competition was divided into two equal categories.

1996 saw eight finalists – from an initial field of almost eighty chefs – compete for the honour of winning SQBLA's Taste of Scotland Scotch Lamb trophies and titles.

Winner Gourmet Section and overall winner of the 1995 Taste of Scotland Scotch Lamb Challenge : Bruce Price, Executive Chef, The Old Course Hotel Golf Resort and Spa, St Andrews.

Winner Classic Section : Paul Somerville, Creebridge House Hotel, Newton Stewart.

Recipes

Scotch Quality
Beef & Lamb
Association Limited

Gourmet Section winner Bruce Price (centre) with
Vic Prow of SQBLA (left) and Bruce Sangster.

Both winning recipes are reproduced in our receipe
section (starting overleaf), together with a selection
of other dishes from some of Scotland's top chefs.

Loin of Scotch Lamb
with Lamb and Parsley Parfait, Encased in Savoy Cabbage,
Presented with Cake of Ratatouille, Creamed Celeriac and Squash
With Leek Ragoût on an Arran Mustard Jus

Bruce Price
Head Chef, 'Road Hole Grill', Old Course Hotel,
St Andrews Golf Resort & Spa, Fife

INGREDIENTS

2kg Scotch lamb loin
(on the bone)
100g minced lamb
50g breadcrumbs
500ml lamb stock
1 egg
120ml double cream
100ml sunflower oil
75g butter
90g leek
225g celeriac
175g egg plant
225g plum tomatoes

225g savoy cabbage
175g green courgettes
50g shallots
100g mirepoix of vegetables
4 squash
2 carrots
10g bunch of basil
60g bunch of parsley
seasoning
15g wheat oat
2 slices bread
mixed pepper
1 teaspoon Arran mustard
50ml white wine

METHOD

1   The 4 loins should weigh 125g each after being trimmed, with all fat removed. Season lamb with salt and pepper.

2   Cook in a hot pan with sunflower oil, this should only take 3 minutes each side. Place in a refrigerator to cool and firm. Drain free from fat, add a little water to the lamb stock and reduce.

3   Add a little oil and butter to a frying pan and sauté minced lamb and shallots until cooked through. Stir in cream, breadcrumbs, beaten egg and basil and reduce if necessary to a farce consistency. Place in refrigerator to cool.

Ratatouille

4   Ratatouille of sautéd egg plant, courgette and tomato arranged neatly as a gâteau topped with toasted oat wheat.

Celeriac

5   Cook the celeriac until soft, drain and purée, add the cream.

Squash with Leek Ragoût

6   Wash leek well, cut into julienne. Cut leek, red onion and squash to cube, sweat. Add cream and chive, season with salt and pepper.

Lamb Loin

7   Butter tin foil and lay savoy cabbage on top, add farce with chopped parsley and lay lamb loin onto farce. Roll up very tightly. Poach for 8 minutes. Remove from pan and keep warm, it should be pink in the middle. Add remainder of oil in pan, add white wine, glaze lamb stock, and pass sauce through a fine strainer. Add Arran mustard and chopped basil. Finally, whisk in butter to finish sauce.

8   Keep warm in oven for 1 minute. Slice lamb into 3 pieces. Arrange the celeriac purée and ratatouille around top of the plate, then pour the sauce at the bottom of the plate next to the lamb.

Serves 4

Roast Loin of Scotch Lamb with Basil Mousse

Paul Somerville,
Sous Chef, Creebridge House Hotel, Newton Stewart

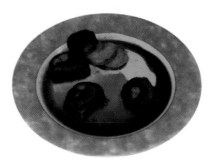

INGREDIENTS

3lb loin of Scotch lamb
250g spinach leaves
50g packet basil
100g cooked chestnuts
2 sheets of caul fat
2 eggs

1 bottle elderflower wine
300ml double cream
300ml lamb stock
4 large potatoes
25g unsalted butter
2 carrots
100g Strathkinness Cheese
2 cloves garlic

METHOD

1   Bone lamb loin, removing all fat and sinews.
2   Blanch spinach leaves, retaining 12 large leaves for later. Process lamb fillet with salt. Add blanched dried spinach and basil. Process until fine and refrigerate. Peel potatoes and carrots.
3   Bring half the cream (150ml) to the boil with the two cut cloves of garlic. Add the grated cheese.
4   Blanch the carrots then layer the potatoes and carrots in a timbale mould with the cream mixture. Season and bake for 30 minutes.

5   Add 1 egg and 1 egg yolk to the lamb mixture and then the remainder of the
cream. Pass through a wire sieve and refrigerate. Season the loin of lamb, spread
some of the mousse on top of the loin and place chestnuts on top. Then totally
cover the chestnuts with mousse. Totally encase the mousse with the spinach
leaves then wrap it in the caul fat and tie and roast at 425°F / Gas Mark 7 for 12
minutes.

6   Reduce the elderflower wine to almost nothing, add the lamb stock and let it
reduce by two-thirds. Whisk in the butter and season to taste. Portion the lamb,
garnish with the potato gâteau and then add the sauce. Serve.

Serves 4

Summer Fruits Marinated in Malt Whisky

Volker Steinemann
Head Chef, Keavil House Hotel, Crossford

INGREDIENTS

250g strawberries
100g raspberries

100g blueberries
100g brambles or Tayberries
200g caster sugar
malt whisky to cover fruit

METHOD

1   Carefully clean and dry all fruit. Place fruit in an earthenware dish.
2   Mix sugar with approximately the same amount of whisky.
3   Completely cover the fruits with the liquid, topping up with more spirit if
required.
4   Weigh down fruit with plate or something similar and cover dish making sure
that it is airtight.
5   Leave in a cool dark place for a minimum of one week.
6   Before serving, gently stir the fruits. These fruits taste best when served with a
rich dairy ice cream as a truly Scottish sundae.

Serves 4

Lamlash Bay Scallops
with a Timbale of Wild Rice and Herbs

Janet Hughes
Proprietor, Grange House Hotel, Isle of Arran

INGREDIENTS

8–12 large cleaned scallops
4 rashers smoked back bacon
6 squashed cloves of garlic
juice of 1 lemon

3 tablespoons chopped parsley
100g unsalted butter
100g mixed wild rice
selection of herbs, chervil, dill &
coriander

METHOD

1   Cook the rice and add 5 tablespoons of freshly chopped mixed herbs.
2   Melt the butter and add finely shredded bacon and cook until crisp.
3   Add crushed garlic, lemon juice and scallops and cook for 2–3 minutes.
4   Make a timbale of rice and turn onto the plate and surround
     with scallops.
5   Serve sizzling hot.

Serves 4

Darne of Salmon with Tarragon

Philippe Avril
Head Chef, Froggies, Glasgow

INGREDIENTS

4 x 200g salmon steaks
480g peeled plum tomatoes
1 bunch tarragon
1 clove garlic
1 glass white wine

salt and freshly ground black pepper
1 leek (cut into julienne strips)
8 medium size potatoes (turned)
8 medium size carrots (turned)
1 tablespoon olive oil
1 tablespoon butter

METHOD

1   Boil the turned potatoes and carrots separately in lightly salted water for the required time.
2   Sprinkle both sides of the steak with salt and pepper. Heat the oil in a pan and cook them on medium heat for approximately two minutes either side. (The salmon must still be pink close to the centre bone otherwise it will dry up too quickly).
3   Take salmon out of the pan and keep warm.
4   Pour the wine in the pan and bring to the boil. Add the chopped tomatoes, finely chopped tarragon, crushed garlic and seasoning and simmer for 3–4 minutes.
5   Meanwhile, sauté the leek in the butter for approximately 1 minute.
6   To serve, pour the sauce onto heated plates and lay salmon steaks and leeks on top. Arrange potatoes and carrots around.

Serves 4

Chargrilled Vegetables with Balsamic Dressing

Mohammad Abdulla & Denis Dwyer
Proprietors, The Cabin Restaurant, Glasgow

INGREDIENTS

1 aubergine
1 yellow courgette
12 asparagus
4 vine ripe tomatoes
12 cloves of garlic
3 red peppers

2 yellow peppers
fresh parmesan
balsamic vinegar
olive oil
coarse salt
freshly ground pepper
salad leaves for garnishing

METHOD

1   Take one of the red peppers and slice into very fine strips. Place in ice cold water and leave to one side.

2   Roast the remaining peppers and remove skin. Blanch asparagus and refresh.

3   Slice the aubergine and courgette and sprinkle with salt. Allow to sit for 30 minutes then wipe with damp kitchen paper.

4   Place on to the char-grill or griddle and cook quickly on both sides followed by the peppers and asparagus.

5   Roast the garlic and quartered tomatoes in some olive oil and place on a tray with the other vegetables. Brush them with olive oil if they seem dry. Allow to cool.

6   To serve, toss the salad leaves in olive oil and place in the centre of a large plate. Arrange the vegetables around and drizzle with balsamic vinegar and shavings of parmesan cheese and freshly ground pepper.

Serves 4

Cloutie Dumpling

Elma Barrie
Owner, Hawkcraig House, Aberdour.

INGREDIENTS

plain flour for dusting
100g vegetable suet
250g self raising flour, sieved
1 teaspoon baking powder
75g caster sugar

450g currants & sultanas, mixed
1 teaspoon ground cinnamon
1 teaspoon ground ginger
1 firm green apple, grated
3 large eggs, beaten
approximately 150ml milk
caster sugar to dust

METHOD

1   Scald a linen tea towel with boiling water, lay it on a surface and sprinkle liberally with the flour.
2   Place all the dry ingredients into a large mixing bowl and stir to mix.
3   Stir in the apple, eggs, and enough milk to mix to a dropping consistency.
4   Pile the mixture into the centre of the prepared tea towel and gather up the edges, then tie into a bundle, allowing enough room for the mixture to expand.
5   Place an inverted plate inside the bottom of a large pan and place the dumpling on this. Add enough boiling water to come about ¾ of the way up the dumpling.
6   Simmer gently for 3½ – 4 hours, topping up water as necessary.
7   To turn out, heat an ovenproof plate. Remove the dumpling from the pan and untie, turn out onto the warm plate and place in a cool oven, Gas Mark 1–2/130°C/250°F for a few minutes to dry off. Dust with caster sugar and serve with whipped cream.

Seed and Oat Crofters Bread

Kate Macdonald
Chef/Proprietor, The Old Smiddy, Laide

INGREDIENTS

350g granary or plain
wholemeal flour
100g plain white flour
225g coarse oatmeal
1½ level teaspoons
cream of tartar

1½ level teaspoons bicarbonate of soda
¾ teaspoon salt
2 teaspoons soft brown sugar
175g sunflower seeds
350ml milk
2–3 tablespoons lemon juice
1 beaten egg

METHOD

1   First sour the milk with lemon juice.
2   Mix all dry ingredients together and bind with milk and egg.
3   Spoon into a 2 lb loaf tin and bake at Gas Mark 6/200°C/400°F
    for 40 minutes or until hollow sounding.

This is excellent served with home-made soups or pâtés.

Scottish Salmon

Stir your imaginations with the thought of silver scales gliding through pure, Highland waters and it's not too difficult to reason why gourmets everywhere declare Scottish salmon to be the finest in the world. Once, Scottish rivers held such abundant stocks of wild salmon that rich and poor could feast on them at will. Poached in vast copper kettles, fresh salmon graced the laird's table and fed the hungry apprentice. The sea captain dined heartily on salmon which had been pickled, smoked and salted for the long voyage.

Today, we too can savour Scottish salmon. Although, sadly, depleted numbers of wild salmon have made it an expensive seasonal delicacy, the Scottish salmon farming industry ensures that the finest quality farmed salmon is available for you to enjoy all year long at an affordable price. With over 25 years of experience, Scottish salmon farmers nurture their fish in the clear, fast flowing waters of Scottish lochs and coastal inlets. Their expert husbandry skills ensure a succulent firm textured salmon with superb flavour.

Indeed, you can unleash your wildest gastronomic designs on salmon. It is succulent poached simply, or equally mouth-watering complemented with a rich French sauce or a spicy dip from Thailand. It is quick to prepare whether you choose to grill, steam, bake, pan-fry or microwave it. Eat indoors or enjoy salmon al fresco, sizzling on the barbecue and add colour and flavour to the traditional repertoire. In either case, a meal can be ready in less than 20 minutes. The versatility of salmon goes on and on. Take the unique taste of Scottish smoked salmon. Smokehouses use closely guarded secret recipes to cure salmon in a way which will inspire.

Increasingly more and more people are realising that Scottish salmon is not only tasty and versatile but equally the healthy choice. At under 200 calories for a 125g/4oz portion (steamed or poached) and containing protein, calcium, iron and Omega 3 fatty acids – which can help reduce blood cholesterol levels as part of a low-fat diet – you can't choose a better food.

But as with all recipes, only the best ingredients provide success and that's why it's important to look for Tartan Quality Mark when buying salmon. It appears as a gill tag on whole fish or a label on pre-packed cuts and smoked salmon, and is your assurance of genuine Scottish origin and the very best quality.

The Tartan Quality Mark ensures that every aspect of the salmon's existence – from the sea loch in which it was raised through to its processing and packing after harvest – is carefully monitored to guarantee the highest standards at all times. Only Scottish Salmon which are reared in accordance with the stringent standards of Scottish Quality Salmon scheme are eligible to carry Tartan Quality Mark, so it is your guarantee that the fish, whether fresh or smoked, is both genuinely Scottish and in peak condition. Make one of Scotland's finest products a regular feature on your menus. Enjoy Scottish Salmon.

The Mark of Superior Quality Scottish Salmon

They say class always shows. One look is enough to tell you whether you've selected the finest salmon there is. Look for the Tartan Quality Mark.

It's your guarantee that every stage of the salmon's existence, from the Scottish lochs in which it is raised to its delivery to store, is carefully monitored to ensure the highest standards at all times. Furthermore, each Tartan Quality Mark Scottish Salmon can be traced back to source, so full accountability is assured.

You'll find it widely available as a gill tag on whole fish or as a label on pre-packed fresh and smoked salmon. So don't accept any compromises when you next buy salmon – insist on the best, insist on Tartan Quality Mark Scottish Salmon.

For further information and recipe leaflets on Tartan Quality Mark Scottish Salmon contact the Scottish Salmon Bureau on 0131 229 8411

The 1998 Taste of Scotland Guide

is scheduled to be published in November 1997.

To reserve a copy at a special post inclusive price, just complete the coupon below indicating your method of payment and send it to:

Taste of Scotland (Guide Sales)
33 Melville Street
Edinburgh EH3 7JF

You will be placed on the priority list to receive the Guide as soon as it is published. For your convenience, we accept ACCESS and VISA.
Tel: 0131-220 1900. Fax: 0131-220 6102

- ✂

To: Taste of Scotland (Guide Sales), 33 Melville Street, Edinburgh EH3 7JF

Please send_____copy/copies of the Taste of Scotland 1998 Guide and debit my ACCESS/MASTERCARD/VISA (please delete as appropriate)

Card No. ☐☐☐☐☐☐☐☐☐☐☐☐☐☐☐☐☐☐☐☐

Expiry Date   Month _____Year _____

Account Name: _____

Signature _____

Please ✓ appropriate amount:

To addresses			
	in UK	£7.75	
	in Europe	£9.00	
	in North America (Airmail)	£10.50	

Note: cheques in £ sterling also accepted

Name: _____

Address: _____

_____

_____

Post Code: _____Country: _____

BLOCK CAPITALS, PLEASE

Post inclusive prices to other countries availabile on request

Comments on meals in places listed in
The Taste of Scotland Guide are welcomed.
Send to Taste of Scotland, 33 Melville Street, Edinburgh EH3 7JF

Establishment visited _____

Date of visit _____ Meal(s) taken _____

Comments _____

_____

_____

_____

_____

_____

_____

_____

Name _____

Address _____

_____

_____

✂ --

Comments on meals in places listed in
The Taste of Scotland Guide are welcomed.
Send to Taste of Scotland, 33 Melville Street, Edinburgh EH3 7JF

Establishment visited _____

Date of visit _____ Meal(s) taken _____

Comments _____

_____

_____

_____

_____

_____

_____

Name _____

Address _____

_____

_____

The Macallan Taste of Scotland Awards 1997

Send to: Taste of Scotland, 33 Melville Street, Edinburgh EH3 7JF

I nominate _____ (Establishment)

for a Macallan Taste of Scotland Award for the following category:

(Please tick one category only)

☐ Hotel of the Year   ☐ Country House Hotel of the Year   ☐ Restaurant of the Year

☐ Special Merit for _____   ☐ Personality of the Year _____

Name _____

Address _____

_____

_____

Date of visit _____

Meal (if appropriate) _____

Closing date for entries: 30 June 1997

--- ✂

The Macallan Taste of Scotland Awards 1997

Send to: Taste of Scotland, 33 Melville Street, Edinburgh EH3 7JF

I nominate _____ (Establishment)

for a Macallan Taste of Scotland Award for the following category:

(Please tick one category only)

☐ Hotel of the Year   ☐ Country House Hotel of the Year   ☐ Restaurant of the Year

☐ Special Merit for _____   ☐ Personality of the Year _____

Name _____

Address _____

_____

_____

Date of visit _____

Meal (if appropriate) _____

Closing date for entries: 30 June 1997

Comments on meals in places listed in
The Taste of Scotland Guide are welcomed.
Send to Taste of Scotland, 33 Melville Street, Edinburgh EH3 7JF

Establishment visited _____

Date of visit _____ Meal(s) taken _____

Comments _____

_____

_____

_____

_____

_____

_____

Name _____

Address _____

_____

_____

✂ -

Comments on meals in places listed in
The Taste of Scotland Guide are welcomed.
Send to Taste of Scotland, 33 Melville Street, Edinburgh EH3 7JF

Establishment visited _____

Date of visit _____ Meal(s) taken _____

Comments _____

_____

_____

_____

_____

_____

_____

Name _____

Address _____

_____

_____

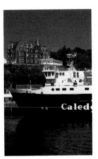

Taste of Scotland Alphabetical Index – 1997

New Member for 1997 ★★

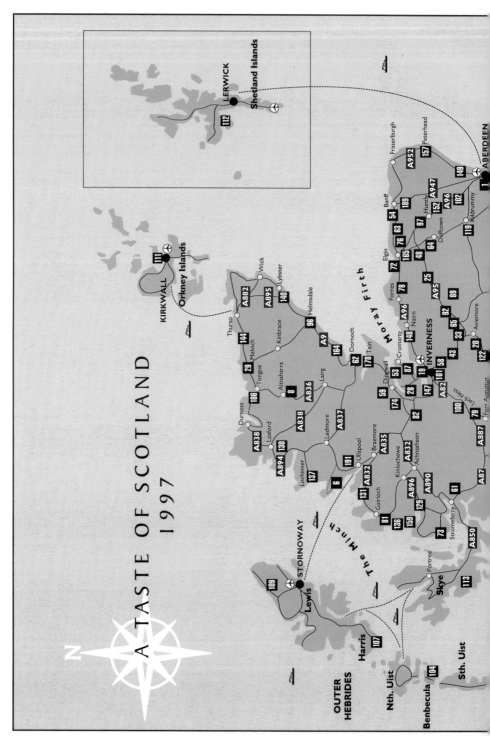

A TASTE OF SCOTLAND 1997

Shetland Islands

LERWICK

112

Orkney Islands

KIRKWALL

111

Fraserburgh

Peterhead

A952 157

ABERDEEN

A947 149

A96 102

Huntly 152

Banff 189

54 63 97 Kildrummy 119

76 Dufftown 64

Elgin 165 48

72 Forres A96 78 25 A95 89

Wick

A882 A895 Lybster

140

Helmsdale

Kinbrace 96

Thurso A9 Dornoch Nairn

144 Melvich 164 Tain A96 92

29 Tongue Kinbrace 178 Cromarty 148 65 33 Aviemore

Altnaharra 8 Lairg 62 Dingwall 87 INVERNESS 43 20 122

186 Durness A836 53 19 Fort Augustus

59 28 147 A82

A838 Laxford Ledmore A837 174 82 A887 79

A838 130 Braemore 191 Ullapool 100

A894 Lochinver 137 6 A832 Kinlochewe A832 Loch Ness

131 Gairloch A835 Achnasheen

81 136 159 A896 A890 61

129 Stromeferry A87

73 A850

Portree 113

Skye

STORNOWAY

Lewis 109

The Minch

Harris 107

OUTER HEBRIDES

Nth. Uist

Benbecula 104

Sth. Uist

Moray Firth

N

270

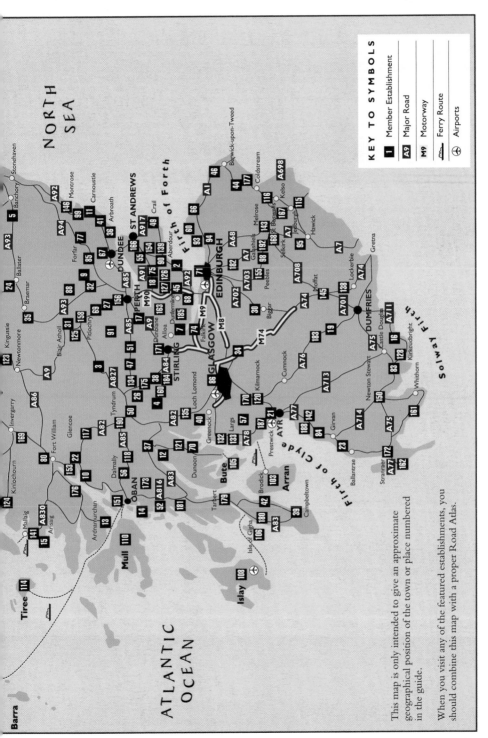

KEY TO SYMBOLS

- **1** Member Establishment
- **A9** Major Road
- **M9** Motorway
- Ferry Route
- ✈ Airports

This map is only intended to give an approximate geographical position of the town or place numbered in the guide.

When you visit any of the featured establishments, you should combine this map with a proper Road Atlas.

The Taste of Scotland Guide 1997

Editorial
Amanda Clark, Angela Nealon, Tracey Waterston

Published by
Taste of Scotland Ltd,
A non-profit making company limited by guarantee trading as Taste of Scotland

Design, Illustration & Typesetting
David Frame Creative, Edinburgh

Printed by
Macdonald Lindsay Pindar plc

With particular thanks for editorial assistance
Charles Maclean, Maclean Dubois (Writers and Agents), Edinburgh
Jim Middleton, David Frame Creative, Edinburgh

Cover Photography
Main photograph courtesy of Argyll, the Isles, Loch Lomond,
Stirling, Trossachs Tourist Board
Inset Photo by Morten Rosvik
Food Styling by Wendy Barrie

Colour Photography courtesy of
Aberdeen and Grampian Tourist Board
Ayrshire and Arran Tourist Board
Kingdom of Fife Tourist Board
Orkney Tourist Board
Scottish Borders Tourist Board
Shetland Islands Tourism

The details quoted in this Guidebook are as supplied to Taste of Scotland Scheme Limited and to the best of the company's knowledge are correct. They may have been amended subsequently and all users are advised in their own interest to check when making a reservation.

Taste of Scotland Scheme Limited accepts no responsibility for any errors or inaccuracies.

Taste of Scotland Scheme Ltd
33 Melville Street Edinburgh
Tel: 0131 220 1900 Fax: 0131 220 6102

ISBN 1 871445 08 6